The Brakes Are Off

MY AUTOB

D0245942

GRAEME SWANN

The Breaks Are Off

MY AUTOBIOGRAPHY

with Richard Gibson

HODDER

First published in Great Britain in 2011 by Hodder & Stoughton
An Hachette UK company

First published in paperback in 2012

1

A CIP catalogue record for this title is available from the British Library

Paperback ISBN 978 1 444 72740 1
Ebook ISBN 978 1 444 72739 5

Typeset in Minion Pro by Palimpsest Book Production Limited, Falkirk, Stirlingshire

Printed and bound by CPI Group (UK) Ltd, Croydon, CR0 4YY

Hodder & Stoughton policy is to use papers that are natural, renewable and recyclable products
and made from wood grown in sustainable forests. The logging and manufacturing processes
are expected to conform to the environmental regulations of the country of origin.

Hodder & Stoughton Ltd
338 Euston Road
London NW1 3BH

www.hodder.co.uk

In memory of my grandparents who are no longer with us –
Les, Lillian, and Wilf x

CONTENTS

ACKNOWLEDGEMENTS

'*The Breaks are Off*? Are you serious?' I asked Gibbo, my ever so patient and wonderfully monotone Brummie ghost, when he called me during the 2011 World Cup to discuss a title for this book. 'Can't I have something like *My Life and Other Funny Stories*?'

'No, you can't,' he said. 'A lot of people at the publishers have put their heads together, and this is the best one they've come up with.'

'How about *An Idiot's Guide to Playing for England*?' I pleaded.

'But that could be any fast bowler from the last 30 years,' Gibbo argued. 'Besides, this has a nice double meaning, given that you bowl off-breaks, and seeing as you did naff all in cricket for so long, then suddenly picked up at pace!'

There's not much of a comeback to that sort of comment. Sitting on a bus outside a massive Indian stadium waiting for Jonathan Trott to finish some more throw-downs, I had to let out a good laugh.

'Okay then, mate, call it what you like,' I said, 'but push for a decent picture on the front cover.'

'Well, that could be a problem,' chirped the five-foot-five wordsmith. 'You're an ugly bastard at the best of times, but when you're bowling, you look like you're chewing a Marmite-flavoured wasp.'

Again, I had to laugh. Gibbo had made two very good points, albeit in a worryingly honest sort of way. First, I had indeed been going nowhere fast for a long time before a lucky break here and there led me to the point at which someone was willing to publish the story of my career. And secondly, yes, I am not the most photogenic man alive, especially when gurning my way through the crease. I relented.

'Okay, mate – call it your brakes-are-off thing and pick any old picture. I'm sure it'll be all right.'

So here you have it. My very own pun-spun autobiography. However, I do believe it's a better title than some my England team-mates have been overheard discussing during rain breaks. I'll give you a few examples and see if you can guess the player:

Cooking Up a Storm
Leading from the Front
Miserable Monobrowed Burnley Paceman

Of course, not all of these titles have made it to the bookshelves, although I am keen to see the last one hit the bestseller list, if only to cheer up Jimmy Anderson on a future tour.

It's been nothing but great fun putting this book together. Even when the two-megabyte-a-week Internet speeds of the subcontinent made Skype nigh-on impossible, I somehow managed to get enough face time with Gibbo to smile my way through stories of the last 30 years. I even managed to convince him to invite me into his lovely home in his adopted Yorkshire, just so I could raid his chocolate biscuit tin, where I was truly shocked but equally giddy to find a 15-year-old Wagon Wheel. Only after eating it did I roll into a semi-hallucinogenic dialogue of the darker years of my career, which hopefully helps fill the pages between the lovely pictures we've managed to dig up!

Thanks, of course, to Richard Gibson, for his amazing patience and rambling phone messages; Roddy Bloomfield, for being an extremely understanding publisher; Mum, Dad and Alec, for their verbal and pictorial contributions; and everyone else who helped get this book off the ground.

Most of all, I have to thank my beautiful wife Sarah and extremely handsome (chip off the old block) baby boy Wilf. It's fair to say that without them in my life, I would be clad in skin-tight jeans, heading for a seaside town somewhere as an Erasure tribute act, telling anyone who'd listen that I could have been.

I hope you enjoy it . . .

PHOTOGRAPHIC
ACKNOWLEDGEMENTS

Hamish Blair/Getty Images, Philip Brown, Stu Forster/Getty Images, Gareth Copley/PA Archive/Press Association Images, Getty Images, Paul Gilham/Getty Images, Laurence Griffiths/Getty Images, Mike Hewitt/Getty Images, Rupert Jefferson, Indranil Muhkerjee/AFP/ Getty Images, David Munden/Popperfoto/Getty Images, Rebecca Naden/PA Archive/Press Association Images, Pete Norton, Clive Rose/Getty Images, Tom Shaw/Getty Images, WPA Pool/Getty Images.

EARLY SNAPSHOTS

My RECOLLECTION of the day I believed I'd ruined my dad Ray's life is as vivid as any of my childhood memories. I was 10 years old and playing a home match for Northamptonshire Under-11s against Derbyshire at Weekley & Warkton Cricket Club, about half an hour's drive away from where we lived (in the posh side of Northampton).

The sense of occasion had been heightened on the journey to the ground by my dad's announcement that we would be stopping on the way to buy some film for his camera – a Canon as I recall, with a lens that was flipping massive, and an ability to take as many as two shots a minute.

'I'm bringing this tedayuh cos ah want te tyek the opportunity te get some photos of yee,' he told me.

Well, we must have stopped at about 10 shops – newsagents, chemists, corner stores, you name it – before eventually getting the right roll to fit this contraption, and undoubtedly he would have been seeking a 24 exposure rather than a 36, in typical northern style. But having finally struck gold, he found himself the prime position to take some award-winning action photos.

We opted to bat after winning the toss and, with me due in at number four, I would not have to wait long for my big moment.

Sure enough, my turn came around pretty quickly and, full of expectation, I headed out to the middle. Unfortunately, I trudged back in despair moments later after I nicked off second ball, turning my gaze as I did so to where my father sat, in anticipation of a sympathetic look.

No such luck. There he was, kicking a fence. It was the kind found in club grounds around the country – wooden posts with metal railings running horizontally, designed to keep the horses out – but this particular fence was having seven bells booted out of it in sheer frustration.

Being a good son, I took my kit off, ignored whatever my coach had to say – I thought he was rubbish anyway, something of a recurring theme in my life – and trotted around the boundary to face the music on the other side of the ground. There was my dad, sitting on a bench at the furthest point from the dressing rooms he could find, with only the horses behind him for company. As I approached he refused to look at me. He completely ignored my existence as I perched next to him and began swinging my feet.

After five minutes of silence – pierced by a couple of meek inquiries along the lines of 'What should I have done with that ball, Dad?' – came the inevitable rollicking. Call it a son's intuition but, despite kidding myself that I was on the threshold of a little pat on the shoulder and a 'Never mind, son, you'll get some next week', I knew it was coming.

'Tha cost me £3.95, did tha fillum,' were Dad's first words. 'An I've got two bloody shots of yee!' He then got up and walked off. And that was the moment that this 10-year-old, without breaking the rhythm of those swinging legs, believed he'd done irreparable damage to his old man.

As it turned out, they were quite nice shots. One of me bouncing out to the middle, and the other walking back again, dragging my bat along the ground with my toes turned in and head bowed.

Generously, my dad stayed to witness the rest of the game, but he refused to take any pictures of me when I bowled. He told me in no uncertain terms I was undeserving of his beloved Canon, and it was destined for the boot of his car.

Only a week earlier, my brother Alec had struck a magnificent 148 somewhere or other, and what seemed like thousands of commemorative photographs were displayed on the dining room table for everyone to admire, while in contrast my measly montage wouldn't have filled a place mat.

It was a good few years later that I discovered the old man had craftily waited for us to take the field to retrieve the camera and get a few decent shots of me bowling. Alas, he had not managed to capture my dismissal of Ian Blackwell, the Derbyshire hero, first ball.

Dad rarely came to watch me play again after that – and only saw me a few times until I played men's cricket alongside him. However, there were extenuating circumstances.

Once Alec, who is two years older than me, progressed beyond the Under-11 team, it meant that we would invariably be playing for the county at the same time in different locations. Therefore one parent had to drive each of us to a game. Dad clearly washed his hands of me after his Lord Lichfield impression went wrong at Weekley & Warkton, and ferried my brother everywhere. As a result, my mum, Mavis, came to watch me. So we grew up with me as Mum's favourite and Alec as Dad's. They will deny it, obviously, as all parents do, but Alec and I know the truth.

By the age of 10, I was already an established fixture in the Northants youth set-up, having turned up for Under-11 nets with Alec from the age of seven. That was the age, in fact, that I made my county debut – it was the final game of the 1986 season and for some reason they were one (minuscule boy) short for a match against Middlesex.

My first set of bowling figures were far from impressive but have nevertheless stuck in my head. Despite barely being able to see over the stumps, I bowled a demon spell of 2–0–31–0, and had a blatant stumping declined. Disgraceful.

It seemed like a man's game to me because I was so tiny. And it would continue to do so for quite a while as I represented that same Under-11 Northants side for the next four seasons. Certainly for the first couple of years, Alec was the big gun of our side, scoring the majority of the runs, and that arguably helped me along; I was probably better than half the lads that were older than me just because I knocked about with him in the back garden. That sibling rivalry definitely brought me on as a player at a quicker rate.

I adored playing for the county and the highlight of every summer was undoubtedly the Under-11 festival at Dartford College, where we would face London Schools, Essex, Kent and Lancashire. That was when I first played against kids like Andrew Flintoff, Alex Tudor and the future Manchester United and Everton footballer Phil Neville.

Spending three or four nights at the Dartford Festival felt longer than a winter tour does now. You would have a game every day and at the end of the week there would be a festival match where the best team got picked. For sport-loving lads it was like the perfect holiday. You would play cricket during the day and ping-pong at night. In fact, we played table tennis so much that I'm sure I was better then than I am now, because these days I doubt I would give my cats a good game.

Dartford's main pitch was unusual because the square was not square at all but round. There were two other pitches on-site as well, so games would be going on simultaneously. These other two were probably about 200 metres away, although because you had to carry your own kitbag, it felt like a trek across the Himalayas. And when you arrived things got even more treacherous: awaiting you were the most dangerous pitches a young kid could ever play on, especially when Tudor, who was already about 5 ft 9 in in his stockinged feet, was whanging bouncers down at you.

I got to know Freddie Flintoff at a very young age because of this festival, and we were always very friendly, off the field at least – because on it, he was a boy with the physical capacity of a bloke. Like Tudor, he would bowl proper bumpers. He was really long and lanky as a kid, with enormous hands. And you could see where he got it from because his dad Colin seemed like a giant to us little people. Fred was an amazing batsman – his power allowed him to smash it all over the place – and he also had the ability to bowl at what seemed like 100 miles per hour.

The first time I played against him was aged 10 for Northamptonshire

Under-11s against Lancashire at Rainford Cricket Club. It was an intimidating experience, which began with the Lancashire coach telling us: 'Be careful today, lads, I've got a couple of Malcolm Marshalls bowling for us!' He wasn't joking.

One of them was Fred, another was Phil Neville, who was already being tipped as a future England international. That came to fruition, of course; it just turned out to be in football not cricket. Well, the pair of them were the absolute speed of light to their contemporaries, and I remember our opening batsman crying at the non-striker's end. When the umpire inquired what was the matter, he whimpered something about the bowling being too fast.

I went in at my regular number four position, missed the first ball, survived a plumb lbw next up – reprieved because umpires tend not to give leg-befores at that age – but really made amends by getting my hobs knocked everywhere by my third. And this wasn't even by one of the feted duo. This bowler was a guy called Lee Radcliffe. Lancashire had the quickest bowlers in the world, it seemed, and being northern meant they were all massive.

Northern fixtures were good for me because my grandma Lillian and grandad Les lived in Warrington, and they were in the crowd that day. They would get in their Mini Metro and drive to all sorts of places to see Alec or me play. Grandad's attitude towards my performances was the polar opposite of my dad's. 'Never mind, son, have an Eccles cake,' he said as I perched myself in front of his car. I was always pleased to see Grandad at my games.

He was at the corresponding match the following summer too. Once a season Lancashire junior teams got the chance to play at Old Trafford and it just so happened the annual fixture was against Northants. Now, the chance to play at a Test ground when you're a kid – a county ground, let alone a Test venue – was pretty amazing. But things didn't look too promising as we drove north, rain bucketing down all the way, and as I stood selecting my twenty pence-worth of pick-'n'-mix at the midpoint service station prospects of the match taking place did not appear good.

Miraculously, however, it did. Not long after we arrived, the wet weather cleared and we played. Some matches, even ones I did well in, are hard for me to recall, but this one comes back easily. Lancashire were 130 for four after 32 overs when the rain returned and I had claimed two of the wickets: Flintoff lbw, and a guy called Scott Richardson, who went on to play for Yorkshire.

It was an amazing day for me. There I was at Old Trafford, with Grandad Les sitting alongside the steps to the pavilion, dead proud that I was competing on the hallowed turf. He always wanted Alec and me to play for Lancashire, you see, and here I was doing the next best thing. I remember walking off the field and seeing him holding court in the pavilion, surrounded by committee members.

'Your grandad's told us all about you,' one of them said to me, as he patted me on the back. 'You're going to play for England, we hear. England captain and a Lancashire regular, you'll be.'

My mum joked afterwards that Grandad would have been trying to talk his way onto the committee. I suspected he was more interested in their cake selection. Unfortunately, Grandad died when I was 14, so he didn't get to watch me as a county or international player, nor did he see his wish come true when Alec played for Lancashire. That was a shame, but whenever I think of him it leaves me with a feeling of happiness.

People associate me with having a laugh, and my mum says I get it from my grandad. He was the most jovial, old-fashioned northern grandad going, a truck driver by trade and an avid sports fan. Whenever we were at their house, he would be watching something on the box, and he was never happier than when that something was rugby league, and Warrington in particular.

Sport and pastries were his first loves. The fondness for the latter stemmed back to the Second World War when he tried to join the army along with his nine brothers but was rejected when it was discovered he had a heart defect. Barred from fighting on the front line, they trained him up as a baker instead, and he became Warrington's finest. He was very proud of his Eccles cakes, and so I never had it in me to tell him that I hated them! Nothing personal, I just can't stand mincemeat or raisins – devil's food, if you ask me – yet I always forced them down regardless because good old Grandad had made such an effort.

Closer to home, Alec and I played our club cricket at Horton House because Northampton Saints, the club Dad joined in 1987, did not have a junior section at the time, and so a chap called Ted Gascoyne was my first coaching mentor. He was also one of the nicest blokes I've ever met. Every club's got a Ted: an above-and-beyond kind of guy. He would be there five nights a week, coaching the Under-11s, Under-13s, Under-15s and Under-16s. Two of his boys, Sam and David, or Bomber as he was affectionately known, used to help out. Years later, when Ted moved away from the area, the two lads eschewed a normal social life to build on their father's legacy.

Short and rotund, Ted was the most convivial man on the planet. Always smiling, if ever there was a game of cricket going on, you'd find him in the nets throwing balls to the less talented lads. He had so much time for everyone. In fact, I can only remember him being angry once and that was when his son Geoff, who was my brother's age, swore. As punishment, Geoff was made to stay at home the next week and have his mouth washed out with soap and water. Literally, we suspected, because when it came down to it Ted was pretty old-school.

For a kid it is so important to feel wanted. You see so many playing football and getting bellowed at by adults from the sidelines these days, but Ted was the exact opposite. He made you want to go and play cricket at his club every day of the week. At the time, we didn't even realise we were learning and getting better, it was such a great laugh.

Ted wasn't very technical – having said that, apart from my dad, I can't remember getting much technical coaching from anyone – but we definitely improved as a team under his guidance. Ted's big thing was to try to get all of us to hit the ball back where it came from and not across the line. Clearly, I didn't listen to a word he said because that's exactly where I've tried to hit everything ever since. But his lasting legacy was the idea that the game was to be enjoyed. If you didn't find it fun, you shouldn't be there. He obviously wanted his teams to win, but it was the sheer love of cricket that kept him coaching, and that rubbed off on the kids.

While most of my county team-mates played for a club called Little Houghton, making them the team to beat in our area, the efforts of the Gascoynes made Horton House ultra-competitive. Quite rapidly, in fact, we reached a standard where we won everything. And this was quite something, because aside from just a few exceptions – us Swanns being two – our team was made up entirely from lads in the local village.

The sense of achievement was tangible when we won our first competition – victory in an Under-13 County Cup final at Irchester, inevitably against Little Houghton. In their line-up was Kevin Innes, who went on to play for Northants and Sussex, and was at the time the best player in the country of his age by some distance. In fact, Innes was at the crease as the game went into the final over with the scores neck and neck. The rules of these eight-a-side contests always kept things interesting, because in addition to scoring runs, you knocked eight off your opponents' total for every wicket, and so there was everything to play for as Andy Oram, a family friend of ours, and a future Northants second-team colleague, ran in to bowl.

Little Houghton had just nudged ahead of us when Innes skied one and the ball seemed to disappear into orbit. It certainly felt like the most towering catch ever as I ran back from cover – in reality, it probably just looped in the air – and clung on in front of all our mums and dads. The parents went up as one, screaming and cheering, and Ted was hugging anyone within grabbing distance as we secured our first trophy. After that watershed moment we seemed to win every year, and when I look back they were really happy days.

Mum, who transported me to practice or a match virtually every night of the week – Tuesdays would be Under-13s, Wednesday Under-15s and Thursdays Under-16s – was a major part of that great time. She would drive me wherever I needed to be, sit down and watch the whole thing, whilst marking books, looking up and clapping with a distinct sense of timing. Then on the way home, she'd listen to me harp on about the runs I'd scored or wickets I'd taken.

Nobody could question the level of her support, yet she also imposed my maiden suspension from cricket. Yes, a family-imposed ban on representing Northamptonshire, which began when I was 12 and lasted for four years. Now, I will admit to being a tad anti-establishment, but this particular ban had nothing to do with me. It sprang from accusations that Alec, of all people, had been abusive to umpires during games. The county attempted to make an example of him for a couple of matches, but my mum wouldn't have any of it.

Anyone who knows my brother would tell you it is just not in his character to show dissent, and I remember Mum going potty after receiving an official letter about it. 'Right,' she said. 'If they're going to treat one of my boys like that, they aren't going to have either of them.' True to her threat, we never played at age-group level again.

Although that felt devastating for a cricket-daft young lad, it was probably the best thing for me because, instead of travelling around the country playing against boys of my own age, I was suddenly thrust into men's cricket every Saturday afternoon. Horton House showed a distinct reticence to let me play, or certainly play a meaningful part if selected, so I moved to my dad's club Northampton Saints in 1991 because their attitude was that if you were good enough you were old enough.

So it proved. Rather than batting number 11 and bowling a token two overs, I went straight into the Saints' second team, opened the batting and bowled regularly. I loved it and within a few weeks I made it into the first team.

From that moment on, my game advanced greatly, primarily because I was competing against seasoned club cricketers at a good standard. I was only pushing 5 ft 3 in at that age, used a size six bat and couldn't hit the ball off the square, yet I adapted my game quite well. I remember right at the end of that season, there were half a dozen people missing in the 1st XI and we fielded a skeleton side at Bedworth. It was the first first-team game I can recall, probably because of the part I played in it and the unusual circumstances. We had turned up with just eight players, and I batted at number seven, but I got about 30 and hauled us agonisingly close to securing a losing draw.

We so nearly saved that match against all odds, but as I walked off that field any disappointment was tempered by the knowledge that I could actually play at that level. It was a weird feeling. This was the team that I had always watched Dad play for, and it seemed like the pinnacle of cricket to a little kid. Yet here I now was part of it and doing quite well.

They say you develop lucky grounds and favourite opponents and I did my best to prove the theory when my maiden hundred in senior cricket followed in the corresponding fixture in 1993. Miners Welfare was hardly the most salubrious of settings, with its pitch plonked in the middle of a public park. Dog turds lined the whitewash like boundary markers and stragglers occasionally had to be reminded that it was not etiquette to walk directly across the field during play. Nevertheless, Bedworth were a competitive team, and in Dennis Oakes, a wily old leg-spinner who had played for Warwickshire in his day, they possessed one of the league's leading bowlers. 'Look out,' Dad had warned me beforehand, 'cos he will try te bool yee while you're not watching. His trick is te let gan before yee are ready.' On this particular day I was ready for anything.

Dad's next piece of advice came out in the middle. He had dropped down to number five, basically to allow me to bat at number three, and joined me when I had 98 to my name. I knew this for a fact because he informed me as he arrived at the crease. 'Remember, I'm forty-three and not very fast between the wickets,' he added.

Of course, the advice went unheeded as I immediately hit one to deep backward point and hared through for two, with Dad shrieking 'Yee bloody idiot' as we crossed for a second time. I turned to look over my shoulder as the ball was hurled to his end and saw a whirl of bat, pads and boots as he dived full length to get in. Thankfully the throw was wide and he'd beaten it, giving me the chance to revel in the glory. Rather than go and apologise, however, I ran around the ground, punching the air in jubilation. Dad, meanwhile, was emerging from his shower of dust. 'Well done, son,' he said, as I returned to the middle. 'But dinnae ever bloody do that again!'

Even in his forties, Dad remained one of the best players in the Central League and was still good enough to represent Bedfordshire, while I, despite losing all sense of coordination somewhere during adolescence – it was as if one day I grew big feet and longer legs, which made me look like Peter Crouch without the sense of balance – was developing something of a reputation as a batsman. Good job, I guess, given that my ridiculous growth spurt meant I completely lost the ability to bowl.

But my approach to batting could not have contrasted more with that of my dad. It was demonstrated the first time we opened together, against Blossomfield at home later that season. Birchfield Road East was a lovely little ground with short, straight boundaries, and on this particular afternoon I made good use of them. So much so, in fact, that after 21 overs of being sledged by just about every member of the opposition I brought up my hundred. If they dropped short I cut hard, when they pitched it up I launched it straight back down the ground. I just smacked it everywhere. Upon reaching three figures I received some fatherly advice from my first-wicket partner, who had meandered to about 35 at the other end.

'Right, son,' he said. 'This is a great chance for you to get a double hundred. Forget what's gone, switch back on and start again. You've got your eye in, so bat sensibly from now on.'

'Stuff that,' I said. 'If I'm getting 200, it's coming in the next 10 overs.'

Seconds later I was caught on the boundary for 107, and departed happy enough because it gave me almost 30 overs to mess about with my mates. Dad, meanwhile, as if to prove a point, batted for the remainder of the innings, finishing unbeaten on 126, and refused to look at me over his cakes and scones at tea.

He still allowed his thoughts to find their way to my ears, however. 'You're a bloody idiot!' he told me. 'Yee could have had 250 there. You're a bloody idiot!'

We never saw eye to eye on this subject throughout my formative years. I always used to tell him: 'No one will remember me for a boring sixty. People just don't remember that type of innings, but they will always remember a flashy thirty or forty.'

'That's rubbish, yee don't knaa what you're taakin aboot,' was his staple reply.

But I was sufficiently obstinate to stick to my guns, and I have continued in the same vein. Of course, I now wish I'd said flashy hundreds instead because my entire career has been blighted by those flashy thirties. C'est la vie, I guess.

One thing I am indebted to my dad for, however, is a love of the game. Cricket was an integral part of our family life and when it came down to it we didn't have a choice in the matter. From the year dot I was ferried to cricket grounds. I was born in March 1979, and before the end of April, when the local league started up, I was dragged off to my first match at his then club Old Northamptonians. Alec was already running around with bat in hand, of course, while I was wrapped up in the pavilion in a huge purple blanket. It was a warm welcome to the rest of my life.

In the Swann family weekly schedule, Saturdays meant cricket. From a young age it was the day I idolised my dad. All kids think their dad is Superman, don't they? But I had genuine evidence to back up my claim, because more often than not he would be the best player on the pitch by miles. It seemed he scored a hundred or pretty damn close to it every week. Who was Ian Botham, anyway? No one compared to my hero.

Such was Dad's reputation that his dismissal was always met by the biggest roar of the day from the opposition. However, their pleasure at his departure could not have been in greater contrast to his feelings about the situation. And this is where Mum came into her own. She learned very early in their relationship that it was best to stay out of Ray's way whenever he was out.

Let's just say that he was not one to respect the traditional sanctity of the dressing room. He would take it out on his cricket bag, and shout and swear without a care for who was in earshot. So the routine for this fraught family time was for Mum to beckon Alec and me over, sit us down in perfect tranquillity on the picnic rug and feed us cupcakes and juice. This impromptu picnic would last what seemed like an eternity – so probably quarter of an hour in reality – and be followed by Dad's reappearance for the rest of the innings.

One of my earliest recollections is putting on his batting gloves and cap after his dismissal, and I can still almost get the whiff of it in my nostrils – unsurprising really, because the smell given off by his Combined Universities cap, one of those traditional ones with the flat peak, was horrendous. Years of sweat build up on old cloth is unlike anything else, but the fact it hummed never bothered me. I would put it on and sit there contented, and by the time I was three I would round up pads and gloves and sit with the rest of the team as if waiting to bat.

My parents met at Loughborough University, on a teacher-training course, the perfect environment for someone like my dad who played every single sport under the sun. It was football and rugby in the winter (before my mum banned him from playing football because his disciplinary record was so dreadful) and cricket in the summer. There was no respite. As soon as the winter season finished, the summer one began, and so Mum's spare time was spent at various sports grounds, both before and after us kids arrived on the scene.

We were used to watching Dad play sport but were never allowed to attend his football matches. We didn't know why at the time but it later became apparent it was on account of his appalling language. Because he was the only Geordie, Mum figured we would have been able to identify the culprit too easily!

Dad was a centre-forward and a good player by all accounts. His father, Wilf, played for the Services – after he single-handedly beat Rommel in the desert – and possessed the claim to fame that he was the only player not with a First Division football club at the time. In fact, my grandad never played cricket. But Dad took it up, quickly found he was good at it, burst into the Blyth first team at a young age and soon went on to play for Jesmond and for Northumberland.

So how did our family settle in Northampton? Well, during his student days, Dad turned out for the Combined Universities against Northamptonshire 2nd XI at Wantage Road, a ground, as anyone travelling there for the first time will testify, that is only discovered with a considerable amount of difficulty because of the maze of backstreets that surrounds it. To do so also requires a modicum of luck. As they battled vainly in their quest on this occasion, apparently Dad turned to Mum and said: 'I'll tell you one place I'm never going to live, and that's Northampton.' So, Sod's Law dictated that the only teaching job offered to him upon qualification was in the town – and 500 yards from the cricket ground to boot.

Long-term indoctrination has meant that even Mum has grown to love the sport. Well, she has certainly come a heck of a way since the first time my dad ever took her to a game: Yorkshire were playing, and she asked, rather loudly, and thus embarrassingly: 'Who's this bloke then, fielding next to us here?' It was Geoffrey Boycott. The whole world knew who Geoffrey Boycott was – other than Mavis Swann, that is.

Now she knows the game inside out, and she has always been great for me. Because she knows I don't like talking about cricket that much, she never brings up the subject. Yet if I do want to talk I can have remarkably intelligent conversations with her. She's switched on and brilliant for me because she has remained one-eyed throughout my whole career. It doesn't matter how well anyone else has done, I'm still better than they are, and that's exactly what you want to hear from your mum. It has certainly helped me maintain my positivity. My glass has always been half full, while my dad is the opposite: an archetypal pessimist.

When my brother scored hundreds as a kid, the first question would be 'How did yee get on?' Dad's second, having barely waited for a response, would be 'How did yee get out?' In contrast, Mum's answer to everything was 'Wow, that's brilliant!' If I did really badly she would always know to talk about something else. With a Geordie dad and a Lancastrian for a mum I have had a very northern upbringing, but their outlooks couldn't have been more different.

Dad continued playing for the Saints until 2001, and that would have been it for him but for the feeling that he had unfinished business in his club career. A meticulous compiler of records, he spent a few years nursing the knowledge that he had scored 96 competitive hundreds – those scored in friendly matches discounted – before the bug bit him again in 2009. He simply had to get to three figures, and two hundreds in his first season back nudged him closer.

Despite his 60th birthday looming on the horizon, he reached the landmark during 2010 in a Northamptonshire Cricket League Division 10 contest between Saints' fourth team and Irchester. I knew he would reach his target that summer, although I was convinced that he would sprint the single required, raise his bat and keel over dead on the pitch. It would have been quite a nice way to go for someone who had devoted his life to cricket, but I'm obviously glad he didn't.

His achievements were recognised with a special award at the league's annual dinner, and I am so proud of him because that is what he always had in his cricket: pride. He played with so much passion, and I hope that has rubbed off on me. His love for the game never waned throughout his entire club career. Good on him.

Although Dad's first teaching post was in Northampton, we moved on to Towcester in 1990 on the back of him getting a job at Sponne School. This was a good move from my point of view because it meant I could just roll out of bed at the last minute and still be on time for the bell.

You know the kind of teacher who is either loved or loathed, with no one occupying the middle ground? That was my dad. He is unmistakably Geordie and Towcester is a very conservative, middle-class town, and anyone with a regional accent is either feared or mocked. His fellow teachers tended to love him, but the kids, especially the naughty ones, hated him because he didn't really care about the boundaries when it came to discipline. If he found out that kids were bullying others, he would happily bully them back to teach them a lesson. These were the days before smacking was banned in schools, but it is safe to say that he wasn't the hippy teacher that swore by the holistic approach. He would stand perpetrators up in front of everyone and yell at them until they cried. I loved that about him.

Not that I was exempt from his dressing-downs. I confess I was a cheeky so-and-so at school and got away with murder, but somehow I survived Dad doubling as my maths teacher for two years between the ages of 13 and 14. In maths we sat in rows of four and I was in the penultimate row, with four girls in the row behind me – four very attractive girls, as it happened – so I was forever leaning back in my chair chatting to them. On one particular occasion it was clear that my dad had had a distinctly bad morning.

'Graeme, turn around and get on with yer work,' he barked.

'Sorry, Dad.'

Two minutes later I was leaning back talking to them again.

'Graeme, ah've told yee once and ah won't tell yee again. Do yer bloody work!'

A couple more minutes passed, and I'd just resumed my chat when I was startled by a huge bang. The back of the classroom housed a full set of metal lockers for pupils to store their books in and the almighty din was the sound of a set of keys, which had flown seriously close to my head, smashing into them. The whole class gasped and put their pens down.

I slowly got up and went and picked up the keys, shaping as if to shy them at the teacher's end.

'Yee dare!' he warned.

I don't know what came over me, but I threw them back at him and in his attempt to catch them he cut his hand. Dad didn't say anything and, with that typical adolescent attitude, I thought: 'Yeah, that showed you – don't shout at me!'

However, this was the first period and that left my dad simmering all day long. While I had completely forgotten about the incident as I sat in the car waiting for Dad to take us home that afternoon – Alec had a spare car key, so he used to let us in – my dad had not. Alec was sitting behind me on the back seat on this occasion – it was obviously my turn to ride shotgun – as I saw my dad approaching in the wing mirror. He was walking through the playground with a huge pile of books.

He opened the boot of the big Volvo estate, popped his books in and quietly made his way around to the driver's seat. He opened the door, sat down and in the same motion gave me a right smack around the side of my face. 'If yee ever show me up leik tha agyen, ah will break yer bloody neckl' he warned. To sum up in teenage parlance, I was bricking it at this point, and needless to say from that day forth I carried on being cheeky in everyone else's lessons, but not in those of Mr Swann.

We didn't play cricket at school. Well, that wasn't strictly true. We did play the obligatory annual fixture in the County Cup, but we were not a cricket-playing school. There was just no appetite for it. So, each year, the sports teacher would come and seek me out a week before the first round and prep me to pick a team.

The games I remember, and for obvious reasons, were against Oundle, a very well-to-do public school, which fell within the county boundaries. Now, my school was a very good, middle-class establishment, the oldest in the county, and one of the oldest and indeed highest-rated comprehensive schools in the country. But it was probably like Grange Hill compared to Oundle.

The Oundle lads' preparation would no doubt have been meticulous, whereas our pre-match planning amounted to me picking my 10 best mates, all of whom fancied an afternoon off lessons. Then, on the morning of the game I would cram my kitbag with every pair of whites and every cricket shirt I owned and hand them out like a Red Cross missionary.

Our dressing room must have been some scene. There in one corner was the biggest 14-year-old we possessed, whose body defied the odds to squeeze into Under-12 gear, and in the other would be one of the lads who had missed out on the free clobber. The only variation from his day-to-day uniform therefore would be a pair of trainers instead of shoes and his tie would be fastened around his head rather than his neck. But from his point of view, a couple of hours messing about at fine leg was better than double chemistry.

When the ball came towards my team-mates, most of them, despite their rough-and-ready exteriors, would stand aside and protest: 'I ain't stopping that, it's too hard!' So you can imagine the impression we made at Oundle.

I remember them being absolutely appalled by the collection of ruffians who'd turned up at their pristine establishment. Agricultural areas seem to breed big lads and this certainly applied to my mates. By the time they'd completed a year at senior school the majority had grown full beards. A by-product of our physical prowess was that we were brilliant at rugby, and beat everyone. But we must have looked like Neanderthals when we turned up to play cricket. I stuck out like a sore thumb, looking more like the opposition with my pretty kit on, matching pads and gloves, and familiarity with the etiquette of the game.

The other lads didn't appreciate such nuances, of course, and so an appeal from an opposition bowler for caught behind, when our batsman clearly didn't hit it, would trigger rather uncouth responses, usually along the lines of 'F--- off! That's not out. Appeal like that again and I'll beat the s--- out of you.' It was sledging at its most undiluted. There was no cleverness about it, and they genuinely would have swung punches at these posh little kids for appealing if our sports teacher, Mr Yuill, had not intervened from square leg.

Victories were rare but one win that I cherished was against Roade

School, one of our two local rivals. Their team was made up of the majority of the lads I played junior club cricket with at Horton House, and I was determined to beat them. I got a hundred, and we did. And I got my highest-ever score against Campion School – our other local rivals, and the target of our jibes because the Jesus Army had its base just outside their village. It was a 20-over game and I made 191.

This mass destruction took place on an AstroTurf pitch, which was sandwiched between two rugby fields, and I was genuinely gutted when my chance to get a double hundred was scuppered in the 18th over when a guy sporting the full trainer-minus-tie look, who had never played cricket before, produced an astonishing one-handed catch at long off. He was probably only standing there so he could be first off for a bat. There was no method to setting fields – school teams in our area often used to employ four mid-ons, not for any tactical reason, but just because that was where the lads that couldn't be bothered stood around chatting.

There was certainly less intensity about these games than those that took place in our back garden. The width of our house in Towcester was just about the perfect length for a cricket pitch. The back patio was made up of concrete slabs, and the cracks in between provided the bowler with some assistance. Our match ball was one of those orange wind balls used for Kwik Cricket.

These days those balls tend to be quite light but this one was dense and hard, so blows to the body hurt. We used to get fully padded up in Dad's kit – helmet, gloves, arm guards, the lot – and prepare for a peppering. Halfway down the pitch was the garden tap, and to liven things up we would take off the hose, turn on the water and flood the playing area, making the ball absolutely fly as a result. This was proper, competitive garden cricket. Serious stuff.

Various targets earned different amounts of runs: the big set of steps up the garden was worth three; if you hit the wall it was one; hitting the window was out. Our one-day games would consist of five overs, and you were required to vary your bowling between an over of seamers, one of spinners, then an over of left-arm, and so on. As a batting side you had three wickets and one of your batsmen had to be left-handed. You get the picture.

Our cat Gus was employed as a fielder and because of his contrasting relationships with us – he hated Alec – would always assist my cause. If you hit the ball and Gus jumped on it, that was a wicket. Officially he was my cat, given to me as an 11th birthday present, and he seemed to know this, so whenever Alec was batting he would leap into action, but when Alec was bowling Gus would disappear to some other part of the garden and ignore him.

The late Gus – christened because he reminded me of Gus Logie – made it to 20 years old before snuffing it. I even got him a signed shirt from the original Gus during a Northants pre-season tour to Grenada. I didn't tell Mr Logie it was for a feline friend, of course, just a mate back home.

We would play for hours on end, or until Mum got fed up with our destruction. The drenched concrete slab caused the ball to gather such speed that the fence behind took an absolute pasting, and we would be banned for weeks at a time for putting new holes in it. We would still sneak out when we could, of course, trying to keep as quiet as possible so as not to draw attention to ourselves.

Unfortunately, silence rarely prevailed for long and the noise that one of my full-blooded pulls made on the large patio doors is something I'll never forget. These doors represented short leg and hitting into them, no matter how hard, was out. On this particular day, Alec had wound me up something rotten and when he switched to bowling spin I pulled it as hard as I could straight into them. Although it was right out of the middle, it was a terrible piece of timing, coming as it did just as Dad peered out from the other side. Needless to say, I was already jumping the fence into the safe haven of the farmer's field as he stormed out.

We would always be outside playing something, be it throwing a rugby ball or kicking a football. But when the temperature was okay we would play cricket. Of course, we fell out as brothers do, but he was my best mate. And from my first competitive match, Alec and I always seemed to be playing together. When I think back to my earliest matches, he was always there. There used to be an unwritten rule that you couldn't play above your own age group, but when I came along the powers-that-be allowed me to play two years ahead of myself. So I played for a couple of years with Alec before he graduated to the Northants Under-13s.

And I've always bowled off-spin. Or I should say that I have bowled it so long that I cannot remember starting. Simply, because I began so young, and was so small, the only way I could get the ball to the other end was to have a huge loop on it. So I don't know whether anyone actually suggested spin bowling. I think I just did what came naturally.

As kids, myself and Alec, who was a wicketkeeper, were a cunning combination. We worked out at a very early age that we could get stumpings off wide deliveries, yet none of our contemporaries seemed to be aware of this. Perhaps it was because all we seemed to talk about with Dad was cricket's finer details that we cooked up such plans.

If you bowl spin as a kid, your opponents tend to charge down the pitch and try to hit every ball for six. So, in anticipation, Alec and I came up with different signals: a flick of the hand to signify that the next one would be down the leg side, or a rub of the chest to warn of one on its way outside off stump. Down the pitch they would charge, only to be duped on their journey, allowing Alec to whip the bails off. In our eight-a-side matches, we would regularly combine for half a dozen stumping victims and I would finish with as many wickets as runs off my bowling.

2

THE UNIVERSITY OF LIFE

DURING THEIR teenage years just about every young English cricketer ends up bowling medium pace at some point. I was no exception, although my stint as a seam-up merchant amounted to no more than 10 matches, the most memorable of which was for the Northants County Colts in a Northamptonshire County League game in May 1998.

Former England bowler Neil Foster was our player-coach, his remit being to organise selection each week and fill in himself where necessary, depending on injuries and call-ups for the senior teams. On this particular occasion he informed me I would have to share the new ball with him because the pair of trialists who were supposed to be fulfilling those roles had pulled out. Our team that day had six spinners in it and I'd drawn the short straw.

As it happened, I couldn't have enjoyed myself more: my 17 overs yielded figures of six for 61. There was I at one end hurling down these dreadful little away-swingers while Fozzy kept beating the bat at the other. Yet somehow I got half a dozen members of the Irthlingborough 1st XI out – including a couple of their ex-county players – whereas former England paceman Foster managed just one victim. So I felt pretty good about my new vocation, and even better when, in pursuit of 215 for victory, we scraped home by one wicket.

The performance certainly had an effect on me, but not in the way one might anticipate. The next day it was back to business as usual and I was in the first team for a televised game against Essex, at Ilford – my first appearance on TV. Naturally, I switched back to spin in pre-match practice. But I was all over the place; the previous day's exertions had completely knocked me out of rhythm and I was sending down double bouncers and all sorts.

Things didn't get much better when it was our turn in the field later that afternoon. Nasser Hussain was playing for Essex and he smacked me for a massive six, as I headed towards figures of 5–0–38–0 in a resounding eight-wicket defeat. Stephen Peters, who I knew from schoolboy cricket, later told me that Nasser got back into the dressing room following his unbeaten 62 and brazenly declared: 'If that Swann lad is the future of spin bowling in this country, then we're f-----!' His judgement, based on the evidence I presented, was fair, though, because I bowled like a drain.

During my youth I always took wickets, but as with many aspiring all-rounders, my main suit fluctuated between batting and bowling as I moved through the system: in county age-group cricket, then for the Midlands and Young England. Primarily, I had risen as a bowler who could bat, but as my batting improved at around the age of 15 I became a batsman who bowled a bit. In fact, for the England Under-15 team a lad from Essex called Jonny Powell was picked as the main spinner, and I didn't mind at the time because bowling seemed too much like hard work. A combination of laziness and the realisation that batting was much more fun meant I hardly put up a fight.

But regular wickets against Wales, Scotland and Ireland meant I kept my bowling going. However, this period also coincided with my rapid growth and it was the one time in my life that my action didn't feel completely natural. I could spin the ball miles but couldn't really control it, and as a result I didn't enjoy it that much.

It was my ability with the bat, in fact, that initially attracted the attention of Northants, and I made my debut for the 2nd XI at the age of 16 years and 46 days as a top-order batsman. Yet when my next chance came a year later, it was as a bowler who batted down the order. Somewhere in between my bowling came back and it undoubtedly improved from netting every day. Of course, when you are young you imagine you are going to open the batting and bowl spin for England. Life is pretty simple. But when you start playing county cricket you get pigeonholed, and because I was the spin bowler I slotted in at number eight. And to be frank, ever since I established myself for the county it has been my bowling that has been my main thing.

My inaugural Northamptonshire 2nd XI call-up came on 9 May 1995, the second day of a Championship match against Gloucestershire at Bristol, after Tim Walton had been summoned by the first team. Upon arrival I was told that I would be batting at number four but, with Gloucestershire 65 for four in reply to our first-innings score of 264, that meant a wait for my chance to impress.

We secured a 111-run lead on first innings but the nerves were understandably jangling as I sat on the balcony at Nevil Road and witnessed Pakistani Mohammad Akram charging in at the speed of light, minutes after I'd implored my new team-mates to lend me whatever protective gear they had arm guards, thigh pads and even a helmet, as I didn't have one at the time.

Alec was batting at number three and we came together at 16 for two, shortly after he was smacked on the gloves by one that had flown off a length.

'Good luck, Graeme, keep your eye on the ball,' he said, heartily.

I did and hit a couple of nice fours but got caught at third man upper-cutting Akram not long afterwards for 14. As I trudged off with us 38 for three, Jon Lewis bade me a West Country cheerio: ''Ere, bloody 'ell, thought he'd be a bi' fas' for you, little 'un.' We won that game by 19 runs but I did not appear again until the following summer.

I was recalled for a 2nd XI Championship contest against Leicestershire at Campbell Park, Milton Keynes, a month after playing against Northants for Bedfordshire. By now I was being picked as an all-rounder, and although I had no great success with the bat in my five appearances that summer, my two three-day appearances returned six wickets for 81 runs.

But it was the summer of 1997, the year of my A levels, when I made my breakthrough proper. I was only still at school because my mum wouldn't allow me to leave at 16. I had no desire to go to university, as my parents had. 'I'll just build up an enormous debt and end up becoming a fat, alcoholic waster,' I told them. 'A degree doesn't mean what it did in your day.' I would say anything to convince Mum that three years staring out of windows during tutorials, thinking of cricket, was not an option for me.

When they were younger, it had been a huge step for Mum and Dad to go to university. They were probably the first in their families to do so, both coming from working-class backgrounds, and my grandparents had worked very hard to ensure that their kids could go to grammar school and beyond. Perhaps Mum thought I should be emulating them; she had already been disappointed that my brother had not gone and he was always much more studious than I was. Dad was undoubtedly more at ease because, having missed out on a professional career in cricket himself, he probably felt he could live one through us.

Mum informed me that while she appreciated my honesty, I had to get A levels as a bare minimum, that was not negotiable, as, whatever happened in the future, they would stand me in good stead. She also warned me that I'd have to work hard for them because with A levels you couldn't get by on a good memory and a gift for blagging it. Of course, that only strengthened my resolve to show her I could. So during my two years of sixth form I copied the essays of girls I'd managed to charm, having chosen subjects that gave me licence to waffle: English, history and psychology.

My 10,000-word dissertation for history was completed over two evenings, and several sittings, on our old Archimedes computer, which was particularly fond of crashing. It was on the attack on Pearl Harbor and the impact it had on the Second World War, and my conclusion was along the lines of 'It's what won it for us in the end because it brought on the Yanks, and about bloody time too.' That was the extent of my analysis of that momentous historical event. Ironically, I have been fascinated by the Second World War ever since, and reckon I'd produce a decent piece of work on it now, but then it was an obstacle to be hurdled asap.

As for my exams, I had done the square root of naff all in terms of revision and was on the first day of exam leave when Mum came into my bedroom, sat on the end of my bed and said: 'Look, son, I know we've had a lot of fall-outs over the past couple of years regarding your education. But just promise me that for the next fortnight you will get your head down, revise and do your best in these exams, because you owe it to yourself as much as anyone else.'

'Mum,' I said, 'I promise I'll do everything I can to make you happy and do myself justice.' And I genuinely meant it.

So that morning of 29 May 1997, Mum went off to work and I went back to sleep, before arising with the best of intentions. Shortly after nine o'clock, I picked up my history folder, ready to crack on with some learning.

The thing about my school folders that set them apart from those of my fellow pupils was that my signature was squiggled all over them. Most kids go through the process of practising for when they become famous but stop when they're eight. I was still doing it at 18.

I had just begun reading the words on the first page – 'Hippocrates, father of modern medicine, born on the island of Cos, circa 460 BC' – and as my eyes reached the end of the sentence, the home phone rang. It was Alec, who informed me that the 2nd XI were playing against Worcestershire in Milton Keynes and that Nick Cook, the captain, had asked for me as a replacement for David Roberts, who had been promoted to the Ones. With Mum's sentiments still ringing in my ears, there was a choice to make. 'Yeah, no problem, I'll be there in 20 minutes,' I told him. I packed my kit as quickly as I could, jumped into Alec's car and drove at breakneck speed.

At the end of that day, the second of the match, my hand was bleeding because it was the first time I'd ever bowled with a Duke's ball. That was my crude introduction to the fact that bowling off-spin for a living was going to leave me with a split finger. On the way home that evening, Alec asked: 'Do you think you'll get in trouble with Mum?'

'I think she'll kill me!' I replied.

Sure enough, when we got in, Mum was pacing up and down, with a face like thunder, screaming at the top of her voice: 'Where've you been? You promised me . . .'

'I've made my mind up,' I told her. 'I want to play cricket.'

'Don't worry,' Alec assured me 24 hours later, on the same journey, after I finished with figures of 26.5–14–54–3 in a six-wicket victory. 'You got a few wickets and blatantly you are going to have a county career.'

Even though it was little more than a throwaway comment, to me it was confirmation of my destiny. When you begin at that kind of level you can't help questioning whether you belong. Alec's opinion clinched it for me.

I promised Mum that I would do my best in the forthcoming exams, and that I would not fail them. Naturally, she had completely given up on me. But I couldn't turn down my opportunity: Northants were willing to invest further time in me and on the back of that performance I was signed up for the rest of that season.

My first summer contract was a £1000-a-month deal. The terms were simple: it lasted exactly three months and I received £3000. Forget the rate of pay, though, I'd landed my first job, and I felt like a millionaire. Compared to all my mates who still worked paper rounds, I was so content. It was everything I ever wanted and even though it upset Mum, I think she knew the outcome had always been inevitable. She was just disappointed that I didn't get my head down. Looking back, I can see her point, and I wouldn't want to parent someone as cocksure and arrogant as I was.

But my career was already developing apace. Two months after I had signed that contract with Steve Coverdale, Northamptonshire's chief executive, I got the call to play for an England Under-18 representative side in a three-day game against the touring Zimbabwe Under-19 team in Sleaford, Lincolnshire.

For this match, the ECB picked a strong XI, a good number of whom went on to have successful professional careers – like-minded souls to me, lads who had taken their first steps towards a life on the County Championship circuit.

We started well on the opening day and I was 70 not out overnight. Now that I was earning my own money, however, I was determined to have the time of my life, and so, it turned out, were the rest of the team. An action plan was devised for that evening and we headed for the big city – well, Lincoln – intent on finding a nightclub.

We piled into taxis and, after trawling the centre in our search, we eventually found one. You can probably imagine the behaviour that followed. We were necking beer, trying to get off with girls and generally dancing like idiots, having a great night.

The sensible ones went back at a reasonable time, and at the fag end of the evening there were just five of us left: myself, Richard Logan, Graham Napier, Michael Gough and Chris Hewison, a cracking Geordie lad who went on to become a copper in Gateshead.

We were well and truly tanked up and, mindful of the late hour, desperate for a cab back to our hotel. I appointed myself minister for transport but, having been told there were no five-seaters available in the office of the biggest rank around, I emerged onto the pavement to see a bloke on his own across the road.

'You've no idea where I can get a taxi from, have you, mate?' I asked him.

He obviously looked at me, saw the big blue neon taxi sign above my head and deduced that I was taking the proverbial. Speaking with a distinctly Mancunian accent, he inquired whether that indeed was the case. 'Noo, noo, noo, I ain't taken' the p---, mate. Mad for it, or wha'?' It was prime Oasis time and I had the accent down to a T.

I walked up the road thinking nothing of this innocent exchange, found a phone box, called for a taxi and, having secured one, began strolling back towards the others. As I did so, I suddenly became aware of all these lads piling out of the pub in front of me.

'What's going on here?' I wondered, naively. 'Bet there's going to be a fight.'

My nosiness enhanced by several pints, I edged towards where this posse was forming. But as I got closer I heard someone shout: 'That's him in the white T-shirt!'

I looked around, then down, and a cry of 'Oh, for f---'s sake' spilled out like a reflex action. Before I knew it, this lad who I'd given the full Liam Gallagher to appeared in front of me and, flanked by his pals, demanded: 'You took the p---; now I want an apology.'

'I am sorry if you think I was taking the p---, but I can promise you I wasn't,' I explained.

'That ain't good enough,' he barked.

Bravado took over. 'Go f--- yourself then,' I bellowed.

Sadly, I was not aware that a couple of his mates had crept into position on either side of me. A big right hook from one of these heavies connected with me good and proper and as I fell, my head hit the kerb. I managed to haul myself back up but got another one for good measure.

I didn't really know what was happening because I was so drunk, and I slumped back down into the gutter with blood pouring out of my eye and lip. Yards away Graham Napier was slouched in a doorway too comatose to do anything about it. Michael Gough meanwhile had legged it up the street to get away and Richard Logan was chatting up some bird – which proved to be par for the course for him – and so it was left to Chris Hewison to step in.

'Cum'n, lads, there's naw need for that,' he protested.

'Do you want one as well?'

Before he could answer, he had been smacked on the nose – it broke instantly and spread across his face.

What a sight we made when we got back to the hotel an hour or so later. Although we were covered in blood and in a complete mess, Hewy and I couldn't stop laughing. Alcohol had numbed both the pain and our brains and it was the funniest thing in the world.

After taking off my claret-stained top and washing my face in a cold shower in an attempt to sober up, I kidded myself that despite how things looked now, it wouldn't be too bad in the morning.

The stupidity of this opinion revealed itself first thing the next day, however, when Mum rang the hotel and was put through to my room. It dawned on me that I was in trouble when I went to speak. 'Aaargh aaah. Aaargh aaah,' I said, rather like you do after having a filling at the dentist's. Having failed to say hello properly, I wanted to keep conversation to a minimun. 'Bloody hell, what're you doing?' Mum asked. I somehow managed to force the words 'Nothing, just tired' through my new inflatable lips.

'Graeme, you've only gone and passed your A levels!' declared the ecstatic voice at the other end of the phone. 'I can't believe it!'

Mum was absolutely over the moon – she had been convinced I would get three Fs – yet I was barely able to thank her for calling with the news. She promised a family meal to celebrate on my return home, but all I wanted to do was get her off the phone as quickly as I could, so she wouldn't twig what had happened.

I staggered into the bathroom to discover the full extent of my deformed face. I was the Elephant Man. My lip looked as though it was halfway on the journey back to Towcester already, complete with a huge gash in it, while my left eye was completely closed. How was I going to get out of this one?

I sneaked down to breakfast to find Hewy, and sure enough there he was, sporting the full panda: two black eyes, a broken nose and all the hallmarks of having gone a few rounds with Frank Bruno.

'What on earth are we going to do?' I asked him.

'Dunno,' he said.

'Leave it to me then, I'll think of something.'

Over the next hour, we somehow managed part one of the operation, namely to avoid close contact with the coaching staff. Word of what had happened spread like wildfire amongst the other lads that morning, but as I went out to resume my innings I was still refusing to take it lying down.

'We'll get ourselves out of this,' I thought, because if the management found out we'd been on the lash the whole team would be in a lot of trouble and I did not want to let that happen. For once, I really focused on my batting and went on to get a hundred. Something like 140-odd. How I did it, I have no idea, because I couldn't see a thing out of my left eye.

While I was on the field I was also out of the firing line, and it was therefore not until lunch that Hewy and I had to face the music from Graham Saville, the coach. He sidled up to us and asked in a direct manner what had gone on. Recognising that we were being chummy, sitting down eating together, he presumed we'd had a ding-dong and had subsequently made peace.

'Look, Sav,' I said, 'that couldn't be further from the truth. It's a remarkable story and you won't believe me when I tell you.'

'Try me!' he said.

'Well, we all went to this bar last night and were being dead sensible. I was driving, so I didn't drink. It was all rather sedate, in fact, with everyone around a table chatting, when Chris leaned over to grab his drink. At that very same moment, I stood up and accidentally headbutted him.'

'Really?' he said. 'Well, what happened to the rest of your face then – fairy godmother?'

'You won't believe this either,' I continued, 'but when we got back to the hotel, after the other lads got out of the car – it being a three-door, you see – I tried to pick up some CDs that had fallen into the footwells in the back. As I turned to get out, I tripped over the seat belt and smashed my face on the car park.'

'CDs and seat belts! Are you sticking with that?'

'Yep.'

'Well, it's a good job you got a hundred,' he chuntered. 'That's the end of it.'

When I got back to Northampton that story was the source of mickey-taking for a month. Alec had relayed all the details to the lads within minutes of being told, and the evidence – a big scab on my lip – was still there when I did my first ever TV interview the following week.

That came during the second Under-19 Test between England and Zimbabwe on my home ground at Northampton. I had been selected on the back of my score in Sleaford and, after I followed up with an unbeaten 156 in a high-scoring draw there, I found myself talking to Ralph Dellor on the BBC with what looked like a beetroot for a mouth. My lips were still absolutely enormous and of a distinctly purple hue. Frankly, I looked ridiculous.

That draw meant we were 1–0 up heading into the final match – England had won the opening contest at Edgbaston by 112 runs after Ryan Sidebottom blitzed the Zimbabweans with 10 wickets.

The final Test was a fairly low-scoring game at Canterbury, which we won, but it was not memorable for anything that happened on the field. What sticks in my mind are events off it.

I was sharing a room with the captain, Zac Morris, a thick-accented Yorkshireman and one of the funniest guys I've ever met. We'd been out on the sauce the night before and I woke up on the final morning of the game, Sunday, 31 August 1997, feeling awful. As I came around at some ungodly hour, I noticed Zac sitting on the end of his bed, eyes rooted to the TV.

'What you doing, mate?' I asked, reaching for my watch. 'It's only seven o'clock.'

'Di's dead, Dodi's in coma,' he said, in his broad Barnsley twang.

Imagine trying to decipher that kind of dialect at such a delicate hour when you've had a few the night before.

'Pardon?'

'Lady Di – she's dead one. Dodi Fayed – he's one in coma.'

It was the equivalent of a JFK moment and I'll always remember where I was and how I found out. An almost surreal atmosphere prevailed everywhere you went that day and I remember driving home from Canterbury in my mum's red diesel 1.4 Metro. That journey would normally take two and a half hours in a decent car. On that evening it took me twice as long, as I chugged away at 55 miles per hour. Every radio station played 'Imagine' by John Lennon on what seemed to be a continuous loop. As a result, I hated it for years.

That came at the end of a remarkable summer for me. My cricketing education had been rapid over the previous 16 months and I had learned a great deal from following in Dad and Alec's footsteps and playing for Bedfordshire the year before. Dad's body had held up enough for him and Alec to open the batting together for Beds at the end of the 1994 season, but there was not enough left in the tank to hang on for me and he knocked Minor Counties stuff on the head in his mid-forties.

Like those two before me, I also opened for Bedfordshire, employing my own trusted method in a first-wicket partnership with former England batsman Wayne Larkins. The most fun way for me to bat has always been to try to hit every ball for four and block as a last resort – sometimes to the chagrin of my coaches – but it's a method I've refused to compromise.

At the other end, Ned had his own distinct way about him, and a calculated one at that – because he was on a bonus of a grand for every hundred he scored. We had 10 games that year and I think he got 11 hundreds. He was truly phenomenal. And the master of kidology, to boot.

Here was this dasher at one end, smashing it everywhere, or at least trying to, while he stood at the other, knocking it around for singles and punishing the bad ball by hitting it for four.

'Ooh, I'm loving watching this, Swanny,' he used to egg me on during our mid-pitch discussions.

To be honest, I didn't really need egging on to chase the bowling, but his encouragement was probably as much for his benefit as mine, as it allowed him to tick over at whatever rate he wished in the knowledge that I would be giving it some at the other end. Regardless of his tempo, his target was to reach three figures. Once accomplished, he would almost inevitably hit the next ball in the air and walk off smiling, content that he could sup a glass of red wine and await his £1000 cheque.

Ned was a lovely, lovely man and a cricketer who taught me a valuable lesson. Namely, how appearances can be so deceptive on the field. He was a really good player, especially against the spinners, but he knew the true value of the con. If he came up against an off-spinner on a helpful pitch, for example, he would jerk at the ball for the first four deliveries of an over, nodding to the bowler in appreciation along the way and offering the occasional 'Well bowled!' down the pitch. Then, the last delivery of the over would be hammered over the top for four or smashed out of the ground for six.

'Good response, that,' I would say. 'Is he bowling well?'

'No, he's bowling a shower of s---, but I don't want those seamers coming back on for a while yet.'

Every game he did it, and yet those Minor Counties captains never seemed to cotton on. It wasn't until he got to about 85 that it would suddenly occur to them that he was destroying their spinner. Personally, I've never been a good enough batsman to toy with bowlers like that, but that season with Ned taught me the importance of judging for yourself. Just because a batsman is blocking you, it doesn't necessarily mean you're bowling well. It can also mean quite the opposite.

I have always found bowling very instinctive and hardly ever decide what I am going to bowl until I am at the crease. I try to anticipate the batsman's movements – whether they're going to come down the pitch, or sweep, or just try to survive – and have always relied on that instinct. Also, as a bowler I genuinely know when I am bowling well because it is more about the way I feel than what my opponent is trying to do, so I tend to judge things from my perspective rather than how someone is playing against me.

It was for Bedfordshire that I first played against my brother Alec in a competitive match. Having grown up as perennial team-mates, it was a strange experience to be on the opposition side against Northants' 2nd XI in a 55-over game at Oundle School on 12 May

1996. To add to the piquancy of this sibling rivalry, I was also ridiculously keen to impress and follow him onto the Wantage Road staff.

I went in to bat with us on 125 for five, chasing 232 to win, but miles behind the run rate. As ever, I went after the bowling and struck 32 at better than a run a ball before, as fate would have it, Alec came on to bowl his ropey offies.

With around 60 runs required for victory, I advanced down the wicket – I am never that fussed when I get out, I tend to put it into context pretty quickly, 'You are an idiot, you got yourself out again' – and was properly embarrassed as I ran past the ball and was bowled. It was mortifying that I had given him licence to take the mickey out of me solidly for years.

I got my own back, however, at the start of the 2004 summer, during Alec's return to Northampton with Lancashire. He had suffered a stinking lbw decision by Allan Jones, to fall for nought, in the County Championship draw that preceded this Totesport League game, and I effected his second dismissal of the trip to exact my personal revenge.

We were defending only 161 and Lancashire were absolutely cruising it when I got a couple of wickets to make things interesting. It meant Alec walked in, and this was the first time I'd ever bowled at him in a competitive match. With Mum and Dad both watching on, a defensive block greeted my first delivery, but next ball he shuffled across his stumps and missed a big turner to be bowled round his legs.

They needed just a few runs to win, but that was irrelevant – I'd only gone and dismissed my brother! My celebrations were reminiscent of Diego Maradona's drug-addled rant at the camera in the 1994 World Cup. I was a crazed lunatic, jumping around all over the place, and everyone joined in because they all knew Alec as a former colleague. I remember looking over to the scoreboard, where Mum and Dad always sat. Mum gave me a little wave as if to say 'Well done, love.' Dad, meanwhile, sat with his head in his hands. Even 20 minutes later, when I glanced again, he had not broken the pose.

Afterwards, Dad said: 'Ah just can't believe it. What did yee get him oot for?'

Two months later, on 25 June 2004, in the reverse fixture at Old Trafford, I caught Alec. It was one of the best catches I've ever taken, diving one-handed at backward point, off Jason Brown. I've only recently discovered that it was Alec's last professional game. I wish, in some ways, it hadn't stuck. He will always remember that innings of 22 as his departure from the professional ranks, and I feel a bit guilty now for my part in it. Sure, in professional sport you know that these kind of things can happen, but it's such a shame when it turns out like that.

Everything fell into place for me but it didn't for Alec. Even the events of that day showed that. I opened the batting and whacked 78 to charge us to our 177-run target in just 27.1 overs. Alec provided symmetry that afternoon when he caught me off Dinesh Mongia, as I attempted another big shot, but he could have had a much better career, and may have done with one more chance – because he was a much better player than his record suggests. I see some guys now and it makes me genuinely angry that Alec is not still playing. He is head and shoulders above half of them.

He is more than happy now as a sports writer on the *Northampton Chronicle & Echo* – journalism suits him because he's a miserable bastard – but at the time he wanted to go on his own terms. He chose to look for pastures new at the end of that 2004 season, at the same time as I made my move from Northamptonshire to Nottinghamshire, but nothing came of his search. His big fear was ending up at Derbyshire. He wasn't having that. 'Because I f------ hate Derby,' he memorably told me. It is not too bad now it has been redeveloped, but anyone who played there at that time will know exactly what he meant. There has never been a less receptive place on the planet to play cricket.

I cherished the top-level matches I played alongside Alec. We had some great times in my early days with Northamptonshire. One of the most memorable games was a NatWest Trophy quarter-final against Surrey, on 28 July 1999, during the days when Surrey seemed to win everything.

There were two reasons for this game at Northampton sticking in my mind. First, a spectator died as we were warming up. In the middle of our running drills, our attention was drawn to the top of the Ken Turner Stand. Just in front of the press box, at the top of a huge flight of stairs, was slumped an old chap. 'Look at that bloke up there, he looks as though he's dead,' Alec said, innocently. It soon became apparent that he had indeed conked it, and two minutes after we had laughed this comment off, mass panic ensued. It turned out the poor old bugger had had a heart attack.

The incident naturally led to us players discussing whether the game would be called off. But our chief executive Steve Coverdale soon answered this question authoritatively with his address to the public over the tannoy. 'We will be putting back the start time by 14 minutes,' he announced. That figure has always stuck in my head. How on earth did they come up with 14 minutes? It seemed so ridiculous. This poor old boy had snuffed it, and they had delayed the match by the number of minutes it had taken for the medics and his family to cart him off the ground!

When the game belatedly began, we batted first and after our captain Matthew Hayden was dismissed cheaply, I joined Alec in the middle. I walked in with the score at 31 for one and we raced things on to 90 by the 14th over. We were having a whale of a time and before we knew it, our partnership was worth 59 off 40 balls. This was shortly before modern scoring rates went through the roof and it was as if we had carried our carefree attitude from the back garden to a cup quarter-final.

Alec had never been thought of as a limited-overs player but on this occasion we were going stroke for stroke, smashing it everywhere and having the time of our lives. Then Saqlain Mushtaq, who had been the scourge of county batsmen that summer, came on and everything changed in the most dramatic way possible. Alec was trapped leg before for 35, attempting to turn Saqlain's second ball to the on side, and I soon followed when I swept to deep square leg, for 42.

Our fun was well and truly over. And things rapidly became serious, as we were bundled out for just 152. We had lost nine wickets for 62 runs in 22 overs. Although I had Alec Stewart caught at silly point by our Alec with my first ball and also did for Ian Ward soon afterwards, we were absolutely hammered, and lost by seven wickets.

Playing with my brother was simply great. My maiden five-wicket haul for Northampton was against Sussex in our final home game of a disappointing 1998 season for the club, and on a pitch which was penalised for being too spinner-friendly. Shortly after we won our third Championship fixture of the season, securing 20 points in the process, the fax from Lord's arrived to confirm that we had been deducted 25 points for an unfit surface which 'displayed uneven bounce and turned excessively early in the match'.

To be fair, it was ridiculous. The strip in question was about three months old – it had been marked poor by the umpires for a one-day game ten days earlier – with huge craters in it. During this particular match it turned so much that I didn't even get a bowl in the first innings. Michael Davies, our slow left-armer, played one of his first games and he and Jason Brown took five wickets each as Sussex were dismissed for a paltry 72.

In the second innings, I replicated their success but only after a crucial intervention from Alec. I had four wickets to my name when James Kirtley ran down the wicket off Brownie and got himself in a right old tangle. The ball got caught up between his legs, and although he had no idea where it had gone he decided to run for a single. It dribbled no further than to where my brother was positioned at silly point. Kirtley was about 11 yards out when he realised the calamitous nature of his decision, and stopped motionless in mid-pitch. But rather than walking up to dislodge a bail, Alec opted for an underarm throw from three yards and somehow missed the stumps!

The whole place was in hysterics and, after regaining his ground, even Kirtley was chortling so much he couldn't face up for another couple of minutes. But I had the last laugh when I dismissed him with my next ball, to seal my glory moment. As I walked off, I thanked Alec for his contribution to my landmark. But as we made eye contact it struck me that his faux pas had not been made with me in mind. Nor had it dawned on him that he might get away with claiming he had carried out a brotherly gesture. 'I would love to pretend that was on purpose, but I can't,' he admitted. 'It was just a s--- bit of fielding.' It was a moment to cherish.

3

TOP OF THE WORLD

M Y SUCCESS with England Under-19 during late summer 1997 led to my first experience of a prolonged overseas tour, in the winter that followed. And what a memorable winter it turned out to be.

I was selected for the seven-week tour to South Africa, which incorporated two Tests and three one-day internationals, with an Under-19 World Cup thrown in at the end. It was the first time I'd been away for any sustained period of time with my mates, and we treated it accordingly. The entire two months were spent in much the same way we would have tackled a fortnight in Ibiza.

We were not paid for our exertions, other than a few hundred quid expenses, but the whole thing was an absolute hoot. Our group was packed with real characters – Stephen Peters, Rob Key, Owais Shah, Paul Franks, Richard Logan and Jonathan Powell among them – intent on having a laugh. Being teenagers, we were still learning life's lessons and some of those were extremely favourable to us, such as the fact that booze was very cheap in South Africa and that the local girls were susceptible to English accents. It was carnage from day one, and how my liver coped with that trip, I'll never know. There wasn't a night of the week when we weren't all out on the gas. Oliver Reed would have quaked in his booze.

On the field, we played some terrible cricket at times but we managed to scrape a draw in the two-Test series, after following on at both Newlands and Fochville. From a personal point of view, my performances were good, and my statistics backed that up: I top-scored with 75 in Cape Town and returned figures of 43–5–139–3 and 42–15–90–4 in South Africa's two 500-plus first-innings scores.

We clung on in each of those matches, but then got absolutely destroyed in the one-day series. It was so bad, in fact, that it reached the point where our tour manager, Phil Neale, and our coach, John Abrahams, sat us all down for a team meeting and read us our fortunes.

'You lot are a bunch of prima donnas; you don't listen, you think you know best,' we were told. (Of course we did, we were a group of 19-year-olds with the world at our feet.) 'You don't agree with what we do, when we train or how we train. You're always whingeing, so do it yourself. You're on your own. Let's see how far you get,' they added.

Of course, they still organised the training sessions, but true to their word they washed their hands of us once our tour matches against the South Africans were over. They simply let us go our own way.

Well, as luck would have it, and it was more luck than anything else, we went on to win that World Cup.

It was anything but a smooth ride through the initial group phase, our struggle summed up by the fact we lost to Bangladesh and only beat Namibia by three wickets – our passage secured by virtue of a superior net run rate to the Bangladeshis'. In the next round, the Super League stage, we beat a very good Pakistan team, one that included Shoaib Malik, Abdul Razzaq and Imran Tahir, then lost to India in a rain-affected contest in Benoni. Surprisingly, Pakistan lost all three of their round-robin matches, but with Australia defeating the Indians, it turned our game against the old enemy into the equivalent of a semi-final – from our perspective at least.

For us it all came down to this contest at Newlands: victory would potentially see us progress as group winners but defeat would send us home. In contrast, the Australians had won their two previous matches so convincingly that they would not have viewed the match in the same manner. Because their run rate was far superior to ours, and they went in with a 100 per cent record, it was almost a dead rubber for them, and in reality, the chances of us pipping them for a place in the final were remote.

Naturally, Australia were well fancied to win the tournament – as they always are – but the only guy from that particular team who has gone on to do well is Marcus North. He was given out caught behind by our wicketkeeper Nick Wilton off Paul Franks to a ball that bounced well short of his gloves. I remember being a bit sheepish about that, but then again it was the Australians after all, and we were in with a shout of getting through.

Our chances of progressing were significantly enhanced when we managed to roll them for 147, and then, during the tea break, Phil Neale, because he is the most organised man I've ever come across, calculated that if we knocked the runs off in fewer than 33 overs we would displace Australia at the top of the group.

In normal circumstances, chasing such a low score would require a sensible approach, but we pretty much teed off from the word go, and the Aussies didn't seem to twig why. Paul Franks, our pinch-hitter at number three, had been smacking it around for quite some time when, at around the 25-over mark, the Australian management finally got a message out to the middle.

But Allan Border and the rest of their backroom staff had realised too late that we could overhaul them, and knock them out of the tournament, with a hasty chase. We had somehow pulled the wool over their eyes and, having gone out to join Franks for the final rites, I celebrated the winning runs as though we were definitely in the final. We won by six wickets and, with just 29.1 overs used, we were indeed in the box seat to qualify. Only a comprehensive defeat of Pakistan by India two days later could deny us. They did win, as it happened, but a clatter of early Indian wickets – they collapsed to 38 for four in pursuit of 189 – prevented them completing the comprehensive result required and our unlikely passage was confirmed.

New Zealand, a team that had reached the final in a similar back-door manner, and one that we had already defeated in the tournament, awaited us at the Wanderers on 1 February 1998. For the first time in my life the magnitude of the game I was about to play hit me. Approximately 8,000 schoolkids had been given the day off to be there, so there was that monotonous high-pitched noise, the kind characteristic of England schoolboy football internationals, reverberating around the ground throughout. But why would we care? After all, this was a World Cup final.

The Kiwis managed a respectable 241 for six but our batsmen showed no nerves whatsoever and we hammered them, knocking their score off with four overs to spare. Stephen Peters hit a hundred and our captain, Owais Shah, finished on 54 not out. They set the stage for my kind of innings and my unbeaten 22 helped us over the line in a seven-wicket victory. We were officially the best Under-19 team on the planet.

As a result of that trip we returned home with our reputations massively enhanced. The semi-final and final had been screened live on TV and, because the England Under-19 team had done well for the first time in ages, a number of us walked into our county first teams on the back of it.

It felt like such a huge moment, and at the time we were the dog's doodahs, or so we kept being told. We would form the basis of the next successful England Test team, the press wrote; this was the England team that would win the senior World Cup in five years, they claimed – and with our bravado overflowing, who were we to doubt them?

As things panned out, very few of us went on to play for England, which was a great shame because there were some very talented guys in the group. In the winter of 2010–11, I was the sole member of that team still flying the flag at international level. Rob Key played for England with a deal of success, of course, but apart from Owais, none of the other lads got past county cricket. Some didn't get much beyond their county second teams.

It might have been something to do with our attitude. As Phil Neale and John Abrahams had surmised, us players were united in the belief that we knew best, and when I look back at those days I do so with more than a little embarrassment. I can't believe some of the things I did and said, but I suppose that's all part of growing up. We were a very immature bunch of 19-year-olds, living in denial of that very fact. The most dangerous people in the world are the stupid ones who think they're clever, but arrogant teenagers who think they know everything aren't far behind them. I was certainly one of those.

Looking back, we went overboard and never tried to clamber back onto dry land. We were happily going out every night of the week until closing time in whatever pub we fancied, necking booze and trying to cop off with birds. Our behaviour was disgraceful. A pint of beer was the equivalent of about 20 pence and hardly any of us could hold our drink, yet we still gave it a good crack every single night.

No wonder some of those boys didn't progress any further. We all thought the rock-'n'-roll route was the way to go, and I certainly took that attitude with me when I was selected on the senior England tour of South Africa the following year. That much could be seen from my reaction to not being selected: if I wasn't playing, I felt I might as well go out and have a good time. But in big-boy cricket that doesn't really work.

Arguably, our problem was winning in spite of an appalling attitude. Such was our proficiency on the social scene that we knew all the bar staff and doormen at the hottest spots in Cape Town that winter. Our notoriety was for off-field rather than on-field action, and after that semi-final victory over Australia we perhaps hit an all-time low.

We went into a bar called Green Man – later renamed Tin Roof – just down the road from the Newlands hotel we were staying in. Our Australian counterparts also happened to have congregated there and in the midst of them Allan Border was sporting their Dick of the Day outfit, a horrendously loud Hawaiian shirt and neon sunhat combination, for his part in their elimination from the competition.

At some point during our revelry, someone decided it would be a good idea to grab Border, wrestle him to the floor and enact an old-school pile-on. So here was a Test legend, the then highest Test run scorer of all time, who had been enough of a sport to change into this outfit and have a quiet drink, being man-handled by a bunch of muppets who saw fit to rugby-tackle him to the ground and dive on him. Talk about a lack of respect.

I certainly wasn't the first man in the pile but nor was I the last. It was hilarious at the time, or so we felt, but, once back to his feet, he must have looked at our team and thought: 'What a bunch of cocky idiots they are.' It makes me cringe with embarrassment to think back to that episode.

By that stage, I had already competed against other players of renown, albeit fleetingly, at the end of the 1997 season. My debut came against Worcestershire in an AXA Life League game on 10 August, just a few days before representing England Under-18 against the Zimbabweans at Sleaford.

In fact, my first ball as a professional cricketer was bowled at Graeme Hick, which was a big thing for me, because he was my dad's favourite cricketer by miles at the time. Thankfully, I was unperturbed about competing against blokes of his calibre and I took two for 28 off my eight overs. The maiden wicket of my career was David Leatherdale, who came down the wicket at me and was bowled through the gate. Then I got Vikram Solanki fortuitously, caught down the leg side by wicketkeeper Russell Warren, a great mate as well as team-mate of mine.

Remarkably, I remained pretty calm throughout my debut, aside from the fielding part. Of all the aspects of my game, batting and bowling were always a breeze for me, but I never really fielded well in those days and I won't pretend I've ever liked it. I've always hated it, in fact, although standing at slip is bearable because I get to talk to two other blokes next to me.

In that game, as the new kid on the block, I was constantly thinking: 'I hope they don't hit it to me now.' Quite simply, my concern was that I could lose the game for us with one misfield. Don't get me wrong, I would have backed myself not to lose it with either bat or ball, but with the fielding it could easily have been a disaster.

As a kid, when you're the best player in your team you're generally the captain, that's how it rolls, and of course when you're captain you choose where to field. So I naturally always chose to field at slip. You can use the excuse that you are keeping a close eye on things and directing the game from there. When I wasn't captain, and couldn't wangle a spot in the slips, I quite liked square leg because you could have a natter with the umpire, and that has always suited my nature. Stick me in solitude at cover or mid-on and my mind goes to some weird and wonderful places. So, when it comes to concentration, my team and I have always been better served if I've been able to go and have a chat with someone, somewhere on the field.

There must be so many young cricketers like that in county second teams, but thankfully they saw there was some talent in me in the batting and bowling departments and I got the gig. On that particular day I was at the mercy of Rob Bailey and patrolled the deep in fear. For 99 per cent of the game it looked as if I would start with a win, but we somehow lost by a couple of wickets. Worcestershire needed 16 off the last over, bowled by John Emburey. To us this was going to be a walk in the park. However, Stuart Lampitt had other ideas and completely laid into him. Embers tried to take the pace off one delivery, but it came out as a waist-high full toss, and Lampitt thrashed it over the ice-cream vans about 200 yards away from the ground. Despite our seemingly impregnable position, we ended up losing the match with a ball to spare.

Incidentally, my debut match turned out to be Embers' last, just 10 days short of his 45th birthday. Defeat is never nice and it had blotted my day, but I walked away happy it had gone well for me personally. So well, in fact, that I featured in the remaining one-day games I was available for that season. Three more solid performances convinced me that there was a county career ahead of me. Returning home as a World Cup winner in February 1998 also increased belief in my own ability.

A by-product of this confidence was that I was developing strong opinions as a cricketer that were perhaps ahead of my years. I have always bucked the trend and actively sought to be different at times, and some of the things I thought during my adolescence I still stand by today.

My main gripe as I approached my first full season of county cricket was the apparent acceptance that Northamptonshire should know their place in the domestic circuit's food chain. This was an attitude that I vigorously rebelled against. I came back from South Africa bristling with confidence, considering myself to be the bee's knees, and walked into an environment with an altogether different atmosphere.

Our plans for the summer were discussed at length in an organised pre-season team meeting. The idea behind it was to identify the games we were most likely to win and how. Considering a batch of five one-day games in just over a week in the Benson & Hedges Trophy, David Ripley, our vice-captain at the time, said: 'If we look to win three of them, then we might get through to the next round.'

Brimming with the petulance of youth, I argued that this plan was plain stupid, and that looking to win all five of them was the way to go. The response from the established players was along the lines of: 'Come on, we've got to play Warwickshire twice, and they always hammer us.'

This apathy really clashed with how I thought about things. I have never seen the point of entering a game, even when an underdog, thinking anything less than 'We can win this.' Naturally, in that meeting I got shouted down and was left really frustrated by the collective attitude of my new team-mates. To this day I am glad I said it, though, and to my mind, the subservient outlook was the reason Northants never won a major trophy during my time there. We had a really good team in 1998 but lacked the attitude of winners. Successful teams will give anything to come out on top, but to us winning was a bonus, and that rankled.

Our team was chock-full of talent: Mal Loye, Russell Warren,

David Sales, Rob Bailey, Devon Malcolm, Paul Taylor, Ripley as the keeper. We had a seriously good cricket team yet didn't even get close to competing for trophies. At the time Warwickshire were winning everything, yet they did not necessarily have the best XI in the country. They won things on the back of Dermot Reeve instilling a belief into his players that you could win any game of cricket, from any position, if you played a certain way. Success should have been within Northamptonshire's reach as the nineties gave way to the noughties, but the entire club ethos was wrong.

It was only when I left to go to Nottinghamshire years later that it really hit home. At the corresponding pre-season meeting in 2005, my first with the club, director of cricket Mick Newell made no bones about his priorities. We want to win the Championship, he told us, and we will deal with the one-day cricket when we come to it.

I thought this attitude was brilliant because there is such a difference between having ambition and merely playing for a good team. No matter what it took, we were going to try to finish top that season, and the boldness of our plan was refreshing because it was the first time I'd experienced it. It was certainly not the sole reason we would be crowned champions that September, but the fact the whole squad had that lofty target embedded in their heads played its part. It felt as if we were destined to win it. And, at the time, 2005 was the proudest year of my life.

It would have been understandable if my early enthusiasm had been sapped by my first-class debut against Cambridge University on 14 April 1998. After all, the start of this three-day match at Fenner's was delayed by snow flurries, and what little play was possible was curtailed at tea on the first afternoon by heavy rain. I didn't even make it onto the field.

Poor weather also interrupted my County Championship bow against Surrey at The Oval, a few days later, when Alec and I became the first brothers to represent Northants in the competition since Peter and Jim Watts in 1966.

Persistent showers meant the final day started with Surrey 88 for one in the first innings of the contest, reducing the match to a scrap over bonus points. I made a pleasing start and had figures of one for 13 from my opening five overs: Nadeem Shahid, my victim, stumped down the leg side. By the end of the innings, however, those figures had taken on a rather different sheen. Ali Brown, later to become a team-mate at Trent Bridge, destroyed me and I finished with 13–1–91–1. He smacked six sixes off me in a savage hundred. Although he might not have made it to three figures at all because Mal Loye jogged over the boundary with the ball off one of his early blows.

That kind of thing is a semi-success for a spinner and, buoyed by it, I truly believed I would snare him again, so my response was to take the pace off the ball, bowling slower and slower as our duel developed. But this proved a real lesson for me because it simply didn't work. It was the first time I'd played against someone who, when you held it back, had the ability to hit the ball even further. A rude introduction it may have been, but as a young spinner you have to find answers quickly because word gets round the circuit fast, and you need to have Plan B ready for the next time.

My figures looked like a car crash but John Emburey told me afterwards that he had admired the way I kept throwing it up. 'That's good,' he said. 'It will take you a long way in this game – just don't f------ do it again while playing for us, will you!' It was a nice way of telling me he thought I had talent but needed to find a different, or more economical, way of expressing it.

As a coach, Embers was brilliant for me. First and foremost he was the one that encouraged my selection. 'This lad can bowl,' he kept telling people around the club while he was still a player. Now, as first-team coach, he had a big say on who played. Our main spinner at that time was Jeremy Snape, who Embers recognised as a good one-day bowler but someone who was unlikely to prise people out in four-day cricket. Intent on selecting a spinner who would bag wickets in the longer game, he gave me my opportunity from the very start of the season.

From my experience on the county circuit, Embers's brain was the best to pick in terms of how to bowl at different players. He knew what fields worked, where certain batsmen would try to hit you and how you could stop them. He simply understood spin bowling. For a young lad who was full of it – I didn't dare talk back to Embers, mind – he was the perfect mentor. I was always cheeky to others but here was a guy I'd idolised as a kid, and I was determined to get as much out of him as I possibly could.

It was never technical stuff, in fact there's not anyone I've come across in the world that stands out for technique – you can either bowl off-spin, ripping it with some semblance of control, or you can't, and once you've got your action, the basics are in place and there's not a lot more to be done – but Embers had a brilliant understanding of the tactics of bowling spin, the awareness of when to try this or that, and how to bowl spin intuitively.

I was a feature of the Northamptonshire team that season, and flourished in the Championship. My 22 wickets cost just 30 apiece and I scored 548 runs, at an average of 34.25, including my maiden first-class hundred, against the champions Leicestershire at Grace Road. When I took 91 off the Derbyshire attack in my very next innings, it strengthened my belief that I was destined to be a batsman who bowled part-time spin. You are fairly impressionable at that age, of course, and my career turned out nothing like that, so our captain, Kevin Curran, must have been sick of this cocksure kid telling him he was wasted down at the bottom and ought to bat at number five. I genuinely believed it as well.

My scores were clearly influencing my thoughts but thankfully a few wise people recognised my staple was the pretty thirty/caught at cover combo, and that wasn't what most teams looked for in a number five. In subsequent seasons they did experiment with me in that position a couple of times in the Championship, and I acquitted myself well enough until a pair against Nottinghamshire at Trent Bridge, the first of my career, secured a permanent relocation to the tail. These days, there is no better feeling for an ageing campaigner like myself than winning the toss and not having to put your kit on for a day or so.

Number eight has also proved a successful position for me, and against Leicestershire that July, I walked out with us in trouble at 124 for six in the first innings. I batted for a long time with one of the top-order batsmen, Mal Loye, and because the ball was swinging a bit it felt as if I was playing the equivalent of a Test match innings, keeping my head down. In reality, I was probably scoring a run every one and a half balls, but the match situation and conditions dictated a watchful approach. Yet, with three figures just a couple of blows away, I flashed wildly at a David Millns away-swinger and nicked off for 92. I had hauled us up to a respectable 274 for eight, but everyone in the changing room was genuinely gutted for me getting so close to three figures. Tongue firmly in cheek, my reply was: 'Never mind, I'll just get one in the second innings, instead.'

Little did I think that this would actually come to fruition, but from an almost identical position, in the brown stuff again at 128 for six, still 32 runs behind our hosts, I grafted first of all with David Ripley and then for what seemed an eternity with Paul Taylor, who, thanks to his similar love of driving fast and hitting the town, was known as my dad within the dressing room. I loved Roadie to death, so I was more than happy spending time out in the middle with him.

In Chris Lewis, Alan Mullally, David Millns and Phil Simmons, Leicestershire had a really fine county attack. Once again, however, I defied them and climbed into the 90s, only this time, when I reached 97 I hit Darren Maddy over mid-on for four to bring up three figures. Easy, the first of many hundreds, I thought; there'll be loads of them along the way. How wrong I was. And quite unbelievably, our efforts failed to stave off defeat as Leicestershire made an audacious assault on a 204-run target and got home in fewer than 20 overs.

Nevertheless, and in spite of my reservations about the lack of belief within it, it was a contented Northants dressing room at that time, and I was really happy to be playing first-class cricket. Professional sport doesn't create utopias but things were friendly enough. Although Kevin Curran divided opinion, particularly among the younger lads, to me the deal with him as captain was simple: if you gave everything and tried your hardest, he absolutely loved you. I responded well to him for that reason. He couldn't give a monkey's what I was like in the changing room. I made him laugh and he loved that, but all he was interested in was me giving everything on the pitch.

Despite having one of the best teams on paper, however, we finished fourth from bottom in that 1998 season, the final one of the single-division County Championship. But I had a hell of a time, adored playing for the club and felt comfortable enough to be myself. I was fairly brash and cocky, but because I was doing well, people tended to tolerate me. That's always the case in dressing rooms. If you are happy to take the mickey and have jokes at your own expense as well, it's great for team spirit.

My performances during a really solid season proved sufficiently good to merit a place on the England A tour to Zimbabwe and South Africa the following winter. It was a very strong squad led by Michael Vaughan, who I had not met prior to departure. I was soon to discover what a brilliant captain he was, on a truly amazing tour.

In Zimbabwe, you played against five different teams, all with different names – a couple of provinces, a President's XI, a Farmer's XI, a Country District XI – yet virtually the same players would turn out each time. That meant you were up against the Flower brothers, the Whittalls, the Strangs, no matter the nomenclature of the opposition.

In one particular 50-over game against Mashonaland at Old Hararians we got bowled out for 159 on a dodgy wicket, and the words Vaughan spoke as we formed a huddle on the outfield before our defence of the target have always stuck with me.

'Right now, listen up,' he told us. 'I couldn't give a f--- if we lose this game. But I will be properly p----- off if you lot don't give it absolutely everything. Try new things, throw yourself around the field, bowl as quick as you can, give it a rip. Then if we lose I will not be bothered.'

He was the first captain I had played under who'd taken that attitude onto the field. He'd thrown down his challenge knowing it would bring out the best in players. It did: Mashonaland only made 86.

I was immediately impressed with Vaughan's leadership, and it was no surprise to me that he went on the full England tour the following year, despite a fairly modest county record on the minefields of Headingley. Nor did it surprise me that he went on to become England captain, and a bloody good one, because he simply knew how to motivate people. There is a skill to that and I always felt very relaxed playing under him. Spirit was always harnessed rather than quashed.

We had a very good team in Zimbabwe that winter – Andrew Flintoff, Steve Harmison and Robert Key some of the primary names. Darren Maddy went on the back of his exploits with Leicestershire and Dean Cosker was the second spinner. I loved every minute of it. It was much more professional than any tour I had experienced but the level of frivolity remained high, as you would expect with the kind of blokes involved.

From a career development point of view, it was a great tour for me because I took 21 first-class wickets at 25 apiece. It told me that I was able to compete not only at home but overseas as well, and when I went back to South Africa for a Test series 10 years later, I still had good memories of bowling well at Newlands, where we beat the South African Board President's XI, and the Wanderers, the venue of our crushing 10-wicket victory over Gauteng, in the locker. I finished with a Michelle Pfeiffer in the first innings in Johannesburg and seven wickets in all, and was even sent in first to knock off the 27 runs we required to wrap up the match.

Unbeaten throughout, we preserved an England A record that had stood since 1994, although it still resembled something like a stag trip at times. Most of my fondest memories involve laughter off the field, and centre around Freddie Flintoff.

One of the reporters on that trip, the *Daily Telegraph*'s Charles

Randall, had called Fred a flat-track bully in print after he got a hundred in that match against Gauteng, and we were out for a drink on a subsequent night when Charlie came over to explain himself.

'You can call me what you like,' Fred tersely replied. 'But I am going to put you in a dustbin.' Without pause for thought, he picked Charlie up, carried him outside and placed him head first into the nearest bin as promised. All you could see were two little legs kicking out of the top. Fred patted him on the soles of his shoes. 'Flat-track bully, am I?'

If it hadn't clicked before, this was the time I realised that the lanky lad I'd played against as a schoolboy had developed into a man mountain. He had the strength of 10 blokes, and that physical prowess had shown itself on another night, earlier on the tour, when we made a trip to a bar in Harare.

A rugby team was having an 'underpants' party while getting merrily bladdered. They all sported briefs, and nothing else, and so Fred mischievously debagged one of them as he strolled past, following it with a friendly thumbs-up to signify the playful nature of his action.

Taking it in good spirit, this lad turned around with a smile and went to high-five Fred. But Steve Harmison, blissfully unaware of what had preceded this action, caught a glimpse of raised hands out of the corner of his eye and got the wrong end of the stick. To a Geordie, once arms are raised it's dust-up time, so in he waded. In turn, some of the rugby players saw Harmy on the charge and suddenly it all kicked off. Before we knew it, the manager was herding us all outside. 'Don't fight in my bar!' he roared.

Out on the lawn it was like a Mexican stand-off. On our team no one really wanted to fight at all, whereas the rugby team seemed considerably keener. Thankfully, Fred put an end to it all. As a pair of lads came at him, he managed to grab them both, secure them in headlocks and sit back down on the grass without loosening his grip.

'Now then,' he said. 'Who else wants a row with Uncle Freddie?'

The two lads were turning blue as the captain of the rugby team turned peacemaker. 'Good on you, lads,' he said. 'Let's all go and have a beer.' Only seconds earlier these farmer types were about to kick our heads in. It was an amazing turnaround but one the cowards amongst us were thankful for.

There were a number of significant developments on that trip – my own aside – with Fred showing himself to be a maturing cricketer of real substance and Vaughan emerging as A-grade captaincy material. The latter's attitude left a resounding impression upon me, and encouraged me to be my own character. Even then, with limited experience of the job at any kind of senior level, Vaughan had a straightforward approach: if it works for you, it works for me.

Much later, it amazed me that Vaughan and Duncan Fletcher had such a good working rapport, because their attitudes couldn't be more polarised. Even though I didn't play in Vaughan's England team, I could understand why they were so successful. You never felt excessive pressure to do well because he made his primary target alleviating it for all those under him. He wanted people to relax and express themselves, whereas Fletch was naturally more conservative.

Vaughan and I first sat in a senior England changing room together on the same day later that year, at the start of the 1999–2000 tour to South Africa. My immediate observations were that it was a divided place: jealousy amongst the players was rife, bitterness about previous selection snubs lingered, and there were a couple of ex-captains still around. Nasser Hussain did brilliantly in shaking all that up, which later allowed Vaughany to take things a step further. I have always wondered whether Vaughany observed that environment on our maiden international trip and vowed that his England team would never be like that.

Certainly, the way we played as an A team was rather un-English, I guess, and Vaughany was the exact opposite of what I expected a Yorkshireman to be. You hear stories about the obstinate, dour Yorkshire way of playing – they have never been known as the most progressive county – so it was a real surprise that this young buck from Sheffield was so Australian in his way of thinking. Or at least how I perceived Australians to be when it came to cricket.

4

MISSING THE BUS

OVER A period of 10 years, every new England call-up received his good news directly from the chairman of selectors, David Graveney. Every new England call-up, that is, except me. It was August 1999, days after Graham Gooch and Mike Gatting lost their jobs on the selection panel, that I was picked for the final Test squad of a disastrous summer. The choice of a certain G.P. Swann of Northamptonshire for the final match of the series against New Zealand at The Oval might have surprised a few people, and it was certainly a surprise to me when I found out.

I was actually on the sauce at legendary Northampton nightspot McGinty's, with my best mate Richard Logan, when Grav called to relay the news. And my very location meant I missed his call. In those days, McGinty's had what it called a mad half hour (it lasted for 40 minutes – can you see what they've done there?) when drinks were cheap as chips and a mishmash of songs would be played 30 seconds at a time. It was a real cocktail of booze and music mayhem: you'd go from the Stone Roses to Bon Jovi to Van Morrison in a flash and the crowd would be heady with delight. And it was during this kind of frenzy, with senses impaired on two fronts, that I was unable to hear my mobile phone ringing in my pocket. It was only later that I noticed the missed calls and went outside to listen to my messages. One, semi-frantic in tone, was from my mum asking me to ring her back.

'David Graveney's been trying to get hold of you. You've been picked in the Test squad,' she told me matter-of-factly.

I couldn't quite believe it, but I was in the perfect place to celebrate, so I steamed back into McGinty's and the drinks were on me.

I always had a laugh with Grav after that initial call-up.

'You're a difficult man to get hold of,' he would say.

'Well, I was in a nightclub, Grav, what do you expect?'

'Yeah, right, Swanny. What were you really doing?'

Just goes to show, I suppose, that when you have a certain reputation, even when you tell the truth, people don't always believe you. He wouldn't have a bar of it, and it would clearly have been a lot more believable had I fabricated some tall tale. As it turned out, there was plenty of time to come up with a cracker for the next time he rang.

It was to be another eight years down the line when I got another Grav call, and I was fully expecting that one because my Nottinghamshire team-mate Ryan Sidebottom helpfully pre-warned me. 'Don't say owt but we got told in changing room today, you're in team for Sri Lanka tour,' he said. 'I'm not supposed to tell you but you may as well know.'

Given my previous experience of such a call, or lack of it, I thought I had better be prepared this time, so I even told my wife Sarah, who I had only recently started dating, that we had to delay going out that evening until I'd received the news. I was staying at her flat, and so we wedged ourselves on the sofa in anticipation.

Typically, Grav didn't get around to ringing with the confirmation on that Saturday night until approximately half past ten, and it just so happened that *Last Night of the Proms* was on TV.

'What are you doing?' he asked during our brief chat.

'Me, Grav. Oh, I'm just sat in watching *Last Night of the Proms*,' I said, with 'Land of Hope and Glory' blaring in the background.

'Yeah, right, whatever, Swanny.'

'No, seriously, Grav, it's a massive tradition for me to stay in and watch it!'

Smiling, I belted out a few lines of 'Jerusalem' for him. He must have thought I was crazy, but I was that happy about being picked I didn't care.

My initial call-up in 1999 was a real surprise but, having said that,

I probably should have seen it coming. In those days, the word on the circuit was that if Christopher Martin-Jenkins wrote your case up in the *Daily Telegraph*, you would be picked. That particular newspaper seemed to be the fifth selector. I had already seen my name in print and was thrilled with the plug but hadn't at that point grasped the correlation between suggestion and selection.

What the next few days confirmed to me, however, was that I was definitely not ready for international cricket at the age of 20. There were signs that the hierarchy knew it too because on the second day of practice for that Oval Test, my batting session was against the spin of David Graveney and Graham Gooch's medium pace. Everybody else had scarpered, and I should've smelled a rat – as if that was adequate warm-up for a Test match.

When I first reported for duty, they were intending to play two spinners, by all accounts. That was certainly the vibe I got. But it then poured with rain for two days, which put paid to that plan, and once they'd decided to have only one spinner, it was always going to be Phil Tufnell.

Our practice for the match was severely disrupted by the wet weather, and more so because the indoor school at The Oval was out of bounds, as it was being prepared for corporate entertainment. We were forced to go to Lord's to train, and that meant driving across London. So Darren Maddy and Ed Giddins, the two other new faces in the squad, jumped in my car and off we went.

We'd had our net and were driving back through central London on the return journey, listening to Radio 1. Our ears pricked up when listeners were urged to stay tuned because, after the news, they would be bringing us a story about an England cricketer who might be 'taking the p---'.

For those not familiar with Mark and Lard, hosts of the afternoon show in those days, they ran a feature called the Teasingly Topical Chart Challenge whereby listeners had to suggest song titles relating to a quirky news story of the day. That day, it was all about me.

Right at the start of the 1999 summer, I had done an interview with the *Independent* newspaper. It was a fairly innocuous chat about the A tour the previous winter, and my hopes and dreams for the season. During our conversation, I was asked how, as a spinner, I hardened my fingers for bowling. Naturally, I went through all of cricket's old wives' tales, such as smearing your fingers in friar's balsam or surgical spirit, or even dipping them in wee. However, as far as I was concerned, I said, and contrary to the thoughts of Nick Cook, my spin coach at Northamptonshire, who swore by the wee theory, none of them really worked.

I had never even tried the practice in question but someone somewhere was clearly keen for their five minutes of fame and suddenly, now I was in the England fold, the story had mutated. Apparently, I strengthened my spinning finger by dipping it in a bucket of urine. Other newspapers had jumped on the back of this and there I was pictured in the *Sun* that morning, under the headline 'ARE YOU TAKING THE P***?'

I had been oblivious to this ludicrous chain of events until we sat in an Oxford Street traffic jam in my sponsored county car, which handily had my name and signature displayed along the side. So, as well as being the victim of my passengers' laughter, I had people on the outside mocking me too. Next to us, a carful of lads, who were obviously listening to the same thing, were sent barmy when they spotted the writing across my doors.

This lot couldn't stop laughing and gave me a selection of V-signs and thumbs-ups as we sat there in the gridlock, remembering to sniff their fingers every time they did so, to maximise effect. That was my first taste of what it is like to be recognised as an England cricketer.

Joking aside, my overall experience that week was far from positive. Mainly because the England team environment was really weird in those days. It was so cliquey, and all about looking after number one. Only two people spoke to me when I first arrived at the ground: Darren Maddy, because I knew him from the A tour the previous winter, and Phil Tufnell, who introduced himself as my fellow spinner. It was hardly the kind of welcome conducive to good team spirit.

Tuffers showed himself to be a diamond of a bloke but, in contrast, other established players were so insular due to fear for their places – Duncan Fletcher had just got the job but was not in charge yet – that it concocted an horrendous atmosphere.

To a young lad coming in from outside it was obvious that it was not a happy dressing room, and therefore nothing like the one I was used to at Northampton. 'I wonder if any of this lot actually enjoy playing for their country?' I thought. It certainly didn't seem like it.

Although I remained on the periphery, I met the great and the good of English cricket for the first time that week, and I remember Sir Ian Botham coming over to me while I was in the middle assessing conditions on the second morning.

'Hi, how are you doing? I've seen you bowl, and they should definitely have played you on this. You could have landed it in this all day long,' he said, pointing downwards. The 'this' that England's greatest all-rounder was referring to was the tiniest little foothole imaginable. One lone foothole, caused by Alan Mullally's follow-through.

'With a deep point out for protection you'd have rolled these Kiwis,' he continued enthusiastically.

I looked down at this patch and thought: 'Is that what you've got to do in Test cricket? Is that the margin for error? I'm nowhere near good enough.'

Even as I nodded my head in agreement with one of the most revered cricketers in history, the truth had registered somewhere inside it. Walking away, I realised I would have to get a hell of a lot better, because there was absolutely no way I could hit that spot nine times out of 10. (As it turns out, and contrary to what aspiring spinners may think – you only find this out when you play for England for the first time – you don't have to hit a minuscule foothole every ball.)

I was the kind of kid that bluffed his way through and I'd never once doubted I was good enough to play for England until this point. And my reaction to the complexion of the pitch simply confirmed that I was not ready. I was terrified. There were no blemishes on the wicket – it was a typical featherbed Oval surface – and as someone who had grown up at Northampton bowling on what resembled an old man's ball sack, knowing that however many revolutions you imparted on the ball it was going to spin square once in every three deliveries, this did not fill me with confidence. Looking at the Wantage Road pitch was like meeting up with a long-lost friend for a finger spinner and here I was confronted with what might as well have been an ice rink. I might have been young and therefore naive, but it certainly struck home that all the advantages I worked with in county cricket had been taken away.

Not playing was actually something of a blessing in disguise because being left out made me a certain tourist that winter. Having been picked as the number two spinner in the country for the final Test of the summer, there was no reason for me not to retain my place in the pecking order when the touring party was announced two days after the match. It would have been bizarre to have been deemed Tufnell's understudy one week and dispensed with the next.

In contrast, if I had featured in what some of the press deemed to be the death of English cricket – defeat to New Zealand plunged us to the bottom of the world Test rankings – things might have been different. I am not sure how I would have done against those Black Caps but I acknowledge I was not ready. And with the benefit of hindsight, playing might have discounted me from going back to southern Africa for the third winter on the trot. Having done well with England Under-19 and England A the two previous years, I knew I could bowl effectively in those conditions.

Until I met up with the full England squad for the first time, cricket, and a rise through its levels, had seemed a doddle. Now I had been thrust into a situation partly, but not entirely, of my own making.

With 53 wickets at a cost of 28.2 runs each, allied to more than 500 runs with the bat, in the County Championship that season, I was the next cab off the rank in terms of the spin department, although in those days you didn't necessarily get picked on the basis of bowling exceptionally well throughout the season. I owed my elevation to a decent A trip and a good mid-season performance in a televised one-day game. Domestic cricket was not widely televised at the time and so my performance in a NatWest Trophy contest against Essex on 23 June caught the eye.

Ironically, I didn't bowl particularly well, and didn't even take a wicket in my five overs. No, it was my batting that drew attention. I went in and struck 30 off only 13 balls, including three sixes, to power us to a comfortable five-wicket win. The fact that we had chased 282 and won with relative ease thanks to my contribution seemed to influence the thinking: 'What an exciting cricketer, let's get him in.'

Echoes of that kind of attitude still reverberate around the county scene from time to time. For example, if a young spinner bowls well in a Twenty20 game on Sky, it inevitably leads to the typical commentator's knee-jerk, 'Why isn't this lad playing for England? He'd be brilliant, la-di-dah-di-dah.' But one game means nothing in the greater scheme of things, and generally selection is a lot more performance-based nowadays. Because you are picked up in the system at an earlier age, your career is monitored more extensively, making selections out of the blue a lot less likely.

That's what was strange about the Australian selection policy in the 2010–11 Ashes. They appeared to revert to how England went about things 10 years previously. From out of nowhere, the left-arm spinner Xavier Doherty was picked, and it was 100 per cent because the press pinpointed him to play: as someone who played with Ricky Ponting at Tasmania; a good left-arm spinner, they said. They talked him up for two or three days. It was as if their selectors read this and thought: 'Oh hell, we'd better pick him.' They no doubt felt under siege from the newspapers and believed that if they picked him and it went wrong, they would be absolved of blame. Then it was the same thing with Michael Beer: 'Well, he got four wickets once – he's our man.'

That is how it always used to seem to me with England. I knew I wasn't really good enough at that point and signs told me so. For example, in net practice I never felt that I could get all our blokes out. I fancied myself against a couple of them, and knew I was a decent bowler, just not a Test-ready bowler. But as a 20-year-old with £30,000 in my pocket for the trouble, I was happy to set off on tour.

Departure was all a bit of a blur for me. The pre-flight media frenzy was a real eye-opener: the signing of 300 bats for sponsors and fundraisers, cameras being shoved in your face and requests from every man and his dog for an interview. I loved every minute of the attention, of course, because being the centre of it has always appealed to my nature.

I knew a handful of the other lads – fellow tour freshers Michael Vaughan, Darren Maddy and Andrew Flintoff were ex A-team colleagues – but most didn't know me from Adam. On tour, you get to know people quicker than you do when you are playing at home because you spend so much time in each other's company, and one of the surprises for me has been hearing people recall me on that trip and say: 'What a breath of fresh air he was, always willing to voice his own opinion.'

Talk about putting the rose-tinted specs on. If that tour was as great as everyone suggests, then I would have played for the next 10 years and not been cast out. The reality, I assume, was that I was seen as a cheeky little upstart.

I have since read that Duncan Fletcher addressed me at the airport before departure and asked me where I saw myself being in five years' time. 'I'll be the best spinner in the world,' I allegedly said. Now, I don't dispute the fact that those words came out of my mouth, but the honest truth is I cannot remember having that conversation. Although it does sound rather like the kind of thing I'd say.

In those days there would have been a lot of bluster behind such statements. When young players talk to coaches, they tend to say exactly what the coach wants to hear. You teach yourself, and are professionally advised in media training, to give certain responses.

Whatever I said to the England coach at the time will have been a by-product of that and the promotion of positive thinking by our team psychologist. My answer would simply have been the one I assumed he'd want to hear – because even at 20 years old I was savvy at saying the right things to the right people, right on cue, for an easy life. As for the outrageous claim, it would not have been through a cast-iron, 100 per cent belief that I would be the best spinner in the world by 2005, just a 100 per cent belief that that was the best thing to say at the time. All emerging players do it and anyone who claims they don't has honesty issues.

During that 1999–2000 tour, however, I did change a little. I recognised that a couple of players would do absolutely anything, kiss anyone's behind, just to get ahead in the game, and it made me feel a bit sick to watch them in action. The result was that I decided never to do the same, but always to be my own man and suffer the consequences. Yes, it led to a lot of hardship over the next few years, but ultimately I stuck to my principles and refused to pander to people just to keep my nose clean. When I don't agree with something I'll always voice my opinion, which is one of the main reasons I later got into strife at Northamptonshire.

The people who are dead honest and tell it exactly how it is in sport are few and far between. In football, Ian Holloway is a rare example, and people love him for it, but he had to fight like hell to get into the position of being a Premier League manager. I've stuck to my guns since that first tour and when things are going well people see my attitude as refreshing. When things are not going so well, I become the Antichrist.

Nasser Hussain thought I was exactly that on the first morning of the fourth Test at Cape Town in early January. Till then, we had struggled against the South African pace attack, most notably when we were rolled at Johannesburg in the series opener, but now we appeared to have turned the tide. Well, in my mind, at least, because after about an hour and a half, we were still none down.

Allan Donald had taken a bundle of wickets in the first Test but

Michael Atherton played him beautifully that morning and I was watching with Gavin Hamilton in the viewing gallery. 'Donald's not getting it through today, is he?' I said to him, completely ignorant of the fact that Nasser, sitting right in front of me, was batting next.

You simply don't say stuff like that, I am firmly of that belief now, because all you do is wind up Mother Cricket. And the England captain, in this instance.

'Swann, f------ shut up. What are you saying, you f------ idiot?' Nasser spat.

'Calm down, Nass,' I said. 'You surely can't believe in rubbish like that?'

He did, and so did I from the moment soon after lunch when Donald began a slump from 115 without loss to 141 for three. One of the trio of wickets to fall, during a session which included 26 runs being scored in as many overs, was that of Hussain. I genuinely felt the collapse was my fault.

At Newlands you have your own separate lunch room next to your changing room, and at tea there was a stony silence. I was sitting with Gavin and Alex Tudor, two of the other guys who were not playing, when Nasser approached, threw his food on the table and, snorting viciousness, said: 'Awright, Swann, you clown, you think you're a comedian – well, make me f------ laugh. Tell me a f------ joke. Come on then.'

Everyone seemed to freeze. But being cocksure, I took up the challenge.

'Luke Skywalker and Darth Vader are having a light-sabre fight one day,' I began. 'De-de-jeesh, de-de-jeesh. Then Vader leans in and says: "Luke, I know what you are getting for Christmas." Sssh-boo, sssh-ba. "That's impossible, how can this be?" the young Skywalker asks. "Luke, I just know," Vader replies. "I have felt your presents."'

Everyone knows that joke now but I am pretty convinced I invented it. When I started off, all the other lads must have thought: 'What an idiot; I bet Nasser's going to kill him.' But then I got to the punch-line and everyone fell about laughing. It was the perfect ice-breaker.

At least now when he swore at me, he did so with a smile on his face.

Nasser liked the fact that I could have a laugh and joke – I think – but as far as the cricket was concerned, I was not viewed seriously. Such a judgement confined me to the nets every day, and anyone will tell you that I am possibly the globe's worst net cricketer because my heart is never in it. I just don't enjoy it.

Being stuffed in the nets twice a day for two hours at a time for a two-month long Test tour is my idea of purgatory and as a result I couldn't have been less enthused about the game of cricket by the end of that trip. Aside from a couple of tour matches, I was never likely to play, so I ended up with Gavin Hamilton – who had been discarded after one nightmare Test of no runs and no wickets – playing stupid games in the nets during play.

We would challenge ourselves to score 50 off 10 balls and every ball we didn't clobber, we would claim to have scampered through for five. It was like two six-year-olds inventing a new game while their dads played club cricket on the other side of the pavilion. Gav is very similar to me in terms of juvenile humour, and dossing about like a couple of little kids was our way of getting through the tour. You get passengers on every trip and I was possibly the greatest passenger England have ever taken abroad.

I had just bought a new three-bedroom house for £60,000, and this was before the property boom took off, so in relation to the man on the street I was earning good money. And for a lad who had told his schoolteachers he wouldn't have to get a proper job because he would play cricket it was a big two fingers up just to be picked.

But the way the tour turned out was far from what I had hoped for, and my way of escaping was to go out drinking most nights. To such an extent, in fact, that all I had to show financially from the trip was a single payment of a couple of thousand pounds off my mortgage when I returned home.

From my point of view there was a non-stop supply of booze at every hotel and if you were never playing – at that age I didn't get hangovers – you could drink all night, get two hours' kip from about five or six o'clock in the morning, then find a little hole in the changing room later in the day to hibernate while the game was going on.

These were the days before Xboxes, and televisions in hotel rooms were limited to about four channels, so touring without competitive cricket was just mind-numbingly boring for me. With nothing to do, my refuge was the recently launched Sky Sports News, and Kelly Dalglish, someone I had a real soft spot for, and a woman who bears a passing resemblance to my wife Sarah.

Every morning, it was like *Groundhog Day* as I awoke to Kelly reading out the same old stories – more often than not concerning a protracted transfer saga of a Division Two midfielder. 'Will Millwall sign Cheltenham's star striker? Or won't they? Orient told to up their bid for Carlisle ace.' By the end of the week I knew every last detail about these players and even though I truly couldn't give a toss about them, I couldn't stop myself tuning in every morning to find out whether they'd agreed terms, passed medicals or gone out on loans. It was just a bizarre existence.

But watching Sky Sports News provided me with one of the funniest moments of my life. It came after the fifth day of the final Test at Centurion, the day that began with me in a frenzy after sleeping in and missing the team bus to the ground. I had already missed the bus on a training day in Cape Town earlier in the tour and by this stage had almost gone beyond caring.

Considering what transpired in the match, with Hansie Cronje's generous declaration, some people might have thought I was down the bookies putting £100 on us for the lads, but unfortunately I was in the land of Nod after a typically heavy night on the beer. So heavy, in fact, that when the hotel manager of the Sandton Sun rang me in my room and asked me if I would like to book a taxi to get to the ground, I sleepily said: 'No, no, it's all right, I'll just hop on the bus.'

'But the team bus left 20 minutes ago, sir,' she said.

'Oh, yeah, no problem, thanks,' I replied, trying to maintain an illusion of cool.

Effing and blinding, I managed to get dressed and ran downstairs pronto. Luckily, I bumped into Laurence Griffiths and Graham Chadwick, a couple of photographers who had become good friends of mine, and although they found my predicament hilarious, they allowed me to cadge a lift with them.

The journey to Pretoria from the Sandton area of Johannesburg, during rush hour, takes over an hour and the traffic in those days was always absolutely horrendous for the last 10 miles as you approached the ground at Centurion. This particular morning proved no different, and, eager to get there as soon as possible, I persuaded the lads to pull out of the gridlock and get the foot to the floor on the inside lane.

Within a couple of minutes we had the England team bus in our sights and, slowing right down as we passed it, acknowledged the lads on board. I waved vigorously at mates like Vaughan at the back and was still waving as we passed the front, where Fletch was gazing out of the window, stone-faced, slowly shaking his head. As he did so, I considered whether he actually wanted to kill me.

Nevertheless, when I arrived at the ground, ahead of the rest of the team, I tried to act as normal as possible, and I was changed and knocking a ball up on my bat as the lads walked in. Nasser Hussain was the first through the door, and he had a withering look on his face as we made eye contact.

'What kept you, lads? I've been here for ages,' I said.

Nasser just shook his head and walked on. Fletch followed and said: 'I think you owe the captain an apology for today.'

I apologised, the game went on, and the rest, as they say, is history. The match will be remembered as the first Test to contain forfeited innings and one shrouded in suspicion due to Cronje's part in setting a run chase of 249, which we completed with a couple of wickets to spare.

The mood at the time was triumphant but it did not save me from being called to the front of the bus by Fletcher on the return journey to Joburg that night, to be told that I had been fined £250 for my tardiness that morning. I accepted the punishment willingly, and Fletcher subsequently announced its severity to the rest of the squad.

'I want this information to stay in-house,' he finished. 'I don't want anyone outside our group to find out.'

So, as had become second nature, I flicked on Sky Sports News upon returning to my room and was greeted by the rolling news bar. Three items ran across the screen in front of me. They went something like this:

DAVID BECKHAM IN PROPOSED £35 MILLION MOVE TO INTER MILAN

ZINEDINE ZIDANE LINED UP IN JUVE-REAL MADRID SWAP

GRAEME SWANN FINED £250 FOR MISSING ENGLAND TEAM BUS

As this reel went round and round, I felt I'd properly made it. I'd been named alongside the greats. Beckham, Zidane, Swann. I lay back on the bed and laughed my head off. As far as I was concerned it was hilarious. Although, on a serious note, my actions meant I had blown my chances of touring for the foreseeable future, and for the entirety of Fletcher's reign, as it transpired.

My guffawing was recognition of a priceless moment of infamy. Nevertheless it surprised me, particularly given Fletch's plea for discretion only minutes earlier. But like politics, sport is full of leaks to the press and someone had clearly passed on the news of my reprimand.

My earlier indiscretion on the punctuality front was a genuine mishap in Cape Town, when I had overslept ahead of training. I've always had this habit, if I'm truly knackered, of turning my alarm clock off as a reflex reaction the second it begins to make its din. My ability to do it in a semiconscious state and then fall back to sleep instantly really is quite something. On this occasion, when I reawoke, it was two minutes shy of the departure time and left me with no alternative but to jump in a taxi.

It is a recurring problem for me even now and on every tour I will be late for at least one or two things. I try desperately not to be – carrying two mobile phones, setting alarms on both and leaving one on the other side of the room so that I have to physically get out of bed to turn it off. But as it only takes you to forget to do that one night – and if you're tired or you've had a few scoops the night before you can be in trouble – I have even initiated a back-up plan. On most tours, the day after a Test match finishes is usually a travel day, which almost inevitably means an early flight, and so I persuade Jimmy Anderson or Alastair Cook to knock on my door one hour before departure.

To be fair, Jimmy is almost as bad as I am but Cooky is a real goody-two-shoes, probably because he's next in line to be captain, and never lets me down. He was a godsend on the 2009–10 tour of Bangladesh, where the problem was never shaking off a heavy head, but having to get up ridiculously early. Without him there was no way I could have got out of bed at 5.45 every morning, which is what you have to do for a Test match over there. It's the witching hour, you shouldn't be awake at that time and my body protests by reverting to shutdown mode.

My timekeeping was undoubtedly something that riled Fletcher, and arguably my immaturity might have too, but not once did I get a rollicking on that tour. The perception is that Fletch and I were at loggerheads for the entire trip, but that is a long way from the truth, an urban myth given credence simply by the length of my absence from subsequent England selections. Sure, there were times when he didn't really talk to any of the players, especially the younger set that included me, but we didn't have a cross word.

At the start of the tour, when I bought into his fielding drills – he was a big innovator who'd always be formulating new ideas on quicker ways to release the ball on throwing, different ways to pick it up, or flick it for a relay throw – I got the impression that he liked me. Once the Test matches started, though, and I was bowling like a drain, I was very much on the periphery. A couple of weeks would go by without him muttering a word to me, but then again, if I was coach in that same situation I wouldn't necessarily be investing time in the 20-year-old class clown. I've never been an advocate of players being patted on the shoulder and told: 'Keep going, son.'

Of course, by the end of the tour he didn't speak to me at all, but that was entirely down to my misdemeanours. There was never any animosity prior to the bus incidents, although I was on the end of a cricket-related joint rollicking with Chris Read for taking the offer of bad light on the second evening of a three-day match against a South African Invitation XI in Port Elizabeth.

This match was wedged between the fourth and fifth Tests and featured some of the recently arrived one-day players. It was getting dark and Greg Smith, who went on to play with us both at Nottinghamshire, kept bouncing Read. Twice he took blows from short balls, in fact, but having come together only minutes earlier on 300 for seven, a lead of 47 runs, we were uncertain whether or not to accept the umpires' invitation to return to the dressing room.

As junior pros on tour we decided the thing to do was to call for a change of gloves and take advice from a more senior man. We wanted to go off, but were we allowed? That is the question we put to Mark Alleyne when he came running out to the centre. Unfortunately, Boo Boo offered the most cryptic response imaginable and one that neither instructed nor advised. He said something like 'You know what's going on, boys' and jogged off. So, none the wiser, we proceeded with the game until Read received another snorter past his lid. After consultation with the umpires, stumps were drawn at 312 for seven.

But we weren't just walking off, we were walking into a Fletcher tirade.

'What the hell are you doing in this changing room? I told you specifically to stay out there,' he roared. 'And you disobeyed my orders.'

We didn't have a clue what to do. We'd made a genuine mistake at worst and here was our coach, the England coach, going berserk. Fletch claimed it had been way darker in the Test match at Johannesburg and some of our batsmen had refused to come off.

More fool them, I thought, if they wanted to face Allan Donald in the bloody dark!

It wouldn't have done much to improve Fletcher's mood when I cut my first ball the next morning straight through the hands of the fielder at point – it would have been absolutely priceless had I been caught, but equally I may have been thrown to the lions at the game park down the road. As it was, the end was not particularly long in arriving anyway, and the match petered out into a draw.

My statistical return from that Test tour was one wicket and one innings in two first-class appearances, stretching across two and a half months. I could understand why on the back of those displays I was not picked for the next couple of years; I couldn't blame Fletcher for leaving me out, as I was not good enough. I was better than some of the players who were put in after that two-year period, but that is a different issue.

The truth is, I don't hold any grudges against Duncan and any suggestion of a mutual hatred between us – for all I know, he might hate me – is inaccurate. Growing older and wiser has made me more phlegmatic about the whole thing. Yes, I could claim I was treated badly. But the primary reason for me remaining on the sidelines was that at 20 I wasn't good enough, and my tendency to wind up the wrong people at the wrong time didn't help matters.

My one beef, however, is that at the start of the 2000 season, when I was playing for Northants against Nottinghamshire at Trent Bridge, Duncan requested to see me for what amounted to a tour debrief. To my face, he told me he was impressed with my work ethic, how when I had an idea in my head I would not give up on it, and he instructed me to keep scoring runs and taking wickets. Admittedly, it was quite a surprise that he had been so positive, but that made it all the more galling when I discovered his words were hollow. My official tour report was, in contrast, a complete stinker. He certainly didn't say to my face what he later wrote. But I guess some people work like that.

This bothered me for quite a while. I just couldn't see why he didn't

front up and say: 'You did this wrong and that wrong.' It would have
been almost cathartic if he'd told me how I'd messed up, rather than
just glossing over it. Of course, deep down I didn't really need telling
and over time you learn from your mistakes – you would be a bit of
a fool not to – but it still hurt when for the next six years they picked
just about every English bloke who'd tried off-spin, and even a couple
who hadn't, ahead of me.

In truth, my first England tour resembled something of a non-stop
stag do. It began in a raucous manner during a team night out in
Johannesburg, when everyone was getting to know each other after
a period of mass change in selection and the appointment of Fletcher
as coach.

Twelve months earlier, on the A tour, Chris Read had shown
himself to be an admirable leader of bar frivolity. For some unfathomable reason he seemed to have made it his business to know every
single university drinking song going before departing on that trip.
Looking at him, you would not suspect it but his vulgar singalongs
gained him notoriety.

Of course, there is a time and a place for that kind of laddish
behaviour, namely on team drinking nights or in the privacy of your
own changing rooms after games. Not, however, in a quiet, respectable restaurant in the plush Sandton complex, where the England
team stays for matches in and around Johannesburg and Pretoria.

The entire touring party was eating at the Butcher's Shop, and after
dinner, with the drink flowing, someone suggested we sing one or
two of Ready's songs. But a request that he lead us in a rendition of
'Coconut Grove', without doubt the most vulgar of his entire set, clearly
left him uneasy given the clientele still present on adjoining tables.

However, Fletcher instructed him to do it, and was quick to tell
anyone advising against it to shush. All I can say is that he clearly
didn't know what he was calling for. That can be the only explanation, because no one would knowingly order that song to be sung
in public.

So under the weight of peer pressure, and having been instructed to go ahead by the England coach, Read began:

> A man came down from the coconut grove,
> He was a mean m-----------, you could tell by his clothes . . .

Every line of this song is repeated by the rest of the group, and suffice to say the first two lines are the cleanest of the lot. Some of the sordid sex acts that this 'mean m-----------' carried out during the song led to grown men crying – tears of laughter were certainly streaming down my face at the time – but looking back at that incident makes me shudder with embarrassment. There we were in this posh eatery, with Read standing on the table leading the chorus. From a PR point of view it was a total disaster. Imagine sitting across the way from the uncouth mob we resembled.

My tour soon went into rapid decline. The knowledge that I would not be playing contributed to the spending of the thousands of pounds that were burning a hole in my pocket in the bars of the five-star hotels in which we stayed. These bars were more often than not crammed with aircrews, and to an impressionable youth, it was all about getting hammered and chatting up the girls.

Splashing the cash didn't seem to matter – I would just get another £30,000 for touring the following winter, right? – and what was the point of being disciplined when it came to nightlife? My entire thinking was fuelled by frustration at remaining on the sidelines.

My general attitude to training was to do the bare minimum. Should I have stayed on and worked on my bowling? Undoubtedly. But I hated being treated like a servant to the others, and so once the routine stuff was over, I would go and put my feet up. I would never condone that attitude in anyone now, but at the time this selfish 20-year-old felt he had done his bit and why should he go above and beyond for people who were selfish themselves?

It was lack of life experience that contributed to a few minor scrapes with team-mates on that trip. Over-enthusiasm for the final word or the cracking of a joke at an inappropriate time could easily have earned me several clips around the ear.

As it happens, I was cuffed by one of my team-mates, but in unjust circumstances. The incident occurred during one of our stays at the Sandton Sun hotel in Johannesburg, and the bloke who punched me was Darren Gough. To this day, I am not sure what his problem was, or what I had done to deserve being cracked. Perhaps he will let me know one day when we are dressed head to toe in Lycra and crashing through walls on Saturday-evening primetime television.

I had not even been with him on the evening in question. I had spent it in the hotel bar, chatting to one of the aircrew and the golfer Ian Woosnam, who was playing some tournament in South Africa. Three sheets to the wind, Woosie was helpfully demonstrating his golf swing using a bar stool instead of a club. It had been hours since I'd seen Goughie, although I had had a chortle before he went off for dinner, when one girl in the bar told him: 'Do you know, you look like a fat Darren Gough?'

However, I was very much aware of his presence at around two in the morning when I went across the foyer of the hotel to the gents. At this point Goughie emerged from nowhere, and as I stood at the urinal, punched me straight in the mouth.

Because of my state of inebriation, rather like in a comedy film, I fell backwards. Problem was I had not yet stopped urinating, so there I was flat on my back with a fountain of wee spouting towards the ceiling. For those of you familiar with Brussels, I was like a horizontal version of the Manneken Pis.

'What did you do that for?' I asked Goughie. But he strode off and left me there, wet jeans, fat lip and all.

Some of the other lads later said that something like that was bound to happen sooner or later because I wound people up too much, and maybe that was true. But not on this occasion.

A couple of days later, Fletch broke one of his silent spells with me to inquire what had happened to my lip. He obviously knew, I think everybody knew, but I just said it was a cold sore that had been split by the sun, and for him not to worry because it was fine.

It was not a big deal, these things happen, and I wanted to move on. But apparently it was a bigger deal to other people. When Northamptonshire played Yorkshire up at Headingley the next season, it was evident that Goughie had gone back and portrayed the incident as some kind of fight.

As he stood at the end of his run, pretending to be a rhinoceros, before charging in to bowl at me, one of the Yorkshire fielders chirped to me: 'Heard you've tried to take on Goughie, lad.'

During the course of that game I pulled him aside to inquire whether he wanted me to tell all his team-mates the truth about the sucker punch he threw on a 20-year-old lad who was never going to stand up for himself and fight back.

'Oh nooo, nooo. Wha' ya talkin' about? I was doin' p--- next to you. Tha's all.'

Boozy incidents filled that tour for me and on one memorable night in Port Elizabeth, Mark Butcher and I got stuck into some Stroh rum. We had just been out for a big steak, as you do in South Africa, and even though we had training the next day, Butch called me over to the bar and told me: 'Right, we're going to drink this here bottle till there's not a drop left.'

So two shots of what in my estimation amounted to neat alcohol were lined up in front of us by the barman. For those of you not experienced in this drink, it is extremely violent. Already on his merry way, Butch threw it down his neck, smashed the glass on the bar and looked at me menacingly, rather like they do in spaghetti westerns.

It was as if he'd been shot as he slipped off his stool and landed face first on the floor. Being an idiot, it only increased my keenness to take a turn, but it didn't quite have the same effect as I had not reached the same level of intoxication. However, I hallucinated wildly and anything else that happened that evening could just as easily have been a product of my imagination.

Wherever we went around the country, I would consult the South African lads, and Herschelle Gibbs especially, on which bars to visit and would drag along whoever I could. My early-evening drinking partner was often Chris Adams. Later on, Butch was always great bar company, playing guitar and singing, while I loved Phil Tufnell to bits.

But it says something that what was probably the most enjoyable day of the trip for me – Christmas Day – was spent with Laurence Griffiths and Stu Forster, two photographers, and their partners up at the house of one of Laurence's family friends in the hills above Durban. I spent most of my time jumping into the pool and swimming lengths with this lovable Labrador. The fact I enjoyed being away from the team for a while and away from the pressures of it all, having a few beers and a Christmas dinner with a couple of what I considered to be proper mates, emphasised what a hard time I was having.

I didn't necessarily dislike anyone in particular but within any group there are guys you wouldn't particularly want to get stuck on your own with. Certainly Nasser at the time was someone I would not have wanted to mix with individually because he was the captain, wore his heart on his sleeve in the job, was desperate to do well for his country, and wasn't my idea of a fun night out. At a meal with him I knew we would talk cricket and he'd pour scorn on my way of doing things. We get on fine now, but his position of authority then made for an awkward relationship.

Talking of relationships, there was always a really strange dynamic between Andy Caddick and Gough. It was something I found really funny yet weird at the same time. They absolutely hated each other but pretended to get on in this pseudo friendship. Their jealousy towards each other's success was something that made me feel uneasy. The atmosphere in general I found strange – I am not sure having two former captains, Michael Atherton and Alec Stewart, in the rank and file helped that – but in spite of everything, that tour did not put me off wanting to be an England cricketer.

Of course it was an eye-opener, because although every kid dreams of playing for his country, you never know how it's going to be until you're actually there. I thought it would be real Roy of the Rovers stuff. I expected players to turn up in their Rolls-Royce cars and the team to be made up of the best, strongest, most confident men in the world. But in reality there were some very fragile characters. Phil Tufnell was one. The Cat's lack of confidence in his bowling was something I would never have expected. Because he was such a brilliant bowler, I thought he'd be super-confident, but he needed someone to tell him just how good he was all the time.

The regime of 2007–08 when I went on my next England trip was incomparable. Perhaps an increased maturity on my part and a complete overhaul of personnel made equal contributions to my perception. Suddenly I was surrounded by contemporaries from youth-level cricket – guys like Ryan Sidebottom and Owais Shah. Things seemed a lot more relaxed and even though Peter Moores is a very high maintenance coach from a work ethic point of view – he lost his off-button in programming – his method of doing things suited me.

5

INTERNATIONAL IMPOSTER

M Y SUBCONSCIOUS has suppressed the memory of most of the cricket played on that 1999–2000 tour of South Africa, and I more readily recall chats with Michael Atherton – the most cerebral cricketer I had met other than Richard Montgomerie – about bands like the Smiths than anything that happened on the field. That, as much as anything, tells you about my state of mind that winter.

England came up against one Kevin Pietersen early on, for example, but I just don't remember him at all from the drawn game against KwaZulu-Natal in Durban at the beginning of December. I know he played in it because he's told me on more than one occasion. In fact, that might have been the last game in which he bowled off-spin seriously before giving it up and becoming a batsman. He played as their front-line spinner and batted at number nine, from where he cracked 61 off 57 balls, with four fours and four sixes. When we batted, he sent down 55.5 overs, for figures of four for 141. We don't get Kev to bowl 55.5 overs in an entire tour these days!

The only guy I remember playing for the opposition in that match was Jon Kent, who I knew from my Under-19 international days. Quite simply, if I wasn't playing in the games I took absolutely zero interest in them, and because that was between the first and second Tests, I don't remember watching the game at all. We were perpetually consigned to net sessions out the back.

While my participation in first-class matches was limited, I did feature more prominently in the one-day matches sprinkled throughout the itinerary. In the second game of the tour against

Easterns in Benoni, I was bowled off my heel by Andre Nel, volleying the ball into the stumps attempting a flick to the leg side, but later returned figures of 10–0–39–1, which contributed to a 19-run victory. And I did well in another 50-over game, a typical mid-tour match in a place called Alice, a township in the middle of nowhere, on a pitch that resembled a sheep field. Makhaya Ntini opened the bowling for the combined Border and Eastern Province side, and went for a few. I hit 29, at better than a run a ball, and followed up with 10–0–38–3, in a resounding win.

However, although I did okay in those matches, I was not included in the limited-overs squad for the series that followed. I was all packed and couldn't wait to get to the airport, in fact, when just a matter of hours after my reprimand for missing the bus on the final day of the Test series, I took a call on my hotel room phone. It was Phil Neale. I was desperate to go home at this point, so the news that Ashley Giles had a bit of a bad back, and I would be required to stay on as cover, was truly painful.

The prospect of making my England bow, after two and a half months on the periphery, should have filled me with joy, but I was absolutely devastated. Such was my mental state at the time I just could not be bothered with that tour any longer. I so desperately wanted to see the end of it, and I remember going to bed that night feeling as miserable as sin.

When I awoke the next morning – having realised I had a very good chance of playing in the first one or two one-day internationals – I vowed to buck up my ideas. My gut reaction to the situation had not been good. The chance of an England cap should have overwhelmed me with excitement, but as I lay on the bed of room 1917 at the Sandton Sun – every time we returned to the hotel on that trip we were given the same room, and mine for all the establishment's splendour felt like a prison cell – sadly it did not. Yes, this is an admission that I found it difficult to feel any positive emotion about standing on the threshold of an international debut. Even after our solitary warm-up match against

North-West in Potchefstroom, when I knew I was a shoo-in to play.

Potch is in the middle of nowhere, visually the South African equivalent of Welwyn Garden City, and we had to drive hours to get there. The coach left early in the morning, something like six o'clock, and I did my usual trick of getting the pillow out and sleeping in the aisle. It was a habit on that tour, mostly because I wasn't getting any sleep at night, but on this occasion it was made necessary by the inhospitable departure time rather than a skinful. Nor was I the only cat-napper on that tour – Test squad members Chris Silverwood and Phil Tufnell were fellow dossers.

If the match was memorable for anything, it was the performance of the North-West opening bowler David Pryke, who, I can confirm, had the worst or most bizarre action there has ever been in world cricket. This chap was carrying a bit of timber, a Mark Ealham-type build shall we say, and as he approached the crease he whipped his arms over, jumped in mid-air and repeated the whip of the arms once more. Any further description I could give would not do justification to how wonderfully manic this guy's action was. We had never seen anything like it. His bowling was like a circus trick, and it's a crying shame that no one has ever posted footage of him on YouTube (at least they hadn't the last time I checked). South African television stations must have an archive, surely?

Even funnier, though, was the fact that this Pryke proved impossible to bat against. The first couple of balls he bowled caused a massive stir in our dressing room. 'You've got to come and see this,' someone shouted. None of the observers could quite fathom how he was projecting the ball to the other end, but he finished with a return of five for 32 from his 10 overs.

Another bizarre incident occurred between innings. Play was delayed something like forty minutes as we waited for the haze caused by the crowd's braais during the interval to lift. South Africans like to barbecue at cricket matches and the smoke was so low and thick that the floodlights could not penetrate it. Ground staff were forced to run out waving rugs, picnic blankets, shirts, beer mats, whatever they could get their hands on, to waft the cloud away.

Once things cleared up I bowled well, and my figures of 10–1–38–2 reflected that. This return with the ball reinforced the belief that I would play in the first ODI at Bloemfontein just a couple of days later.

Unfortunately, my England debut wasn't a big event in my life at all. A by-product of the circumstances, I guess. It certainly didn't feel particularly special to play, and contrary to what might be expected of a young England cricketer, I did not ring home excitedly to tell my parents when I received the news. Perhaps it was because I knew I was on borrowed time: my brief for staying on had been that I would be required until Gilo was fully fit again, and he was by now back bowling in the nets, albeit gingerly. Him doing so only served to emphasise I had been chosen because there was no one else, rather than earning a spot on merit. So, far from making the hairs on the back of my neck stand on end, my England debut made me feel like an imposter.

It was just not a memorable day for me, which is such a shame. I remember my England Under-19 debut, my Northants debut, my Nottinghamshire debut and later my Test debut with great fondness. In fact, I consider my first game back in the limited-overs team, against Sri Lanka in Dambulla in October 2007, as more of a debut than my official bow seven and a half years earlier in Bloemfontein. Because I felt as if I belonged and wasn't just keeping someone else's seat warm.

I take a tremendous amount of pride in playing for England, yet I certainly didn't relish playing on 23 January 2000. To be in that team made me feel like a bit of a fraudster, a bit of a charlatan, an uninvited guest. These feelings were the culmination of everything that happened to me over that winter, my antipathy towards the set-up not helped by its unhealthy disregard towards anyone from the outside. It was not an environment to make newcomers feel welcome. At the time Nasser took over it was a very selfish, cliquey dressing room. It was not until England started to get a bit of success under him that he was able to stamp his authority on things a bit more. New players, people like Michael Vaughan and Andrew Flintoff, began to be introduced as part of the shake-up and that's when it shaped into more of a team.

As it happens, we absolutely trounced South Africa in that opening match of the series, winning by nine wickets, after chasing down our 185-run target with more than 10 overs to spare. From a personal perspective, I bowled five overs for 24, neither particularly badly nor particularly well. One ball ragged square, found its way through Jacques Kallis's gate and past wicketkeeper Chris Read for four byes. But it did me few favours. Soon afterwards, Nasser took me off, and by way of explanation said: 'I am putting Graeme Hick on because he doesn't turn it as much as you.' I've never asked Nasser what he meant by that, nor have I comprehensively worked it out, but reading between the lines I reckon he was saying: 'I'm putting Hicky on because I think you're rubbish!'

As I made my way to deep square leg it dawned on me that if Hick was bowling, he was taking my overs, and therefore I wouldn't bowl for the rest of the innings. It was particularly frustrating because we'd rolled through their top order. And as I was contemplating my lot, as if to rub it in, someone from the crowd threw a boerewors (a big South African sausage for the uninitiated). It was a good shot, hitting me on the back of the neck and landing at my feet. This was a very Afrikaner-dominated crowd, and I had been getting a load of abuse from them. Not very intelligent abuse, but abuse nonetheless. So I picked up this piece of meat and shaped to throw it back.

'What're you gonna f------ du?' one of them goaded.

I simply took a big bite out of it and held it triumphantly above my head. My actions were greeted by great roars of 'Jaa', and the fact that they seemed to love the banter encouraged me. Being a naive young pup, it was only later it occurred to me what this thing could have been marinated in before it had been lobbed in my direction. But the interaction with the fans felt good at the time because, after hurling the boerewors back into the stand, I got a standing ovation from that section of the crowd every time I touched the ball. Undoubtedly, this was the first time in my life I recognised the power of getting the crowd on your side – if someone is willing to throw one of their prize sausages at you, all you have to do is bite, chew, smile and they're won over. Not that it has happened to me since, mind.

I've always tried to take that lesson forward. I shake my head in disbelief when I see people trying to take on a baying crowd. How can you possibly win? The only other successful way to deal with it – if someone is shouting abuse – is to put your hand to your ear, as if you haven't heard them. This works particularly well in Australia. The heckler immediately repeats what they've said, and it usually sounds even more moronic second time around, so a laugh and an appropriate gesture in response – to show you've got one up on them – usually turns things around. Suddenly their mates are laughing at them rather than you.

Hussain and Nick Knight both hit half-centuries as we cantered home inside 40 overs, and that meant I was the one England cricketer to maintain a 100 per cent record for the best part of the noughties. I was released from the tour a couple of days later, and jettisoned to county cricket. However, I am a firm believer that everything happens for a reason, and remain equally convinced that having seven years out, watching other people failing while working out my own game and strengthening my resolve, made it a darn sight easier when I eventually got in there again. By my next international, I had come to terms with everything that had happened to me early in my career, and any pressure had long since disappeared.

On my long-haul return from Johannesburg, despite the fact I was travelling solo, our team manager Phil Neale told me that I had to wear my England blazer on the aeroplane. Suited and booted, I was booked into the aircraft's business-class bubble, and the hostess in charge clearly took pity on me as I sat there, uncomfortably dressed, looking about 14 years old.

Glancing at my badge, she asked what school I went to and why I was travelling on my own. When I explained I was part of the England cricket team, she patted me on the shoulder and said: 'Yeah, of course you are, darling.' And off she wandered. Even the British Airways cabin crew seemed to know that England and I were not meant for each other.

However, she did offer me a first-class meal – a choice between rock lobster and smoked salmon – so I seized it. It was the first time I'd ever had lobster and champagne on a flight, and the banker who sat next to me naturally demanded the same treatment, only to be given short shrift by this woman. 'No, sir, for you it's chicken or fish,' she said, sternly. Clearly there were some benefits in wearing the three lions that winter after all.

6

NORTHAMPTON THROUGH (AND THROUGH)

NORTHAMPTONSHIRE WAS a great club to be at around the turn of the millennium. In those days county staffs numbered 30 and we had a cracking set of blokes. The make-up of our squad made it feel like you were playing with your mates, and there was a complete absence of selfish players. I looked forward to turning up at the ground every day and when I recall those days the sun always seemed to be shining.

There is no doubt I was happy with my lot during the summer of 2000, and it was a particularly good season for the club. For a start, we secured our first league title for close to a century – the Second Division crown representing the only top-place finish for the club since the Minor Counties triumph in 1904.

Matthew Hayden was our overseas players and captain, and led from the front with more than 1000 runs, while Darren Cousins was outstanding with the new ball. Snapped up from Essex, he took 67 Championship scalps at a cost of less than 20 apiece, making him one of the surprise packages of the season. Then again, surprising people was something he was good at. Once this contented dad of two crossed the threshold of the dressing-room door, he became one of the funniest blokes you could meet, and he also boasted the best collection of European porn I have ever seen.

The majority of the rest of the wickets were shared between myself and Jason Brown, our off-spin alliance totalling 98. After the winter I'd had it was brilliant to feel part of a team again; a friendly atmosphere prevailed around the whole club and I loved my cricket that year.

Team spirit was strengthened by our friendships away from the club. A large group of us lived in a little enclave in the town. Fast bowler Richard Logan was my housemate; 50 yards up the road David Sales had an identical house to mine, and John Blain lived with him; Russell Warren was two doors further down; my brother Alec was around the corner; Michael Davies and Michael Strong lived together 100 yards further on.

Our group of eight were pretty much inseparable. We would go out on Wednesday, Thursday, Friday, Saturday nights and then head off to the snooker club on Sundays, before taking Monday and Tuesday off to recover. Here was a group of what amounted to young professionals, I suppose, all single lads having an absolute ball.

Off we would head to the Northampton nightspots, in fake Ralph Lauren shirts – you could always tell because the man on a horse looked more like a monkey on an armadillo – white jeans and Patrick Cox shoes. We would get into some serious scrapes, and I remember once almost missing a match with a swollen knee after slipping on the alcohol-soaked floor at McGinty's while re-enacting MC Hammer's moves.

County cricket was a very sociable scene back then, and so in turn was the 2nd XI Championship. Because playing staffs were larger in those days, your second team would always be made up of contracted players, or of ten plus a trialist, and that in itself made it competitive. It also meant that you gained mates at other counties, and on away trips there would be nights out planned in advance. The cricket was taken seriously, and you would all report in official uniform – day one was a red shirt, two was a blue shirt, three was cream, all paired up with your blazer and trousers. You would also pack night-time clobber for each day – games at Belper would mean a night out in Derby and another in Nottingham, for example – and you had to have different stuff because it was a time when smoking was still allowed in pubs, and at the end of the night you stank of cigarettes. But thank God Jäger Bombs had not been invented pre-2000 because they would have ended a few careers.

This group of ours had come through the youth system, and the step between the youth and senior set-ups was playing for the Northants Colts team in the Northamptonshire County League on a Saturday afternoon. You weren't permitted to turn out for your club team, so I wasn't allowed to play for the Saints, which really used to hack me off because I loved the club and wanted to help them win the league. But playing with your mates was the next best thing.

One of my favourite memories of our local league encounters came one Friday afternoon in 1996 when our coach, Neil Foster, told John Blain, Richard Logan, David Sales and me that it was our lucky day: 'Because we've got four trialists coming to play tomorrow, and that means you've got the weekend off.'

For an aspiring 17-year-old county cricketer, with a penchant for partying, you might as well have said: 'Here's five litres of vodka and a straw. Happy drinking, lad, get it down you as quickly as you can.'

We steamed into town that night and were still steaming next morning when we congregated at Salesy's house at around 11 a.m. Mobile phones were only recently on the scene but we all had one and they soon began ringing, one after another. Logie's started going off first and his immediate reaction was: 'I am not answering that. I've got a good idea who it'll be.'

Sure enough, ten seconds after Logie turned off his phone, Blain's started to ring. 'Oooh, Jeeesus, a'm noh answerin' tha',' declared our resident Scotsman. Of course, as he was turning his off, mine began ringing, and by now I knew the drill. Sales, however, whose night out had only come to its conclusion a couple of hours earlier, had quite a different take on things.

'You lot worry too much,' he said. 'Fozzie will just be ringing to have a laugh with us.'

So when his phone rang, he didn't hesitate. 'Hello, Fozzie, how ya doin'?' he greeted him.

'Get the lads together,' he was instructed. 'All four of those trialists have pulled out, so you are all playing.'

'Get lost, Fozzie, you're not getting us that easily!' Sales said.

'Be there. This is serious, and you'll be sacked if you don't turn up,' he was warned.

With our kit housed at the ground, we had twenty minutes to get ourselves down there. Salesy could not drive for obvious reasons, but somehow we got there and, despite being in horrendous states, managed to get our kit on. The sobering realisation we had to play was horrible.

The fact that we were batting first against Bletchley at least gave some of us the chance to detox a bit. But the loss of an early wicket meant that Sales was called into action earlier than he would have wished. The rest of us watched as our number three batsman walked to the crease, rocking from side to side as he did so, took guard and almost collapsed forward, he was so drunk.

His level of inebriation suggested he didn't stand much of a chance in the contest about to unfold, and that view was strengthened when the bowler, Ishtiaq Ahmed, beat him all ends up outside off stump with his first delivery. Well, I say beat him, Salesy probably missed it by 12 inches. Naturally he received a serve from the bowler. 'You're a disgrace, you fat git,' or words to that effect.

This only served to rile our drunken hero. 'See that grandstand behind you?' he inquired, pointing over his opponent's shoulder. 'The next ball you bowl's going over it!'

Now, anyone who has been to Northampton will know that a hit over the top of that main stand is truly massive. But Sales remained true to his threat, and that is where the ball disappeared. Subsequently it disappeared to many other parts too as he proceeded to hit 101 off just 41 deliveries, with the most amazing stroke play I've ever witnessed.

The ball after getting to a hundred, he tamely chipped to mid-on, walked off and, passing me on my way to the middle, said: 'I quite enjoyed that, Swanny.'

Apparently, he then strolled straight into the changing room, put down his batting gloves and, having dropped off to sleep, snored like a wildebeest for the next couple of hours while we scraped to 250.

Ultimately his efforts proved in vain as Bletchley chased down our score, the mouthy Ishtiaq hitting 159 to have the last laugh. But that afternoon highlights for me what a player David Sales has been. For my money he is the best player not to have played for England in the modern era. Given his phenomenal talent, quite how he has never played is beyond me. I first encountered him at Under-13 level in a national finals day at Sherborne School, and even in those days he hit bigger sixes than most men could. When I played for England Under-15 against the national Under-16 side he was the best player by a country mile.

Yet for some unfathomable reason, his home county, Surrey, did not sign him up and their loss became Northants' considerable gain. From my perspective, I was over the moon, because if he was on my team it meant I did not have to bowl against him. He is one of those players you have to get out very early because otherwise he'll get a big hundred, or 200, or 300.

It was cruel that he sustained ligament damage in his knee, playing volleyball on the England A tour of West Indies in 2001, but I think the other problem in regard to international recognition was that his face just didn't fit, and the Duncan Fletcher regime didn't look kindly upon him. Perhaps he was even tarred by my brush because of the Northamptonshire link – arguably that might have mucked up a lot of potential careers.

Even now when I bowl at him, he strikes the ball more sweetly than anyone else I've ever played against. In my opinion he should have played at least one-day cricket for England, if not all forms of the game, because on natural talent alone I have not come up against anyone as good as him.

However, I think he might have been better served had he left Northamptonshire. There was a perception within the game that he never wanted it badly enough, that he was not sufficiently motivated to play for England. People perhaps judged he was not prepared to go the extra distance required, that he was content in his comfort zone and lacked the desire to better himself. Sometimes a willingness to move clubs and challenge yourself in a new environment can be viewed by others as an ambitious career step.

David actually had the chance to leave a few years ago, and was going to come to Nottinghamshire, or so he said – I was something of an intermediary for him – but it turned out he was just using the interest as leverage to get a better deal at Northampton. Mission accomplished, he stayed put.

There was a real sense of camaraderie during our promotion season and the commitment to the cause meant people would muck in for each other. All this was quite a contrast to the attitude displayed by Pakistan fast bowler Mohammad Akram, our overseas player in 1997, who proved to be a dreadful signing. With ball in hand, he was seri-ously sharp when he wanted, but the story goes that he walked into the changing room after the first day of the County Championship season, yanked off his boots and sighed: 'County cricket – it's a hard game.' The perplexed expressions of his new team-mates told their own story. He was released mid-contract.

To say we had a never-say-die approach during the 2000 season would be putting it mildly, and our turnaround in fortunes was rather remarkable. Bottom of the table at the start of July, we won six of our next seven matches to claim promotion. As the summer got drier, we came into our own, particularly on our spinner-friendly wickets at Wantage Road.

I was a permanent fixture in the side but injury prevented me from playing in the penultimate home game, against Gloucestershire, so Alec was drafted in as a like-for-like replacement for me. By trade an opening batsman who bowled occasional tweakers, he was told by director of cricket Bob Carter and Hayden that he would revert to number seven and bowl off-spin in this particular game. He hit an unbeaten 61 and followed up with match figures of three for 42 from 28 overs, a fair effort from a part-timer, as we made it five wins on the trot.

'It's a good craic every now and again, but you can keep that kind of job if people are expecting you to get wickets,' was Alec's assessment, and indeed I was back for the drawn final home match against Essex that delivered the Second Division title.

Pitch liaison officer Phil Sharpe was in attendance for that match and had sufficient misgivings about the amount of turn Jason Brown and I were gaining from the surface to form an inspection panel. It was deemed to be no more than 'sporting', however, after Hayden crashed a big hundred, to put the challenge for the batsmen into context and obtain a sizeable first-innings lead.

A lot was made of the pitches at Northampton in those days, but all I can say is that they weren't doctored – honestly – apart from the odd one or two that blatantly were. Nevertheless, the pedant in me would always strenuously deny accusations that they were raked, and I could do so in the knowledge that they were not. No rake ever went near the square for any untoward purpose. To admit to that would have done a huge disservice to our groundsman, David Bates. Although the joke doing the rounds in our dressing room at the time was that our groundsman, David Bates, a Yorkshireman and a cracking lad, wore an old pair of Curtly Ambrose's size 15 bowling boots during pitch preparation and that may have led to some accidental scarring around a length.

Batesy was permanently accompanied by his collie dog Ned, who achieved notoriety the following year when so poor was our season that he gained more votes than any of our players in the *Northampton Chronicle & Echo*'s player-of-the-season award.

Ned had free run of the ground and would regularly do his business on the outfield at night. Living in denial of the fact, Batesy used to insist: 'No, it's not Ned. We've got an urban fox.' Everyone deserves a chance in life and so this claim was not authoritatively challenged until one evening after a game when, having a beer on the balcony as the sun set, a group of us watched as Ned circled the ground in his usual manner, then stopped about 20 yards in front of the pavilion and dropped the biggest Douglas Hurd.

'Batesy, we've found that urban fox!' we roared. It was magical.

*

Statistically, my 2000 season was okay – 41 Championship wickets complemented by more than 500 runs – although I wasn't picked for any of England's winter commitments. However, I ended up joining the A tour to the Caribbean three matches in as a replacement for county colleague Jason Brown, who was picked after having a very good year and was then promoted to the full England tour when they opted to take an extra spinner to Sri Lanka.

That winter, England A competed in the Caribbean's domestic four-day competition, the Busta Cup. It was a trip that made a couple of people. In Ian Ward's case, it gave him a Test chance against Australia the following summer. Ryan Sidebottom did very well too and made his full international debut just a couple of months after we got back. Personally, my own performances were pleasing and my 18 wickets, half of them in a man-of-the-match display against the Windward Islands in early February 2001, came at 20 apiece.

That emphatic innings victory over the Windwards took place on St Lucia and, because it finished inside three days, it gave us what felt like a day's proper holiday in a prime holiday resort. Our itinerary for that tour took us to some picturesque places, and Anguilla was simply gorgeous. It also contained one of those old-school pitches you hear about in the Caribbean – one in which you can see your own reflection on the first morning. We bowled first against the Leeward Islands and I swear the slips were 45 yards behind the stumps. It was like the top of a lake and the ball barely came down once it went past the batsman. For the catch I took to dismiss Stuart Williams, off Alex Tudor, I might as well have been standing at third man. It was lightning-fast before lunch, but when the shine disappeared so did its pace.

The trip also coincided with my first ever glimpse of Chris Gayle. When he hit Sidebottom for six over extra cover off the back foot inside the opening hour in Kingston, I thought: 'Who's this cowboy? He'll never go anywhere.' Good judge me, clearly. But he was one of my five victims in the match, caught by Vikram Solanki at slip after lunch, as we beat the eventual champions by seven wickets.

Unfortunately, we lost in the semi-final to Guyana. Their middle order comprised Shivnarine Chanderpaul, Ramnaresh Sarwan and the imperious Carl Hooper. We played at the old Bourda ground in Georgetown, which was absolutely packed to the rafters every day. It felt as if 20,000 people were there and reminded me of old Tests I'd seen on the TV in years gone by.

The intensity of the cricket replicated it too. Now, I am never one to blame umpires for results, but we were cheated out of that match ridiculously. I must have had three blatant bat-pads caught by John Crawley, but each time the umpires, quick as a flash, would go: 'Nut owt, nut owt, nut owt.' To say that this wound us up would be an understatement.

If that was a lesson in keeping your cool, Hooper gave me another valuable one, the very first time I ever bowled to him. Sidebottom's follow-through had left a decent foot-hole and the first couple of balls I bowled to Hooper pitched in it. Knowing the ball could go either way out of that crater, he twice prodded at it, and nodded at me in acknowledgement. Any sense of respect was obliterated with the third ball, however, when he leaned forward and flicked his wrists, an action which incredibly sent the ball sailing over my head and what seemed to be 50 yards beyond the boundary. Unperturbed, I pitched the next ball in the same place and this time he lap-slogged it for six. Hooper was the first guy I had ever come across who, when everything was in my favour, was almost impossible to bowl at. What a class player he was.

He'd arrived at the crease with Guyana on 33 for four, 260 runs behind, but a big stand with Sarwan swung the game the home side's way and after trailing on first innings we had no option but to pursue outright victory. In drawn matches, the team with the highest first-innings score progressed, and in chasing the game we lost by seven wickets.

Jimmy Whitaker, now an England selector, was our manager and following our exit from the tournament he entered the changing room with both good and bad news. The bad news was that there wouldn't be a 747 aircraft available that could house our full touring party and all our kit for another two days. However, the good news was that we wouldn't be stuck in Guyana – we had to jet over to Barbados to wait for it. Shame.

A group of us, including Chris Read, Paul Franks and James Foster, ended up spending one of the days on the infamous Jolly Roger booze-cruise boat. We played spoof with various forfeits for the loser, one of which involved Read playing dead. He couldn't have made it any more theatrical, walking into the middle of the boat, where he produced a pirhouette and collapsed face down, a position in which he stayed for 15 minutes. No one batted an eyelid.

Another of the forfeits was to go out and dance mega-enthusiastically to whatever tune came blasting out of the speakers – it was only ten in the morning and the party was in its infancy. So with more than 100 other revellers looking on, Franksie – who had had peroxide put through his hair in Guyana, making him look the spitting image of eighties pop star Yazz – strolled into the middle straight-faced and gave it large to 'Mysterious Girl' by Peter Andre. The rest of us were in hysterics, but rather than ending up the subject of mass humiliation, he proved the perfect ice-breaker for others, who soon flocked onto the dance floor. When I look back, that was great fun and came at what seemed to be a brilliant time in my career.

Eventually at Northamptonshire, however, I stopped enjoying my cricket and that was almost entirely down to one man: Kepler Wessels. I have to admit, though, that even prior to his arrival as coach in the summer of 2003, I'd tentatively considered leaving the club because I felt I was not quite progressing as I should be, the dressing room had begun to fracture and certain other things irritated me.

In fact, my brother Alec's release by the club in September 2001 really upset me. There was always a day at the end of the season when the entire squad would report to the ground and everyone would sit in the changing room to be summoned to the chief executive's office, one by one, to find out whether you were being offered a new contract or not. That particular year I received a phone call asking me to go in a day early. Naively, failing to put two and two together, I assumed the request was because of a pay increase, and so toddled in and signed my new contract as in previous years.

It was only the next day, when Alec called to tell me he'd been let go, and considerably after the ink was dry on my signature, that I twigged. It irked me that the hierarchy had acted in such a cold, calculated fashion, making sure I went in first so that I would not kick up a fuss and refuse to sign by way of protest. This followed the release of left-armer Michael Davies the previous year, just 12 months after he had gone on an England A tour. One season plagued by an attack of the yips and he was cast off. In between, Richard Logan, my best mate, had opted to leave for Nottinghamshire.

In my opinion we were allowing players with value to leave and replacing them with players who weren't as good. That was a source of disappointment, although I perhaps didn't realise at the time that the drip of homegrown players departing the club had started as far back as 1998 when Richard Montgomerie, earmarked as a future captain ever since graduating from Oxford University, was dispensed with. His move to Sussex was arguably the start of the exodus.

Northamptonshire fragmented further over the winter of 2001–02 when the girl due to get married to Toby Bailey pulled the plug on the wedding just a fortnight before their big day. When it became public that she had begun seeing Russell Warren – a really good mate of mine, a Northampton lad, and a team-mate both then and previously with the Saints – it led to segregation of the dressing room. I was caught in the middle because the girl in question was best mates with my girlfriend at the time. Yet my firm view on the situation was that it had absolutely nothing to do with me, so I was not going to take sides. I had not been as close to Toby as I had been to Russell previously but I was determined to stay neutral, and that decision means I get on famously with Toby now.

At the time, however, there was a lot of nonsense flying about, and because I vowed not to change how I acted towards anyone, a large portion came in my direction. Having spent so much time with Russell previously – he was my travelling partner for away games – it was natural to continue my relationship with him. Doing anything else would have felt wrong. With hindsight, the start of the 2002 season would have been easier to negotiate had the situation been resolved the previous winter. But our head coach, Bob Carter, made it clear that as it had nothing to do with cricket, it should not affect what we were doing on the field. He believed outside issues should be dealt with away from the dressing room and we should get on with what we did in our day jobs. But in the real world that attitude doesn't necessarily work, so we had to function as best we could with a divided squad.

An example of this division came when Rabbit and I arrived for a game at Trent Bridge. Our car was first there and so we walked in and claimed our usual spots in the away dressing room, which at Trent Bridge was actually two rooms divided by an archway. So when the rest of the team arrived and clocked that we were in the left-hand side, they all proceeded to get changed in the right. It was farcical. Russell and I had palatial comfort in one side while thirteen people were sharing pegs and bumping into each other in the other.

Mal Loye, who'd previously been really good mates with Russell, got heavily involved in the fall-out and, having sided with Toby, vowed never to speak to Russell again. It even got to the point where, when batting together, Mal completely ignored him, refusing to chat in between overs and remaining at his end. Mal and I are not exactly what you call mates, we never have been, and this behaviour only exacerbated the 'us and them' scenario. The split within the team was fairly clearly defined – it was me and Rabbit, and everyone else.

It was an unbelievably weird atmosphere, and one created by people who had needlessly involved themselves in other people's business. There seemed to be an obsession with the exact date on which Russell began seeing this girl – the assumption was that he had been having an affair with her while Toby was still with her – but I never delved into it because I really didn't want to know. It was nothing to do with me, and yet I was astonished by the number of lads, John Blain being an example, who got too involved for their own good. Sticking up for your mates is all very well, but the campaign to get Russell kicked out of the club took it way too far. The result was that the 2002 season was engulfed by disharmony, and after Russell was jettisoned to the second team to placate the majority, he was released in September and took the chance to move to Nottinghamshire.

Selfishly, I also considered a switch, but for different reasons, primarily a feeling that I needed to make more money out of the game. I was on about £30,000 a year at the time, and believed I could get £55–60,000 elsewhere, and still have enough years in me to secure a benefit. Yes, I admit they were pretty shallow reasons for wanting to leave, but I also reckoned that we were not going to win anything either, and as a player I've always believed in competing for trophies.

I actually spoke to Jason Gallian, then captain of Notts, but didn't follow through on their interest. Although leaving was an option, my desire to do so was clearly not strong enough, and when Kepler was appointed I believed I owed it to myself and the club to give it a fair crack. After all, it was still my club, one I had supported as a kid, and I considered that a new start might give us a better chance of progressing as a team.

Staying put was possibly the worst decision I ever made – or the best, depending on how you look at it. Because had I left for Trent Bridge two years earlier, things might have turned out completely differently. I might have played a couple of years for Notts, struggled to get in their first team and been lost to the game for ever. I always look at things with the same philosophical attitude, and there is every chance that if I had taken that plunge I would now be writing this book on behalf of Paul Franks.

When it was revealed that Kepler would be taking over as manager for the 2003 season, I genuinely considered it to be a boost for the club. I knew he was a no-nonsense, hard-nosed coach and thought he could instil an atmosphere which would enable us to win stuff. But his methods did not work with me or with Northants whatsoever.

From the off, he seemed to regard me as a massive troublemaker. The first words he spoke to me came during a training session. He and Nick Cook were walking behind me when he beckoned: 'Hey, Swann. I hear you like to do impressions.'

'Yeah, I do,' I said, turning my head. 'Can do one or two cricketers, as it happens.'

'Oh, that's good,' he said, completely deadpan. 'If you ever do me I will f------ kill you!'

I giggled, and I'm sure he was doing it to be friendly, but even in jest he was very intimidating. And as early as our first exchange, I wasn't sure if it was going to go the right way.

Our first County Championship game under Kepler was against Yorkshire at Headingley, in early April 2003, and it ended in an innings and millions obliteration. For the record, the actual number of runs was 343, making it Northamptonshire's biggest margin of defeat for 82 years. The pitch was like a road, it did absolutely nothing untoward, and we got bowled out cheaply in the first innings.

My memories of it are all the more painful because Ryan Sidebottom hit me smack on the big toe, to dismiss me lbw, with an inswinging yorker. As soon as it hit me I knew the toe was broken. I endured the most horrific shooting pain and could feel blood oozing out of my toenail into my boot as I walked from the field, seeing stars as I went. I felt as though I was going to pass out because I am a genuine wimp when it comes to things like that.

Back in the changing room, I pulled off my boot to discover a claret-stained mess of a sock. As physio Andy Roberts began his assessment of what was inside, Kepler wandered in. Given the angle the toe was pointing at, it was obviously badly messed up but our new coach's advice was explicit: 'Just stick an injection in it so that he can bowl.'

'Bloody hell,' I thought, as he left the room. 'Now that is old-school. It's the first game of the season, and I've broken my toe.'

Yorkshire's doctor was called to give me the injection but, after taking one look at the toe in question, he refused to do so. His belief was that I could properly damage it if I carried on, and that the best course of action was to keep off it altogether.

In the end a compromise was reached. The medics cut a large hole in my trainer and it was agreed that I would play on with my big toe sticking out. I bowled 26 overs in Yorkshire's first innings, and even played against Gloucestershire in our first home fixture a few days later, but the result of walking on the outside of my foot was damaged ankle ligaments, which forced me to miss a stretch of matches.

Things had not begun well with the new coach but I pledged to fall into line with his demands, even though some of the targets set for me seemed wholly unrealistic. On being dropped to the second team relatively early in his tenure, I was told only five wickets and hundreds were good enough to merit a recall. So, you can imagine that being bowled first ball offering no shot to Surrey's Tim Murtagh appealed to the darker side of my humour.

This was also a time when Monty Panesar was emerging as a talented spinner. In future years, when we were picked in England squads together, there was an abundance of references to us re-forming our old county partnership. However, the truth is that I didn't actually play with him a great deal. In fact, we only played in the same Championship team seven times between 2001 and 2004, mostly when we fielded three spinners, and therefore we did not necessarily bowl in tandem. On one of those occasions, in the end of June 2003, Monty didn't even get on as I claimed career-best figures of seven for 33 against Derbyshire.

I never felt under threat from Monty for my place in the long term, because I always took it that I was a first-team county cricketer and no matter where I went or what I did I would be playing first-team cricket. That may have been something of an arrogant assumption, and looking at my figures around then it probably was, but it was just how I viewed myself. Even when my relationship with Kepler degenerated to such a degree that he told me the only reason I kept my spot was because there was no one else, I knew I was a better spinner than most people in the country.

For me, there was more competition with Jason Brown in my earlier years. Brownie was a genuinely good bowler, it just went against him that he couldn't bat, but we played together on a lot of turning pitches and that worked really well for the team in our two Division Two promotion years of 2000 and 2003, when we shared 98 wickets each time.

Monty's rise to prominence followed my departure in the winter of 2004–05. During his early days on the staff, everyone loved this innocent young kid from Luton. It would be unfair to say he was wet behind the ears in those days – he was absolutely drenched. But he would turn up and bowl, want to bowl all day, and was brimming with natural talent.

The thing I remember most fondly about Monty was his fielding. Nick Cook, our madcap second-team coach, would hit skiers before each game and for every catch you dropped you had to take off an item of clothing. Poor old Monty used to get down to his pants within about fifteen seconds. His attempts were truly amazing and these drills were a sight to behold. As he stood there, balls would drop five yards to either side of him. But to be fair to Mont, he has worked his socks off over the years. You won't believe how good he is now compared to how bad he was then. When we were in Australia in 2010–11, he took a spectacular diving, one-handed catch at square leg in a tour game before the first Ashes Test, and after seeing him as a kid, that was the equivalent of me sitting down tomorrow, learning Mandarin, and then being able to address the public of China in a political speech in five years' time. Where he has got to considering where he has come from is phenomenal.

Despite our County Championship promotion of 2003, I maintained misgivings about the new regime, although I convinced myself that the situation would sort itself out and that there would be a future for me at Northampton. However, things took a nasty turn early the next summer.

After defeat in a home Championship game against Kent in mid-May, my former England A colleague Rob Key asked me how I felt at Northants, because they sensed I was unsettled. Official approaches for players had just been made compulsory and he had been instructed by his superiors to sound me out on whether I would consider a switch, so they weren't wasting their time. In full knowledge of the protocol, I asked him to instruct Kent to write a letter to Northants, and I would then speak to their coach and chief executive once it had gone through the official channels.

Being wanted by another county was not something that consumed my thoughts – although I admit it was nice to feel appreciated – so it wasn't until a couple of weeks later, when I was batting in the nets at Northampton, that the issue raised its head again. I noticed David Sales, who was now captain of the club, deep in conversation with Kepler, who was holding a piece of paper, which, it soon became apparent, was the official correspondence from Kent.

I'd only faced a few deliveries when Kepler hauled me out of my net to ask bluntly: 'Who do you want to play for, Kent or Northamptonshire?'

'You are putting me on the spot a bit,' I countered, as he showed me the letter.

'Well, you're not playing here again until you make your mind up,' he warned, and with that sent me on my way.

Although I did play on, our relationship, which might previously be described as strained, was now untenable.

Midway through every season, we would be called in for a meeting, to assess how things were going from both player and management perspectives. I had always insisted on one-year rolling deals because I felt that put me in the best position in terms of bargaining power when it came to wages. But being able to tell Kepler I was not going to sign the one offered to me that summer was one of the most satisfying moments I had in my final two years at the club.

Things got pretty dark for me for a while, and the low point manifested itself one morning when I pulled into the car park, put my head on the steering wheel and thought: 'How can I go through this again?' Turning up for work was making me utterly miserable and for all I know a doctor would have diagnosed clinical depression. At that lowest ebb I would happily have given the game up, and if someone had offered me a chance to work on a cruise ship for six months I'd have set sail.

For someone whose glass is always somewhere between half full and overflowing, this was not right, but Kepler really did grind me down. When you consider that this was my boyhood club, one that I'd always dreamed of playing for, it was a tragic shame it got to this point of violent happiness that I was leaving. The whole situation deteriorated rapidly because I didn't want to be there, and he certainly didn't want me in his team because he viewed me as a disruptive inconvenience.

Things were destined for the bitterest of conclusions even before he chose to make me a scapegoat for our poor performances. Suddenly, it became routine to use the local media to question my attitude. On one occasion he claimed he had tried to help me with my bowling but I had ignored his advice and been stubborn. This was total rubbish as far as I was concerned. Here was a man who was prepared to make me look like an absolute git by lying about me in print, and I hated him for it.

When I challenged him about his actions, he simply replied: 'As coach I will use any method I see fit to get the best out of my players.' But there was not a method on the planet he could have applied to get anything out of me; I simply didn't want to play for him.

Strangely, I had my own column in the *Northampton Chronicle & Echo* at the time, and for a while I thought about retaliating with a made-up story about him. But the whole sorry episode made me take a look at myself. What was I doing? How had it come to this? I might as well just go quietly, I thought.

But doing so was a real test. The rest of the team were instructed by Kepler to avoid hanging around with me, to stop laughing at my changing room jokes and to give me the cold shoulder. On one occasion I walked into the dressing room – I am renowned for thinking players get to grounds too early for any game of cricket, and I've never been one of the first on parade – to find an unusual scene. All the other players were already present and changed. My entrance was greeted by a deathly hush. Nevertheless, I walked over to my usual spot, which was next to Tim Roberts, a really good mate, and a lad I'd played cricket with since I was 10 years old. I took the plunge and asked him what was going on, thinking someone had died or something.

In his undiluted Northampton accent, he replied: 'We're not allowed to laff at ya, lad. Can't be seen to socialise wiv ya.'

He was giggling as he said it. I looked around at the other lads but they were all avoiding eye contact, staring at their bags and stuff, rather than look at me.

'You're joking,' I thought. Inside I was fuming.

This occurred on the first day of a Championship game, and throughout the next few days people ignored me, paid me lip service or tried to wriggle out of conversation as quickly as they could. After lunch on the first day, I went back upstairs to the changing rooms and for some reason happened to have a cream cake in my hand. I don't know what I was doing with it, but without thinking I aimlessly chucked it over my shoulder. Would you believe the timing? A millisecond later Kepler walked into the changing room. Thank God, it didn't hit him. He didn't utter a word, but the way he looked at me – as it flew past his nose and hit the wall – made me feel more frightened than I've ever felt in my life. I had visions of him ripping my head off with his bare hands.

The atmosphere was such a contrast to half a dozen years earlier when Matthew Hayden had promoted togetherness. It was Hayden, in fact, who had pushed for us to establish a team song. In Australia, the singing of the team song after victories is an established cricket tradition, but the concept felt very otherworldly to us. We all fell into line, though, and because there were a lot of local lads in the team at the time, the most natural thing was to employ one of the Northampton Town football songs as our own, tweaking the words slightly.

It went like this:

> The fields are green, the sky is blue,
> The River Nene goes winding through,
> The market square, the cobblestones,
> That shake the old man to the bones,
> A finer town you'll never see,
> A finer town there'll never be,
> Those city lights don't bother me,
> Cos from Northampton, I'm proud to be.

You didn't have to be a Cobblers fan to know this song; you would have known it from growing up in the town. Such was the turnover of players and influx of Kolpak signings in those years, however, that the closing line was now a bit of a joke. Only Tim and I remained of the Northampton lads. Ironically, at one point earlier that season I was instructed to write out the words to the song because not enough of the players knew it. That act in itself showed the way the club had gone, and I wasn't clear whether they wanted me to provide an Afrikaans translation.

Once it went down the Kolpak route, stripping itself of local players for whatever reason, the club lost its homely feel. It was no longer the same place. Whenever I walked in during my early years on the books you would hear laughter in the corridors, and after-hours the office staff would have drinks with the players, but now it was all change and there seemed to be a sense of fear pervading the place.

If you bring in a South African coach it is probably going to be par for the course that he will want to bring in South African players, but it seemed that the players coming in were not always as good as the ones they were replacing. Toby Bailey, for instance, was a brilliant wicketkeeper and had been groomed to be long-term keeper ever since I'd been there. Under Kepler he was shipped out because Kepler's son Riki, who joined as an 18-year-old, kept wicket. There was no doubt Wessels junior had some talent with the bat but he certainly wasn't a wicketkeeper of first-class standard.

Things like that became a bit soul-destroying for me, but no one else seemed to be seeing it the way I did. Others were buying into the new regime, perhaps scared for their own places. As a result, I found myself drifting away from guys who'd previously been established close mates. I had been through loads with David Sales, for example, but our relationship was now much more distant. Others whinged about things amongst themselves but weren't doing anything to try to challenge what was going on. Meanwhile, I was becoming more and more ostracised.

One of my final games for the county was on 22 August 2004, a one-day hammering inflicted by Hampshire at Milton Keynes. We lost by 67 runs despite needing only 239 to win. Our pursuit never got going. We were 17 for four at one stage, but I went in at number five and played my natural game. I hit 59 off 46 balls, with three sixes and five fours, but was not able to alter the course of the contest. Not much was said in the aftermath by Kepler but in the newspaper the next day he had a real go at the performance, claiming that he constantly faced pressure to play local players but this proved they couldn't score any runs.

I remember thinking: 'Hang on a minute, I am the only one who got any runs, and I'm a local.'

There were other clear indications that this was no longer the club I had fallen in love with. Steve Coverdale, the long-standing chief executive, quit after it emerged our financial administrator, Sue Woodward, had been putting her fingers in the till. It was all a bit of a laugh that she had bought herself a nice villa in Spain, but the club ended up suing her for the loss of a six-figure sum.

The County Ground, where Dad dropped Alec and me off during

the summer holidays to cheer on Alan Fordham, Nigel Felton, Allan Lamb and Curtly Ambrose, no longer held its magic for me. As kids we were proper little cricket geeks. We would watch a session, then play our own games round the back of the stands, just as others had done before us. It was something of a Northamptonshire ritual, you see, and Mal Loye and Russell Warren did exactly the same before they joined the staff. Mal always made me laugh when he recalled his trips down there because whenever he went, he would make sure he was watching when Rob Bailey came in to bat but would clear off round the back to play when it was David Capel's turn.

But driving to the ground now on the occasions I have to play there, I never feel the same as I did when I was a kid. It was my club, I really felt that, yet now I can't even stand the sight of the ground, which is a real shame. I've since spoken to other people who left during that period and no one can believe how different things are. Sure, times change, people move on, but I am convinced that these changes were all for the worst.

7

TIED UP IN NOTTS

W HEN IT came to leaving Northamptonshire I had a few irons in the fire. However, while Kent had revealed their interest earlier in the year, and I had nothing against them, I didn't really want to go there. On the county circuit there are grounds you get a feel for and others you dislike; because I had never enjoyed bowling there, and never actually done well there, Canterbury was a real turn-off. I couldn't see a future down there for me.

Every single week of that summer of 2004, or so it felt, a mate from another county would sidle up to me at the bar after a game to ask if I'd consider joining them. Word had clearly got round about my unrest and coaches were instructing players who knew me to put the feelers out. From all these quiet words, I learned there were about eight counties who were actively seeking to speak to me.

Keen to get something sorted, I asked athletes1, the company who acted for me at the time, to get out into the marketplace and come back with some firm offers. Yet a few weeks later when I rang back to check progress, having heard nothing, I was told lots of calls had gone in but nothing concrete had come back. So, because I'd got closer to deals myself while chatting over a pint, they were hoofed into touch.

At that time, Mike Hussey recommended his agent called David Manasseh, who I remain with to this day. Our first conversation began with him saying: 'I'm glad you're on the phone because I've had county chairmen asking about you for months. But I've told them all you are not one of mine, so couldn't comment on your availability.'

I left my future in his hands and very quickly the equation became simple – a straight choice between Lancashire and Nottinghamshire. When Mick Newell, the Nottinghamshire director of cricket, travelled down to see me at a Northampton hotel, he said all the right things to win me over. I left that meeting feeling as though he had offered me the world. He might as well have. To this day I don't know whether he had been advised by someone who knew me but I suspected he had because it was uncanny. It was everything I wanted to hear.

Nottinghamshire had Stuart MacGill as their overseas player during their Championship promotion season of 2004 but, Mick explained, they were already planning for an assault on the Division One crown, and those plans included me as the sole spinner and MacGill's overseas berth being sacrificed to bring in a new captain, New Zealand's revered leader Stephen Fleming, in place of Jason Gallian.

Far from wanting to suppress my personality, as my previous coach had, Mick was keen for me to be myself in the changing room. They were getting rid of some people who had created disquiet and wanted to replace them with good blokes, who liked a laugh and a joke, and see where that took them. I was sold on the spot. I told him as much at the time but felt I owed Lancashire the courtesy of hearing what they had to say too.

When I spoke to Lancashire's Mike Watkinson he offered me the polar opposite of Mick's impassioned speech. Whereas Mick filled me with excitement, made me feel important and convinced me he was a coach worth playing for, Mike told me he considered himself a bloody good spin coach, and emphasised the work he had done with Gary Keedy. Indeed, because of Keedy's presence, and the fact they hoped to sign Muttiah Muralitharan that winter, he couldn't even guarantee me a place in their first team. But I was more than welcome to pop along if I fancied it. If the choice had been 50–50 before speaking to either of them it was now 100 per cent Notts.

My decision became one of the most badly kept secrets on the circuit. We played Surrey in a one-day game about a week after I had informed Northamptonshire of my intentions, and Martin Bicknell had obviously heard from his brother Darren, who was at Nottinghamshire, that I was on my way.

Towards the death of the Surrey innings, as I was bowling, Bickers, stationed at the non-striker's end, whispered: 'Off to Trent Bridge next year, are we, Swanny?'

I didn't think another soul in the world knew, other than the limited few I'd told. Naturally, I looked at him sheepishly.

'Don't worry about it, mate,' he continued, in hushed tones. 'It will be a good move for you.'

I respected the fact that he was being discreet. 'Good on him,' I thought.

Yet the truth was he'd let the cat out of the bag, and I didn't have to wait long to discover that fact. Later in the day, early in my innings, he beat me outside the off stump and the close fielders boomed: 'Well bowled, Bickers, you're tying him up in Notts!'

I am not sure if Usman Afzaal, my partner at the other end, even noticed, but at that point I should have been past caring anyway. I had made my choice and I wasn't going back on it.

When it had been narrowed down to two options, my gut feeling had initially swayed me towards Old Trafford because I knew the ball turned there and it would be easy to bowl spin. My brother Alec had been there for three years and I knew it was a good club. But the more I thought about it, the more it seemed to make sense to move up the M1. After speaking to Mick they could have played on sand and I would have still gone there – he made me feel so wanted – but well before that my dad had given me some considered, constructive advice.

Dad reckoned playing at Trent Bridge every other week would make me a better bowler. His reasoning was simple – because it was a Test ground we would often have to play on the edge of the square, therefore I would be tested regularly bowling to short boundaries, and it wouldn't do me any harm learning to tighten up. I had always been able to turn it and take wickets, but this was a chance to improve another side of my bowling.

I had developed as an attacking off-spinner, and one of Dad's mates was responsible for that. The chap in question was John Wake, the first-team spinner at Northampton Saints. He and Dad grew up in neighbouring pit villages in Northumberland, although Wakey with his moustache and mop of curly hair was a double for one of the Scousers off *Harry Enfield's Television Programme* rather than a typical-looking Geordie.

I'd watched Wakey in action from a young age, and both his approach and advice rubbed off on me. I never had any spin coaching as such but he was a great bowler to learn from. I would study him from the sidelines, and he also regaled me with tales of when he first went to Australia to play grade cricket. He bowled very straight, old-fashioned, Ray Illingworth lines with heavy leg-side fields when he arrived in Australia, only to be asked what on earth he was doing. His team-mates demanded he got the ball outside off stump because, they said, he would not get wickets in their conditions unless he did that and brought in a man at slip. He acquiesced and years later drummed it into me that I should be looking to pitch it outside off stump to hit off stump rather than bowl straight. It was ingrained in me at an early age – this was the way to bowl, and most importantly the way for me to get more wickets.

Wakey was very feisty on the field, and so he and my dad forged a ridiculous comedy duo. In one famous game in which I was playing – the Saints lads always bring this story up at our annual Christmas drinks – Dad stormed off the field despite being captain, directing an offer to Wakey to take over amongst a host of expletives. Dad took refuge on the bench at fine leg until a set of four wides came his way, and all was soon forgotten.

It was Wakey's general attitude towards the game that really influenced me, however, and there is one particular away game at Lutterworth that I recall for two reasons – firstly because our Alec, in retrieving one of our wayward balls, tried to climb a metal fence and slipped, resulting in him being temporarily suspended upside down by his tracksuit pants until a friendly passer-by hauled him free. The second was because Saints batted first and got millions, but from the start of their reply Lutterworth blocked out for the draw.

That kind of approach irked Wakey, it was not the way he liked to play at all, so with the game petering out towards a stalemate, he began negotiations with the two not-out batsmen on how many they would like to chase off the last 15 overs. After realising he was deadly serious, they nominated something like 65, and so he ran up and bowled 10 lots of four wides, employing a man off the field at fine leg to keep throwing the ball back. He was fully prepared to compromise just to give Saints the chance of winning the game.

I would love to say that this particular tale had a romantic ending, and that we won off the last ball, but in truth I cannot remember what happened, and that hardly matters anyway. To me, the adventurous approach did. Central League matches were 50-over affairs and could be won, lost or drawn. But the latter result was never really an option for the Saints because they were always prepared to lose to win. It is undoubtedly why I can't stand draws, and will always go for it if there is a chance of victory.

Now circumstances were offering me a chance to test myself against the odds, and Dad's advice proved sound enough. Just as he'd suggested, it is very rare we get near the centre pitches, certainly in Championship cricket, and the fact that Trent Bridge was not a ground renowned for taking spin meant doing well would catch the eyes of the powers that be.

Quite honestly, moving to Nottinghamshire turned me into a better bowler in numerous ways. Of course, other things like age and experience have contributed, but having Chris Read as a wicketkeeper helped me massively, in terms of talking about bowling different lines and lengths. He is very astute when it comes to stuff like that. Because it doesn't turn at all until about day three and a half, I learned that, particularly in the first innings, contrary to Wakey's advice, it was necessary to bowl really straight. Having always been someone who pursued wickets, I also developed the knack of attacking even when being defensive.

Working hard for rewards is nothing new to a seasoned spinner. The art is hard work anyway, and you tend not to get your five-wicket hauls in 15 overs. It normally takes twice as long as that, so I was happy to get stuck in on these challenging pitches. As an inherently lazy person, I can't pretend the fact that seamers would be hogging the ball for the first six weeks of the season didn't appeal to me too when I first made the switch. Not bowling a ball also meant getting to chat in a slip cordon with Stephen Fleming and David Hussey, with old man Mark Ealham positioned at gully. Flem and Huss are two of my best mates in the game and Ealham's a very funny bloke, who would talk about all kinds of subjects, ranging from the size of the lunch portions, to how much salt chef had put on the food, to what was for dinner tomorrow.

September 2004 was a double watershed moment for me as it turned out. As well as signing for Nottinghamshire on a three-year deal, I was summoned to Loughborough to see the England and Wales Cricket Board academy director Rod Marsh.

People tend to assume that it was a breakdown in relations with Duncan Fletcher in South Africa 1999–2000 that went against me when it came to international selection over the following years. But a bust-up with Marsh at the ECB academy in Adelaide was more significant in my mind.

When it was launched in the winter of 2001–02, quite a lot was made of English cricket's new academy system – which effectively replaced the annual winter A tour – and we got paid about £15,000 a man to go Down Under. Andrew Flintoff and Robert Key were also in that inaugural intake and like me considered it to be an opportunity to stake another claim for full honours. In fact, the three of us sat at Sydney Airport upon arrival in Australia discussing the fact we'd all been given another chance and needed to grab it. We made a pact to do just that.

Yet only a matter of hours later, shortly after we checked into the Adelaide facility, I was about to stuff up. We were herded into a dining room for our induction. Former Australia Test player Wayne Phillips, one of the coaches, introduced himself and then Rod explained what he expected of us all during our stay.

With the formalities out of the way, Kirk Russell, the physio, then mentioned that Robbie Williams was playing in town the following week and that should any of us want to go he would put the tickets on his credit card. As Robbie had recently left the worst band in the world at that point, he was now all right by me, and I was seriously considering the proposal when Rod, in his broad Western Australian accent, demanded: 'Who the f--- is Robbie Williams?'

Now, to this day I don't know why I did it – I never will, and looking back it makes me laugh out loud even though I concede it shouldn't – but I just looked at him quizzically and in a mock Aussie drawl replied: 'He's a f------ singer, you ignorant c---!'

You know when you've totally misread a situation? Rather than roars of laughter, my response was met with a collective gasp. Phillips clasped his hands to his mouth as if to say: 'What the hell have you done?' And although I tried to claw my way out of my self-dug 100-metre hole by explaining again in more polite terms what Robbie Williams did for a living, the damage was done. As everyone dispersed, some of the other lads were truly astonished at my outburst.

My stay had begun on the worst possible terms and it didn't get any better. As it transpired, this particular academy trip did less for my England ambitions than the England tour to South Africa by miles. I will happily admit that my attitude stank. I just didn't want to be there, didn't see the point, didn't embrace it and made that all too evident with my behaviour. These were the people you had to impress to get in the full England squad and I was doing anything but.

Andrew Strauss was my room-mate out there – but the only similarity between us was a liking for Hootie & the Blowfish. He'd never previously heard of them but now loves them thanks to me educating him.

In cricket terms, of all the players who have surprised me with how well they've done as we've come through the England system, Strauss is probably my number one. If you had written down the names of the guys on that trip and asked me who was likely to have the longest Test careers he wouldn't have made the top five. Yet he has had the best career of the lot, so that speaks volumes for him.

Batting-wise I always knew he could play, but something told me he would never get picked – because he's not the prettiest batsman and his record was not phenomenal in county cricket. Once offered the chance, though, he never looked back.

I got on with him that winter but we couldn't have presented more of a contrast in our attitudes. He made the most of every waking minute to throw himself into the cricket, trained hard and embraced the ethos of the academy fully. I did the exact opposite.

I believed it was the biggest waste of time going, and hated every second of it. We were treated like kids, locked in rooms no bigger than a downstairs bathroom, with two beds and a cupboard wedged in. Plus it was just non-stop cricket. There was no time for anything else. It really irked me.

To be fair, some other people thought it was amazing, and I've since spoken to Jimmy Anderson about it and he loved every minute of the time he was there the following year. But to me it was like being in a school team on tour for six months. It might have been perfect for a 17-year-old lad but I resented being treated like one.

Our diet was ridiculous; you were not allowed to eat any fat and there was no butter on the table at meal times. So one day I went down to the local shop, bought a tub of Flora Light and took it into breakfast with me. I got in a whole world of trouble for that. Rod went absolutely mad because our fitness trainer outlawed anything of the sort. 'You shouldn't need it,' we were instructed. 'Just put jam on.' That argument was pretty hollow to me because I don't even like jam.

From a cricket perspective the trip gave me a chance to show I could do well, but my reaction certainly didn't endear me to Rod. What actually riled me most was the fact we appeared simply to be copying the whole Australian system. Now when I look back I see that was because the Australian system worked, but at the time it was a bugbear for me.

So strong was my opinion that I am not even sure I wanted to play for England badly enough to kowtow to people. It was like being in the army, and the one reason I didn't join the army is that I absolutely hate all that discipline, that hierarchical structure. Well, to be honest, it wasn't the only reason I didn't join the army . . .

Three years on, however, not long after the permanent academy facility at Loughborough was built, I received an instruction from Rod to report for duty once more. This time, I eagerly got changed and made my way to the nets, but I had only bowled a couple of deliveries when another of the coaches, John Abrahams, came over and cut me short. I had not been called in to bowl, he told me. Rod wanted to speak to me in his office.

'What do you actually want out of the game?' asked Rod, now one of the ECB's four selectors, in his opening gambit.

'I want to play for England,' I replied, because by this stage I truly did. A few of my mates from that 2001–02 group had gone on to do very well. Fred was obviously the golden boy of the Test and one-day teams, Strauss had begun his international career in a blaze of glory and Robert Key had just scored a double hundred against the West Indies at Lord's. Their feats had strengthened my resolve to get in, and thankfully Rod was willing to give me a second chance.

'I am not a man to hold a grudge,' he informed me. 'Even against someone who calls me an ignorant c---.'

He continued: 'I've spent the summer studying county cricket and you are the best spinner. Full stop.'

My mouth ran away with itself in apology. 'Oh Rod, I'm glad you brought that up, I'm so sorry, I don't know why I said what I said all those years ago . . .' The whole garbled sentence took about a second.

He shook my hand, laughed and told me: 'Go and take some wickets!'

From that moment I got on famously with Rod. Getting to know him over those next few months at Loughborough, I thought he was a different bloke. In fact, I loved the academy when it was in England that winter of 2004–05.

The fact that it was at the university meant we became glorified students. We lived in what were effectively halls of residence – well, a huge house about 50 yards from the students' union – trained our tits off five days a week and went home at weekends. We ingratiated ourselves with the uni lot, particularly on Wednesday nights when all the sports teams would go on the sauce after their games. Actually, the fact we joined in the revelry didn't go down particularly well with the rugby and football lads, because those of us who weren't married or engaged were up for some fun. I had an absolute whale of a time, and went out with one of the tidiest girls on campus prior to heading to Sri Lanka after Christmas.

During that academy tour, the thought of getting back into the England team was firmly in my head, and I strengthened my case for inclusion, or at least believed I had, with some runs and wickets. We drew the Test series against Sri Lanka A 1–1, winning the first comprehensively after I claimed a five-wicket haul in the second innings. In the second match I weighed in with a futile 71, sharing a big partnership with Matt Prior, to get us close to chasing down our 285-run target despite being reduced to 22 for five at one stage, as the hosts dismissed us to take a share of the spoils.

I genuinely believed I had a chance of playing for England in the Ashes during that memorable summer of 2005 – or at least making the squad. I got nowhere near, of course – although I was twelfth man for the first couple of days of the Edgbaston Test, with typically disastrous consequences.

You just couldn't make this up. As luck would have it, on my return to sharing a changing room with Duncan Fletcher after five years away, I pulled a muscle in my back. So as England fought their way back into the series, serenaded by thousands of drunken Brummies, there was I receiving treatment on the physio bench. Fletch must have looked at me and thought: 'What an imbecile.' There were no pleasantries, no breaking of the ice; once again he didn't have anything to do with me. But that's not unusual because as twelfth man the last thing you do is hobnob with the coaching staff. They're too busy trying to win the game.

The noise in the ground that week fuelled my determination to get back into the fold. When Andrew Flintoff bowled *that* over at Ricky Ponting, one of the best ever in Test cricket, the atmosphere was simply amazing.

But going through the whole summer of 2005 without coming close to a recall disheartened me once more, particularly bearing in mind the quality of the guys getting picked for one-day tours around then. I didn't have a problem when Shaun Udal was selected, or even Gareth Batty, but when guys like Jamie Dalrymple and Alex Loudon were called up I considered my England chance gone. It almost felt as if the selectors were mocking me. My mates certainly were. Every time I went down the pub they would give me a hard time about who was getting picked ahead of me. That's mates for you.

In contrast, things with Nottinghamshire could not have gone any better. Everything Mick Newell promised was delivered. Having targeted the County Championship title, in September we secured the club's first in 18 years, in the penultimate round, after dangling Kent a poisoned carrot at Canterbury. Kent had to win this particular rain-affected contest to retain their own hopes of silverware and were therefore compelled to chase a 420-run target in just 70 overs. Needless to say, our hefty victory was greeted joyously, in stark contrast to the incandescent reaction of the great Shane Warne, captain of Hampshire, our nearest rivals. According to him, it was the dumbest thing he had ever seen in his life.

I was happy with my 30-wicket haul in Division One, although my season's statistics became somewhat tarnished in the final game of the season against Hampshire in what would have been a title showdown but for our win over Kent. Our celebrations were still in full flow when we arrived in Southampton – let's just say there were

11 visiting players nursing the biggest hangovers in the history of cricket, and this game certainly did not take place on a level playing field – and Flem asked them to bat first on a soaking-wet wicket.

Now, if it had been the game to decide the title I reckon we would have had them eight down at lunch, given the favourable conditions. As it was, Hampshire closed the first day on 424 for four. David Hussey, who had enjoyed such a sterling season, was given the game off by Mick not because he was treated any differently as overseas player but because he was so drunk. He was required to come on as sub a couple of times and on both occasions he went into the slips and dropped catches. It was brilliant fun.

But we suffered for it in the scorebook. They piled up 714 for five, their highest ever Championship score, breaking a record that had stood since 1899. My figures were one for 145.

We lost by an innings, of course, but the thing I loved about Notts was highlighted in that week. We had been so professional and strived so hard all year to win, and rather than peddle out clichés about the next game being the most important after doing so, we savoured the achievement. Mick's attitude was that as we had worked so hard all year, we deserved to enjoy it, so nobody left the bar on the eve of the game until everyone had bought a round. We just sat and talked cricket together. The bond and team spirit was something to cherish; it was as good as anything I'd known.

Mick was amazing for me and true to his word gave me free rein to be myself. That's not to say there weren't teething problems that first summer. In a Championship game at Glamorgan in late August – shortly after I'd knackered up a game against Surrey by running out Mark Ealham – I went in with a lead of exactly 100 with four wickets intact and decided it was time to tee off. However, having advanced down the pitch to only my second ball from Robert Croft, I picked out midwicket beautifully, and as I trudged off, Mick absolutely fumed.

One of the most fidgety watchers you will ever come across, Mick on this occasion had wanted someone to get a partnership together and edge us towards a win. My attitude couldn't have been more of a contrast, and that had caused a seismic reaction.

The old changing rooms at Cardiff were horrendous, housed as they were in a 1950s-style prefab building. Mick, frothing at the mouth and looking as if he wanted to punch me, frogmarched me downstairs to the shower block – I thought I was off to the gulag – and roared: 'There are 10 blokes here trying to win a Championship and you're f------ around! What are you f------ doing?'

'Oooh, calm down, Mick, sorry,' I protested.

Admittedly, it didn't help that we had slipped from 231 for two to 283 all out against the bottom-placed side, but thankfully we ended up winning comfortably to go three and a half points clear at the top of the table, with a game in hand.

Nevertheless, Mick told Darren Bicknell to take me to one side afterwards and have a quiet word. Darren explained that Mick wanted the best for the club and that my decision while batting was a poor one. My defence was that he would love my approach one day. I'm still waiting for him to acknowledge that day has come, mind.

Two months earlier I'd crashed 62 from 25 balls in a Twenty20 game at Headingley, and only got out when, confronted by Yorkshire off-spinner Richard Dawson, I became obsessed with playing the reverse sweep. I connected nicely with a couple before top-edging one, and when I walked off we were 101 for one, well on course for our 181-run target. I expected rapturous applause but as I sat down with the other guys, Mick rapped: 'If you play one more reverse sweep, I'm going to rip your head off!'

Later, after victory was completed and he'd had time to chill out, I explained that as I'd grown up on spinning pitches, the reverse sweep was a bona fide tool for me when batting. I was adamant I didn't want to give it up, and therefore we came to a compromise that, as long as I practised it regularly, I was allowed to play it in games. As far as I am aware, I am the only member of the Nottinghamshire playing staff who is – because it drives Mick mad when other people get out attempting it.

Typically, he was the sender of the first derogatory text message when, after getting 20-odd in my first game back for England in Sri Lanka in the autumn of 2007, I pulled it out of the locker and failed to clear the inner ring. But to me it is one of the best shots in the game, so I will never stop playing it.

Mick desperately wants his team and his players to do well and to win every game. And he is very good at picking and preparing teams to that end. His cricket brain is terrific but perhaps his primary skill as a coach is man-management. Yes, he kicks the dustbin when things aren't going well and disappears into his office with a slam of the door, but that just shows he cares. And he was rewarded with silverware for identifying and moulding that team of 2005.

He had begun that process a couple of years earlier when Nottinghamshire and Northamptonshire were not miles apart in terms of talent. If anything, Northamptonshire would have been superior. But belief at Trent Bridge was key, and the fact that they'd been fairly mediocre for a few years was not dwelt upon. It was as if they'd said: 'To hell with it, from now on we're going to be winners.' In terms of attitude it was the first time I'd been in a team that believed they could actually win the County Championship, and the fact I was in new territory is why I retain such a fondness for that summer: we set out at the start of the year to do something and we did just that.

Our winning formula was based around bowling first, dismissing the opposition – of the eight matches at Trent Bridge that year, we fielded first in all but our final one – and trying to bat just the once. Our openers Darren Bicknell and Jason Gallian both had superb seasons and they ensured we regularly got off to great starts. Then Flem and Huss would weigh in with big scores at rapid rates, which would buy us plenty of time to bowl teams out again. It was Flem's idea of a perfect game of cricket.

Unfortunately, it was not so perfect the following year, when disaster struck at the season's end. During 2006 we simply never scored enough runs; Gall and Bickers both had poor trots and as a result we were forever three or four wickets down early; the knock-on effect was the bowlers only got three or four hours' rest before getting back on the field again. It was a cumulative thing and was the difference between being a fresh, happy team and one that struggled.

Yet it should not have ended the way it did – in relegation from Division One. After all, it was far from a prolonged survival battle. In fact, it was not until the final couple of rounds of matches that we got sucked into the equation at the bottom, and needed three points from our final match against Sussex to stay up.

As the end of the season coincided with my elbow problem flaring up for the first time, I was sidelined for the finale – I couldn't straighten my arm for love nor money – and Sky Sports invited me to commentate. Because Sussex were in with a shout for the Championship, and we were an outside chance for the drop, it had been chosen for live TV.

It was a painful experience as Sussex piled up 560 for five declared, a score that reaped us a single bonus point. Even then, though, because of events elsewhere between Durham and Yorkshire, our required tally for survival dropped from three points to two. Agonisingly, we should have already had those two in the bag but David Alleyne, our wicketkeeper, dropped a regulation catch offered by Robin Martin-Jenkins.

Nevertheless, we needed only 200 runs in our first innings to guarantee our top-flight status for another year, and were cruising at 143 for three when little Mushtaq Ahmed, who was later to become a great mate of mine, came on to bowl. Lord knows how we managed it, but from that position we somehow contrived to be dismissed for 165, which meant we both failed to gain the point we were cruising towards and, with more than two days remaining, were destined to lose the match.

I was left helpless, sitting in a commentary box, gobsmacked (which is obviously not the best thing to be when operating a microphone), fielding questions about a ludicrous situation. If you'd offered any

side an equation of eight points from the final two matches for
survival they would have taken it, but we'd failed, and as I sat in that
Sky box the realisation sank in that I would have to go back to play
against Northampton the following year. At that time I couldn't think
of anything worse. Apart from perhaps Derby and Bristol. And guess
what? They awaited too. Goodbye Test grounds, welcome Division
Two and the dumps of English cricket.

As it turned out, we played Leicestershire at Oakham School and
Derbyshire at Chesterfield, two of the prettier settings on the circuit,
and 2007 proved to be a fun and rewarding season. Although the
standard was noticeably worse – it was the first time I had detected
a difference between the divisions; some teams were four-out, all-out
and therefore not good enough to play in the County Championship
– we had to discover a winning formula again.

Having received the kick up the arse our complacency deserved,
we made an immediate return as runners-up to Somerset, and
retained our competitiveness for the next three years, culminating
in another title win in 2010. At some clubs, there would have been
a knee-jerk reaction in 2006 and Mick Newell would have got the
bullet, but thankfully the Sir Alex Ferguson of county cricket – the
comparison because of longevity rather than grumpiness – remained
in his post.

My new life in Nottingham also allowed me to fulfil another childhood dream. All young boys want to be rock stars or fighter pilots
at some point, and seeing as I was never going to jump into a jet
plane, being in a band was the more viable option.

So when former Nottinghamshire spinner Andy Afford asked
me, at the end of an interview for *All Out Cricket* magazine, whether
I fancied a shot at being a frontman, I jumped at the chance. They
had a drummer, a bass player and a guitarist, so all they needed
was someone to sing. There had been loads of times over the years
that I'd had similar conversations with mates down the pub and
nothing had ever come of it. But Andy was true to his word, and

next thing I knew we not only had practice sessions organised but gigs booked.

Andy somehow persuaded the landlord of the Southbank pub in Nottingham city centre that if he bought us £500 of sound gear we would go and play some gigs there, blagging him that we were brilliant and had been rehearsing for ages. The truth was we hadn't so much as shaken a tambourine in anger. But Dave the landlord went for it, and so we spent many nights that winter practising at Newark Cricket Club, our first tunes banged out in the pavilion when the rest of the ground was under water.

Following our first session we went away to think up cool band names. Unfortunately my best effort, The Fuzz, was, as you'll agree, dreadful. Thankfully other offerings were far more creative and we owe being called Dr Comfort and the Lurid Revelations to Andy. For the uninitiated, Dr Comfort was a psychologist in the 1970s who wrote the bestselling *The Joy of Sex*, a book that became the equivalent of a romping manual for a generation of previously prim and proper housewives. Hence, the lurid revelations.

As band names go, it is right up there, not least because everyone always asks: 'What sort of name is that?' One that gets people talking, that's what.

The band is completely cricket-centric. Andy is now back at Notts working as spin-bowling coach, our guitarist Eddie is a development officer at Trent Bridge and Jim Hemmings is ex-England bowler Eddie Hemmings's son. Because of our connections, we even managed to blag using the Long Room in the Trent Bridge pavilion as our practice venue, to save us the trek to Newark. It always made me giggle when we started jamming in there because there's a portrait of an old codger on the wall, some player of yesteryear, who stands 10 feet tall alongside us. He's got the kind of weird boggle eyes that seem to stare at you wherever you move in the room, and so when I was screeching along to Guns N' Roses' 'Sweet Child O' Mine' I'd convince myself his expression became more and more perplexed with every note. As if to say: 'What the hell is happening in my clubhouse?'

Being a lead singer is another opportunity to indulge myself as the centre of attention. We had mastered just five songs for our first gig at the Southbank, so we played them all twice, sandwiching a ten-minute instrumental in the middle. Thankfully, it went down a storm. I persuaded all the Notts lads to pile down there; so many people turned up that the door staff had to operate a one-in, one-out policy. Sky Sports cameras turned up, and Dave's investment of £500 resulted in his pub taking something in the region of £11,000 on one Sunday night.

However, even before being recalled by England I'd always been wary of others thinking I do not concentrate sufficiently on cricket. My belief has always been that it is counterproductive to do nothing but live and breathe the game, and this is one of my escape routes, but having such hobbies does give people rope to hang you with. The moment something went badly, I feared accusations that I couldn't give a stuff and I'd rather be off gallivanting on stage. Nothing could be further from the truth.

At school, I was a proper music geek, with a devotion to Oasis: I had every B-side, every alternative recording, every Radio 1 and XFM live session, and hunted down rare Japanese imports just for the different B-sides. The Gallagher brothers were real heroes of mine and I would have no end of arguments with my dad, who was disgusted by this lager lout Liam who swore all the time. No matter how hard I tried I could not get him to see that Noel was not the better frontman for the band. Agreed, he might have been a better singer but he was not the better frontman. If I could replicate Liam in any way on stage I would take it as a compliment. I don't shout and swear as much as him, but I loved his swagger and his don't-give-a-damn attitude: 'I am how I am and if you don't like it, tough.'

I would forever be singing in the car or school common room but I never showed any inclination to perform until Tim Roberts, who I played junior cricket with, went off to Durham University and returned as a crack guitarist. He inspired me to take it up.

One day when my car was in for service, I walked home past a guitar shop I had driven by a thousand times previously. On impulse I popped in and, because I am not one to do things by half measures, bought everything that was recommended to me by a bloke who clearly saw me coming. I had the acoustic guitar, the acoustic-electric guitar, an amp, a mic, everything. I could have put Live Aid on in my front room by the time I'd got home.

BBC radio reporter Alison Mitchell, another Northamptonian, gave me my first lesson on a fretboard and I regularly strummed alongside Michael Davies, who had bought a guitar some time earlier but only began to play when I took it up. We would spend time at each other's houses, order pizza and play horrendous versions of 'Wonderwall' and 'Whatever' until our fingers could take no more.

I've improved a bit since, of course, and the guitar has been a brilliant way for me to unwind in hotel rooms after a day's play. Sarah even allows me to play up to four minutes a week – as long as the soundproof doors are sealed.

Nothing compares to being up on stage performing, though, when you can see the crowd getting drunker and drunker as the night rolls on. Musicians always make a point of saying how amazing it feels to be in a full stadium with words penned in your own bedroom being sung back at you by the crowd. I totally get that, but despite several attempts – my compositions are all officially tosh – it is not something I will experience.

These days I feel a bit of a charlatan when it comes to Dr Comfort because, other than our first six months together, when we rehearsed once or twice a week, I have hardly seen the rest of the boys. Since I've been back in the England team it has been a case of them rehearsing for months on end, then me turning up two days before a gig, having a sing-song and giving it a cheery thumbs-up. It's always fly-by-the-seat-of-your-pants stuff. It'll be all right on the night, and all that.

A few years ago, when we played as support act to Mark Butcher's band at the Professional Cricketers' Association dinner in London, it was almost like being a proper rock star. It felt very rock 'n' roll to hand in the dressing-room rider, although while Butch's lot had asked for a bottle of whisky and a bottle of vodka, and got Jack Daniel's and Stolichnaya, the bourbon we'd asked for was Tesco's own (we'd properly scrimped on it). Our set list was supposed to contain half a dozen songs but I ended up encouraging the crowd to call for half a dozen encores, and by the time we'd cleared off there were 20-odd stray beer bottles strewn about the stage. I shouted my way through it but the dream was lived for one night.

Just a couple of weeks before flying off for the 2010–11 Ashes, we played to 600 people at a charity dinner in London, below the mighty Keane on the bill. I even got up on stage to sing 'The Lovers are Losing' with Tom Chaplin. Thankfully, he had asked me to choose a song in advance because Keane songs are difficult due to the high notes. Sure, Tom can reach them but I certainly can't for love nor money. Being a frontman rather than a genuine singer, I was really nervous as I got up, but I managed to get through it, and the proof was still on YouTube the last time I looked.

Singing high notes is a subject I will never improve on but the body can be trained to do things better with practice and that certainly can be applied to my bowling. Spinning the ball hard has always come naturally to me, more so than just putting it on the spot, but the big difference these days is the ability to do it with control. In my first few seasons on the professional circuit, I was still prone to bowling bad balls and that meant plenty of downs interspersed with the ups. But if you do something for 10 years you should get better at it, and that is what I know happened to me as a spin bowler.

Experience is a big thing for a spinner and when you arrive in situations you've been in before your mind takes over. Some guy might walk in to bat who you've got out previously, and memories of that can help you. I know from the way I treat spinners when I bat – if they are young I look to crucify them, as I remember how I felt at 19 – that it gets easier as you get older. The first few times people go after you, you don't really know where to go, but if you are good enough you work it out eventually.

Now I am able to assess my career progress with a sense of perspective, the truth is, despite my urge to get back onto the international scene in 2005, I wasn't good enough to bowl for England and do myself justice until I'd had a couple of seasons at Notts. I am not sure how I know, and it is not as though I could pinpoint the exact time by charting my career on a graph, but I just know. Once established at Trent Bridge, everything seemed to knit together. Statisticians wouldn't be able to locate point X either, because in terms of my season averages I may not have been a great deal better. But I arrived in a zone where, mentally, I knew I was going to bowl well every day rather than wondering whether I would. And that's a massive thing for a spinner.

Having said that, in 2007, the year I was recalled, I cannot believe there were many people who had better numbers in one-day cricket. My 20 wickets cost 23.25 each at an economy rate of below four runs per over. My 10 Twenty20 wickets came at 12 apiece. I went at only a run a ball.

Mick Newell told me a few times that summer that he'd spoken to the England selectors about me because I was the best spinner in the country, in his opinion, and that I would get a shout sooner or later. Be ready, was his message, but I still didn't fully believe it would happen. 'Good on you, Mick,' I thought, 'but I am not sure you understand just how black my name is.'

As it turned out, it wasn't quite as black as I thought because that September evening I got the phone call I'd waited seven years for. The one from Ryan Sidebottom that gave me the heads-up I was in the Sri Lanka tour party.

There were certain other factors in my favour in 2007, most notably the fact that Duncan Fletcher's time in charge of England ended in the spring, upon exit from the World Cup. The fact that he was replaced by Peter Moores, who had been coach of England A's Busta Cup campaign back in 2000–01, enthused me. You can never be certain, but Peter was, I believed, a coach who rated me. For once I thought the stars were realigning in my favour.

Sure enough, less than six months into a new era, here I was picked to go away with the full England team once more.

Ironically, I was also picked at a time when I craved it least. Don't get me wrong, I love playing for my country, and always will, but I was finally at peace with the fact I'd not been picked for so long. It no longer bothered me because I had found a great club in Nottinghamshire, loved playing cricket again and had just met my wife, Sarah. The England cricket team wasn't playing a big part in my life because it hadn't been in my life for so long, and there was plenty of other stuff making me as happy as a fat lad in a cake shop.

During the previous close season, given that I did not anticipate a resumption of my England days, I had accepted an offer from BBC Radio 5 Live to be a regular on Gabby Logan's Saturday morning show. I was already penning an irreverent look at my life in Swanny's Diary in *All Out Cricket* magazine, and forging a media career seemed like a sensible thing to do. At that point I was looking to play for five or six more years and considered it a worthwhile way to expand my experience. I'd also done some Sky Sports commentary and stepped in as a summariser for the Beeb for Twenty20 finals day on a couple of occasions. The fact that the Gabby Logan gig was unrehearsed, and took only five minutes out of my life, also appealed. My segment even had its own ditty, a doctored version of the 1950s Robin Hood theme tune – *Graeme Swann, Graeme Swann, riding through the glen . . .*

I was still fairly new to the role when one week, having stayed over at Sarah's flat, I forgot all about it and slept in. So when the phone rang, I leapt up and perched myself on the end of the bed.

'Who are you on the phone to?' Sarah asked, midway through this interview.

'Ssshhh, I'm live on the radio,' I responded.

'Oh, shut up, you idiot,' she said, walking off to the kitchen, to be greeted by my voice again when she turned on the wireless.

Top right: I've been chasing a sunglasses sponsorship for 30 years now.

Middle right: I've always pulled faces when I bowl. At the Dartford Festival with Northants Under-11s, 1990.

Below left: Alec and I following a County Cup victory for Horton House Under-13s. Parents complained about our tactic of stumping opponents from wide deliveries.

Below right: Playing for Horton House Under-13s in the regional finals at the cracking John Player Ground, Nottingham. It's now a David Lloyd tennis centre.

I loved playing cricket alongside my brother Alec at Northamptonshire.

Playing football against a local side while at Northamptonshire. Nick Johnson, the club's commercial manager, had asked us what kit we wanted to play in and I obviously shouted the loudest!

Me, Freddie Flintoff, Daz Maddy, Matt 'Steamy' Windows and Rob Key on the 1998–99 England A tour to southern Africa. The tour had an amazing social side to it.

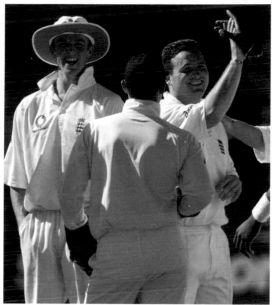

They say first impressions are important. Well, I managed to stuff up mine with both Rod Marsh (*left*) and Duncan Fletcher (*right*).

An early appearance in England whites, against a South African Invitation XI in Port Elizabeth, January 2000. Chris Read and I received a real dressing-down from coach Duncan Fletcher for accepting an offer of bad light. Had he been armed, I think it would have been curtains for me!

The England one day squad in South Africa, January 2000. Falling asleep on the hotel verandah that afternoon contributed to my withered-lobster look.

I never hit it off with Kepler Wessels. Our working relationship broke down completely in 2004, leading me to consider giving up cricket altogether.

Happier times at Northamptonshire with Mike Hussey. A great overseas player and still a great mate.

Hitting out for Northamptonshire. Jack Russell looks on from behind the stumps.

Looking like Pat Sharp for Nottinghamshire, 2005.

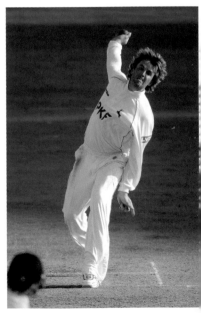

On-tour fun with Ryan Sidebottom, Sri Lanka 2007. I'm not sure what Siddy is doing to me but the elephant didn't seem to mind.

Back in England colours after a seven-year absence, Sri Lanka 2007. Things went amazingly well for both England and me.

An old-fashioned picture taken during 'Mougust' 2007. Our facial hair raised a fair whack for Paul Franks's benefit year.

Above: The frustrating Test series in the Caribbean. West Indies were nine wickets down in Antigua. This one evades Paul Collingwood at slip.

Left: Alongside some illustrious company on the honours board at the Antigua Recreation Ground, following my maiden five-wicket Test haul in February 2009. The match was drawn.

10. M. MURALITHARAN (S.L) 5/31

11. C. AMBROSE (W.I) 5/94

12. C.A. WALSH (W.I) 5/83

13. W. AKRAM (P) 6/61

14. W. AKRAM (P) 5/49

15. J. LAWSON (W.I) 7/78

16. G. SWANN (E) 5/62

Above: Pre-Ashes 2009. The series I had been waiting more than 20 years for.

Below left: Escapology in Cardiff. I saw none of the heroics of Jimmy Anderson and Monty Panesar.

Below right: Andrew Strauss on his way to a century against Australia at Lord's, 2009.

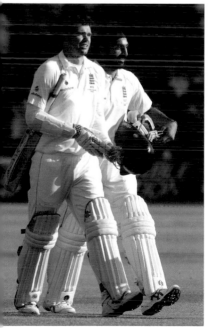

Michael Clarke was our nemesis in 2009. His form had deserted him for the return series in 2010–11.

I took the last wicket in the victory over Australia at Lord's – Mitchell Johnson bowled – when it should really have gone to Andrew Flintoff. This was Flintoff's last truly epic performance in an England shirt.

No one was more surprised than me when I turned one through the gate to dismiss Ricky Ponting at Edgbaston. I bowled like a clown thereafter.

'I thought you were pulling my leg these last few weeks when you said you were talking to Gabby Logan,' Sarah later admitted. She thought it was code for speaking to my mum or something.

It is fair to say Sarah was equally unimpressed by my performances on the cricket field, particularly in the first match she attended: a televised one-day game against Gloucestershire at Trent Bridge at the end of August 2007. I whacked 59 off 33 balls, opening the batting, and then claimed career-best figures of five for 17 as we won by a whopping 116 runs. It was, undoubtedly, the best one-day game of my life.

Sarah had been sitting with the other wives and girlfriends drinking white wine all afternoon. When I got to her afterwards, she was half-cut but I was nevertheless eager to find out what she'd thought of my display.

'I couldn't tell which one you were,' she claimed.

'I was the guy that got a fifty and five wickets!' I said, exasperated.

'Oh. Does that happen every week?'

Luckily Sarah James, erstwhile clinical research associate, was not on the England selection panel at the time. A fortnight later we watched *Last Night of the Proms* and waited for Grav's call.

8

MY TURN AT LAST

WHEN WE landed in Sri Lanka for a short one-day tour in late September 2007, I was determined that the trip would be everything that my previous tour was not. My general approach was to fit in and enjoy every minute of it – I could probably have counted them had I wanted to, given we were only away for two and a half weeks or so – and not be downhearted about remaining on the sidelines. I had waited so long for this opportunity, the last thing I wanted to do was blow it.

In fact, one moment that occurred before a single ball was bowled in that five-match series summed up my mood. We were based in a place called Dambulla, right in the heart of the Sri Lankan jungle, and staying at a real honeymooner's hotel, a truly amazing place, the grounds of which were full of wildlife.

In Sri Lanka wildlife generally means monkeys, elephants and snakes. Thankfully, only the monkeys came near the hotel guest rooms, and they were so tame that they'd swing onto your balcony, push open your patio doors and be off with your fruit basket in a jiffy, ingenious creatures.

Having got wind of this, bored one day I got my video phone out and left a trail of Mars bar bites all the way into the room, up onto the bed and next to my pillow. My cunning ploy worked and that moment, when the monkey sat there nibbling chocolate on my bed, summed up what I believed I would get out of that tour: it would be light-hearted, I would enjoy myself, and chill out.

Monty Panesar was the established spinner at the time and so my selection for the opening one-day international, in addition to being a complete surprise to me, was also somewhat controversial. Although I had bowled well for Nottinghamshire at the end of the season, I hadn't taken a wicket in the six overs I sent down in a comprehensive warm-up win over a Sri Lanka Cricket XI in Colombo.

My selection was a genuine shock because I had not expected to play, unless we went down an unlikely road and fielded two front-line spinners. So when the team for the first ODI was announced – I have always been the same when a team is read out, I never listen for anyone else's name properly, only for whether my own one pops out somewhere in the bottom half of the order – I was not expecting to hear 'Swann'.

It gave me only 24 hours to prepare for the match, too short a time to allow pre-match anxiety to build up. Only later did it hit me, such was my own focus in practice that day, that Monty had been left out, and indeed it wasn't until we got onto the field for pre-match practice the next day that I noticed he had a bib on and would therefore be twelfth man.

I was the sole spinner in an attack that conceded 269 for seven in that opening day-nighter, a total that we were quite happy to chase. One of those seven wickets was my first in international cricket, that of Kumar Sangakkara, who came down the wicket and was beaten by one that spun past him, and was stumped by Phil Mustard. Things had gone pretty well for me, the ball gripped and bounced from the off, and I finished with the respectable figures of 10–0–47–1.

Whenever I have gone anywhere around the world, my mum has always reminded me to bring back a stuffed toy. In Australia, for example, I've bought kangaroos or koalas, and this time I thought it would be a nice touch to buy an elephant, not for my mum but for Sarah. However, the look on her face when I presented her with Kumar, an orange, pink and purple patchwork jumbo, was one of abject horror. He has since been consigned to the guest bedroom in our house, but although he might not be important to Sarah, he is to me because of what he represents.

I bowled quite well, at opponents renowned for their ability against spin, and chipped in with a quickfire 24, but we lost by 120 runs in the end. Yet in a big defeat like that my performance was arguably the best of a bad bunch, and so I had made a good impression. When people first come into an England team they are half-expected to disgrace themselves, so the fact I hadn't was taken as a positive aspect of the game by the press. Several journalists were crowing about how well I had done. In my mind I hadn't done *that* well. But what the heck, I thought. After an interim of approaching 3000 days waiting to double my cap tally, I was quite happy to take the plaudits.

Even greater praise followed as we won the next two matches in Dambulla, and I had a couple of dream games. In the first of the two, I contributed 34 with the bat and then returned figures of 10–3–27–2, in the first away victory by an England team over Sri Lanka in 26 years – the margin a comfortable 65 runs.

When you are in good form you tend not to think too much about what you are doing, and that was certainly the case for me. When things aren't going well players fall into the trap of over-analysing, but this scenario was the exact opposite. I'd felt so at ease with my county form at the end of that 2007 season that I just relaxed into things. When you are not quite there, and you're searching for a bit of rhythm, the batsman seems huge, the pitch is tiny and your area to land the ball in shrinks drastically. However, at that point I knew exactly what was coming out of my hand, so all I ever thought about was how I was going to get the batsman out or how I was going to stop him scoring. I was lucky to be in that frame of mind, my body felt completely natural, and so I just let things happen.

The wicket was nice to bowl spin on and in the third match of the series I used it to my advantage, and reaped a greater personal reward. Just as in the previous contest three days earlier, Ryan Sidebottom and Stuart Broad shared four wickets inside the opening 15 overs, and we never relinquished the pressure their bursts created. A fifth-wicket partnership of 43 between Tillakaratne Dilshan and Chamara Silva was broken when the latter attempted to sweep me but only succeeded in deflecting the ball onto his boot and up into

Phil Mustard's grateful grasp. Jehan Mubarak and Farveez Maharoof both offered return catches, and my quartet was complete when Dilshan clipped to midwicket to be last but one out for 70. I walked off in the knowledge that I had deserved my wickets rather than got lucky. Sometimes you can bowl like a drain and grab three or four but this was not one of those occasions.

Sri Lanka were dismissed with more than six overs of their 48-over allocation to spare but, despite posting only 164, it turned into a good match because we lost a lot of wickets. In the end it needed a 40-run stand between me and Broady to see us home. And I picked up my first international man-of-the-match award for my all-round contribution.

It was my bowling in particular that pleased me and seven wickets in three games made me feel rather good about myself. In fact, it was almost a shock when I failed to take one in the next match in Colombo, which confirmed us as series winners. Truth is that when you arrive at international level you do not expect to get wickets. Now here I was just a few days later bitterly disappointed with a blank in the final column.

Having played a part in securing an unassailable 3–1 lead, I missed the final match with a tweaked hamstring. It was the first time I realised how much more physically demanding international cricket is in comparison to county cricket. The intensity of the games takes that little bit extra out of you, and after four of them in 10 days my body was just not able to deal with it. Despite getting through a full season with Nottinghamshire, it was a real shock to the system.

It was irritating to have to miss out when I was on such a high but I nevertheless came away from that tour absolutely buzzing. I had gone out with doubts over my ability to dismiss international batsmen, but I returned with an expectation to dismiss them every single time I bowled. Until you get your first wicket, it is impossible not to wonder whether you really will be good enough. Then you discover the different set of principles you assumed necessary – that only magic balls are good enough for international wickets – are not necessary after all and that the game is the same apart from the increased pressure. Once you know all this, the whole world opens up.

Now, no one could describe me as being short on confidence, but discovering that I didn't need to do anything different filled me with belief that I would be more than a one-tour wonder this time. Doing well and taking wickets made me feel so much more at ease, and although I had only been away for three weeks, I arrived home transformed. I had departed as a county cricketer and now felt like an England player.

The whole England set-up felt drastically different from the previous one I'd experienced, and that put me at ease. Peter Moores is a coach who could never be accused of lacking spark. He is 100 per cent energy, all the time, and while some might suggest that can be a weakness, it is also his greatest strength. He lives and breathes the game, and on this trip it just felt as if everyone was pulling in the same direction. None of the cliques that had been prevalent last time revealed themselves. We were all there to do a job, and I felt a worthy part of what was going on, rather than a hanger-on. It also made a world of difference to have been picked on performance rather than because I'd had one good Under-19 Test match and someone thought I might fit in with Lord MacLaurin's vision to haul English cricket off the floor.

In this environment there was no selfishness, no bitchiness, no looking out for number one. Nor were there massive names in the squad as with the previous generations – no Hussains, Stewarts, Goughs and Athertons – but this England XI would have beaten the previous one nine times out of ten, because it felt like a team. And I felt part of it.

My mindset had altered so rapidly that a jolt to the system was inevitable, I suppose, and having considered I would not only be picked for the return to Sri Lanka for the Test tour in November and December but also make the XI, it was a setback when only the first part materialised. In direct contrast to the limited-overs trip, I fully expected us to play two spinners in the Test matches, and therefore anticipated making my debut.

But my input into the three-Test series was restricted to the nets and a 16-a-side game against the Sri Lanka Board President's XI. And I didn't do myself justice in that match at the Colombo Cricket Club because of a damaged hand. A problem with my spinning finger had hampered me before but this was the first time I'd encountered it abroad. It stemmed from a net session a few days previously when, after bowling a ball to Paul Collingwood, I looked down and noticed a big hole in said finger. I sported an elastoplast for that warm-up game, but things just didn't feel right and I didn't bowl well.

The pitch was ridiculously flat and my one wicket, in a Board President's XI score of 500 for five declared, made over two weather-interrupted days, was Chamara Kapugedera, one of their three centurions. So favourable were the batting conditions that only Michael Vaughan and Kevin Pietersen were actually dismissed in our reply of 315 for six – the other top-order batsmen retired out to give others a hit.

Even when I was left out of the first-class fixture against the same opponents over the road at the Nondescripts Cricket Club three days later – Steve Harmison had been called onto the tour late, after proving his fitness in South African domestic cricket, and was thrown straight into the action – I still expected to form a spin alliance with Monty Panesar in the Test series.

Unfortunately, that didn't happen, so I ended up carrying drinks for three games, and it almost felt like back to square one – how it had been in South Africa all those years previously. The difference was that this time, rather than feeling relieved I wasn't playing, I was actually narked. Not only did I genuinely believe I was good enough now, but there was a convincing case for playing two spinners, and yet we were going into these Test matches with just Monty. We consistently picked three or four seamers on wickets that were their deathbeds. I just couldn't understand where we were coming from.

I actually spent more time on the field than I would have wished in the opening Test in Kandy, however, after Kevin Pietersen chipped his fingernail catching Sanath Jayasuriya off Ryan Sidebottom in the third over of the first morning. Now, any bowler will tell you that batsmen go to any length to get out of fielding, so it was no surprise that I ended up as substitute for two whole sessions. The outfield was ridiculously bumpy and that made me look like a complete clown. But to be perfectly honest, I wasn't particularly interested in being there anyway. Down at long on or long leg, baking hot, every time the ball came to me it bobbled and hit me on the shin or wrist. No runs were leaked but I rarely picked it up cleanly.

All along I kept looking at the pavilion, wondering how Kev's poorly pinky was. I was even back out for the second innings, one that seemed to last for about a month from my vantage point, and claimed my first catch in Test cricket off Monty: Jehan Mubarak came down the wicket and tried to smack it over the top but skied it instead. Given the way I fielded, the fact I held on must make it one of the best catches of my career.

Having started the match well when Matthew Hoggard took a bundle of wickets with the new ball, and secured a 93-run lead on first innings, we could not maintain our grip on the game, and lost at the death when, with the light receding rapidly, Muttiah Muralitharan came on to take the new ball and split a determined partnership between Ian Bell and Matt Prior that had threatened to salvage a draw.

Earlier, Muralitharan had become the most successful bowler in Test history, surpassing Shane Warne's 708-wicket haul, on his home ground of Asgiriya, when he dismissed Colly in the first innings. The match stopped momentarily as Murali's achievements were heralded. Fittingly, someone had penned a pop song to mark the special occasion – although it was all drums and keyboards with a curiously simple ditty that lacked any rhythm whatsoever. It went: 'Muralitharan, Muralitharan, the greatest spin bowler the world has ever seen!'

Jimmy Anderson and I still give a rendition of the Murali song occasionally now. I spent a lot of time with Jimmy on that trip, it was when we really clicked, and another impromptu singalong actually landed us in hot water with Mooresy. The pair of us, along with Stuart Broad, were amongst those not playing in the final Test at Galle, which was hosting its first match since the tsunami had washed it away two years previously. With nothing in particular to do for a while we sat in the air-conditioned dressing room with eighties tunes blaring out of the iPod. We were laughing, singing and joking to the cheesiest songs imaginable, and Mark Garaway, the analyst, was laughing along with us. He had his camera out, making a video of us, and gave us the thumbs-up as we pratted about.

We were not entirely sure how, but we were shocked later when we discovered that somehow or other Moorsey got to see the footage.

We were still 1–0 down in the series, this match had been delayed by wet weather, and Sri Lanka proceeded to stack up 499 for eight declared. Mooresy was so fed up with how things had gone on the field that we were pulled aside and told that it was our fault. Sri Lanka had, apparently, wiped the floor with us on first innings because we were singing along to Rick Astley! Years earlier I would have told the coach where to stick it and refused to take such a bizarre rebuke, but thankfully I had matured to a level above laughing in his face at the very accusation. I've still got the bite mark on the inside of my lip, although I fell down the stairs guffawing when we got out of the room. We actually slumped to 33 for six in reply, and were eventually dismissed for 81, but Alastair Cook hit a second-innings hundred to stave off defeat.

Naturally, the evenings were more pleasurable than the days for me on that tour, most of them in that final week spent in Steve Harmison's room at the Lighthouse Hotel. I couldn't wait to get home by this stage, as I wasn't playing, and was looking forward to Christmas. So every night when asked if I was coming to the Harmison Arms, the answer was yes. Harmy turned his room into a pub that week. He would order 50 beers from reception in the morning, have the bath filled up with ice and leave the bottles to chill while we were down at the ground. Then we'd all pile in during the evening. He'd just chill out on his bed as we drank his ale, watched *Auf Wiedersehen Pet* and *Only Fools and Horses* DVDs, and played darts.

In January 2008, we headed to New Zealand, and with the limited-overs games preceding the Test series it meant that I was back in the team and able to focus on my cricket again. We won the back-to-back Twenty20 matches convincingly but came unstuck in Wellington in the opening match of five one-day internationals.

We were undoubtedly undone by local knowledge. The Westpac Stadium, also known as the Cake Tin, is primarily a rugby venue which doubles up for cricket by having a drop-in pitch inserted. As a result, the grass in the outfield is really fluffy, so when you hit the ball along the ground, it merely dribbles to the fielder. It absolutely strangled our scoring, and we managed only seven boundaries in our measly 130 all out. We couldn't work out how to play there – despite batting all but two balls of our full 50 overs – until Brendon McCullum and Jesse Ryder provided a demonstration. The way to go was simple: you took the outfield out of the equation. Everything went aerial from ball one, and although they lost four wickets, New Zealand knocked off the runs in next to no time.

That was a bad start, and we also lost the second ODI at Hamilton. Well, I say lost; we actually got completely destroyed. Hamilton, for the uninitiated, is Hicksville, New Zealand. The Waikato Chiefs rugby union team are based in the town and we went to watch one of their Super 14 matches. There was a guy who sat in a crane behind one of the sets of posts with an electric chainsaw, which he revved up whenever the opposition got anywhere near him. Strangely, this ceremonial act seemed perfectly normal to the locals. The boy racers' vehicle of choice was also eye-opening. Every night posses of utes would tear through the streets.

As well as being one of the more intimidating places on the

international cricket circuit, it was also where my run of games as an England one-day player was unceremoniously ended. We were actually going well, having scored 85 for two after 15 overs, when rain interrupted the match. When it later resumed as a 36-over-a-side contest, we were rolled for 158 and New Zealand's target was adjusted to 165 under the Duckworth-Lewis system.

This time Ryder and McCullum smashed it everywhere – and we hurtled to a 10-wicket defeat in 18.1 overs. I didn't get on to bowl until the game was gone, at 103 without loss, and was powerless to stop its course to an inevitable conclusion. My two overs cost 27 runs and, following our massive rollicking in the changing room afterwards from Peter Moores, I was the fall guy.

Inevitably someone has to get dropped after that kind of defeat, and using an old principle I was vulnerable – last one in, first one out and all that. It was the easy option. Looking back, I shouldn't have been dropped as they played the rest of that series without a front-line spinner, which is crazy in any game of international cricket. Players rarely concede that they should have been left out, of course, but I genuinely think it was a bad decision because it meant Owais Shah was our only slow-bowling option.

I was annoyed, but I did not want to appear so, because I considered touring with England an honour, and at that stage it was possible that my role might be limited to bits and pieces with the one-day team. I had to be ready to prove myself when my chance came again, so I vowed to enjoy touring as much as I could.

As things turned out, we won the next match in Auckland with our all-seam attack and then posted a whopping 340 in Napier on 20 February, in what was one of the most amazing one-day internationals ever played. For lots of reasons.

It was rocket hot and New Zealand maintained such a ferocious pace in their pursuit that they passed 300 with more than six overs remaining and with seven wickets in hand. But somehow we kept the series alive by taking wickets, slowing the scoring, and Luke Wright held his nerve bowling the final over. We even missed a run-out that would have given us victory off the final delivery, but a tie maintained the 2–1 scoreline heading into the final match. Perhaps the greatest significance that match held for English cricket, however, followed in the minutes immediately after the thrilling finale. It was the first time that cracks started to appear in the relationship between Peter Moores and Kevin Pietersen.

For some reason, Mooresy decided that we should do a training session straight after the game. And when I say straight after the game, I mean straight after the game. Frankly, it is the most ridiculous thing I have ever been involved in. The lads had just fought to the wire in an amazing match, which had reached the final ball with all three results still possible, and physical and mental exertions must have taken their toll given the temperature and pressure of the situation. They would naturally have expected a few minutes to put their feet up – but Mooresy kiboshed any such thoughts when he announced that the whole squad was to return to the field of play.

'Those New Zealand boys will see us running on the square, and they will s--- their pants, because they'll know that we mean business,' he claimed.

S--- their pants? More like p--- their pants. The Kiwi lads thought it was absolutely hilarious as we trooped out into the middle with our fitness trainer, Marques Church, with a good percentage of the crowd still milling about. Our opponents sat there watching us from their dressing-room balcony, beers in hand, laughing their heads off. They couldn't believe what they were seeing, and I have to say it's the most humiliating and degrading session I have ever been involved in. For half an hour as we shuttled back and forth we had to ignore their mocking laughter. There was no escape because once we had traipsed out there we couldn't sheepishly wander off, we were there on public display. And if I had been amongst those Kiwi lads I would have been laughing the hardest.

Personally, because I wasn't playing in the game, I was due to do fitness work anyway, so this was my lot that evening, but I could not believe Mooresy made the whole team do it. It was absolute lunacy.

Nor has it been forgotten. That one session resulted in a lot of resentment towards the coach building in a number of players. Even now it is joked about in the England dressing room. Whenever we have come off the field following a really demanding day, someone inevitably comes up with: 'Right, shall we go and have a run around the square?'

Because I hadn't managed to get a game in Sri Lankan conditions, I considered the chances of me making a Test debut in New Zealand to be absolute zero, even though the opening match of the series at Hamilton was a two-spinner pitch. New Zealand went in with both Daniel Vettori and Jeetan Patel, in fact, and ended up victorious in a game that from an England perspective was memorable for Ryan Sidebottom's hat-trick and Alastair Cook's two stunning catches in the gully but nothing else. New Zealand truly outplayed us.

Considering the backdrop of me being stuck on the sidelines, it was perhaps not ideal timing for Sarah's first venture on tour – and it almost brought about the end of our relationship, as is the case with so many cricketers and their partners, who come out expecting it to be akin to a holiday and have to stomach the shock that it is not.

For a girl who has never been involved before, three weeks in New Zealand, on paper at least, looks like the most amazing deal you could wish for. But very soon that girl discovers three-quarters of it is going to be spent in a hotel room doing nothing – other than trying to console your cricketer boyfriend after his rubbish day, that is. Then there is the pressure on partners to go and watch on match days. There is an unwritten rule that they are expected to come along, even though I would never be bothered whether Sarah does or not. I would rather she did what she wanted.

It certainly didn't help that the grumpy bugger she had come to see was becoming even grumpier because he was not playing, and it got very close to Sarah bailing out. It even reached a stage where she was phoning the airline at 2 a.m. one night, to assess when the next flight home was, while I simultaneously helped pack her bags.

Yet going through that kind of situation, experiencing the downs with the ups, can help a relationship. You quickly set some boundaries. Naturally, it is great to see your missus, but for the five nights of the game you want to stay in, have some room service and be asleep by ten o'clock. Happily, these days Sarah deals with that and she'll even order the room service for me, so it arrives shortly after I get back. We tend to do absolutely nothing on match nights, and she now treats it like a cricket tour rather than a holiday. That is perfect for me.

I thought Sarah was a good craic from the moment I met her at a house party in Nottingham the previous summer, but couldn't even remember her name afterwards. She appealed to me because she hails from Newcastle – not that she's got the accent – and so I started telling her my Geordie jokes. One had a bit of a dirty punchline, so being a gentleman, I changed it to a cleaner version. 'That's b------,' she said, before informing me of the blue alternative. But it was not until a few months later, when we were surreptitiously set up by a mutual friend, that we got together. I moved into her flat about three days later – because she had better parking and made absolutely amazing poached eggs.

I'd spent six months playing club cricket in Christchurch a couple of winters earlier but my return to New Zealand held few fond memories. I had waltzed back into the England team on a high, and perhaps being omitted again just six months later gave me a necessary kick up the arse and ensured I didn't get complacent. Not that, with my background, I have ever fallen into the trap of taking my international place for granted.

As you will have gathered by now, I am not the best at dealing with being on the periphery of a team, but this group of England players made things more of a laugh. The biggest one, a rapturous affair, came through my hotel room wall one night about 10 seconds before my mobile phone beeped with one of the group text messages our operations manager Phil Neale sends.

On each tour you have team photographs taken and the players are then required to sign the 50 copies in their appropriate slots. They are then sent off to sponsors and charities and so on. On this occasion, the photos had been left in the team room for the past couple of days, and we had been told to go in to sign them at our leisure. Phil then went through the lot to make sure all were complete, only to find some rather random squiggles. Normally Ryan Sidebottom or I would be the likeliest candidates to sign something stupid, but neither of us had caused the normally mild-mannered Phil to lose his rag this time.

The message on my phone's screen was simple: 'Whoever has signed Keith Collingwood can they please f------ come and change it!' The laughter from the other side of the wall belonged to Collingwood, who swore he was not the culprit either. What had made him laugh, though, was that he does have an uncle Keith. Chuckling about that kept me going for a few weeks.

Another Durham man, Phil Mustard, was also a fine source of amusement on that tour. He was late for just about every bus departure – funny how that sticks in my head – but he didn't get fined, which was a nice touch from the management. If he had been, he would have forfeited his entire tour fee.

When it comes to taking an opportunity to have a good time with both hands, Colonel, as he is known, is right up there with the best. If there is fun to be had, he will grab it. Anyway, a couple of days after losing the decisive match in the one-day series, we were in a minibus heading back from training in Dunedin when it was announced on the radio that New Zealand's new wild boy Jesse Ryder was going to be sidelined for three months after severing a tendon in his hand punching through a glass door at a bar in Christchurch. This had occurred at 5.30 a.m. on the Sunday morning, and we were all aghast – Peter Moores and other members of the management were listening with us – at the thought that Jesse was still sinking shots at that time.

'Aye, Jesus Christ, that is strange,' said the Colonel. 'He was fine when I left him at five.'

The beauty of Mustard as a bloke is that he was completely oblivious to the fact that he'd just dropped himself in it. And he would do it time and again. Every flight we had on that trip was the morning after a match finished, and because we have an alphabetical seating plan for travel days, Mustard and Moores were obviously next to each other on planes. Now, the Colonel is the kind of bloke who seeps alcohol through his pores. It simply pours out of him, and he would never think of popping some chewing gum to disguise it, so he'd take his place next to the England coach, who would be beavering away on his laptop, put his head back and knock out some Zs. Goodness knows what Mooresy thought as he snored through the entire journey.

Talking of uncomfortable positions, the whole squad was placed in one on that trip by our fitness coach Marques Church, a Kiwi who sported very strange facial hair, in the build-up to the tied Napier match. He sat us down in the changing room at the ground and gave us a collective rollicking about not being fit enough. Did we really want it enough? Were we the athletes we wanted to be?

'Which one of you in this room doesn't want to be the best you possibly can? Which one of you wouldn't train every day until it kills you, to achieve your goals?' he demanded.

To his credit, Owais Shah put his hand up and replied: 'Let's be fair, Marques, no one is going to own up to that, are they?'

However, the point of Marques's rant was that he wanted us to compare our fitness at that point with another point in the future. He wanted us all to commit to getting fitter with a technique he said he'd used in his rugby days.

'I am going to take a photo of you all with your tops off,' he told us. 'Then in six months' time we will take a similar one and we will see how your body has developed and changed through our training programme.'

Everyone looked at each other with uneasy expressions on their faces. This sounds a bit iffy, I thought. Uneasy whispers circled the room but it was one of those times when you knew you had to fall in line or have some explaining to do to the coach. It was very much voluntary in the compulsory sense of the word.

At least it gave me a chance to do one of my party tricks – blowing my diaphragm up to make myself look pregnant. Marques didn't get the joke, unfortunately, despite the comic look on my face.

He did take those photos of everyone as he pledged, but we was not around for the proposed August shots because, when he got back from that tour a member of Vodafone's management rang our staff at Loughborough to reveal there was a problem with his dongle. In just a month in New Zealand he had run up a £23,000 Internet bill.

Vodafone, our team sponsor, needed the hard drive off the laptop to check whether or not there had been some clerical mistake. Unfortunately, there was not, and when it was discovered that Marques had downloaded a load of child pornography, he ended up doing a six-month stint inside. It has troubled me since to think that somewhere within the bowels of one of Her Majesty's clinks there might be a digital camera with the torsos of the England cricket team being used as prison currency. You can just imagine it, can't you? 'I'll give you an Anderson and a Broad for 200 smokes.' I sometimes wonder what my snap would have fetched. A tea bag and a copy of *Gardeners Weekly*?

My own stock rose once more during that summer of 2008 back in England when I regained my place for the NatWest Series against the New Zealanders. It was a nice feeling to be back in the team, and we got off to a perfect start with a resounding 114-run win at the Riverside on 15 June, the game in which Kevin Pietersen twice switch-hit Scott Styris for six.

That stroke, and whether it was indeed legal, stirred up some controversy in the opening days of the five-match series but, after the MCC green-lighted it, it came an even bigger one. It took place towards the end of the penultimate match, at The Oval, when captain Paul Collingwood became embroiled in a row for not reprieving Grant Elliott, who was run out following a collision with Ryan Sidebottom.

It was nip and tuck when, with the Kiwis 220 for seven in the 44th over, chasing a target of 246, Elliott blocked the ball down and, as batsmen tend to, ran over the top of it. Siddy quite naturally went for it, Elliott careered over the top of him as they collided, and both ended up on the deck.

Now, it is the accepted norm that you don't run the batsman out in that situation. But in this instance we did – Ian Bell threw to Kevin Pietersen, who took the bails off at the bowler's end. Umpire Mark Benson then asked Colly whether he was going to retract the appeal, as Elliott received treatment on the field. To be fair to our captain, there was a lot of pressure from other players that we should not. The opinion seemed to be that Elliott had run to block Siddy and that was that.

Elliott voiced his disapproval as he headed for the dressing room and the issue was simmering throughout the final few overs, until we reached the last ball and New Zealand, with one wicket intact, needed two to win. Number 11 Mark Gillespie hit it straight to me at cover and although there are different versions of what happened next – both the bowler Luke Wright and Kevin Pietersen swear blind they were waiting at the top of the stumps, though they are not in the video replays I've seen – I picked up and shied at the stumps.

Unbeknown to me, Stuart Broad, who was backing up, had come charging in, so when I missed the target he wasn't in a position to stop the ball. In a flash the scampered single became the couple they required for victory. I maintain I was only 50 per cent to blame for it, because had any one of them got to the stumps or backed up properly we would have tied rather than lost.

Afterwards the New Zealand lads went absolutely potty, shouting stuff at us as we left the field and shutting the dressing room door on Paul Collingwood as he approached it. That really annoyed me. Minutes later I went into the press conference and suggested that rather than being chastised, I should be given credit for averting a third world war and the irretrievable break-down of diplomatic relations between England and New Zealand. Yes, I cost us the game, but I had saved Colly's life, with the Kiwi air force on standby in their biplanes.

New Zealand's ire stemmed from the fact that such ungentlemanly conduct was contrary to the spirit of cricket. But some of our lads reminded Baz McCullum that only months earlier he had run out Muttiah Muralitharan in a Test match when he had gone down the other end to congratulate his partner Kumar Sangakkara on reaching a hundred. They were very much in a people-in-glass-houses situation, but looking back it was poor of us, even if it was the sort of thing that happens in the club game every week. On a Saturday afternoon it would be out ten times out of ten but in international cricket you have to take the moral high ground and say not out, despite the fact that the batsman is taking advantage of that by blocking the path to the ball. I say that if he wants to take that line, we should go back to the old-school rules and allow dump tackles.

But let's face it, we play so many games that even the most enthusiastic cricket watchers in England don't give a monkey's about some. When I didn't play for England I could never keep up with the number of games played by the national team; unless it was in an important competition or against the Aussies, each game merged into one. This was one such game and my way of dealing with it in the aftermath has been to remind myself that no one will remember it in a few years . . . except me. Oh, and Colly, of course. To add insult to injury, match referee Javagal Srinath banned him for four matches for maintaining a slow over rate for the second time in a year.

That meant England were under the captaincy of Kevin Pietersen for the first time for the final match at Lord's, one we had to win to share the series. This match was also notable from a personal perspective as it was undoubtedly the best I had bowled in an England shirt up to that point. Scott Styris could barely score a run off me towards the end of my spell – he hit four singles from my final 16 deliveries at him – and significantly it was the first time I ever enjoyed bowling at Lord's.

Success eludes you at some venues and so you don't enjoy going there, and Lord's had been one of those for me. It had never really turned, the slope is tricky to get used to, and I had never had much success. But ever since finishing with figures of 10–0–33–2, I have relished bowling there.

Despite his lull, Styris went on to smash the seamers at the death of the innings and his assault in a glut of 61 runs in the final five overs helped New Zealand post 266 for five. Having looked as if we might contain them to 220 at one point, we went on to lose the game and the series, but it was my finest performance to date.

That very fact rankled at the end of that 2008 summer when we played against South Africa and I was dropped. Such was my feeling of deflation that I had not been selected after such a pleasing display that I briefly considered that my Lord's outing might actually be the last time I'd ever bowl for England.

The irony of the last match being my best gnawed at me, and to make matters worse, the man who effectively replaced me was my Nottinghamshire team-mate Samit Patel. If anyone was going to miss out at the start of the second NatWest Series of the summer, I didn't expect it would be me because my previous performance was so good. But I was consigned to sitting and watching five games because Peter Moores and Kevin Pietersen, now permanent captain following Paul Collingwood's resignation, fancied a batting all-rounder who offered a spin option. Kev talked Samit up from the start and, to be fair, Samit did well in that series as England romped to a 4–0 win.

Samit and I, despite being team-mates at club level, were not exactly close. We worked well together for Notts, particularly in one-day cricket, but I had a few issues with him dating back a couple of years previously when he told a few porkie pies about me. I found out and confronted him and he had the gall to repeat his stories to my face. It was only after a couple of minutes of heated argument that he suddenly backed down and apologised.

He'd claimed that he'd confronted me about my contributions to the team and said that he should be playing instead. This was all news to me. It was a very bizarre and surreal episode and it left me feeling very wary of him. Afterwards, even though relations improved over a few seasons playing together, I still found things awkward.

Samit has had some well-documented issues with his weight and fitness since, including being dropped from the touring party to the West Indies in 2009 when he fell below the minimum fitness standards required by the selectors. Having returned to favour at the start of the 2011 summer, however, it is now up to him to really knuckle down, get himself in better shape and make the most of his undoubted potential. Maybe, like me those few years back, he'll realise what he's missing out on and make a pact with himself to sort himself out a decent international career. After all, cutting out a few packets of crisps here or there is hardly the most difficult thing to do if it's the difference between a tour to Australia and a winter spent having bowling-machine sessions with the Notts batting coach (even if Paul Johnson is an absolute gem of a bloke).

Having had a good season with Notts, I found traipsing around the country as a non-playing member of the squad very dispiriting. Poor old Tim Bresnan suffered the same fate in 2010 – spending a couple of weeks fully fit but not playing a single match – and it is soul-destroying, frankly. For the record, I am the worst twelfth man on the planet, and am probably universally recognised as such by my team-mates. Good on the people who say it is a frightfully important role within the team environment, and that you should be the best twelfth man your country could ever produce, but for me the frustration of not playing doesn't allow me to fulfil the role as I should.

I just find that sitting on the sidelines with three other blokes leads me to talk incessantly, joking around and generally playing the fool. I guess it's my way of dealing with the inner feelings of hurt, and indeed embarrassment, about being publicly told you're not good enough to get in the starting XI.

Immediately after the final scheduled match in Cardiff was washed out, Samit and I returned to Nottinghamshire, and back into a double-pronged assault on silverware. Once again we had got ourselves into serious contention for the County Championship title, and we also faced a showdown against Sussex at Trent Bridge for a one-day pot. In a winner-takes-all match on 14 September, the Pro40 crown and the £44,000 prize money was at stake.

Until England lost to Ireland in the 2011 World Cup, I did not have a game in my experience to compare this one to. It was simply the most irksome of defeats, more so because of the prize that was wrenched from our grasp. I walked off the field convinced that there was no way we should have lost. But somehow we had contrived to do so.

We batted first and our 226 was a solid total, particularly with the ball turning on a late-season surface. Samit and I exploited that and when we had both bowled out, having shared six wickets, Sussex were reeling at 130 for eight in the 30th over. What happened next beggared belief.

With 10 overs left and nothing to lose, given Sussex's seemingly hopeless position, Murray Goodwin chanced his arm and somehow changed the course of the game. Our bowlers began to panic and, from a position of complete control, all of a sudden couldn't bowl any dot balls. Number 10 Mohammad Sami got lucky quite a few times, miscueing it over fielders' heads and that kind of thing, but Goodwin didn't mishit the ball once. He just kept pumping it. Until finally, having whittled the requirement down to 15 off the final over, and three off the last ball, he smashed Charlie Shreck for a huge six.

Just as they had when they won the Championship title and consigned us to Division Two in 2006, Sussex were celebrating joyously on the Trent Bridge outfield. It was painful to witness and Matt Prior kindly reminds me of this on a regular basis. A few of us made a point of making fun of Sussex for being a one-man team, our argument being that they would be nothing without Mushtaq Ahmed, and our taunts were validated when in the first year after his retirement they were relegated themselves. However, Matt does have that ridiculous chase to throw back at us.

Defeat did not knock us out of our stride in the Championship race, however, and just three days later we headed down to The Oval to crush Surrey by an innings. That meant we went into the final game of the season as leaders, and another comprehensive victory would guarantee the silverware. But Hampshire, our opponents, were also in with a sniff of the title if they won and results went for them elsewhere, while Durham, although 10 points behind us, were always favourites in my mind because they faced already-relegated Kent.

After winning the toss, we began well by dismissing Hampshire for 203, but we shot ourselves in the foot when we only secured an eight-run lead on first innings. It should have been an advantage of three figures after we negotiated our way to 172 for three, and when they made a better fist of their second innings, setting us 442 in 76 overs, the dream was over. We had a little go for it – I even opened the batting – but we were never realistically going to get there, so we ended up losing out to Durham. Popular opinion afterwards was that Notts had thrown the Championship away, but I truly expected Durham to get a full victory and so they did. Despite the double disappointment, we considered 2008 a good season but, having fallen at the last in two competitions, you couldn't help dwelling on how an extra point here or there might have won us something.

9

FOOL'S GOLD

KEVIN PIETERSEN'S captaincy era – following Michael Vaughan's decision to tearfully step aside in early August 2008 – undoubtedly opened in a blaze of glory. The England team played unbelievably well in that one-day series win over South Africa, that much could not be denied, but, put into perspective, there was not a better time to play them. Since I became an international regular, it has become clear to me that the prime time to play limited-overs matches against any team is when you have just lost to them in a Test series. While the winners naturally ease off, having achieved their primary objective, the losers regroup, determined to start afresh. New Zealand had turned the tables on us earlier that same summer, we in turn did it to South Africa, and Australia twice hammered us after Ashes victories. Whether it is consciously or subconsciously, players always place emphasis on Test cricket, and the answer in my opinion is to schedule one-day series first – that way both teams maintain their focus to the last.

Whatever the order at the end of that summer, however, all that had gone before could not prepare us for the next few items on the itinerary. Our home fixtures with South Africa preceded the biggest pantomime season English cricket has ever witnessed. The first stop was an October trip to the Caribbean to play in what was billed as sport's biggest-ever purse for a one-off team event: Texan billionaire Allen Stanford's 20/20 for 20 concept. A single cricket match with £20 million in prize money – of course it was too good to be true. It later transpired that the ECB had jumped into bed with this bloke after quite a number of rival cricket boards had turned him down.

Midway through the English season, at the announcement of this mouth-watering annual fixture in Antigua, this fella Stanford clambered out of his helicopter and onto the nursery ground at Lord's, waving at people as if he was royalty. And as he ostentatiously showed off his wedge of dollar bills crammed into a Perspex box, the England entourage hosting him smiled back as if he was exactly that. It was all so showy from the start, and the publicity shots of KP with Stanford that day summed up the whole fiasco for me.

Now, Kev is not exactly known for wearing decent clobber but the suit he turned up in for the press conference that day was truly, phenomenally awful. I cannot believe a human being with mirrors in his house would end up wearing the pastel blue, Miami Vice whistle he rocked up in. Who suggested to him that he looked half-decent in it, I will never know. As with the event itself, you couldn't shake the feeling that somehow it just wasn't right.

Some might have argued it appropriate to prepare for our 1 November showdown with the Stanford Superstars, a match that would make the playing XI US dollar millionaires on the spot, exactly as we did, with talks by a former SAS man – Who Dares Wins, and all that – but I am still not sure what our two-day bonding exercise at the Leander Club, Henley, was all about. My confusion arose from the attitude of our ECB bosses at the time. Soon after this bash-for-cash was announced they were intent on convincing us that this unprecedented match, where the winners would pocket £620,000 per man, was not about the money at all, and that it was actually a big-pressure game that would prepare us for other tasks ahead. Indeed, the bigger picture was what we should focus on, they said, and the special forces bloke reinforced the ethos of standing up to big challenges. But frankly it was ridiculous, because it patently was about the cash.

The SAS guy was fascinating, talking about his adventures in far-flung corners of the world, and all the challenges he had overcome, but I didn't see what the hell it had to do with the Stanford Series. To be honest, most of us had the nodding dog on when we were ushered back into this room for part two on the second day. The previous night we had gone out for a group meal, and inevitably followed it with a few beers, so the fact that we were sitting in a baking-hot room being addressed by the most soothing, velvety voice imaginable had its inevitable effect.

In the run-up to the game, the entire management – including Peter Moores and Kevin Pietersen – emphasised at every juncture that this was not about the readies, and their message was still being repeated as we gathered in Antigua for our week-long jaunt. At one point they even tried to argue that in playing this match we would be doing our bit for grass-roots cricket in the Caribbean. It would have been better if everyone had just admitted that the game was all about the $20 million and treated it like that. A far better mission statement would have been 'This is going to do your bank accounts no harm at all, lads; let's go all out to win it!'

Naturally we were conscious of how it looked playing for such a ludicrous sum just as the recession was hitting the UK big time, but there was no way around it for us. Our job was to represent England whenever asked to do so by our employers, for whatever series they organised around the globe. We had been selected in much the same way we would have been for a Test or one-day tour and were reporting for duty. It wasn't the players who negotiated the prize fund or the long-term deal to go back every year.

When Alastair Cook was interviewed a few days after our get-together at Henley, he was asked directly whether it was all about the cash. 'Of course it is,' he said. Later, when asked by a journalist what I would do with my share, I revealed my intention to decorate the downstairs bathroom and buy a pink Ferrari. I was being flippant, of course, but by this point I was becoming frustrated that people had deluded themselves that this wasn't about money. Or at least that is what they were conveying publicly. During the build-up in Antigua, for example, Kev sat four or five of us down and told us we mustn't talk to the press in the way that we were, that the game was not about the money, it was about this, that and the other.

Yet from the second we'd arrived, the whole island was talking about the riches of this game, and the minibuses had pictures of KP and Chris Gayle on the side alongside the slogan 'One Game, One Chance, $20million'. It was rammed down your throat all the time, and to make matters worse a lot of people had already come to the conclusion that we would win. The West Indies weren't as good as England, the argument went, and as this wasn't even the West Indies team, of course we would beat them. There was an assumption that we would turn up, play a couple of warm-up games against Middlesex and Trinidad, and thus be ready to topple big Al's Superstars.

Even amongst ourselves we were doing too much to tempt fate, and one incident 24 hours before the game made me feel particularly uneasy. The 11 of us who had been picked for the match were called to our meeting room at the Verandah resort complex where we were staying to be addressed by Andrew Flintoff. His concern was the way the cash was to be split among the victorious side. The financial details of the deal were that the winning team took $11 million, the two boards shared $7 million, and the remaining $2 million was divided between the non-playing members of the squad and the backroom staff. The losers got nothing. However, Fred decreed that above and beyond that we would each plough a hundred thousand back into the pot so that the other four lads – James Anderson, Ravi Bopara, Alastair Cook and Ryan Sidebottom – got more of a pay day. His argument was that we had gone out there as a squad, but selection was out of our hands, and therefore it would be fairer to give the non-players a bigger share. It was put to us in such a way that no one dared say no, but I walked away thinking: 'Christ, it must be a nice position to be in, where you can just write off a hundred grand.'

Walking away from that meeting, a number of guys were unhappy with the ultimatum, and let's just say that the differences in earnings between some of the England players were brought to light as a result of it. Some of my colleagues were considerably better off than me if they could afford to siphon cash like that. However, I did not consider the new proposal to be wrong per se, only in terms of its timing. As a superstitious sort, I do not believe in talking about what might be, only what is directly in front of me. In this instance, we shouldn't have given any serious consideration to what we might do with the money because it was not ours yet. Doing so was messing with the cricketing gods and said to me: 'You lot ain't winning anything here.' Cricket has a habit of biting the presumptuous on the arse. The second you dare suggest you are going well in a game is usually the time you lose two wickets in quick succession. To me Fred's suggestion was the right thing to do, but was made at the wrong time. I wouldn't have had a problem handing over some of the winnings, but it might have been better to have had that conversation in the event of us winning.

There were other issues that affected the squad too. Some of the lads were bothered about the fact that while the Windies were playing under another moniker for this groundbreaking match, we were still called England. I have to say it didn't bother me one jot – after all we were the England team. What would a different name have changed? We were the same blokes who had represented England the previous summer and would do so in the winter that followed.

We weren't playing for national pride, were we? It wasn't like playing a proper series for your country when you feel everyone is supporting your cause. If we had won that game no one back in Britain would have been doing cartwheels. There would have been a fair few players in county cricket, good honest pros, aggrieved that they had missed out while a chosen few had trousered a preposterous amount. The difference in, say, an Ashes series is that you feel others are in it with you, desperate for you to win. On the other hand, the fact that I knew they were not on this occasion made me feel that the pressure was off, so I might as well enjoy myself.

Mike Atherton observed in *The Times* that I was the one person who was treating it how it should have been treated. I was out all the time, chatting to the press in the bar most nights, and generally relaxed about the whole thing. He was spot on, but that was probably as much to do with the fact that I had left Sarah back in Nottingham. Because we were only there for a week I assumed that partners wouldn't be in attendance, so imagine my surprise when most of the other lads turned up with full families in tow, and we made our way to a holiday resort on the other side of Antigua upon arrival. She was livid with me later when she realised she'd missed out, but I am not sure how she would have coped with the ant problem in my room, to be honest.

There were problems from a cricket perspective throughout the week. The Coolidge ground Stanford built had not hosted many games of cricket, the pitch was slow and the outfield long. That meant low-scoring games at the start of the week, including our win over Middlesex when we successfully defended a run-a-ball score. I was not included for that match but I always maintain that Twenty20 is a spinner's game and the conditions were begging for pace to be taken off the ball. Thankfully, the think tank of Pietersen and Moores recognised it too, so I was recalled for the one-run win over Trinidad & Tobago that preceded our big showdown.

In addition to the two warm-up games, we had a couple of practice sessions under the floodlights. The lighting from those erections was horrendous – every time the ball went aerial it completely disappeared into the night sky, and so the first few games featured some absolute howlers from the fielders. Trouble was that catching became a complete lottery. You thought you were underneath the ball but then, out of the darkness, it plunged to earth two yards to the side of you. This made catching practice cracking fun, if a little precarious, and not what you would expect in preparation for a game of such potential riches.

It was a measure of Stanford's power on the island that he rectified the problem for the showcase match. The proximity of the international airport across the road had restricted the amount of light that could be emitted, yet when it came to the crunch he opted to stuff the consequences – what consequences – and have proper lights, so he took off the eyelids that caused the restriction. Of course, they

worked much better after that but the fact he felt empowered to defy
the authorities reinforced his image. He just did what he wanted,
when he wanted, including wandering into our dressing room whenever he liked, which upset quite a few of the boys. His mugshot was
even on the restricted area security list, right next to that of Kevin
Pietersen. This was the big Allen Stanford Ego Show and we were
pawns in it. When he sat Emily Prior on his knee during that England
v Middlesex game, Matt wanted to confront him. I imagine he would
be in a pretty long queue these days. It was an embarrassing episode,
and the whole week made me cringe. Not one thing that happened
there makes me beam with pride.

The Stanford Superstars had been at a training camp for six weeks
drilling for this match, whereas we were ill prepared – 'ill' being the
operative word, as a few of the lads went down with food poisoning
a couple of days out. Now, if Stuart Broad goes down with anything
like that you can guarantee Luke Wright will have it soon afterwards,
and vice versa, and so it proved here. It was coming out of both ends
for them and they really were in a bad way in the 72 hours leading
up to the big match.

Naturally they were forced to miss training, and on the way back
Samit Patel claimed to have come down with the same thing. So he
was excused training the following day. Yet when we got in that
evening from a floodlit session we spotted him coming back from the
hotel shop with two dozen Bounty bars. 'I've been so ill, I can't keep
anything else down,' he explained. 'The only thing that will stay down
are these things.' So there you are – if you ever have horrendous food
poisoning, or even a hangover, try it; apparently it's the way forward.

As it was, we got annihilated in the game, our score of 99 put into
context when Chris Gayle came out and smacked us everywhere.
Such was his speed out of the blocks, I only just got on to bowl. The
Superstars had reduced the target to 29 from 12 overs by then, and
although I managed to bowl four dot balls, Gayle hit me approximately 150 yards over long on – one of the biggest sixes the world
has ever seen – and that was that for me.

Actually, the best thing about the whole week was the fireworks display that greeted our 10-wicket defeat. It must have set big Al back a few bob – not that it was his money, of course – and would have given Sydney at New Year a good run in the extravagance stakes. As we watched those explosions in the sky, little did we know what was to unravel over the following months. When you factor in his arrest, and that people had been swindled out of their life savings, it was actually a godsend we lost. Can you imagine how uncomfortable it would have been to be in the position of having to give that money back?

Had we cashed the cheques, I've also considered that my next big career decision might have taken me down a different route. In the aftermath of the terror attack on Mumbai that same month, I cannot say for sure I would have gone back if I'd had in excess of half a million quid sloshing around in my bank account. In that position, I reckon I would have said: 'Do you know what? Sod it, I'm not going.' At least money didn't cloud that issue for me.

That Stanford trip was always all about money, you see, and how ironic that I returned from it out of pocket after all that had gone before. My deficit was racked up on a night out with six couples and a few single stragglers. We went to a nice restaurant and after the meal we played credit-card roulette, a game in which everyone throws their credit cards into a napkin, for the waitress to pick out one by one. The last one is used to pay for the lot. Of course, Muggins had to foot the bill and thanks to my cloudy maths – which had deteriorated after a bottle of New Zealand Sauvignon Blanc – I miscalculated it to be about £250. Imagine my surprise when I got home to find it was something like four times as much.

10

A VERY TRICKY PROPOSAL

Had Kevin Pietersen stayed as captain in one-day cricket things weren't looking good for me. Having finished the 2008 summer out of the side, it struck home that I was far from an automatic choice and when we arrived in India in November I was omitted once more as the seven-match series began. Again my loss was Samit Patel's gain, with Pietersen and Peter Moores putting their faith in him as the team's sole spinner. They seemed to be intent on bolstering their batting and that made me expendable.

They had got away with that policy on home soil against South Africa, and Samit would have been pleased with his performances, which included a maiden five-wicket haul in the win at The Oval. But it remained in the back of my mind that the wheels might come off for him when we got to the subcontinent because he is not a genuine spin bowler. He's a batsman who bowls a bit of spin, and in conditions where the pressure would be on to perform against the best players of slow bowling in the world, I thought he would get found out a bit. So it proved.

Aside from my personal observations, however, I just couldn't believe that we were not finding room for both of us when I looked at the pitches that were being served up. Our tactical thinking seemed to be flawed, and frankly speaking I considered it ridiculous that for some reason we believed we could go in and blast out their stellar batting line-up with pace. The theory was that the Indian batsmen didn't like it short, but on their own wickets the ball sat up rather than rushed through and they absolutely murdered us.

In the opening defeat in Rajkot, India's 387 for six was the biggest total conceded in one-day internationals, and another sizeable loss followed in the second match in Indore. I was not selected for either of those but their outcomes prompted a re-think and I did get in for the third match in Kanpur, where I bowled pretty well, to take one for 47 from my 10 overs. That match and the following one in Bangalore were both shortened by the atmospheric conditions: fading light handed India victory on the Duckworth-Lewis method in my first game and rain interruptions altered our chase to a stiff 198 in 22 overs in the next. We never looked destined to win a game nor got into a position where we were likely to, and in the fifth game in the series, in Cuttack on 26 November, we were placed at a severe disadvantage once more.

A Pietersen hundred and a late blitz by Owais Shah pushed us up to 270 for four, which we considered to be quite a competitive score. But the dew on the ground was absolutely ridiculous. Virender Sehwag hit the ball to all parts early on and as a result it ended up soaking wet. The seam itself was drenched and because I try to spin the ball hard I just could not hold the damn thing. We'd already all but lost the game so I sent down two or three overs of seam instead, and even had the temerity to bowl a bouncer at Suresh Raina towards the death. I considered it might be my only chance to bowl a bouncer in an international match. So I just did it.

We were 5–0 down in the series and facing a whitewash, with only games in Guwahati and Delhi to come, as we set off back to our hotel in Bhubaneshwar. It was a two-hour drive – one that was interrupted by Stuart Broad's announcement that 'something was going on'. While everyone else was either asleep, chatting or having a beer at the back, he had been roaming on his phone.

'They say there's been a terrorist attack at the Taj Mahal hotel in Mumbai,' he told us.

It was a familiar landmark to all of us, as it was where we had stayed just a fortnight earlier and a place where we were due to return just a few weeks later for a Test match. It was also where half our team kit was housed.

The severity of the atrocities revealed themselves, and graphically at that, at the conclusion of our journey. Back at the hotel in Bhubaneshwar, we wandered into the bar to find the entire staff watching the television. Now, rolling news footage in India is nothing like it is back in Britain. When they claim to be reporting live from the scene, they are actually reporting live from the scene, unlike here where producers have a three-second delay that buys them time to edit or blank out stuff that's too violent for viewing. Presented before us were images of people getting shot and others being dragged across the street with blood pouring out of their heads. TV crews climbed through windows in the hotel and reported things like: 'We think we can see people in the lobby with guns to their head.' It was absolutely frightening.

At that very moment, before any of us had discussed anything, my thoughts were concrete: 'We're definitely going home.'

To me there were no two ways about it, yet when it became a formal issue the next day, Giles Clarke, the ECB chairman, made a big push for us to stay. Everyone to a man in our squad – nothing to do with the fact that we were five games down, although that didn't help – presented the same clear message. Simply: get us out of here.

A lot of foggy information came out in the 24 hours after those Islamist extremists devastated the city of Mumbai, but the very fact that they were attacking westerners – it seemed to us that Brits and Americans had been targeted – led us to the conclusion that we were not safe. At one point, my paranoia convinced me that the terrorists knew we were there on tour and I imagined a big arrow pointing towards us. So while other people might have been perturbed by the presence of tanks and army personnel outside our hotel when we awoke the next morning, I actually found it reassuring.

My view was that we were not there to fight for our country, so we needed to be removed from the situation. What on earth were we doing even thinking about playing cricket when the hotel manager, and his wife, a couple who had looked after us so well just days earlier, had been executed in the lobby of the Taj? Cricket was no longer the priority for anyone, so we flew home in dribs and drabs on whatever aeroplanes the authorities could fit us on.

Quite honestly, when I learned the tour was being called off I could not have been happier, and everything that had happened over a horrifying 48-hour period made me do a lot of thinking about life. It was at some point in those couple of days, in fact, that I decided I was going to ask Sarah to marry me. I cannot claim it was the only reason, but thoughts of 'What would have happened had we been at that hotel and been murdered?' filled my head. 'I love this girl with everything I've got,' I kept thinking, 'so why aren't I committing to her?' I decided that I would do just that as soon as I got back home to Nottingham.

My proposal is a beautiful story of romance, as it happens. Well, actually it's not, but it's the story of my proposal, so take it or leave it.

On the night of my return, Sarah was on her way to the Angel Ball, an annual charity event at Colwick Hall, a Georgian-style mansion, just a couple of miles from where we live. It was about 9.30 p.m. by the time I walked through our front door, but she had left my tuxedo out on the bed with a ticket, and a note saying 'See you there'. So while playing around with Max and Paddy, our kittens, I formulated final plans for the impending big moment. Originally, I had planned to drop my bags and allow the words 'Will you marry me' to be the first I uttered as I got through the door but that option had obviously been scuppered, so I modified it to walking into the ball, finding the relevant table and popping the question surrounded by all our friends.

I threw on my tux, turned up at the ball, looked at the table plan and strolled in. It was a very sedate crowd – the usual sights and sounds you would associate with that kind of ball were evident, both laughter and champagne flowed throughout the room. However, in the far corner two tables gave off a distinctly different vibe. They were home to absolute carnage. Somehow it looked like Christmas, New Year and 21st-birthday parties had been rolled into one. People with heads down on the table had streamers hanging off them, others were under the red-wine-stained tablecloth and those that were upright were singing, whooping and high-fiving as I wandered over. Yep, you've probably guessed that these were the tables where Sarah and our closest mates were sitting. They had begun their drinking activities well before the event itself and were hammered from the moment they arrived.

While I was in India I'd had my head shaved, and lost a lot of weight, because of the heat out there, the combined effect being that I was now a doppelgänger for one of the Polish footballers in *Escape to Victory*. Unfortunately, that is as close as things got to a film-star moment. As I tapped Sarah on the shoulder, she turned round, took one look at me with one eye open and indiscreetly asked the others: 'Who the hell is that?' Thankfully, before anyone could answer, she did a double take. 'Graeme?' she inquired. By that stage she had forgotten I was even coming home.

The moment had gone, I think you'll agree, so I decided to leave it for a more appropriate time, which quite clearly was a few hours later, at approximately four in the morning, round at my mate Jack's house. Sarah and I ended up in the front room together alone, so I opted to ask her there and then. I didn't even get down on one knee – good job because I wouldn't have balanced for long enough – it was more of a flop on the couch.

It clearly made a resounding impression on her because a couple of hours after saying yes, Sarah checked whether my proposal had really taken place. She was not entirely sure. Perhaps she had expected something more dramatic, but I have never been one for overblown romantic gestures. Although I must admit that I always feel sorry for Sarah whenever any of her mates get married and the bloke has gone to ridiculous lengths to make the moment special. One went to Vienna, another hired a private helicopter, so there is a small amount of guilt about the way I did things. But anything else just wouldn't have been me, and let's face it, she's a lucky, lucky girl!

We had had only a couple of days at home to get used to our new engaged status, however, when pressure for the England team to return to India reached fever pitch. I had been aware that the issue was dominating the agenda on channels like Sky News, and that the debate was almost non-stop, and so I turned my phone off and avoided watching TV for a while, in the hope it might all go away. I knew it wouldn't, of course, and when I switched communication back on, one of the first calls I received was from Kevin Pietersen.

Because Giles Clarke had been so adamant about us staying put, and that there was no danger to us whatsoever, I had anticipated we would be asked to go back from the moment they confirmed us on flights home. By now Kevin, the captain, was obviously on board with his superiors because he informed me that he had been asked by Geoff Miller, the chairman of selectors, to ring round and check on availability. 'Will you make yourself available to tour?' he asked.

The ECB hierarchy tried to convince us there were strong reasons to return. It was for the good of cricket, they said. The truth was it was for the good of their bank balances. We knew as much because we were told that if we didn't go back it was going to cost English cricket £25 million, and that was money that would have to come out of county cricketers' wages. The whole situation made me feel very uncomfortable.

I'd not spoken to any of the other lads since I'd been back in Blighty – it was a conscious decision not to – instead I canvassed opinion, first of all from Sarah, and then my dad. Sarah told me she didn't really know anything about the situation but felt she didn't want me to go back because her hunch was that it was not safe. That gut instinct mirrored my own and I had more or less decided I would stay put when I called Dad for a second opinion. I told him I needed his advice but that I wouldn't necessarily follow it. I simply wanted his take on the whole thing.

Immediately, he told me to put the safety aspect out of my head. 'How much do you want to play Test cricket?' he asked.

'It's everything I want. It's all I want to do. All I've ever wanted to do.'

'Right,' he said. 'If you don't go, how much is it going to impact on your chances of playing in the future?'

His questions found their way under my skin. In subcontinental conditions there was no way England would not play two spinners, and if the same squad did head back, then I would be guaranteed the opportunity of fulfilling my dream. If I opted out, someone else would go instead, and if they did well, I might never get another chance. These facts started playing on my mind big time.

Sitting in my back garden, on one of December's first days, wrapped up but content to be experiencing the cold British winter, I went through that potential playing scenario. With regard to off-field issues, I quickly came to the conclusion that security would be ramped up to over-the-top proportions, and the fact that I desperately wanted to play Test cricket helped me to my answer. My dad had never really given me much advice – he has always let me get on with things, and I have never been someone to take advice from other people – but I just thought he was right. He was very honest. 'Of course your mum and I will worry about your safety but we think you'll be all right, and if it is a good move for your career it is something you've got to do.'

Then the Prime Minister, Gordon Brown, called us 'brave and courageous'; leading political commentators reckoned we returned with great credit; we were applauded for a gesture made towards the people of India; we were great sporting ambassadors. Yet, if I am 100 per cent honest, there was no show of solidarity from me. I went back to receive my first England Test cap when there was a threat it might never materialise otherwise.

Even then, as a squad we did not commit to anything beyond attending a holding camp in Abu Dhabi, our numbers swelled by the presence of academy players, added in the event of some of the original party withdrawing their labour. Despite my personal resolution, however,

I couldn't completely shake the following thoughts: 'Is this really the right thing to do? Are we going to get blown up?'

Had it been a few months later, after the Sri Lankan team bus had been attacked in Pakistan, then there would have been no way I would have considered it. Scepticism about player safety in Asia had been on the agenda for a number of months prior to this tour, following the refusal by a number of countries, including ourselves, to travel to Pakistan to participate in the Champions Trophy that September. During this time, the International Cricket Council chief executive, Haroon Lorgat, and the head of the ICC's security specialists Nicholls Steyn came over to try to convince us that Pakistan was indeed safe. Even to the point where this Nicholls Steyn guy said he would happily take his mother-in-law there for this trip. I'm guessing she must have been fairly happy to pass on that one.

Their logic concerning why we would be safe was mind-blowingly naive. As cricket was so big in Pakistan, they reasoned, no one would do anything to upset the apple cart. It was the equivalent of football in England, they said, and perhaps even more of a religion to its people. Any act against the sport would be sacrosanct. Now, I don't have a background in the military or intelligence services, but I considered this a fairly porous argument. Fundamentalists aren't going to give two hoots about a few games of cricket if their principal objective is to attack western civilians. That being the case, an English cricket team would be a perfect target.

Whilst we gathered in the United Arab Emirates, training at the Sheikh Zayed Stadium, our security adviser, Reg Dickason, a man respected and trusted by the whole group of players, went ahead to India with Hugh Morris, of the ECB, and his namesake Sean Morris, then chief executive of the Professional Cricketers' Association. The original Test venues of Mumbai (for obvious reason) and Ahmedabad, because of its proximity to the Pakistani border, had been scrapped and Chennai and Mohali proposed, so safety assessments were required on our behalf. Immediately, those with a grasp of Indian geography questioned the choice of Mohali, being just about the same distance from the Pakistan border as Ahmedabad but it turned out it was because they could offer the most robust security arrangements. If we were going to be attacked, it was the easiest place to defend, the argument went. Reg and the Morris men undertook their whistle-stop tour and arrived back on the Sunday, intent on convincing us things would be tight enough.

When Reg and Hugh Morris addressed us that evening, it was an unusual position to be in. They talked us through their findings, and asked us to decide whether we were willing to continue on to Chennai. It rankled some guys, particularly those who'd been involved with the Zimbabwe issue a few years earlier. They had been guaranteed by the ECB that they would never be put into that kind of position again. Post-2003 World Cup, there would be no more decisions to be made on non-cricketing grounds, they were assured, and yet here they were in the same sort of situation once more. There were some seriously hacked-off guys, and half a dozen still wavered as midnight approached. But a united front was eventually reached.

My reasons for going back were purely selfish, I admit that, but I wish others had been more upfront. Money does strange things to people and I couldn't shake the feeling that we were going back to keep the Indian board sweet. As I listened to justifications for continuing south, I thought: 'This is nonsense.' If people were frank and said from the word go 'Yep, this is a money deal', it would be a lot easier to accept. When you are told in one breath that it is nothing to do with money, then in the next that we'll get fined a shedload if we don't go, it just narks you off. Pretending it is about far bigger issues when it is patently not is wrong, in my book.

I had bitten the bullet and decided to chase my ambition of becoming a Test cricketer, and once I took those steps on Indian soil I couldn't have felt any safer. Talk about security. Anyone who has ever toured India will know that half a dozen people are required to carry out any one job. Suddenly, instead of six people it was 15 and they all had machine guns and wore camouflage. We were treated like absolute kings, and protected like heads of state.

The reaction from the Indian public made it all feel worthwhile too. Again, I am not saying I went back for any other reason than I have admitted to in these pages, but seeing how happy they were gave me some satisfaction that I had done a good thing no matter how that point had been reached.

Nor was there pressure to perform: we had no warm-up games because of the disruption, and next to no practice in the build-up. But the press reaction to us being there at all was overwhelmingly positive and our own journalists especially wrote that the results would pale into insignificance when placed against our gesture. It was not the winning but the taking part that counted given the circumstances, and it was quite a novel feeling that we lost and did not get obliterated for it in print.

Any lingering doubts that I would indeed make my Test bow in Chennai were removed a couple of days out when in net practice I bowled Kev three times, with spinning deliveries that snaked through the gate. It was absolute confirmation we would play two spinners, and this time when I heard my name read out I was absolutely made up. 'This is why I am here,' I thought. 'The deliberation's all been worthwhile.'

11

A TEST OF CHARACTER

FORGET ANY notion of humanitarian gestures, the morning of 11 December 2008, at the Chepauk Stadium, was the primary reason I had gone back to India. To be handed my Test cap by Sir Ian Botham in the dressing room was the fulfilment of a boyhood dream. England had used 595 players in Test cricket when I was first selected in a squad, and I was now officially the 641st. For the feeling alone it was worth the wait, and I was desperate to get out onto the field of play. The words with which Beefy sent me on my way were pure class: 'Good luck, mate. Having seen that pitch, if you can't get wickets out there you never will.' No pressure, then.

We won the toss and batted first against a backdrop of 3,000 police officers stationed around the ground and 300 commandos forming a perimeter on the boundary edge. A hundred-plus opening stand between Andrew Strauss and Alastair Cook ensured we got the two-match series off to a decent start, and guaranteed that we would post a half-decent total. Patience is a valuable virtue in Indian conditions, but from a personal point of view, it seemed as if I had to wait ages for my turn to bat, and it was not until day two that I got to the middle. Even then it was to take my place at the non-striker's end, as Jimmy Anderson had holed out in the deep sweeping, and crossed in the process. Typically, I did not waste time when I did get to face, and was off the mark first ball when I turned a delivery from Harbhajan Singh off my hip. But, after unsuccessfully attempting to reverse-sweep my fourth ball for four, my sixth went through the top a bit and looped to slip. In contrast to its build-up, my first Test innings was ridiculously short, but at least I wasn't out for nought.

Although my contribution to our 316 all out was minimal, when I bowled it all started to happen for me. It was shortly before the tea break on the second day, with India 30 for one, that I was thrown the ball by Kevin Pietersen. My response, as I positioned myself at the end of my run, was an unfamiliar one, and one that I ultimately had no control over. As I stood there, my knees started knocking together, and for the first time since my debut against Worcestershire 11 years earlier I was properly nervous. My beans were going, the ball felt really alien in my hand, to the extent that my hand no longer felt like my own. As a result my first delivery was a rank long hop that Gautam Gambhir cut for four.

Despite starting life as a Test bowler with a boundary, upon returning to my mark, I considered it a good thing that the first ball was out of the way. Determined not to look a complete idiot, I tried to calm myself with the thought that it couldn't get any worse – although looking back, I am not sure why I discounted being hit for six given what I had just served up. As it was, the delivery that followed resulted in a big kerfuffle for a bat-pad catch on the leg side. And the third was even better as the left-handed Gambhir padded up and the ball struck his pad in line. Excitement spilled out of me because I knew one thing for sure – he was out. I began jumping up and down appealing excitedly to Daryl Harper, the umpire, more in anticipation than hope, because although he took an eternity to raise his finger, I knew what was coming. The look on his face told me as much.

After all the uncertainty about whether I was truly going to be good enough at this level, I had taken a wicket in my first over. I had waited all that time to play and the feeling that overwhelmed me as my team-mates congratulated me was stupendously ridiculous. It might easily have been mistaken for relief but it was simply unadulterated elation. Whatever happened from that point onwards, at least I had a wicket in international cricket, and celebrating it felt just like any other wicket I'd taken before. Well, any wicket I'd ever taken before multiplied tenfold. It was ten times more exciting, it was ten times as important and I must have jumped ten times higher in the air. Or so it felt. The only thing I could compare it to was my experiences as a kid when a good night's sleep used to incorporate dreams of scoring a goal for Newcastle United at Wembley. This had displaced it, however, as the best thing I could ever imagine.

Having waited nine years between my first England tour and my maiden Test scalp, it did not take long to double my tally. It was the London bus syndrome, in fact, as it was just three balls later that I managed to snare Rahul Dravid in the same manner, leg before wicket, this time when a delivery turned from outside off to beat his defensive push. Once again, I beseeched Harper to raise his finger and, after he did so, and I'd received my pats on the back, I meandered off for tea having bowled one over more in Test cricket than I had when I woke that morning. As we made our way back past the hordes of security personnel into the changing rooms, I had an amazing warm feeling inside me and figures of 1–0–7–2 up on the scoreboard.

Grabbing wickets in my first over of a spell for England has been a recurring theme for me ever since. People are always looking for explanations for this trend but the truthful answer is I honestly don't know why. I remember that during my Bambi-on-ice growing phase I would come on and send down all sorts at the start of a spell. My radar would be all over the shop, with double bouncers followed by full tosses, a source of great agitation to my dad. He told me that it just wouldn't do and that my first over always had to be spot on. You cannot afford to bowl such a loose first over, he argued, because it allows the opposition easy runs and releases any pressure on them. A good start is certainly something I've striven for ever since, but I can't give any other reasons why I have been so successful at the start of spells, other than that I can now land the ball where I want. That has simply come from bowling this stuff in first-class cricket for more than a decade.

John Wake, my off-spinning mentor at Northampton Saints, told me recently that his theory on my speed out of the blocks is that it's because I am an optimist, and fully believe that I will take wickets from the minute I come on to bowl. Because you believe you can, you often do, is his general thinking. And he is right in the assessment of my attitude, as I always think about getting the batsman out. Whenever I have the ball in my hand I believe I have a chance, and that includes the very first delivery. I aim high from the word go. Unlike a lot of bowlers, I have never come on with the intention of simply getting the first over out of the way, and perhaps that, allied to the fact that batsmen expect you to ease yourself in, has worked in my favour. It is nice that I have struck so often in the first over of spells, and it's an easy line for the commentators when it happens, but it is just the way things have turned out. Don't get me wrong, I would happily bowl 15 overs for my first wicket in every Test match I play. But there really is no definitive explanation for why I have maintained those successful starts. Other than the fact I've practised black magic since the age of 15. Not sure if that has anything to do with it!

Back to the match in question, however, and in that final session of the second day, inspired by Andrew Flintoff's ferociously fast spell, we picked up three more wickets and India were struggling on 155 for six at the close. Afterwards I was asked by the press how satisfying it had been to dismiss some of the best players of spin bowling in the world, but for me the level of the challenge didn't come into it. This was a Test match and I was playing in it. That was what mattered to me. It could have been played in Timbuktu for all I cared. At that point I wasn't even thinking about the fact that it was India and I was up against revered players of spin. However, that certainly did come into my head in the second innings when it was turning square yet Sachin Tendulkar was playing with such ease.

Andrew Strauss's second hundred of the match and another from Paul Collingwood helped us develop a 75-run advantage on first innings, setting India a challenging 387 for victory. When we went back out to press home our claims, however, we were to learn exactly how good this Indian batting line-up, and Tendulkar in particular, were. It was humbling to witness first-hand just how amazing he was. Everyone knows he has been the best player going in the modern era, but when you actually bowl to him on a wicket in your favour, and he appears to know what you're thinking the minute before you think it, it's like playing poker against a full-time professional. Whatever he does, you struggle to come up with an answer, and yet with conditions in the bowler's favour it should be the other way around.

Virender Sehwag set the platform at the beginning of the Indian chase with a blistering counter-attack of 83, which I thankfully managed to halt. A couple of deliveries earlier he had carted me over the ropes at midwicket, but unperturbed I maintained my rip on the ball and when one turned out of the footmarks it earned another lbw success. It was also perilously near to the close of play, which came with India 131 for one.

We were given the perfect start the following morning when Rahul Dravid nicked behind off Flintoff, but that simply marked the start of the masterclass as Tendulkar was roared to the crease by a sizeable fifth-day crowd. As it happened, it was the first time I'd ever bowled at Tendulkar – we both missed the start of the one-day series that preceded the Tests – because the only other time he was at the crease when I came on, during the final match in Cuttack, Sehwag kept the strike. Well, this innings in Chennai turned out to be just about as good as any in his career – he acknowledged as much afterwards – and from where I was watching I can confirm it truly was a phenomenal knock. The way he manipulated the field was pure genius. Now, I didn't think I had particularly very good fields throughout that Test because to my mind that wasn't the strongest aspect of Kev's captaincy, but it wouldn't have mattered where I positioned my men because, once set, he seemed to hit everything to where you had just moved them from, regardless of where the ball pitched.

Various members of the Indian top six weighed in with runs – Gambhir hit a half-century before he steered to gully off Jimmy Anderson, while I had V.V.S. Laxman claimed at short leg from a climbing off-break – but it was Tendulkar who provided the measured guidance to the finishing line with his remarkable, unbeaten hundred. Yuvraj Singh joined him for the final flurry and we had no answer to the fairy-tale script. Normally this kind of defeat would have led to stinging criticism in the press, but as promised, the England team was applauded after this game, and not just for donating half of our match fees to the relief fund for the victims of the Mumbai terrorist attack.

Those who had spoken of a duty to the game of cricket in the build-up had been rewarded with an enthralling contest, and a positive result, which is something we knew would be difficult to force in our bid to level the series in the second Test up at Mohali. It was always going to be a big ask, given the conditions in the north of India at that time of the year. Early-morning fog prevented play starting promptly. Every day we would leave our hotel in Chandigarh at 6.30 a.m. and there would be a blanket of fog over the ground when we arrived, thick enough that you could not see the stumps from the changing rooms, and it remained a problem until deep into the morning session. At the other end of the day, with natural light fading fast in early evening, we lost something like a fifth of the scheduled playing time.

India won the toss and batted first, and were set fair for a massive score at 320 for one, but once again I removed Gambhir and Dravid in quick succession, this time after both had hundreds to their names, and then the prize scalp of Tendulkar, all in a 19-run spell. This time, he played a false shot and was out lbw. I would like to think it was, in part, due to my clever bowling rather than just a cock-up, but let's face it, 95 per cent of the time batsmen get out it is because they have cocked up. It's just an honour to know that one of Tendulkar's cock-ups was off my bowling. When you consider I had walked off the pitch a week earlier astounded at how good a player he was, it was such an exciting feeling to have got one over on him. Here, things were more in his favour than mine, yet I somehow got him out. Cricket doesn't always make sense, of course, and this was one of those occasions.

As might have been expected, the match fizzled out into a draw but there were some complimentary comments aimed in my direction from both colleagues and critics alike. Andrew Strauss, my former Adelaide academy room-mate, reckoned he had seen a marked improvement in my bowling during that trip, while Andrew Flintoff acknowledged I should have been given a chance earlier in my career. To be fair, these guys had been playing for England for a while, and on central contracts at that, so probably hadn't seen me bowl much for six years or so. I had definitely improved over that period of time, but how much of that improvement had been made during the past 18 months I was uncertain.

I was buzzing when I got back to England. For one thing, I now felt much more part of the England team. Twelve months previously, I had been on the tour to Sri Lanka and felt like a spare part as a squad member. People who are in the team don't view you in the same way if you're not playing, and nor should they. But now, returning with a couple of Test caps under my belt, some wickets and some encouraging write-ups in the papers, I had an overwhelming sense of satisfaction. Some, Scyld Berry of the *Sunday Telegraph* amongst them, even went so far as to say that not only had I established myself on the tour but I had established myself as the number one spinner ahead of Monty Panesar. That was not something I gave much credence to but it was nevertheless pleasing to be thought of in an increasingly positive manner.

For the first time in a while my career seemed settled and I knew what was in front of me. We were due to head to the West Indies in early February and I considered myself a cast-iron certainty for a place on that tour when the squad was announced in mid-January. There were no fears whatsoever that my name would not be on the list when they held that press conference at Lord's to reveal the names of those who would be heading to the Caribbean. That was a nice, if unfamiliar, feeling.

12

MUTINY IN THE CAMP

T HE OPENING days of 2009 were some of the most dramatic and newsworthy for English cricket in living memory, but the events in question took place nowhere near the field of play. Yet as Kevin Pietersen's rift with Peter Moores played out in public, I was one of the few people in the country not to have followed the details of this fractious relationship and its complete breakdown. It had been evident from reading the body language of the pair in the previous six months that their dynamic was not natural – and there were mutterings about Moores from others, not just Kev – but it was nonetheless a complete shock when I belatedly discovered what had occurred over the festive season.

Struggling with man flu, I had been consigned to bed for the New Year, and was still not fully functional when I turned my mobile phone back on. A barrage of around 50 text messages flooded my inbox – a couple of early ones along the lines of 'Are you going to be the new England captain? Ha ha!' Only when I scrolled through them, however, did it become apparent what had been going on and so I turned on the TV to catch up on the latest state of play.

Over the next couple of days, despite that time of year being prime football territory, English cricket dominated the back pages of the newspapers. One of the things I read was that after Kev had effectively cast aspersions on Moores's ability as a top-level coach, all the England players had been called and asked their view on the situation. My place in the hierarchy of English cricket was clearly not yet established enough on the back of a couple of decent Test performances – either that or those in question did not have my phone number to hand.

It amused me that the whole dressing-room set-up was being analysed at this time. There were graphics in the papers to show who liked who within the dressing room. It was quite eye-opening to see who the press clubbed together. Apparently there was an Andrew Flintoff clique and a Kevin Pietersen clique, and according to those in the know, I, rather like Switzerland, had steadfastly stuck to being neutral. The truth was that in India pre-Christmas I hung out most nights in either Fred or Steve Harmison's room, playing darts and watching northern comedies on DVD. But one newspaper said that I was everybody's China, and I was pleased to take that because I knew full well I wasn't.

Let's be honest, very rarely do you get everyone pulling in the same direction in a dressing room. At that point there were two or three big characters who didn't like each other and that's how it was. I wouldn't say it was a split dressing room as such, because it wasn't anything like the state it was in when I first played for England, with all the chips on shoulders and big egos. But there certainly were some clashes of personality.

Kevin had decided Mooresy was no longer the man for the job, and had tried to get him fired, only for it to go spectacularly wrong for him too. I guess once his ultimatum to the board was leaked rather than kept in-house, the ECB had no choice but to take the most decisive action possible.

Several months earlier I would never have guessed this situation could have arisen because I felt Moores was doing a fairly decent job. But the second that Kev was made captain the previous August something had to give because captain and coach were so diametrically opposed. With the two of them removed from their positions, following extensive discussions at Lord's, it became another huge event to follow up the Stanford saga and the Indian terrorist attack. Pantomime season was in full swing and there was a certain resonance in the traditional lines of 'He's behind you', 'Oh no, he's not.'

If this situation had been brewing in India, and by all accounts it had been, I didn't pick up on it. You could tell that the two of them didn't like each other, that was fairly transparent, and there were others similarly at odds with the coach, but within a dressing room you always get people that don't get on particularly well. From my perspective, I felt a bit sorry for Mooresy because undoubtedly it was he who got me back onto the international scene, and he'd done a fairly good job. Sure, there were things he did as England coach that I did not agree with whatsoever, like that crazy post-match training in Napier, but I liked him as a bloke; his commitment and energy towards the job could never be questioned, and my feeling was that he had been hard done by.

Yet Kev was adamant that Moores was a county coach who could not cut the mustard at the top level. When a captain goes renegade like that, I am not sure how you should handle it, but it was probably for the best that they changed the captain as well, because out of all the disharmony we ended up with the right man as captain of England, and a world-class coach as well. Perhaps the ECB saw the ruck as a bit of a watershed moment and moved to draw a line beneath the whole affair. There was probably quite a strong element within the ECB who would rather have had Andrew Strauss as captain anyway, and his appointment as leader for the tour of the West Indies was equally well received by the players.

After the Lord's announcement that Strauss would be captain and Andy Flower interim coach for the tour of the Caribbean, a team meeting was called at Loughborough. Its sole purpose, as far as I could tell, was to make sure that Kev would toe the party line and go along as one of the rank and file, because at that point there was a lot of talk that he would refuse to play for England again. It was never specifically made clear that the get-together was for his benefit, and that of the ECB, but it certainly felt like that. Not that it was much hardship for me – Loughborough is only a stone's throw away, and I was heading home again after half an hour.

There is no doubt that Kev is a good player, a really fine batsman, but he was never the right man to be captain, in my opinion. Strauss was. Some people are better leaders of men and Kev for all his abundant talent is not one of those natural leaders. In contrast, Strauss is one of those guys who demand respect, and on a daily basis you never really fathom why. He just does. He always says the right things, whether it be in team meetings or press conferences, and his word is never questioned. As the old cliché goes, if you were in the trenches you would pick him to be in charge, and his captaincy is founded on leading from the front. That is not to say he cannot be hard-nosed if necessary, and the thing I particularly like about him, perhaps the reason I prefer his captaincy to Kev's, is that he is very level-headed on the field. Probably because I am quite volatile and lose my rag fairly easily, the captains I've enjoyed playing under are the ones that don't get flustered out in the middle even when the pressure is on. I need someone who can calm me down, but Kev could get quite wound up. At one point in India his leadership was reduced to a period of screaming 'F------ bowl f------ straight' at everyone.

Andy Flower was also a very popular appointment because he had been involved for the previous couple of years as batting coach under Moores. His promotion seemed fairly natural and the fact that we had all either played with or against him in county cricket meant that everyone knew him really well. This was an important factor at a time of such disruption. At Loughborough that day we were encouraged to move forward together as one under the new Flower–Strauss management team. Some things happen very naturally, and amazingly from day one of working together – even though their partnership has been quite organic and it has grown – they clicked. The two of them bounce ideas off each other really well, they are not afraid to try new stuff and they have both got a grip on how to man-manage the team. They proved a great foil for one another.

Reputations don't come into it with Andy Flower if he believes someone needs knocking into line. He is not afraid to tell a few home truths, irrespective of the player or their record. He will just say: 'That is not acceptable, that doesn't work in this team.' In the West Indies he was only interim coach, of course, and after the first Test debacle at Sabina Park the ECB were probably hastily looking around the globe to assess other candidates for the job. But the tour got better as time went on and thankfully Andy got the job permanently, because he has proved to be an exceptional coach.

My early experiences of the new regime were not particularly good, though – having departed for the Windies in January 2009 fully expecting to play in every game, I didn't even make the first Test. We had two warm-up games, and I was left out of the first, a resounding win against a St Kitts Invitational XI – something I didn't pay much attention to at the time – but suffered like the rest of the attack against West Indies A days later, on an unbelievably flat wicket. Lendl Simmons decided to bat like Garry Sobers for nine hours and finished up with 282 in a score of 574 for eight declared.

I had nothing to show from 41 overs, but with the performances in India to fall back on, my confidence that I would be the first spinner picked did not diminish. So when Straussy knocked on my door two days before the first Test in Jamaica it gave me quite a jolt. Whenever the captain comes calling, immediately the thought is 'Oh, Jesus, what's he doing here?' Because you've either done something that you shouldn't have – I knew I hadn't – or you're about to receive bad news about selection.

'Look, we are only going to play one spinner here and we are going with Monty,' he explained. 'We just feel that with what he has done over the past couple of years he deserves another crack. Yes, we think you bowled better than him in India but his record earns him first chance.'

There is not a lot you can say to that, so I told the new England captain that I respected him for coming to tell me in person but was naturally disappointed.

Sometimes you become a better player in everyone's eyes by not playing, and this was one of those occasions, because those who didn't play in that game, in which we were blitzed for 51 and lost by an innings, came to the fore during the calls for changes to the side.

Although I ended up as one of the lucky ones, it was far from a smooth transition back into the team because originally I still wasn't going to play in Antigua. Only when the second Test venue, the Sir Vivian Richards Stadium, proved more of a sandpit than a cricket ground did I get my chance.

We had played football on the outfield the day before and whenever you tried to stop, your feet dug six inches into the ground. It was a ludicrous surface and the match was only 10 balls old when umpires Daryl Harper and Tony Hill terminated it. As soon as the groundsmen started to dig up huge areas of the run-ups we knew the match wasn't going to start again, not at its original venue anyway, and word soon reached us that we would be starting a new Test match at the old Recreation Ground at St John's two days later. We'd netted there the previous day and did so again the following day, when I made what was to prove a telling mark on selection. I bowled really well at Strauss in the nets, and afterwards, when he'd finished batting, I noticed him wander straight over to talk to Andy Flower. Their conversation continued after they repositioned themselves at the back of the nets, and I could see them watching me bowl. My immediate impression was that they might be thinking about playing two spinners, but when I got back to the hotel that evening – well, I say hotel, it was more like a hovel – I had another visit from Strauss. This time the news was more positive. 'I want you to prepare as if you are playing tomorrow,' he told me. 'I am not saying that you definitely are playing, but please prepare as if that's the case, and don't go out and have a glass of wine with Sarah. Sorry.' It was Valentine's Night but Sarah understood.

Sure enough I played, as a direct replacement for Monty, and there was another alteration to the side that had been named 48 hours earlier, with Steve Harmison recalled in place of Ryan Sidebottom. Harmison is much more of a hit-the-deck bowler than Sidebottom and the presence of a football pitch marking that went straight across the square, and therefore straight across the pitch, influenced the selection. There were even fears that the game would not last the distance, because when we'd netted on an adjacent strip, a couple flew from that length and others had shot low.

Some of us joked that the match would be over in a day and a half, but we could not have been more wrong. Andrew Flintoff received the only ball in the game that misbehaved, and that contributed to him getting a pair on a real flat one. Everyone else just backed up the truck and scored run after run – it was an absolute road. Afterwards a lot of people annoyed me when they questioned why our bowlers weren't aiming for the halfway line. It was not that we didn't hit the right area; we did. Harmy hit it with about half a dozen deliveries in quick succession and we all scurried to have a look at the little dots it created, but none of them caused mischief.

For me it was a triumphant return to the side, because I took a maiden five-wicket Test haul in the first innings, and three in the second, and we came agonisingly close to winning. West Indies were nine down at the end, clinging on, when the sun finally went behind the pavilion Having my name up on the honours board, alongside some other notable feats at the ground, namely Brian Lara's two world-record scores, made it a great Test for me. As they no longer play Test cricket there, mine might well be one of the last names ever to go up.

Leading into the game I had felt in good form, and had done so stretching way back to that Test series in India. Yet my return of five for 57 came at a price. We dismissed West Indies for 285 but with plenty of time remaining in the contest, and with the heat and Andrew Flintoff's hip injury taken into consideration, we did not enforce the follow-on despite our 281-run lead. Everyone was quite buoyed by our performance, but the next day, the fourth of the match, I awoke suffering pain in my elbow. An intermittent problem, which had started in my first year with Nottinghamshire and surfaced every blue moon, had resurfaced. Basically my elbow just locked up at funny angles now and again, and on this occasion I couldn't straighten my arm at all. I couldn't get it past about 30 degrees when I went out to bowl before play, and that meant I could not produce my customary whirl with my arms in delivery.

'I've got a bit of bad news here, skip,' I said to Andrew Strauss, after my painful trial. 'I can't bowl.'

I explained that it was a recurrent problem and that seemed to cheer him up. 'Well, that's okay then,' he said. 'What do you normally do to fix it?'

'I have two weeks off,' I told him.

Obviously that was not an option, so over the next 36 hours I had constant treatment, took more codeine than is recommended for any mammal smaller than a rhinocerous, underwent a couple of cortisone injections and had to modify my action – instead of the usual whirl, I threw my arm out to the side and then bowled. It meant I could hardly put any spin on the ball in the second innings, but the cortisone's anti-inflammatory properties did their trick and the numbness somehow helped me through that game. But it was still a short-term solution and it seemed a cruel trade that I had been allowed to get five wickets and my elbow was now cooked. My instinct was that I needed an operation and was in all probability out of the series.

Even crueller was the fact the scoreline remained 1–0 to West Indies after their 10th-wicket pair negotiated the final 10 overs to secure a draw. Getting so close to victory on a surface that was as flat as a fart was a great effort. In fact, over a year-long period we were involved in a number of Test matches in which either ourselves or the opposition needed just one wicket to win. That's the beauty of the game, I guess. In Antigua, in addition to my problem, Fred didn't bowl as much as we would have liked him to on the final day because of his own niggle – he played no further part in the series – but we couldn't blame it on injuries, it just wasn't meant to be.

During the days of discussions with the medical people that followed, the piece of bone that was causing me grief dislodged itself. Although I desperately needed to get the problem fixed in the long term, I was able to play in the next Test in Barbados relatively pain-free. On the negative side, the pitches seemed to be getting better for batting every week, but I managed to claim another five-for, which although expensive was pretty decent in the context of the contest.

We piled up 600 before pulling out, and were trumped when West Indies replied with 749 for nine declared.

Unfortunately my elbow flared up again in the final Test in Trinidad at the beginning of March, a match that we so nearly won to square the series. During my bowling spells I was okay, but resting in between caused a problem, as the first few balls of the next spell would bring absolute agony. Tears were rolling down my cheeks at the end of my run-up at one point. I just couldn't believe how much it was hurting. I have pictures of me from the Queen's Park Oval in which, even when appealing, my left arm is ramrod straight but my right is bent. Luckily, however, even before this latest setback, during consultation with Andy Flower it had been deemed prudent to get the problem attended to as soon as possible, and that meant heading to America when the Test series finished.

After West Indies had achieved parity with our 546 for six declared, we showed our intent by scoring in excess of six runs per over and thus allowed ourselves two sessions to dismiss West Indies once more. This was the match when Jimmy Anderson really came into his own as leader of the attack. He reverse-swung the ball in a way that a lot of cricket luminaries didn't realise he could. As team-mates we knew he could, of course, but it was pleasing that he was able to show it in a match situation, and that was the point at which he established himself as the spearhead of our Test attack. Monty and I chipped in with wickets at the other end and we came agonisingly close to victory once more. But the series just wasn't meant to be for us and they finished on 114 for eight to secure the Wisden Trophy.

We had almost closed out two Test matches but couldn't quite manage it, so we ended up losing 1–0 having played much the better cricket. Considering the shambles that had preceded the tour and the fact that our loss could be pinned on getting blown away in one innings in Jamaica, it actually wasn't as bad as it seemed at the time. We also knew our opponents would not hold the trophy for very long as they were heading to England that summer and would be beaten 2–0. We knew that as soon as it swung and nipped around in our conditions they would struggle to handle it.

The majority of the rest of the squad were staying behind for the one-day series but, after a few post-Test drinks, I slept in the lobby of the hotel that night before catching a red-eye flight to the States next morning. Jimmy Anderson made sure I changed into my travel gear in the early hours and escorted me down to the lobby, where I kipped on the couch. For once, when Phil Neale came down to facilitate departure he must have been pleasantly surprised, although the forward planning was not my initiative and rather uncouth.

My elbow discomfort first began midway through the 2005 season, my first with Nottinghamshire, revealing itself when I went to bowl in practice and failed to get it down the other end. It just locked, something it was prone to do once every 12–18 months. Previously rest had proved a satisfactory remedy but while the initial problem was just one piece of floating bone, bowling over time had exacerbated things and more and more pieces had become dislodged. In the end, when I got the scans ahead of what really was career-saving surgery, the fragmented bone count was up to 29. Thankfully, the world-renowned elbow surgeon Shawn O'Driscoll managed to take out all but three – those that remained were too close to the nerve for extraction.

When I was packed off to the Mayo Clinic in Rochester, Minnesota, I quite naturally worried whether I would ever be the same bowler I had been before, and whether things would feel the same, but it had reached the point where the elbow needed fixing, so I had no option. I was to spend a week over there before the operation itself and the ECB's arrangements ensured I was made as comfortable as possible. One of the girls at Lord's even notified me via email that she'd checked the temperature out in Minnesota. 'Just to let you know, it's quite cold,' she wrote. 'It's only five degrees, so would you like a coat sending out to you?' Five degrees? That's not too bad, I thought, and as I had a couple of jumpers in my case declined the offer.

What I didn't realise was she meant five degrees Fahrenheit. Anyone who has ever seen Minnesota Vikings play will know the kind of cold I am on about – they always seem to play in snow – and what turned out to be minus 15 Celsius really did hit me hard as soon as I walked out of the airport doors. It was only five metres to a cab and I swear to God hypothermia had set in by the last metre. I had shrunk in places where you really don't want to shrink.

I spent the first few days there in a hotel because a week of meetings had been scheduled with Dr O'Driscoll before the operation, and he wanted a clear picture of what he was dealing with. The place where he is based is truly amazing. Mayo is more like a city but is considered a hospital. Everyone within the city limits seems to work in the medical industry, and all visitors tend to be ill insurance claimants on a trip to get fixed. All this meant I experienced some quite disconcerting sights during my evenings out at restaurants. For the first three I was out on my tod, and would head off for a steak or a burger, with a book tucked under my arm. Dotted around me would be tables full of families who had come to visit sickly relatives and there would always be some guy on a drip, wearing hospital pyjamas with his arse hanging out. It was the norm in this town for diners to look as if they might drown in their soup. I came to terms with this surreal situation pretty quickly, as I sat trying to concentrate on my Tom Clancy novel.

Later, Julie Pearce, one of the ECB's physios, came out to join me and kept me company at my hospital bedside the day before the operation. The fact she did meant she witnessed one of the most bizarre moments of my life. Dr O'Driscoll had previously, during small talk, mentioned that his pastor was from England, and was a huge cricket fan, therefore would I mind if he dropped by and said hello? Of course not, I told him, it would be nice to meet a fellow Brit.

'Are you religious, then?' said Julie, as we awaited his arrival.

'No, I'm not, but I felt it would be a bit rude to say no, and he likes his cricket apparently,' I replied.

Anyway, when this chap popped in he proved to be a lovely bloke and knowledgeable about the game; he used to play at school before he upped sticks to America. He was also passionate about his church. Having had a good chinwag, he was about to go when he made one final request.

'Would you mind terribly if I said a prayer for you?' he asked. 'In light of the operation you have coming up.'

'That'll be fine, thanks very much,' I told him, thinking he meant that he would go back to his congregation the next day and wish me good luck during a service. Oh, no. Instead, he put his hand on my forehead and, with his eyes closed, began in the most dramatic way possible: 'Dear Lord up there in the sky . . .'

I didn't know what the heck to do. My eyes made contact with Julie, who sat open-mouthed, a mixture of shock and happiness etched on her face. In my uncertainty, I plumped for this: you know when you are at school and it's time for the Lord's Prayer in assembly, so you put your hands together and make a kind of fist. His good wishes went on for about a minute, and I had to lie still and silent for fear of cracking up. Safe to say that within 30 seconds of him leaving the room we were in hysterics. Of course I was grateful for his visit – I may have ended up on a cold grey slab if he hadn't looked after me that day – but I wasn't prepared for the American-style send-off.

When I came round after the operation, I was away with the fairies for a couple of days, and my lucidness only returned 48 hours later. I wished I'd known in advance how I was going to be because I could have written a couple of concept albums on those Vicodin pills. Previously, whenever I saw Hollywood stars addicted to painkillers I was sceptical how anyone could become addicted to paracetamol, but when you actually take these things you understand they are major-league drugs.

Even after I landed back at Heathrow, as Dad drove me along the motorway, all the rear lights of the cars ahead were dancing and jumping up and down to the music. It didn't help that Pink Floyd were playing on the stereo, I must admit, but I was glad when it all wore off, because constipation is another side effect, and there was an unpleasant fortnight ahead.

My main concern was getting my right arm moving again, and this process began immediately – unlike broken arms, which are left to set, rehabilitation for this kind of surgery is necessary straight away, and I was forced to wear a machine on my arm which massaged the joint. Its frequent buzzing really got on my nerves – it annoyed Sarah, Max and Paddy too, so they emigrated to the spare room for the next fortnight – but the 24-hour treatment had the desired effect. Moving the arm back and forth caused considerable pain initially but the important thing was that it had me back bowling two weeks later, a phenomenal recovery speed, and I could straighten the joint again, something I hadn't been able to do with confidence, or completely pain-free, for the previous four years.

13

COUNTDOWN TO THE UNMENTIONABLE

As a sportsman, when you are faced with an operation, it is perhaps only natural that concerns begin to spin around your head regarding the after-effects. For me these were fairly straightforward. Number one, am I going to wake up from this? Two, am I going to be able to bowl again? Three, if I get to number two and the answer is no, what am I going to do with my life? Form a supergroup and tour Japan?

But the recuperation went so well that I was confident about stepping up a level and testing out the elbow in competitive action sooner rather than later, and even ahead of initial estimates. It certainly felt okay in the nets at the start of the 2009 domestic season and was deemed ready to be given its road test exactly a month after Dr O'Driscoll had fished out the offensive material from the elbow.

On my competitive return, a home one-day win over Leicestershire, I claimed three wickets and followed up with five more in the County Championship innings victory over Worcestershire that began two days later. For it all to go so well, and for me to be playing again within such a short space of time, was an absolute treat – the decision to miss the one-day series in the Caribbean had been vindicated and I was fit and raring to go at the start of my first English summer as a Test cricketer.

However, even my imagination, which is renowned for working overtime, could not have dreamed up the role I would play in the first Test against the West Indies at Lord's in early May. Their left-handed opening batsman Devon Smith had experienced a few problems against me earlier in the year and this was still fresh in the mind in the reciprocal series. I've always enjoyed bowling at left-handers anyway, but Smith's demises against me – he hacked at me in Antigua and I dismissed him in the first over of my spell in Trinidad – were latched on to by a number of people, and one with some clout, England captain Andrew Strauss. Perhaps the nature of the dismissals in the final three Tests of the winter – bowled or lbw – led some to exaggerate my success in our duel. The way they talked it was as if I had dismissed him every time I bowled to him. The assumption was I had him in my back pocket, but the reality was I did for him three times in six innings. Nevertheless, I recognised that he was not as comfortable against spin as he was against seamers.

Strauss spotted that susceptibility to the spinners too, and this led him to seek me out for a quiet word after I came off the field unbeaten on 63 at lunch on the second day, my maiden Test half-century. We were eight wickets down and he wanted me to be mentally prepared – because I would be taking the new ball.

'I want to open with you. It might not be for long but please bear that in mind,' he said.

As I ran back out through the Long Room to resume my innings, I did so with the biggest smile on my face you could imagine. The smile still lingered, in fact, when I trotted back to the pavilion three minutes later, having not faced another ball, after we lost two wickets in two balls to close the innings at 377 all out. But I sprinted off to get my bowling boots on, excited about what was to happen next. As it turned out, I only bowled two overs from the pavilion end, and not particularly good ones at that – I have never gripped a new ball that well – before being hoofed off.

Even though cut short, the experiment of me opening up garnered some criticism. Michael Atherton was particularly strong against it. Writing in *The Times*, he deemed it a joke that Jimmy Anderson didn't start off in the early-season English conditions. *Guardian* cricket correspondent Mike Selvey reckoned 'cricketers are always encouraged to think outside the box, or whatever the vogue management-speak is, but Andrew Strauss went so far beyond its borders that he required a different postcode'.

Yet this whole affair showed that Andrew Strauss and Andy Flower are strong enough characters not to give a toss what the press think. Sure, kowtowing to popular opinion in the media is something other captains and coaches have been guilty of from time to time but this pair have never have been on a PR mission. They probably anticipated adverse publicity for their decision but they had a reason for doing it, and frankly couldn't give a stuff that people were upset with it. Generally, if they reckon something might work, regardless of how ludicrous it might look to anyone else, regardless of the potential backlash, they will do it. That is one reason they are such good leaders.

Of course, for years to come I will be able to regale anyone within earshot of the time I opened the bowling for England on a Lord's green-top in early May, and finished as man of the match. To be honest, my first Test at cricket's traditional headquarters simply got better as it went on. Smith was still in when I was recalled into the attack for the 20th over, with West Indies 99 for two, but I got him with my first ball, bowled through the gate, and followed up by having Shivnarine Chanderpaul caught at slip by Paul Collingwood with my second. I finished up with three for spit in the innings, Graham Onions grabbed five wickets on debut and we rolled them for next to nothing.

Our spin-bowling coach, Mushtaq Ahmed, had put me into a really positive frame of mind heading into the game with a pep talk, not about my bowling but my batting, strangely enough. During our chat he told me that he hated it when I tried to bat properly, and that in India a couple of times the previous winter, he believed it actually contributed to me making low scores. He was right about my attitude certainly, because for some reason in spite of my natural instincts, I had put thoughts of being cavalier in Test cricket out of my head. But Mushy let me know in no uncertain terms that this was totally wrong.

'When I used to play against you for Sussex, you used to try to hit me for six every ball and that meant you were really tough to bowl at,' he said. 'If you get out, who cares? Go out there and play your shots, and see what happens.'

That endorsement was still ringing in my ears when I got to the crease, and at number nine I felt I had the freedom to express myself. Having resumed on the second morning on seven, I sensed their bowlers were a bit knackered and I decided to throw caution to the wind. I was pleased with the result and even happier with a double I completed with the ball after West Indies followed on. Having got Chanderpaul first ball in the first innings, I snared him once more, which was particularly satisfying because he had been proper difficult to shift out in the West Indies. He's a very good player and the mode of the dismissals – caught at slip and caught at bat-pad – was a nice little one-two for a spinner.

There were six wickets in all for me, and a slip catch in each innings to complement my earlier runs. To pick up the man-of-the-match cheque for this tally on my home Test debut proved a sweet career moment. Six months earlier I had not played a Test match and yet here I was at Lord's at the start of the season, with Mum and Dad watching on, and Alec half-cut in the Long Room in someone else's ill-fitting jacket, to witness it. 'Herr-lo Gwaeme, well boweled,' Alec said, from behind a lop-sided grin, as I wandered back into the pavilion. That, I thought, was a nice touch at the end of a week of contentment.

The innings victory at Chester-le-Street that wrapped up the anticipated 2–0 series success the following week was more typical of a spinner's lot at that time of year in England. The fast bowlers dominated in helpful conditions and my contribution to the 20 wickets was, well, a 20th share, Devon Smith lbw early in the second innings. Next, winning momentum was maintained in the NatWest Series when we overcame the malfunctioning of Headingley's new drainage system to win the final two one-day games in Bristol and Birmingham.

*

We seemed to be playing the West Indies permanently throughout the first half of 2009, so it was brilliant foresight to have them scheduled as warm-up opponents for the World Twenty20 as well. We won that match at Lord's with ease, having defeated Scotland similarly at Trent Bridge the previous day. But we had considerably more trouble with another of the minnows when the tournament opened on 5 June 2009. It was a night that the Netherlands players will never forget. Nor will I, but for a very different reason.

It felt strange to be left out of the opening match, having played against the Windies on the same ground, and especially since Twenty20 to my mind is a spinner's game. You are always involved in the action, you have a lot of fun, and tend to be a rich source of wickets. The reason for my omission, so I was told by the hierarchy, was that they wanted Adil Rashid to experience a big-match occasion in case he was needed later in the competition. It wasn't a case of 'you are bowling rubbish, so we are dropping you', but it was disappointing not to be playing nevertheless.

To recap, I hate watching cricket when I have been left out for a game, and I would much rather just go home, so there was no way I was going to be a good twelfth man that night. It's not that I have a bad attitude and ignore people, it is just that I am so easily distracted, and want to crack jokes with the other non-playing members of the squad, act the fool and generally be stupid. That doesn't go down well when you miss vital calls from the field. So one of the other lads ousted me from the edge of the pitch where the dug-outs were and dispatched me back upstairs to the dressing room.

It was quite a nervous place because the game wasn't going well, we had not scored anywhere near the runs we should have at 162 for five, and they mounted a good chase. When you are off the field like that it is quite an eye-opener to see how the management react when a game is going badly. I felt slightly awkward being there – a bit like a spare part – as the mood swung this way and that with every good or bad over. Right up until the last ball, when they consigned us to a shock defeat and began our problems against associate countries in global events.

Allegedly, our defeat was good for the game – that cliché is always chucked out there when results like that happen, and I hate it. Sure, it's good for them, don't get me wrong, and I am sure that those Dutch players had a good night smoking their cigars on the dressing room balcony at Lord's, beers in hand, but I've never bought into the theory that such surprises keep sport interesting. If Stoke City beat Manchester United, it's good for the Premier League, we are told. No, it's not; it's good for Stoke, for that week. But just as in our case, you can be sure that the better team lost at the end of the day. Fair play to those Netherlands lads, they excelled themselves, but England played poorly. These teams should be competing in the World Cups and World Twenty20s, don't get me wrong, they definitely deserve to be there – world tournaments should be global competitions, the clue is what it says on the tin – but if you are on the losing team, don't spend your time taking your hats off to that kind of opposition, spend it looking in the mirror and reinforcing the fact you shouldn't have lost. Where did it go wrong? That is the question you should be asking.

When you are not playing in the game you have absolutely no control over what happens and so even though you are still part of the squad, you are completely detached from events. A bloke is talking rubbish if he says he feels defeats like that as much as those who have been on the field. You don't. And I didn't. The guys who played the game really felt the loss, or in this instance a sense of humiliation, although the entire squad suffered the consequences. We win together and we lose together, and we knew in the aftermath we would be taken apart by some in the press and have the mickey taken out of us in general. But there was no mass despondency – certainly not for me, because my bag was packed, after all it hadn't been unpacked – and we were ready to move on. Yes, the result mucked us up at the start of the group, but the fact we had another game two days later gave us the opportunity to put it behind us.

We seem to make a habit of not starting world tournaments well, but we played some decent 20-over cricket in the week that followed. We enjoyed a comprehensive win over Pakistan at The Oval just two days later and, after a blip against the impressive South Africa, followed that with another victory over India at Lord's. Both ends of the spectrum were visited that June – humiliation at the hands of unfancied Holland and then victory over world-beaters India, the reigning champions. The thing was that we knew we had the capability to beat the best teams on our day but we lacked the conviction that we could do it either consistently or against certain opponents. Perhaps Pakistan's triumph in the final, after recovering from heavy defeat to us, showed that we didn't need to feel like underdogs in ICC tournaments any more.

We certainly stepped up on the big occasion against India at Lord's on 14 June when we needed to win, and in the face of a rather volatile atmosphere. Because we have such a large Indian population in this country, India are always really well supported when they play us over here. Even the British-born among them seem to stick to their heritage and fly the Indian flag when they play us, and during the warm-ups it was a bit of a shock to be booed by sections of the crowd as we lapped the outfield. In your home ground, apart from in Australia, where the Barmy Army completely drown out the Aussie supporters, I cannot think that the home team can be made to feel like the away side anywhere else in the world.

Consequently, emotions ran quite high in that game, and a lot of passion came out in our players in a direct response to our pre-match greeting. Some of the abuse towards us was from those with unmistakable British accents and Ryan Sidebottom, in particular, was really fired up. 'They're born and raised in London and they're f------ booing us, bastards,' he chuntered.

Two wickets for me in one over, those of Ravindra Jadeja and Yuvraj Singh, the latter brilliantly stumped by James Foster, were quite important in the grand scheme of things and helped check India's progress towards their 154-run target, but it was Siddy who bowled really well towards the end of that game and closed it out for us. The three-run win was all the sweeter because we had been annihilated in India in the one-day series a few months earlier. Even though it came in a different format of the game, this was a revenge of sorts and it eliminated the holders from the tournament.

The Netherlands debacle aside, we did well defending decent-sized totals throughout the World Twenty20, and I maintain that we would have won against West Indies to qualify for the semi-finals had the game been allowed to go the full distance. We were on a bit of a roll in the tournament, and had good recent history against them in all formats, so they weren't one of the sides we felt we would struggle with. We would have gone close to winning the whole thing, in my opinion, had it not hosed it down in that crucial game at The Oval. Our score of 161 for six was decent enough but after it rained they ended up with a reduced requirement of 80 off nine overs. With all 10 wickets in hand, they were always on the better side of that particular equation, and despite losing their fifth wicket still 35 runs shy, they knocked us out.

So, although there were some encouraging signs in that tournament, we hadn't at that point adopted the freedom of expression Paul Collingwood insisted upon when we headed for the Caribbean for the next World Twenty20 the following year. Enjoy yourself and be damned with the consequences was our mantra for that trip. If there was a positive option we were encouraged to go for it, in the knowledge that the rest of the team would back us up. In the 2009 event we did not yet have that carefree attitude, but not much time was spent looking back on our elimination because there were far bigger fish to fry.

You always know there are serious assignments ahead when you are booked on a team bonding mission. And so our pre-Ashes plans began in earnest when we set off from St Pancras station on the Eurostar to Lille. We were on a weekend trip to Flanders, where we visited the First World War battlefields, and held a ceremony to commemorate the lives of a number of prominent English cricketers taken there. The entire England Test squad, and all of the backroom staff, were accompanied by four active soldiers from the Ministry of Defence and a war historian. Stuart Broad was selected to lay a tribute – a stone cricket ball – at the memorial of one of them. Colin Blythe, a left-arm spinner, had in excess of 100 Test wickets when war halted his career.

It was a rewarding cultural experience, of that there was no question, but it also offered the squad a chance for a get-together away from the public glare back home ahead of what is by far the biggest challenge we face as an England team. Whenever you organise these things, the best bonding you can ever do, in my opinion, occurs when you have a meal together and your employers pick up the tab – particularly for the booze.

So, on the evening of Friday, 26 June, we went suited and booted to a lovely little restaurant in Ypres, where we had a decent feed and a few bottles of New Zealand Sauvignon Blanc. Afterwards all the boys ended up in a bar next door, and as there was an English army barracks down the road, there were a number of squaddies keen to partake in a drink or two with us. The stuff we were necking was absolute rocket fuel: two Belgian beers called Duvel and Bocker, the former being a tasty 8.5 per cent.

Before we knew it, it was 4.30 a.m. Everyone was completely obliterated as we began the stumble back to the hotel. And that was only the start of our problems. Shortly before the coach was due to depart for the trenches first thing next morning, I got a knock from Alastair Cook to warn me I was in danger of being late. I surveyed my room, which I'd somehow managed to turn upside down in my sleep, located my clothes and, without time to brush my teeth or have a wash, ran down the corridor, pulling on my T-shirt as I went. When I clambered on board, reeking of alcohol, there were still a few others missing. It was clear that there were plenty of losers in the sporting contests with our new friends David Duvel and Boris Bocker. Four or five guys ran to the bus with seconds to spare but Andrew Flintoff didn't make it.

When we got back from the trenches – it had been a very sobering day during which we got a feel for what went on in the Great War – I don't think I've ever felt physically worse in my life. Fred might have just been coming round himself for all I know, because as we passed down the corridor, he opened his door and, stark naked, with one eye open above his mischievous grin, asked: 'All right, lads? Have I missed owt?'

Fred was reprimanded for his no-show and in truth the management probably wanted to make an example of him as a senior player. One thing I loved about Fred was that when he did something he did it properly, there were no half-measures, but he was unfortunate in this instance because there were a handful of us who escaped being punished for punctuality by the skin of our teeth on that get-away. There could have been a few lads contemplating fines on the distinctly ropey train journey home.

There were some serious consequences of that trip for me, however. War is something I've always been fascinated with – it's less than a century ago that this all happened and the people involved were our ancestors of two or three generations ago. To witness these trenches was a shocking reminder of how lucky we are, and how ridiculously scant life was for them. Once in those burrows, there was little hope of coming out again. The ones that did survive were walking miracles. It was a scabby little network of what amounted to rat runs, and at some points you would have been within 50 yards of the enemy. A German could have thrown a hand grenade in easily, and that would be the end of you.

This sombre contemplation put things into perspective for me. Here we were on the brink of the 2009 Ashes, a series that was being billed as do-or-die. How ludicrous that seemed as we tried to digest what life must be like when things actually are do or die. What are five games of cricket compared to what those troops had to endure in the Battle of Ypres, or what our modern forces go through in Afghanistan? We moan about schedules and the fact we're knackered all the time, but we've got it so cushy compared to those fellas. I always try to remember that, and it's why I wear my Help For Heroes bracelet when I play. It's the least I can do. It is absolutely nothing in the grand scheme of things, but it is the reality check that ensures I enjoy what I'm doing.

And I enjoy nothing more than an Ashes series, and after the World Twenty20 was over, we were eventually allowed to talk about it. We had this team thing, you see: the usual 'one game at a time', 'focus on the series in hand', 'can't and won't worry about what is looming on the horizon'. Sure, that's all well and good, but deep down when I left the group environment and went to bed at night I wasn't envisaging a one-day international against West Indies at Edgbaston next Thursday. My mind was on July and walking out against the Aussies at Lord's.

Like most of the country, I simply couldn't wait, and the wait for me felt excruciatingly long. Ever since I'd been picked and done well the previous winter, this had consumed my thoughts. I had been desperate to play in the Ashes since I was a kid and this was like a revisit of my childhood. I had the kind of feeling in my stomach I get in the run-up to Christmas. You know, that excited feeling you are supposed to stop having when your age reaches double figures? Here I was at 30 with that same glorious agony. Annually, December felt like the longest month of my life, and here I was with a sense of déjà vu in the build-up to the series. You should never wish the time away, my grandma used to tell me, but I would have given anything for the first half of that year to have disappeared quicker than it did.

Personally, I loved it all, and our profiles undoubtedly went through the roof – it was my first experience of being mainstream news. Ahead of England v Australia you are on TV all the time: Sky Sports News counts down the days to the start of the first Test, and even mundane functions can find their way onto SSN's ticker bar. 'Graeme Swann went for a wee today at 7.03 a.m., Jimmy Anderson followed at 7.07 a.m., and we can confirm that Andrew Flintoff will be having a dump at five to eight,' claims the roving reporter at the team hotel. It is both surreal and brilliant to be part of.

14

A PLACE IN HISTORY

N OT IN a million years would I ever have imagined that I'd play for England in an Ashes Test in Wales, but there you are. The hype for the 2009 series had been building to a crescendo in the first few days of July, reminding us all exactly how big a deal it was to everyone across the British Isles. It meant as much to me too, being the first Northamptonshire-born cricketer to feature in an Ashes since C.T. Studd in 1883, but one good thing about starting out in Cardiff was the location of our team base that week. We stayed in the lovely St David's Hotel in Cardiff Bay, a tranquil spot with a nautical theme, and that allowed us to switch off briefly from the fervour that gripped the Swalec Stadium. We were quite high up there and when you looked out over the water it didn't even feel as if we were in the UK. You could lose yourself in the serenity of it all, although it failed to stop me bouncing off the walls every night.

From a long way out, a school of thought developed that we would play two spinners in a home Ashes Test for the first time since 1993. It did so because Sophia Gardens had developed a reputation for offering exaggerated turn – on the basis of just one county one-day game. A televised Friends Provident Trophy match between Glamorgan and Essex two months earlier had promoted the theory that the ball would fizz and spit off the surface. Leg-spinner Danish Kaneria cleaned Glamorgan up with four wickets and the 20 overs of spin sent down by Essex that day cost a miserly 43 runs. Yes, there was some prodigious turn on offer and the batsmen struggled to cope with it on that dry, limited-overs surface. But quite unbelievably, from that everybody deduced that the pitch for the Test match was going to absolutely rag square too, that Monty Panesar and I would bowl in tandem and everything would be over in a couple of days.

But I refused to be hoodwinked. Glamorgan had splashed out to get this prestigious maiden first Test on their new-look ground and needed it to last five days to recoup their money. So if the groundsman had prepared a Bombay pitch he'd have been hung, drawn and quartered. Therefore, while everyone was talking of this absolute Bunsen awaiting us, I was fully expecting a low, slow pitch, and that is exactly what was served up.

People had seen one spitting cobra of a surface and reacted in a knee-jerk fashion when they really ought to have used their grey matter. I'd played at Cardiff a lot over the years and although the wicket has changed over time, whenever it has turned, it has turned slowly and kept low, a combination which means it is far from impossible to bat on. In fact, it is one of the easiest places on the circuit if you are merely trying to stay in because of its lack of pace and bounce, and that turned out to be handy when we were asked to negotiate the final day to save the game. Had it been the dustbowl that everyone had anticipated, with all due respect to Jimmy and Monty, there is no way they could have batted on it for a dozen overs.

Before any of us got the chance to assess the conditions, however, there was the pre-match rigmarole to get through. Several anthems were belted out by Sean Ruane and Katherine Jenkins, and we then lined up on the outfield to be introduced to various dignitaries. Cue me completely miscasting one of them as he passed down our team.

'Hello, Graeme, good luck,' he said.

'Thanks, Mervyn,' I replied.

Seconds later, Jimmy Anderson nudged me. 'You bloody idiot, you've just called him Mervyn.'

'Well, that's his name, isn't it? Mervyn King, the governor of the Bank of England, we've met him before.'

'Is it b-------,' Jimmy said. 'It's Paul Russell, the chairman of Glamorgan.' To this day I'm still not sure who he is, but he didn't half look like the bloke in charge of this country's cash.

Jimmy is my regular travel partner for home Test match days and it was while driving him into the ground that week that we both vowed to sign up to Twitter. It had obviously been around for quite a while but we had only just become aware of it, so we decided, once we became au fait with how it worked, to have a Twitter war to see who could get the most followers by the end of the Ashes. It was a big thing to us, gave us a bit of a laugh and was soon picked up on by a number of newspapers. Although I have destroyed him on the follower stakes since, he pipped me over the summer and I had a forfeit to complete in September. I can't remember exactly what it was, it might have been to take his wife Daniella out – or is that what I wished it could have been?

I did not actually get onto the field for the first of that summer's 25 scheduled playing days, 8 July, and that suited me just fine. There had been a lot of talk about us wanting to get in the first punch at the start of the series, but that was all media spin. Ultimately, the first thing you aim for in a contest of that importance is not to have a stinker. My nervous energy was channelled into the outcome of the toss – I was desperate for us to bat first, because I always like bowling last in a game and it also meant I could sit around in my shorts, watching us bat all day. That appeals to my innate sense of laziness, so I was a happy bunny when Strauss won.

The opening day was one of jockeying for position and might have been better from an England perspective but for the dismissal of Kevin Pietersen in the evening session. It was his demise that everyone seemed to be talking about after we closed on 336 for seven. Because he had been dismissed sweeping, the media homed in on Kev rather than considering the other six wickets to fall. Perhaps people were looking for a scapegoat after we appeared to lose the initiative. Geoff Boycott, as anyone well versed in the game will know, is always ready to offer his own very blunt opinion, and he ranted about Kev being like a spoilt child, and someone who would play any shots he liked. It was arguably no surprise that the critics had a go, fuelled by the frustration of a slump to 241 for five when things had appeared so comfortable during a wicketless afternoon session. But as a team we didn't see it like that; it was just a wicket that had fallen. If it had been against Sri Lanka or South Africa it would have not got anywhere near the exposure, but because it's the Ashes you have to take the rough with the smooth.

We resumed on day two on 336 for seven but before play Andy Flower reminded Stuart Broad and me that we were both positive batsmen and that maintaining such an attitude could wrest back momentum following Australia's late wickets the previous evening. So when Broady fell 19 runs later, I walked to the crease intent on playing in my usual way. A couple hit the middle of the bat early on – I guided my sixth ball down to third man for four, and crashed the next one on the up through the covers, both off Mitchell Johnson – but it was one shot in particular, a chip over the leg side for three, that made me stop and think: 'Hang on a minute, what made me do that?' The thing is, I wasn't really thinking about what I was doing; I was playing completely on instinct. Undoubtedly, I get buoyed by the crowd in these situations and during that over they were on their feet, signalling fours with their hands. Soon afterwards Nathan Hauritz was brought on and twice I charged down the pitch to hit him for four and I made it three in a row with a reverse sweep that brought up the team 400.

I loved every minute of my first Ashes action, partly because it was alongside Jimmy, my best mate in the team. When you are batting you have two men standing on either shoulder. The man on the left shoulder tells you to do the sensible thing, and get your head down, and the guy on the right dares you to do the ridiculous. Unfortunately for me, and certainly for my statistics, the guy on the right has a hell of a lot more sway than the guy on the left. But he has also provided some fun. The best shot I played in that innings was a straight drive over Ben Hilfenhaus's head for a one-bounce four. By that stage I had determined that anything full was going aerial, and it was one of those innings where everything I tried came off. The partnership of 68 runs in nine overs only came to an end, in fact, when Jimmy got carried away and uncharacteristically walked down the track to attempt to smack Hauritz for a straight six. Nevertheless, we were buoyant when we took to the field with 435 on the board.

The mood didn't last long, however, as the match turned into a procession of Australians arriving at the crease, taking guard and scoring hundreds. Any momentum we thought we gained with our first-innings score had been countered and we painfully discovered that our total was probably 150 runs short. Any spring my unbeaten 47 had put into my step was flattened by the fact I bowled like an absolute idiot. A cut had emerged on my spinning hand in the nets a couple of days previously, and instead of covering the split with a plaster or just getting on with it, following consultation with the doctors I attempted a new method to protect it. It was decided that I would put superglue over my knuckle, which would create a resin shield over it and stop the wound opening up. It certainly did its job but the downside was that it restricted my feel for the ball. After sending down half a dozen balls in the nets it felt okay, but I still cannot believe I was experimenting with new stuff like that ahead of the biggest match I'd ever played. Why didn't I practise for three hours solid beforehand to make sure it felt comfortable rather than try it for a few minutes? What was I thinking?

It was not until the following day, after I'd bowled a dozen overs or so, that I ripped the thing off and decided it would be better to bleed everywhere. Obviously, it hurt a lot more but at least I could feel the ball and land it where I wanted. Not that I managed to halt the procession. People suggested it was ominous that Ricky Ponting was in such good touch, but quite a few of them were hitting it well, and that was more of a worry. Simon Katich and Marcus North both reached three figures and Brad Haddin's hundred was a brilliant effort.

Faced with a 239-run deficit, we made a bit of a hash of things at the start of our second innings, which meant that we had to occupy the crease for in excess of five hours of the final day with only five wickets intact. Naturally, our successful rearguard action from a position of 70 for five was viewed as an amazing achievement, but the way Paul Collingwood played proved how flat and slow the wicket was, and suggested we should never have found ourselves in that situation in the first place.

Everyone who batted between midday and the point at which I went in at 159 for seven had run down valuable minutes on the clock, and I urged myself to bat for a couple of hours. Unfortunately, however, when I walk out with a preconceived plan I am next to useless. There were 25 minutes remaining before tea and Australia seemed intent on bouncing me out. Trouble was I just didn't know what to do in response, and the result was that Peter Siddle pinned me three times in one over. With men positioned at short leg, deep backward square leg and fine leg, every time he dug it in I had nowhere to go. I couldn't duck under it as I normally would because the ball was not getting up high enough, nor hook, because of the obvious perils that entailed. So I ended up letting it hit me time and time again. Once on the arm, once on the head, once on the hand. I had no other alternative and thought: 'If that's sensible batting, thank God I'm not a batsman. It's rubbish.' If the pitch had been quick I would have had my head knocked off, but as it was the ball just hit me and fell straight to the floor.

When you are trying to save a Test match, and the biggest match you have ever played in, however, you really need to have a plan for this kind of thing and so at tea I sought answers from others. Fred came straight out with the solution. 'Swanny, I've played cricket with you for ten years and I've never seen you do this before. Why don't you just watch the ball and block it?' he asked.

Amid all my concern about offering catches, I had overlooked the point that the ball was not getting up. Once I had grasped the fact, it became a lot easier to get in behind it, and I batted for 73 minutes in total before I played an absolutely ridiculous shot to a back-of-a-length ball from Ben Hilfenhaus. I tried to pull, even though it wasn't short enough, and was lbw. Perhaps it was the man on my right shoulder again telling me it was all very well blocking but there was a 70 not out to be had.

My departure put more pressure on Collingwood, but when he was caught in the gully at 6.03 p.m. it caused a shockwave in our dressing room because it had looked as though he could bat for five days if he wanted to on that pitch. As a player with no backlift, it was custom-made for him, and so was the situation, given his great fighting qualities. But what happened next will go down in Ashes folklore. Not that I witnessed any of it first-hand. When I got into the changing room, I sat on my chair and took my pads off. From my position, I could not see the pitch – it was in the back room and there was a wall between me and the viewing area. On the television above me was the German Grand Prix. Now, I am not particularly a fan of Formula One – give me motorbikes any day, ta – but for some reason I started watching this race and, because I hadn't heard roars or groans behind me for 20 minutes, and because I am a superstitious sort, I vowed not to change my position while we were doing well. I felt that if I stopped watching it even for a second we would lose the match.

Obviously as the minutes ticked by I became more aware of what Jimmy and Monty were up to outside because word was getting back from the front of the dressing room. In fact, towards the end things got really tense. Our management worked out that we needed to bat until 6.40 p.m. to ensure that there was not enough time for Australia to bat again, and with us just a few runs in front, the 10th-wicket pair in the middle needed to be aware of this. So our twelfth man, Bilal Shafayat, was dispatched to take new gloves to Jimmy. It served the extra purpose of wasting a couple of minutes at a time when Australia were well on course to send down more than their obligatory 15 overs in the final hour. No one ever admits it, but that's the kind of thing you do in those situations.

Later, of course, we made it clear there was genuine confusion after Jimmy signalled to the balcony again shortly after Bilal's trip to the middle. In swigging a drink, he had got his new gloves wet – they were that drenched they're still drying out now – but his waving was mistaken for injury and so our stand-in physio Steve McCaig was dispatched to check him out. Ponting had already given Bilal a vehement serve, so was in no mood for the appearance of another of our backroom team.

'What the f--- are you doing on here, you fat c---?' he asked him.

He couldn't tell the truth, of course, but it was not that which upset Steve so much. Afterwards, in the midst of a vibrant dressing room, having pulled off this great escape, Steve sat there with an ashen look on his face, staring at the floor. Steve is an Australian, you see, and when asked what the matter was, he replied: 'One of my real sporting heroes has just abused me.'

I have never subscribed to the theory that getting out of jail like that feels like a win. It simply is what it is – a feeling of relief that you head to the next Test at 0–0 rather than 1–0 down. It is a tired old cliché to say that results like ours at Cardiff feel like wins. Whenever you watch *Match of the Day* you hear comments like 'that one point will feel like three'. Nonsense. To me, it felt as if we'd scrambled to a draw, and it was a great feeling, don't get me wrong; you feel far happier leaving the ground than the opposition do, despite the fact they have had the better of the game, and everyone knows that. Their dead-cert victory had been snatched away from them by us clinging on, but we were no better off than we had been on the morning of 8 July.

By this stage, concerns were also developing about the fitness of our two biggest-name players, Andrew Flintoff and Kevin Pietersen. But the first I knew of anything untoward with Fred was the night after Cardiff's conclusion, following a benefit dinner for Andrew Strauss at Lord's. When I got back to the team hotel, one of the journalists, Dean Wilson from the *Daily Mirror*, phoned me to inquire what I knew about Fred's intention to retire from Test cricket at the end of the summer. I knew nothing, to be perfectly honest, and told him so, but I also texted Fred to warn him that I had been asked. I got a thank-you in reply and then found out the story was true at 9 a.m. the next morning when Fred confirmed to the team that the splash on the back of the *Sun* was indeed correct. This series was to be his last hurrah.

It is always a shame when someone announces their retirement, primarily for them, but with Fred I felt the shame went beyond that because he'd been such a bloody good player. However, as a team-mate you certainly don't want to play with a tear in your eye, and so we had to concentrate on our own personal and collective perform-ance. No doubt Fred wanted it to be his Ashes, and wanted to be remembered for winning the Ashes for a second time almost single-handedly. His intention was to go out with a bang, so for him it was great that the Lord's Test that followed his announcement that Tuesday will always be remembered for the epic part he played in it. It was the best I've ever seen him bowl for England, to be fair, and also the fastest. He was just awesome. In one way it was unfortunate that it wasn't the very end for him because it would have been a great way to bow out, and if he had known how his knee was going to be after that effort, and how the rest of the series would pan out for him, he might have walked right there and then.

His career had not come to a premature end in terms of age, it was probably the right time for him to go give or take a year, but the number of Test matches he managed to play was scandalously low for a guy as talented as he was. It was such a shame that his body could never keep up with the schedules and I suppose it was no surprise given the rigours he put it through. Other all-rounders have tended to ease back on their bowling – Jacques Kallis being an obvious example – but that would just not have been Fred. He gives his all with the ball, and no human body could have coped with that kind of intensity after so many operations. As it was, after seeing a knee specialist in the build-up to the second of these back-to-back matches, with Steve Harmison put on standby, he passed a fitness test on the morning of the game to feature at the great ground one final time.

From an England perspective, the greatness of Lord's has proved an habitual problem, and in our team discussions that week we tried to put our finger on why we had such a bad record there over the generations. It wasn't rocket science to work out that other teams came over and rose to the occasion. From the second you arrive to the second you leave, the place enthrals you, and opposition players became inspired by it. In contrast, my feeling was that if you'd played a lot of county cricket, it was easy to become blasé about it. To my mind, we needed to appreciate that this really was something out of the ordinary, something magical for us too. I offered up my observation as we sat chatting on the grass a couple of days out from the match.

'Look around you,' I told them. 'Soak all this up. This isn't Headingley or Derby or Leicester on a cold Tuesday in April; this is Lord's, the best ground in the world. We are playing against Australia, and this is as good as it gets, so let's love every single minute of this week. The architecture, the paintings in the Long Room, the whole history of the game is here.'

Deep down I love the traditions of cricket, and I wanted us to feed off that and feel part of history on the eve of us adding our own chapter. You can smell the heritage of the established Test grounds and I love wandering around and seeing pictures of cricketers in their proper woollen jumpers – I cannot stand the fact we have these appalling newfangled body-fit things that fail to keep you warm and are simply designed to get sponsors' names and players' numbers on the back. If anyone can prove they have been scientifically designed for higher-performance sport, I will eat my hat.

Of course, we were only too well aware that Australia had not been beaten in a Test at Lord's for 75 years, but I wanted to get across that we should enjoy what was ahead of us. If my speech had any effect on our team then I am glad. I am not saying it was all down to me that we overturned that hoodoo, but I would probably settle for 95 per cent.

On the night of Strauss's benefit do I bumped into Stephen Fry in the Lord's museum. He is one of my heroes of comedy – Fry not Strauss, that is – and to stand there talking to Lord Meltchett about *Blackadder* whilst looking at the original Ashes urn through the security glass made it a special start to that special week. I get totally star-struck at times like that, and the fact that someone I'd seen so often on TV actually knew who I was and talked back about his passion for cricket made it a surreal experience. I found him to be a bloody nice bloke and he told me that the whole country was behind us, 'my dear boy'. 'I don't want to put any pressure on you, but everyone wants you to win these Ashes back, and my entire well-being and happiness depends on it.' It was a lovely moment. In his role as the after-dinner speaker an hour or two later, he stood up and, rather than recite anecdotes from his life, read out an essay he'd composed about what cricket meant to him. Although the only line I can recall was about the 'sound of leather smashing against Graeme Swann's body', he held the audience spellbound with his prose.

Given the events at the end of Cardiff, we knew that the best thing for us in the next game would be to bat first, because as an opposition bowler the last thing you want to do is bowl first again after you've endured a day of disappointment like that. We got our wish after another wrong call by Ricky Ponting. His bowlers, and Mitchell Johnson in particular, really struggled on the first morning. I don't think any of them had bowled on the Lord's slope before, and it takes some getting used to. They found it challenging to put the ball in the right place, and Strauss and Alastair Cook smashed it everywhere to help us dominate from the start.

Australia failed to separate them before lunch – although wicket-keeper Brad Haddin dropped Strauss – and the effects of this were twofold. Firstly, it is always a psychological bonus to go in no wickets down, and secondly, at Lord's, it meant the rest of us could absolutely trough in the food hall. The food really is amazing, as all cricket aficionados know, and on a day like that you just don't want to leave. The bowlers don't get to have their puddings unless the batters are doing their jobs, so the chance to indulge in some chocolate lumpy-bumpy was just wonderful.

Cook eventually fell for 95, and a number of other wickets went down in the final two sessions. In fact, when Strauss, unbeaten on 161, shouldered arms to the first ball of the second day, we were 364 for seven, and struggling to match our score in Cardiff. Although we'd started off well, we had to settle for 425, which was 10 runs fewer. It was bizarre in one way because it felt as if we had dominated more here, but thankfully our total was put into perspective when we bowled them out for 215. Jimmy got a couple early on thanks to his ability to swing the new ball, including the prize wicket of Ponting, to leave Australia 10 for two.

Not that Ponting was too keen to exit. He was given out caught at slip, after consultation between umpires Rudi Koertzen and Billy Doctrove about whether the ball had carried, but he argued that he hadn't hit it. However, Ponting's dismissal was one of those when, if he hadn't hit it, he was out lbw anyway. Tough, that. In any case, if you're a batsman who never walks – and openly admits to never walking – you can't complain if you get a bad decision every now and then. If you don't walk when you've hit the ball and survive as a result, then you have no right to complain when you get a harsh decision. You should just walk off. To me, not walking is tantamount to cheating – if others see it differently, it's their prerogative – so you have no right to curse the world when things then go against you. Ricky Ponting is by no means the only one who does this, of course, but it is my pet hate. If you are not a walker, fine, but clear off when you get a bad one.

The seamers did a fine job on that second day and Australia closed on 156 for eight. Next morning, while standing at slip, I was into Strauss's ear about whether we would enforce the follow-on. The lazy side of me wanted him to resist the temptation – after all, it would mean another Lord's pudding – but from a business point of view, as a spinner bowling last was what I really wanted. Any spinner would be lying if he told you he prefers bowling when it's not doing anything, and on the final couple of days the surface would be at its most receptive.

After Strauss declined to enforce it, we developed our lead on that Saturday afternoon, but it came at a cost as Kevin Pietersen's Achilles injury – which had passed a pre-match assessment – was clearly getting worse, and he limped through his partnership with Ravi Bopara. It became fairly obvious at that point that he would not take any further part in the series, and I considered this would be a massive loss for the team because the Aussies feared Kev, or always seemed to give off that impression whenever he batted. Undoubtedly, it was because of what he had done to them in the past. People talk about the Flintoff factor, and there is no denying it came out at its strongest against the Australians, but at the time I thought losing Kev would hit us harder. By the end of the game he could hardly walk, and we knew that was that.

Australia were eventually set a world-record 522 runs to win and we set about dismantling them for a second time. To be fair, however, the Aussies had reason to feel aggrieved at three of the first four wickets we took at the start of their innings. Phillip Hughes was claimed low down at slip by Andrew Strauss, and there was a dispute as to whether the ball had carried. I was next to him and stand by my belief that he caught it despite TV replays casting doubt. Simon Katich had already been dismissed, caught in the gully, but the eagle-eyed would have noticed Fred had overstepped and he should have been reprieved by a call for no-ball. Yet, the worst of the trio, in my opinion, was off my bowling, and provided me with a belated first wicket in the series. I assumed that Mike Hussey had got a regulation nick to slip, we all did, and it wasn't until we got off the field that night and somebody quizzed me about it that I discovered the truth. When I was told he had got nowhere near it I was completely bemused. I thought he'd smashed it. But looking at the replay, quite incredibly, the ball landed in the foot-holes, spun past the edge and went straight into Paul Collingwood's hands.

Following Cardiff, we knew there was only one weak link in their top seven and that was Hughes. The fast bowlers got together with our bowling coach, Ottis Gibson, before the series and came up with a plan to expose his fallibility by bowling short and in at his armpit. The idea was to really cramp him, and it unsettled him a treat. We knew it was important to get the others early, otherwise they would score big. Marcus North had proved this with his effort the previous week, but even though I bowled like a chop in Cardiff I had seen something in his game that made him vulnerable. Because he had a big, high backlift I suspected he would be susceptible to the ball that went straight on from around the wicket. So it proved here. The ball I bowl that goes straight on, called the square spinner – I rip over the top of the ball and it might as easily be called an under-spinner – goes on a bit like a flying saucer. With its natural slope, Lord's is a good place to bowl it to left-handers, when operating from the Nursery End, and having estimated he would be a candidate for bowled and lbw, I was delighted to be proved right by a delivery that clipped the pad and cleaned him up. As Hannibal from *The A-Team* was so fond of saying: 'I love it when a plan comes together.'

That left Australia at 128 for five, but we knew it was still a very good wicket, and so did Michael Clarke and Brad Haddin, whose batting on that penultimate evening was exquisite. I was feeling really good about my bowling, getting some decent drift, but Clarke used his feet so well that every time I tried to take the pace off the ball he was at the pitch of it and piercing the off-side field. They ran us ragged that evening and the fact they reached the close requiring a not-impossible 209 runs made us feel the heat a little.

Driving away from the ground that night, I considered the game to be a lot closer than others might have thought.

'What do you reckon?' I said, turning to Jimmy in the passenger seat. 'Are we going to do this?'

'I hope so, mate,' he said, with a smile on his face.

We looked at each other and laughed but didn't talk about it after that for fear it might curse us.

The atmosphere was terrific throughout the entire five days of the match but the noise on the final morning as we made our way through the Long Room on our quest to take five more Australian wickets really was something else. When there are two to three hundred members in there, you feel the buzz reverberate as you pass through. They make a nice corridor for you and you get an enthusiastic round of applause. But this morning was like no other. The whole country seemed to anticipate an England victory despite the game seeming rather more in the balance on paper, and when we'd arrived it was a nervous team that entered the dressing room. Yes, Australia had to break a world record to overcome us, but it looked as if they might just do it. If we needed settling down, Andrew Flintoff found the perfect remedy. As we strode down the stairs, Freddie turned round to the rest of us and said: 'Watch this.' A dozen paces later, he stopped as he entered the Long Room and, waving his arms in the air, at the top of his voice he shouted: 'Come on, lads!' In an instant he whipped those toffs into a frenzy. None of us had ever heard them roar so loud, and it was just hilarious. The old men were screaming and shaking their fists in the air, giddy with excitement, as we walked through laughing our heads off.

Beforehand we had been nervous, no doubt, and I viewed it as a manifestation of my own nerves when I incurred a pre-play injury – a massive egg on my forehead. It occurred in slip-catching practice when I got hit flush by a ball which I went to take and throw back in one action. Trouble was I tried to throw it back before I had actually caught it – I moved my hands at the wrong time and it just hit me. But Fred's actions, both shortly before and shortly after 11 a.m., settled us all down. The giggles had barely subsided when Haddin was caught at slip in his opening over.

Not long afterwards, having wondered if Clarke would ever make a mistake when advancing down the track, he provided me with an emphatic answer when he left his crease in an attempt to hit through the off side and simply missed a full toss. He was probably trying to hit a bit too square and the ball landed in the foot-holes, turned and bowled him. It was a wonderful feeling. That was almost the moment that told us we had won. From then on there was an inevitability about the outcome. We had a brand-new ball, Fred was bowling at the speed of light from the Pavilion End – and you wouldn't have backed any tail-ender in the world to survive.

Mitchell Johnson played really well for his 63, but Nathan Hauritz and Peter Siddle were simply blown away by searing deliveries that nipped back down the hill. I knew Fred had a ropey knee, but that morning it was not apparent to me how much pain he was in because he was bowling so fast. It was a Herculean effort and he emphasised that with un-Fred-like celebrations. When he got down on one knee in his messiah pose in response to Siddle's stumps being splattered – a celebration I am still not convinced about – it emphasised his willingness to milk the moment. He knew there wouldn't be many more moments like that and he had done it all on one leg, so it was a special effort.

When Johnson missed a heave to leg 18 minutes before lunch, it gave me the honour of claiming the match-sealing wicket, and left me in the knowledge that I'd bowled much better than in the first Test in Cardiff. It was a sweet win, terminating Australia's three-quarter-of-a-century impregnability at Lord's, but there were no lavish celebrations from me. A few of the younger, trendier lads like Kevin Pietersen and Stuart Broad headed into London to make sure they were photographed in the right nightclubs by the right celebrity magazine or newspaper, but my belief has always been that when you win as a team you should stay with the team and have a few drinks. First and foremost I like to share victory nights with the special little group that has achieved something. So I just got drunk in the Landmark Hotel bar. Also, because I am inherently lazy I don't tend to pack any special going-out gear, and unless they'd let me into a nightclub with flip-flops and shorts, I would have been struggling.

At the end of July, wet weather in Birmingham cut the length of the third Test in half, with only 30 overs possible on the opening day. Andrew Strauss was in the thick of the action, however, even before the toss at Edgbaston, with his suggestion in the pre-match press conference that Australia had lost their aura. It was a comment that stirred up the visiting press something chronic, but it was pretty much right on the mark. From my point of view, I had not played against an Australian team before so I hadn't gone into the series thinking they had an aura in the first place. Then again, I never think like that about any team I face. And those, like Strauss, who had been whitewashed in 2006–07 recognised that this was not the team that had inflicted those five heavy defeats. Take out names like Shane Warne, Adam Gilchrist, Matthew Hayden, Justin Langer and Glenn McGrath and you're never going to be the same. That's just the way it goes, isn't it? It was hardly controversial to suggest that this Australian team was not as good as their predecessors – and that is what Strauss meant. But reminding our contemporaries of the fact made for very interesting mind games, I guess. It was a bit like someone slagging off your mum. It shouldn't really matter what anyone else says, but it clearly got their goat.

Although it poured down for the majority of the first three days, Jimmy Anderson bowled like a dream in the first innings and we rolled Australia for 263. In contrast, however, I didn't perform at all well with the ball, apart from a brief spell on the fourth evening when I got Ponting out with the best ball that has ever been bowled in Test cricket – or at least the best ball that had been bowled in Test cricket in the previous 10 years, as I modestly, if somewhat flippantly, claimed at the time. Technically, with Australia still in arrears on that fourth evening, it briefly opened the possibility we could still force victory.

It was nearing the close of play when he came out to bat, and I gave him a bit of a working over. He later, rather favourably, compared it to the great over Andrew Flintoff bowled to him on the same ground in the previous home Ashes. Although I would stop well shy of that, I did have him lunging forward and shuffling around with bat and pad together during those six balls. I had what I believed to be a stone-dead lbw appeal turned down but, undeterred, two balls later I went wider on the crease, ripped it and it just came out perfectly. The ball drifted, dipped and then turned square to bowl him through the gate. For an off-spinner that is the dream dismissal. I won't pretend that it didn't surprise me when it happened on the biggest stage against such a good player, but I was more than happy it did.

Because of this particular over, however, the expectation was, from the media at least, that I would take six wickets and win the game for England on the fifth day. But I wouldn't have got six wickets if I was playing against the Bromsgrove Under-11 team. Up until then I had taken a few wickets in Test cricket but I certainly hadn't taken match-winning hauls. Sure, I got the wickets at Lord's on the final morning, but I had not single-handedly rolled through a team. Yet once that Ponting ball turned square, the pressure was on, and I bowled like a novice.

In truth, it would have been a struggle even if I had bowled well, because essentially it was a third-day, fairly flat pitch and Michael Clarke, their best player of spin, went on to get a hundred. No sooner had I sent Ponting packing than I backed it up with my worst over of bowling in any cricket I could remember. The lucky recipient was Mike Hussey, who cashed in when I dragged one down and followed up by dispatching two more fours from full tosses that slipped out of my hand. There cannot have been a shorter penthouse-to-outhouse journey for an international spinner, and when we walked off that evening I told Huss, who is a big mate of mine, that he owed me big time. Up until then he'd barely made a run in the series but now I'd helped him get his eye in and he would keep his place in the team with that innings. Nor was he shy in confirming that it was the worst bowling he had ever faced. Truth is, despite it being only a fortnight after Lord's, I did not feel in rhythm.

My friendship with Hussey dates back to our time as team-mates at Northamptonshire but we naturally retain our competitive instinct on the field. A lot has been made in recent series of the conduct of the England and Australia teams towards each other and there have even been accusations that we have been too matey. One incident in

Birmingham, however, was seized upon as pure, unadulterated sledging. Sorry to disappoint, but the words exchanged between Mitchell Johnson and me at Edgbaston were not. The incident came on the fourth day during a period in which Stuart Broad and I swung merrily with the bat. Now, the Edgbaston crowd are notoriously loud, and those in the Eric Hollies Stand were getting right into it, loving every minute. At this point Johnson started chirping Broady, but because of the atmosphere he couldn't hear what he was saying. Then Johnson said something to me, so I walked up to him and said: 'You what? I can't hear you, it's too noisy.' For those watching on TV it looked as if I was squaring up to him, but all I advised him during our brief exchange was that there was no point in putting a deep square out and then bowling bouncers because I was not allowed to hook if he did that. 'But,' I added, 'if you bring him in, I promise I'll keep flapping at it for you.' It probably looked as if I was giving him a right old serve, and a couple of the papers the next day were all over it, suggesting I had sent him packing, but I had done no such thing.

One game up with two to play, we headed to Leeds with a growing sense of anticipation that we would regain the precious urn. In fact, there was an excitable element of the media pointing out that victory would seal it with a game to go. A number of us in the team started believing our own press, unfortunately, and amidst the mutterings of 'yeah, we can win this' we completely took our eye off the fact that we were playing opponents who we'd beaten only once, opponents who should have trounced us at Cardiff and easily hung on for the draw at Edgbaston. And as it turned out, they absolutely pulled our pants down at Headingley.

It was complete chaos from first to last. At 4.30 a.m. on the eve of the game, we found ourselves semi-naked in the street, outside the Radisson hotel in central Leeds, following a fire alarm. One of the other guests had left a pair of wet smalls on a lamp – I didn't think that actually happened outside of cartoons – an act that set off the smoke alarm. In my dazed state, for a moment I thought it was something to do with terrorists because, instead of a blaring siren, the alarm was a menacing voice which repeatedly said: 'There has been an incident, please make your way to the nearest exit.' As a result we spent an hour in the cold and wet, with all the drunks and vagabonds of the city staggering past, when we should have been tucked up in our beds.

Then, when we turned up at the ground we discovered that Andrew Flintoff was not playing – there was his bag in its normal space in the changing room, but it was all packed up neat when you would usually expect a mountain of messy kit. The decision had been taken by the management the night before that his body could not get through the strain of back-to-back Tests, but the rest of us didn't know until that morning. And to cap it all, shortly after Andy Flower sat down to explain the situation to us, and that Steve Harmison had been called into the team instead, Matt Prior suffered a back spasm at the start of our football warm-up. He went down like a sack of spuds, as if a sniper in the crowd had got him. In the space of 24 hours the mood had swung from overwhelmingly positive to an acknowledgement that all the wheels were falling off.

We won the toss and batted first once more. Strauss was plumb lbw first ball to Ben Hilfenhaus but was somehow reprieved with a not-out from Billy Bowden. But there was no need for the Australians to rue that for long. They kept the ball full and we collapsed at the start of what was a pretty abysmal two and a half days for the England team. I was among those in and out before lunch, and we were dismissed for 102 not long into the afternoon session. In contrast, Australia then came out and smashed it everywhere. Ironically, I felt I bowled really well. The ball came out of my hand beautifully, although my figures of nought for 64 weren't very impressive. However, those for Stuart Broad – six for 91 – came at a time when some knowledgeable so-and-sos were calling for him to be dropped.

Broad is a great lad, someone I get on really well with, to the extent that we acted like two kids in the playground on the third morning, with the game gone. After Australia claimed a 343-run lead on first innings and scythed through our top order once more, Broady and I had some real fun with the bat. Despite it being a completely lost cause, we were encouraged by Andy Flower to fight that morning, and duly smashed it everywhere. The directive suited us down to the ground. Since Broad has been at Nottinghamshire we have always had this thing about the proper Notts way to bat. Go hard or go home is the motto. We adopted it for what turned out to be one hour of hilarious batting.

From the moment we came together at 120 for seven, we acted like 10-year-olds, and completely egged each other on. We shared 108 runs in a mere 12.3 overs. It was, we were later told, the second-fastest three-figure stand in the history of Test cricket behind New Zealand's Nathan Astle and Chris Cairns, in similarly futile circumstances against England in 2001–02. Although that is a nice statistic, it is the fun we had that I more readily recall. If we were going down, we were going down swinging, and it turned into something of a hitting competition. After Broady hit Stuart Clark for four fours, he wandered down the pitch and cockily asked me: 'Did I just get 16 in one over? How many have you managed?'

Sure enough, I took up the challenge in Clark's next over. 'Did I just match you? Did I just get 16 off that over? Were my shots better than yours? Can you do 20?'

It was proper schoolboy stuff. At one point we agreed that for three overs neither of us was allowed to block a single ball; we made a pact to swing at everything and see what happened. The crowd were going ballistic and the only shame about it was that, like all good things, it had to come to an end. It did so when Broady holed out in the deep, but even then, having brought up my fifty with a top-edged, hooked six off Peter Siddle, I was gutted to be given out caught behind off Mitchell Johnson because, one, I'd started to think about getting a hundred, and, two, I swear I didn't hit it. I flashed at a wide one, hit the ground and Billy Bowden reacted to the noise.

*

After that overwhelming defeat, Andy Flower called a big meeting to discuss where it all went wrong and how we were going to rectify it. This is not something we normally do until after the dust has settled on matches but in the circumstances it was felt necessary, and it was not as if we had anything else planned! For two hours that afternoon, as Australia celebrated levelling the series via an innings victory, Andy and Andrew Strauss regained control of the situation. Rather than rake through the defeat itself, they focused on the issues in the build-up. Fred had stormed off before the game unhappy at not being picked and we began in chaos, after the toss had been delayed to check on Matt Prior's fitness, so they wanted to put what had happened into perspective. Without doing so, there would have been a danger of things spiralling out of control. They reinforced the fact that in some ways we were in exactly the same situation: if we won the following week at The Oval, we'd win the Ashes.

In addition to providing clarity on the state of the series, this session was designed to establish how we were going to work on our games, and what would best help us prepare for the following week. Initially during those talks I felt that an urge to play a Championship game for Notts might just be a knee-jerk reaction to impress the coach. If I played I wanted it to be for the right reasons, so I said that I was knackered and wanted a week off. The alternative was for me to play nine days consecutively. But on the drive back to Nottingham that evening, Sarah asked me whether I was sure about sitting out. On second thoughts, I felt that getting some bowling under my belt wouldn't do me any harm, so I called Andy to ask if he minded if I did play after all. He then rang Mick Newell to tell him I was available, while we stopped off for a takeaway curry as we arrived in Nottingham.

The after-effects of the rogue rogan josh I purchased nearly terminated my Test summer there and then. The next morning, when I was supposed to be preparing for a Championship match against Warwickshire at Trent Bridge, I had to phone the England doctor, Nick Peirce, to tell him I couldn't get out of bed. It is the worst I have ever felt in my life – I spent the next few days in the bathroom, and even endured the inglorious procedure of providing stool samples for my doctor.

With only days until preparation for the fifth Test was due to begin, I was in a right state. But what my spell of solitary confinement did do was prevent me thinking about cricket, beyond the consideration of whether I would be fit or strong enough to emerge from my pit. Rather than worry about how I was going to get some wickets at The Oval, I lay there being fed soup I could barely keep down. Even when I recovered sufficiently to get to London, I remember bowling in training the day before the game, sending down about 20 balls and then almost collapsing in the changing room from exhaustion. Obviously, I hid this from people because I didn't want to give anyone an excuse to leave me out.

That net session on the square at The Oval, just a few strips down from the Test pitch, began with me bowling to Andrew Strauss. My first delivery spun about a foot past his edge, and with smiles etched on both our faces we simultaneously looked across at the match pitch. In terms of appearance it was exactly the same, and from my perspective this was perfect because it suggested it would not be the absolute road that The Oval can sometimes provide.

What the Australians did during their practice heaven knows, but how and why they didn't play a spinner in that fifth and final Test I'll never understand. My first theory was that they couldn't have had anyone bowling spin in the nets because if they had they would have seen the same thing as us: the ball was blatantly going to turn. Perhaps they thought that it was different from the Test wicket, or that having won so convincingly at Headingley with their battery of seamers, it was prudent to preserve a winning team. Whatever their conclusion, they got it wrong, and it was the greatest decision for English cricket possible when they elected to omit Nathan Hauritz for that game.

Yet the way we batted in the first innings made Hauritz's exclusion appear rather irrelevant. Having won the toss for a fourth time in the series, we allowed a position of 114 for one to deteriorate to 307 for eight when I nicked off to signal the close of play on day one. Broad was still in, though, and it was hoped if he teed off once more we could get somewhere near 400. In the event, however, while various commentators were applying the old adage about waiting to see how Australia batted before judging whether it was a good score or not, we were genuinely disappointed to be finished off for 332.

Australia had meandered to 73 without loss in reply when from nowhere Broad bowled like an absolute legend. Almost with a click of his fingers – or rather a rap of Shane Watson's pads – he eased into one of those spells when you know something is going to happen every ball. Even though few balls had misbehaved previously, the crowd roared him in and suddenly the pitch resembled a minefield. Ponting chopped on, Hussey was leg before to one that shaped back in and Clarke jabbed to short cover. It truly was a phenomenal spell – his four wickets for eight runs in 21 balls opened up the contest and ultimately allowed us to take a grip on it. I weighed in with four of the cheaper wickets of my career – two of which I am now willing to wrap up and send back to Australia, because having had several chances to view the replays I don't deserve them.

Once again, I hoped to exploit Marcus North's high backlift from around the wicket, but the ball that did for him was one of those optical illusions thrown up to bowlers from time to time. When my arm ball was halfway down the wicket, I thought 'this is going to be LB'. So when it struck pad, or at least when I thought it struck pad, I immediately turned around to appeal. Everyone around the bat went crazy, in fact, in anticipation of it being given. But North, a lovely bloke who I'd played against since we were kids, had a rueful smile on his face as he walked off shaking his head. 'What's he doing?' I wondered. To me, he was absolutely stone-dead lbw, so imagine my surprise when I saw the replays at tea and it revealed the thickest of clunks off his bat. Then Stuart Clark, who had slogged me around Headingley, was caught at short leg for what appeared to be a regulation bat-pad. To be fair, he only missed it by about a foot and a half. Before the Umpire Decision Review System these were the decisions that went your way now and again, and there is no doubt quite a few went our way that summer.

Although fortune favoured us on both those occasions, with the way Broad weaved his magic, there was a certain inevitability that we would bowl them out cheaply that afternoon. He deserved his fifth victim – Brad Haddin's off stump extracted – and that spell bowling in tandem with him was as enjoyable as our batting alliance had been at Headingley. I finished with four for 38.

It preceded what to my mind was the most fraught period for us in the entire Ashes series. When we had clung on at Cardiff six weeks earlier, it was completed against the odds, whereas here the tables had turned and there was an expectation on us to drive home the advantage when we batted a second time. With a 172-run lead there should have been no pressure, but that can trigger its own problems. And when we were reduced to 39 for three with more than three days to go, negative thoughts inevitably crept in. 'Hey, what if we only get 260 ahead here?' Stuff like that.

But it was at this point that Jonathan Trott came to the fore. It was quite a time for him to make his Test debut, and he had quietly compiled 41 in the first innings. Not many of us had played that much against him previously so we were unsure how he batted, and indeed how good he was. He had given us a glimpse of his ability on the first day, but we were soon to discover the idiosyncratic way he likes to construct innings. Quite simply, he disappears into a bubble; it is as if he is in another dimension as he scrapes away at the crease with his boot. He seems completely unaffected by what is going on around him. Whatever I thought of him beforehand was nothing compared to how I rated him after that effort. He proved himself to be a far better player than I had imagined. He simply batted serenely and, seemingly impervious to any pressure, laid the foundations for the team to develop a huge lead.

Trott continued at his own pace throughout the third day, sharing in an attritional stand of 118 with Strauss for the fourth wicket, and marking his debut with a hundred of his own. He batted for so long that by the time I walked to the crease in mid-afternoon the ball had really begun to turn. Marcus North, an occasional off-spinner, was undoubtedly Australia's main threat with the ball at this stage and had really got it to spit.

Moments earlier, I was sitting on the balcony with my pads on and joked to Strauss: 'I can't believe nobody has reverse-swept him yet!' True, the ball was popping through the top but he didn't have a point.

'You are an absolute buffoon, Swann. It's the most dangerous shot in the book,' Strauss countered.

We had a jokey argument about how it was a valid shot because of the gap square on the off side, and of course when I faced up to him all I could think was 'Watch this, Strauss!' It took me until my third delivery to try it and although I missed with my first attempt, persistence paid dividends. Those before me had created the kind of scenario I love. With a lead already in excess of 400, I was basically given licence to carry on where I left off at Headingley. I knew we didn't have a great deal of time to bat because we wanted to bowl that evening, so I put my foot on the gas.

For example, the ball before tea I came down the track and hit North over mid-off for four. I'd pulled the previous one to the boundary too and reasoned that the Aussies wouldn't be expecting it because it was such an un-English thing to do. We tend to bat for tea in this country, but on this occasion I plumped for the element of surprise. Of course, my colleagues gave me no credit, insisting that I didn't know the interval was coming.

'I did,' I said, 'that was part of the—.'

'Yeah yeah, of course you didn't.'

There was a great deal of cynicism within that England dressing room because people are so scared to try anything that's a bit off the wall, especially with a bat in their hands. It's safety first for the majority, so my approach to batting bemuses as many as it amuses.

However, during that tea interval Strauss emphasised the need for as many runs as possible in the next hour. The exact instruction was for myself and Trott 'to go through the gears'. Obviously, first gear was to look for the ones and twos, with the odd boundary thrown in, increasing the tempo until we were foot to the floor. Unfortunately, however, I don't really use gears – there are only two ways of batting for me: you either try to hit the ball or you try to block the ball. The atmosphere was amazing, and I just kept going for the audacious. Two balls before I was out, in fact, I walked down the wicket to Ben Hilfenhaus and cracked him over mid-on, possibly my finest-ever stroke, even though I say so myself! I absolutely loved it. So much, in fact, that I watched the replay on the big screen three or four times, while pretending that my gloves needed refitting. It was when I considered repeating the stroke two balls later that I succumbed – not expecting the short one that would have knocked my head off, I just chipped tamely into the air.

Having set Australia another world-record chase, this time of 546 in more than six sessions, we conceded 80 runs without reward that evening. Of course, we were firmly in the driving seat, but it didn't stop Jimmy and me asking each other tentative questions on the drive to the hotel.

'You reckon they can do this?'

'Nah, of course they can't. Can they?'

We knew we *should* win, but there is always a little worry in the back of your mind in that kind of situation. Lose, and you become national pariahs. If they were able to bat for two days they would win the game, and if you are on the wrong side of that kind of result, and lose the Ashes as a consequence, it is something you have to carry around with you for the rest of your life. But nothing disturbed my sleep that night, probably because, after my food poisoning, I was still not 100 per cent.

The difference between the Oval and Lord's Tests, however, was that here it was a nightmare for a new batsman coming in – a few balls were going through the top, and it was swinging and spinning. I knew that if we got an early wicket we would go on to do it and I had every belief that the seamers would pick up a couple in the morning. So it was a pleasant surprise to be asked to open the bowling, and doubly so when I got Katich out in my second over.

Before we went out Strauss had told me to be prepared because I would be bowling all day. Of course, I didn't mind that in the conditions, and I made the perfect start when Katich padded up to my quicker ball. Our plan had been to get a new batsman in early, and we made it a double bonus when Broad trapped Watson leg before three balls later. Both openers had departed and Watson's scalp was crucial because since being called in for the third Test at Edgbaston he had been Australia's most consistent player. If he got through the start of his innings, he inevitably got to 50, it seemed, and because he was in form you expected a hundred was around the corner.

Suddenly, we had Ricky Ponting and Mike Hussey in the middle, with the latter on a king pair. Early in his innings he looked ill at ease against me; I beat the edge a few times, the ball spun and he generally rode his luck. For an hour and a half before lunch there was no panic from us whatsoever. But we did not take the chances we created.

Paul Collingwood was always brilliant for me at slip but for once he failed to react to a sharp chance from Hussey, in the 20s, and then put down Ponting off me after lunch. I went round the wicket and bowled a quicker one, which Ponting edged, the ball struck Colly on the boot and bounced up, but as he went to grab it his hat fell in front of his eyes and left him flapping at thin air. As time went on, their experienced third-wicket pair looked more and more comfortable, and the scoreboard began to take on a different complexion. Once they were past 200, I inevitably started to do the maths. Successful chases of 500 are unheard of but, nevertheless, the little voice inside my head said: 'You're kidding me, this can't be happening.'

The pitch even began to look as if it had gone to sleep, so we needed something inspirational from somewhere in that afternoon session. Thankfully Andrew Flintoff chose his moment to step up to the plate. Now, Fred is not renowned for his run-outs – though he is a very good fielder with an unbelievable throw – and he was only fielding at mid-on because he was injured, and couldn't bend down properly at slip. The fact he was the fielder may even have encouraged Hussey to call for a quick single when he tucked a Steve Harmison delivery to Flintoff's left at 217 for two.

I reckon I viewed that incident from the best position in the house. Because I was at gully, I naturally stepped round to back up at the batsman's end and recognised the second he let go of the ball its projection was wide of the stumps. However, because we had worked on the ball for reverse swing, it began arcing in absolutely perfectly towards its target. I could see its flight path all the way and when you are in line like that you just know when it's going to hit. My assumption was correct and the moment Fred's sidearm sling uprooted the off stump – direct hits are mostly out anyway – I knew Ponting was short of his ground. Everyone in our team just knew and mobbed Fred. It had not come about in the way he might have imagined but it gave him the opportunity to produce another of his messiah poses, in recognition of his final say in Test cricket.

It was a truly great moment, the defining moment of that last day. We were always going to win, I am convinced of that, but we did need some magic at that point and who better to provide it than Fred, because his whole career was defined by match-winning performances in Ashes games. Not for performances for England per se, because his record against some of the other countries wasn't great, but against Australia he always brought his best with him.

Ponting's dismissal completely altered the momentum of the contest once more, and brought in Michael Clarke. Because he had proved so effective using his feet throughout the series, we had come up with a plan for me to bowl around the wicket to him. It was something our spin-bowling coach, Mushtaq Ahmed, had stressed: sometimes changing the angle you're bowling from changes what the batsman thinks, and they will do something outside their own comfort zone. Clarke had been playing with such ease when I bowled over the wicket, I switched my angle of attack immediately.

Sure enough, just five balls after we had terminated Australia's healthy third-wicket partnership, Clarke skipped out of his crease to me and turned to leg, only for the ball to ricochet off short leg Alastair Cook's boot into the hands of Strauss at leg slip. A flip onto the stumps barely raised a murmur from the other close fielders initially as it was presumed Clarke had stretched to make his ground. But as Billy Bowden walked in from square leg, Matt Prior said: 'Surely that's worth a look upstairs?' Others backed him up, and even though none of us were particularly hopeful, as time passed we started to think there might be something in it. In truth, we were still buzzing a bit from the run-out of Ponting and had expected this to be a two-second courtesy check, but the longer the delay went on, the more we switched our attention to this latest effort.

I even asked Clarke: 'What do you reckon, mate?'

'Dunno, mate, you never know d'ya?'

Normally, ask an Australian that kind of question and he would be brimming with positivity but this non-committal response made me think something was indeed amiss. So we started looking up at the changing rooms and our stats analyst, Gemma Broad, Stuart's sister, who was watching the television footage. It clearly got her excited, and she put her finger up to signal to us what she thought. Nah, she's a girl, she knows nothing about cricket, we probably thought, despite her being more clued up than most of us. Then, all of a sudden Richard Halsall, our fielding coach, burst onto the balcony with both arms in the air, and that told us what we needed to know before the decision was revealed on the big screen. Some of the crowd near the changing room also saw his reaction and an excited buzz resonated around the ground, which developed into a crescendo as the word OUT was displayed on the electronic scoreboards. Clarke had been Australia's best batsman by a country mile over the course of the series, and we got lucky.

Those two run-outs within a five-minute period completely

changed the atmosphere in the stands and when Marcus North was out 20 minutes later, stumped, trying to sweep me, the noise was deafening. But it was not until the demise of Brad Haddin – the one player remaining who could get a quick hundred – that I knew the game was ours beyond doubt. As an off-spinner you take responsibility for three positions – the apex of midwicket, close midwicket and mid-on – because if a player is going to get caught off you in the outfield, 90 per cent of the time it is going to be in one of them. As Haddin is a guy who likes using his feet, on a turning pitch it is worth dropping your midwicket back two-thirds of the way to the boundary because a mishit will carry, and so it proved. Haddin was lured into the trap and as soon as he went aerial I knew Strauss would not have to move a muscle and sprinted off towards him in celebration before he had completed the catch. I hadn't quite reached him when he turned to the crowd and did his silly little jump, like a little kid who didn't really know what he was doing.

Not that any of us had planned our celebrations. Nor was there much time to prepare for the ultimate one once Steve Harmison, who had done next to nothing in the whole game, summoned up some of his old hostility. Three wickets in a four-over spell turned what had been a very stressful, hard-working day into one with a party atmosphere. Australia were nine down, and as the crowd roared big Harmy in, I stood at gully, urging him not to add to his tally. For purely selfish reasons, I wanted the glory of taking the last wicket. As I'd bowled all day I felt I deserved it.

Ironically, I succeeded in getting the wicket, my fourth of the innings, when I wasn't even trying. Centurion Hussey was so well set that we pushed point back, intent on allowing him a single so we could bowl at their number 11, Ben Hilfenhaus. We knew we would snare him sooner or later. Of course, we knew we might get Huss if it did do something off the pitch, but our primary target was to get him off strike. As it was, the ball that did for Hussey, the second of the 103rd over of the innings, didn't spin much; it just bounced and he prodded forward. Bat-pads are sometimes so blatant that only a geriatric umpire can deny you, so we didn't wait for Asad Rauf's confirmation. As Cooky clutched the ball it was the most ridiculous feeling.

It was as close to pure ecstasy as I've ever felt. It was as if I had just scored a volley from 50 yards to win the World Cup final. I veered off to my right and slid on my knees somewhere near cover, and as Strauss picked me up, it was just pandemonium. Glorious, crazy pandemonium. The whole ground was going absolutely mental. If you watch video re-runs of the moment you will notice that everyone followed me and dived into a big huddle apart from Cook who, having caught the ball, was running in the opposite direction stuffing it in his pocket. He had heard from his old school coach Derek Randall, who had caught the ball that sealed the 1977 Ashes win – the dismissal of Rod Marsh off Mike Hendrick at Headingley – that his biggest regret was throwing the ball into the crowd. So Cook had quickly decided he was keeping this one. It took me a year of badgering him, during which I constantly called him a tight-arsed bastard, to bring it back and donate it to the Lord's museum, its rightful place.

Sometimes you look forward to something so much that it's a bit of a let-down. You feel you really ought to be enjoying it more. It can happen in any walk of life – like when your first kid's born or when your team wins the FA Cup (if only). New Year's Eve is a classic example. You might feel you should be having the best night of the year but you're not. In convincing yourself you are, it all becomes a bit phoney. I feared it might be a bit like that when we won the Ashes, but it felt better than I could possibly have imagined. It was like all your Christmases, birthdays, your first kiss, meeting your wife and your wedding day all rolled into one. Ten other blokes leaving that field no doubt felt the same thing simultaneously. It was ludicrous.

Half an hour later, as I walked around the ground, already drunk because I'd downed half a bottle of champagne (I was on that many painkillers, it didn't take much), confetti filling the air and 'Jerusalem' bellowing around the stands, I looked up to where my mum and dad were sitting and it was just magical. I could see my mum crying and next to her Jonathan Trott's mum Donna was crying too. My dad was standing there with his arms aloft cheering and it felt so good that this was a proud moment for them too. It might sound a bit mushy but it seemed as if I was repaying them in some way for all those times they had gone out of their way to drive me up and down the country, especially my mum. It was nice that in retirement they'd had the chance to travel round and watch this great Ashes series.

I couldn't see Sarah anywhere during our laps and didn't until all the partners came into the changing room later on. Apparently she'd been at the bar getting a bottle of wine in, surprise, surprise. When Sarah came in we just sat giggling and looking a bit goofy. There had been a major clean-up before the families were allowed in to congratulate us. With all the kids about to arrive, I had to hide some of my pants that were lying around. Given some of the stains in there, you wouldn't want children getting hold of them.

My favourite cricket picture – of me, Cooky and Jimmy sitting in my favourite spot in the Oval dressing room, with our caps on, arms around each other, smiling, while Cooky held up the urn (the actual one not a replica) – was taken that evening. We actually talked about stealing it and swapping it for the replica, but I think someone would have twigged considering the stand-in they give us for presentation ceremonies is no different from the ones you can purchase for a fiver in the Lord's shop. They haven't attempted to recreate the majesty of it – it's got a barcode on the bottom, for Christ's sake.

In Ashes of yesteryear both teams used to share a drink together daily after play, but Australia captain Allan Border put a stop to that practice in the early 1980s. Nowadays it is just at the end of the series and that makes it quite a special time. It was nice to be sociable with the opposition, welcoming them into our dressing room after being at each other's throats for five matches. Even though we had competed against them intensely over a seven-week period, I didn't know many of the Australian team very well, apart from Hussey, although I did develop a kinship with Nathan Hauritz, my opposite number. I'd not met him before but we would chat throughout the series about off-spin, stories from their tour and general observations on life. And when we all sat around chatting on the evening of 23 August, it struck me that we were all doing the same thing, we just had different badges on our chests.

A big thing is made of the hatred English sportsmen have for Australians, but that is a big misconception; we don't hate them at all. Sure, there is a great rivalry, and the supporters like to feel that, but as blokes I like their team. Normally there are one or two excep-tions, guys you might consider to be absolute gits, but in that 2009 team there weren't any. In fact, Mitchell Johnson was the biggest surprise to me because you'd expect him to be ultra-aggressive, almost like a football hooligan, because of the way he conducts himself on the field, but when you get talking to him he's as soft as you like, almost like a big kid.

Obviously, a few of the older players had known each other a while and it was a nice touch when Ricky Ponting picked up one of Andrew Strauss's brand-new bats, one that he was dead proud of, looked at it closely and declared: 'What a piece of s---!' With that, he dumped it into the ice box where all the beers had been chilling and there it sat in two feet of cold water while we all supped, much to the amuse-ment of our lads. We'd told Strauss it was a plank all week.

Sharing a drink with the opposition, in recognition of both team's efforts, was a fitting end to seven weeks of drama. I have always been one to enjoy watching my mates on the opposition do well, as long as things aren't going against us or the scoreboard is ticking round too quickly, so I was pleased for Mike Hussey in that Test. I got to know him well at Northamptonshire and shared a triple-century stand with him at Bristol in 2002 when I got my career-best 183 against Gloucestershire. I said before the series began that the ideal thing for me would be to get him out to win the Ashes and I got my wish. Ironically, I would have had him for 55 earlier in the innings but Colly dropped a goober at slip. That might not have been enough to preserve Huss's Test place, such was the immense pressure he was under. As it was, that hundred made sure he was on the team sheet for their next Test, and highlighted how small the margins are in top-level cricket.

15

RECORD BREAKER

TALK ABOUT inappropriate timing. Just two days after the greatest day in many of our lives, the England team that reclaimed the Ashes were dispatched to Belfast for a one-day international against Ireland. It was the most ridiculous scheduling any cricket board could ever have come up with. Had the fifth Test gone the full distance, the ECB would have had to call in another XI because none of us would have been in a fit state to make it up to Manchester for the flight.

Well, when I say the England team, I actually mean the England team minus its leader. Because at the start of that Oval week, captain Andrew Strauss had strolled into a team meeting with a smirk on his face.

'Why are you laughing?' he was asked.

'No reason,' said Strauss.

Seconds later, he was followed by a rather stern-looking Andy Flower. Although we had other things on the agenda, Flower said he wanted this game against the Irish to be treated seriously, and not to have the mickey taken out of it, as he feared would happen. He was right to be fearful because in the grand scheme of things I could not have given two hoots about that game.

'This is a full international and it will get us ready for the one-day series against Australia,' Flower insisted. 'I expect to see ultra-professional behaviour. I don't expect you to treat it as a trip away on the lash.'

Then he dropped the bombshell: 'Andrew Strauss won't be going; he'll be staying at home for a few days' rest.'

That explained the smirk, of course, and we all got stuck into Strauss for somehow organising a great escape.

'It's very tiring on the mind, captaining you chaps,' he insisted. 'A couple of days' R&R will set me in good stead.'

Even during the course of that epic Oval win, however, a nucleus of us were convinced that we would be reprieved at the last minute and a shadow side dispatched in our place. Alas, such instruction from Andy Flower was not forthcoming, and we were packed off to Stormont. The only positive aspect about that, certainly from my perspective, was that it kept the whole team together. With our bosses not inclined to organise a booze-up (if the scheduling was anything to go by, they couldn't in a brewery), we were left to our own devices on that front, and we gave it our best shot.

Because of the way the 2005 Ashes win was celebrated – both in terms of its boozy nature and subsequent series results – there was a reticence towards excessive revelry. Andy, in particular, was very keen to play down our achievement and clearly didn't want us to celebrate in the same manner. Yet I couldn't have disagreed more with that. If you win something, and win it well, you should celebrate as hard as you possibly can. Who cares what anyone else thinks about that? The onus is on you to perform afterwards, of course, and if you don't then you're accountable. But that shouldn't preclude you from basking in the aftermath of your career-high achievement. If I went out and won Wimbledon, I wouldn't be throttling back because I had an Australian Open six months later. Not that I'd ever win Wimbledon: my second serve is shambolic.

So when we were in Belfast, a few of us took the opportunity to celebrate properly as a team. I remember going to one bar and Jimmy and I had a competition to see how many pints of Guinness we could sink. Safe to say, we both had a good stiff at it. Thankfully, I narrowly made it out of the taxi before throwing up in the flowerbeds.

The day of the game was frankly too wet to play a game of international cricket but Ireland were understandably as keen as mustard to have a shot at the Ashes winners. Sold-out signs adorned the entrance but to me it had a real minor counties feel to it. I know because I've played minor counties cricket – there were temporary stands, a few tents and a well-lubricated crowd. Don't get me wrong, I didn't want to lose, but the setting, in addition to the timing, was totally uninspiring.

The ball was soaking wet, we simply couldn't grip it when bowling, and the pitch was a horrible, slow, sticky thing. It was ridiculous that we were playing there at all but particularly in those conditions. Sure, had we lost the Ashes, disappearing out of the country for a couple of days would have provided a safe haven from the lynch mob. But it's clear that something is wrong when 95 per cent of cricket fans are questioning the schedule. Actually, on second thoughts 95 per cent is a conservative number. I don't think I've met anyone outside the Irish Cricket Union who thought that fixture was a good idea. Having experienced the England captaincy for the first time recently, I will have to make my smooth-talking the equal of the estimable Strauss so I can get out of those kind of games too.

Anyone venturing into our dressing room from the cold and wet would have discovered a dozen blokes hiding under shirts and jumpers, getting in any sleep they could because everyone who had played in the Ashes had rightly had a good soak with the black stuff. And it was a turgid game to watch. After we managed 203 for nine from our full allocation of 50 overs, Ireland were set a revised 116 runs from 20 overs, and failed by three runs. Having overseen the defeat to the Netherlands, no wonder Paul Collingwood claimed he was relieved to have got the game out of the way. His feelings represented those of the entire group.

In fact, the entire NatWest Series that followed the Ashes had a touch of 'after the Lord Mayor's show' about it, but it also served to highlight the disparity between our Test side and limited-overs performances. The Test campaign had been topsy-turvy in the sense that in each game one team completely dominated, but in the one-day series Australia monopolised that domination. We were useless.

I even got dropped for a couple of games after we went 3–0 down. There were a lot of changes around that time, with players like Strauss, Collingwood and Jimmy Anderson taking little breaks to recharge their batteries ahead of higher-profile events. But my omission for the matches at Trent Bridge and Lord's was purely on selection grounds.

Let's be honest, I'd missed that much cricket during the eight years I didn't play for England that I didn't want to miss anything else. Of course, I would happily have sidestepped the Ireland game and have my stats from it scrubbed – I don't recall what they were nor am I in a hurry to find out – but if it's a full international with meaning, then of course I want to play. When I was persuaded to have 'a valuable week off' in the summer of 2010, to sit out the one-dayers against Bangladesh, it was horrible. You feel a million miles away from the rest of the team, no longer part of things, and you don't know what to do with yourself. It is excruciating watching it on TV because you'd much rather be on the field, so I would always prefer to be playing and moaning about tiredness than consigned to home.

It was pleasing that, having been recalled for the penultimate match of the series, I made an impact in the seventh and final one at the Riverside on 20 September. We were 6–0 down, and it was the eve of our departure for the Champions Trophy in South Africa. With these two facts in mind, the easy line being peddled in press conferences was that a win would provide us with momentum for that tournament. But you can discount what players say publicly in that situation, because it is absolute tosh. The reason we wanted to win that match up in Durham was to avoid a series whitewash. We certainly didn't want to suffer that humiliation.

It turned out to be a landmark match for me as it was the scene of my first five wickets in a one-day international. A couple of successes with the new ball gave us early control and it was one of those days when it spun square. I was clearly in excitable mood too, as when I bowled Brett Lee to complete my five, I mimicked his own wicket celebration of jumping and kicking his heels to one side.

Bloody stupid thing to do to a bloke who pings it around your ears at 90-odd miles per hour, especially as we were yet to bat. Thankfully, however, for once we didn't get as far down as me, despite an almighty wobble in pursuit of 177. We reached three figures without loss but followed up with a collapse of six for 56 before getting home. Even then I feared that Brett was intent on retribution when he sidled up to me for a quiet word at the presentation ceremony.

'Loved your celebration, mate,' he whispered.

'Yeah, don't know why I did it!' I countered in cowardly fashion.

'Nah, nah, don't worry, it made me laugh.'

We were to renew acquaintances with the Australians a fortnight later at the Champions Trophy, where despite arriving at the last minute, we acquitted ourselves well. Our pace bowlers demolished the Sri Lanka top order at the Wanderers to set up an opening win, but it was the second Group B match against South Africa two days later that sticks in the mind.

That game at Centurion was one of the few times in international cricket that Owais Shah batted as I know he can. For years I had expected him to push on – he was the same age group as me coming through the system and had always shown the potential to do so. Unfortunately, the potential hadn't bloomed. Over the years, Owais has been the kind of infuriating player who always gets out at exactly the wrong moment. He has never been the dominant player for England that he should have been. That's a great shame, because he has as much talent as anyone in the country with the bat in hand. When you talk about natural batsmen you would put him up along-side David Sales and Ian Bell. Whereas Bell will have a 15-year career for England, I fear Owais will look back on one unfulfilled. But in this particular game Owais batted like the absolute genius he can be – he smashed their attack everywhere, and never allowed their spinners, Johan Botha and Roelof van der Merwe, to bowl at him. He dictated to them completely, and picked the right deliveries to pump out of the park. He really deserved a hundred but fell two shy, having laid the foundations for a big score alongside Paul Collingwood.

Nevertheless, that base allowed Eoin Morgan to take the game away from the tournament hosts. He absolutely marmalised their bowling and showed what I already knew: he is a serious player. When you bowl at someone regularly, even if it is only in the nets, you get a feel for how good they are, and when in form Morgs is absolutely brilliant. He is such a natural striker of the ball and hits it miles for a little fella. He can put you wherever he wants and sometimes it is more by good fortune than planning that you get him out. His innings of 67 had a whopping strike rate of 197.05 and his six count of five was just one fewer than that of Owais.

I was confident South Africa were never going to chase 324 down and although Graeme Smith did his best, cramp scuppered him. Afterwards, Andrew Strauss got annihilated in the South African press for refusing to allow him a runner, but let's put the record straight: he had no choice in the matter. It is true that Smith went to Strauss to ask for a runner – and also true that Strauss was not inclined to grant him one – but it was the call of umpires Steve Davis and Tony Hill. They intervened in the chat between the two captains and advised Smith that batsmen with cramp do not qualify for a runner. It's in the rules, or at least it was until a subsequent change was made. To allow one seems crazy to me. Cramp is basically a fitness and conditioning issue, so what we were saying was that it no longer mattered whether you were physically fit enough to bat through 50 overs. The ICC were right to outlaw them two years later.

Despite the bitter recriminations, however, we progressed to the semi-finals with our 22-run victory, with a dead-rubber defeat against New Zealand in between. Perhaps inevitably Australia awaited to contest a place in the final. Unfortunately, the match, once again at Centurion, took on the pattern of so many of the previous ones in that past month. We were six wickets down for 101 and only thanks to Tim Bresnan's rescue-act 80 did we manage to climb up to 257. That score proved insufficient on that pitch and Australia lost only one wicket, in a resounding win. Shane Watson, who throughout the summer made 50-and-out his speciality, managed to go on for once. We certainly saw his ability to up the tempo that night and one of his seven sixes – a flat effort over midwicket off Tim Bresnan shortly after he celebrated his hundred – was ferocious. I reckon the ball was travelling at around 150 miles per hour as a South African lad came bundling down the grass bank trying to catch it. It hit this kid flush on the forehead and poleaxed him. His mates were so drunk that they were oblivious to the fact and carried on clapping and cheering. When the replays were shown on the big screen it drew a collective *ouch* – a blow like that would have ended me.

Once again we had failed in our quest to win a limited-overs trophy, but some evidence of progress in 50-over cricket revealed itself when we returned to South Africa on tour the following month and, with two wash-outs reducing the number of one-day matches to three, became only the second country after Australia to achieve an away victory against them in a bilateral series.

But our main focus, or certainly mine, was the Test series and one significant change to our tactical approach rather dismayed me. Andrew Flintoff's retirement had caused a rethink in terms of the make-up of the England team and when it was decided that post-Freddie we would go in with four bowlers for future Test matches I believed we were making a mistake. Having got used to playing as one of five bowlers, I was convinced that it worked for us. However, the management were convinced we could adapt to a four-man unit.

So on 16 December we headed into the first Test at Centurion, a ground where the pace bowlers normally do the damage, with me as one of a quartet, and naturally therefore with more emphasis on a containing role. The pitch can be a little up and down, and quite quick, so to claim five first-innings wickets was heartening. My successes generally came from trying to bowl tight, and significantly for the rest of the series my haul included a couple of their left-handers early on.

I made the perfect start when Ashwell Prince succumbed to his first ball from me, and only my second of the series, and J.P. Duminy followed to the fifth ball on the second day. I felt those dismissals set the tone for how that pair played against me for the remaining three matches. I certainly had the rub over Prince, and arguably over Duminy as well, from those initial edges to slip.

In response to South Africa's disciplined 418, we slipped to 242 for eight, a position from which I decided to throw caution to the wind. I approached my innings exactly as I had those in the previous summer, in fact, and Jimmy Anderson and I put on 106 in less than a session. It was up there with the most enjoyable batting I had ever experienced, comparing favourably to my top time at Headingley with Stuart Broad. The big difference, though, is that Jimmy is rather more sensible.

At one point he came down the pitch to inquire professionally whether I was going to attempt to pull or hook Morne Morkel.

'Nah, he's a bit quicker than the others and there's a man out – I don't think so,' I said.

Sure enough, next ball Morkel bumped me and I instinctively flapped at it, connected beautifully and sent it flying for a one-bounce four. Whereas Broady would have laughed about that, all I got from Jimmy as he passed was a few four-letter words. But he soon got into the spirit of things and, egged on by me, hit his first international six via a lap-slog off their left-arm spinner Paul Harris.

Not only did we have a blast out there together, we ran them ragged too, and ultimately our ninth-wicket stand was what got us to within 62 runs of their first-innings score. Such was my confidence that I even considered a hundred might be on the cards, but if that was to happen it wouldn't be by me creeping over the line. My attitude of carrying on regardless has led to many downfalls, and arguably I could have had a dozen first-class hundreds behind me at that point of my career – if I'd been a boring git. I've lost count of the number of times I have been caught on the boundary in the 90s, and one of the most (or least) impressive of those came in a County Championship game in 2007 when I reached 97 with consecutive fours off Grant Flower and then, with six men on the boundary, picked out long off. Never mind, I would never have lived with myself if I'd nurdled singles to get there. And here I picked out deep square leg to be last out for a Test-best 85.

The game appeared a dead-cert draw from that point, and indeed we were cruising on the final day when Jonathan Trott and Kevin Pietersen got involved in a stupid mix-up that resulted in the latter being run out. Even then we headed into the final hour odds on for a stalemate at four wickets down, but a collapse caused a panic, and when I was ninth out to one that nipped back from Morne Morkel – nip-backers have been the bane of my career – there were still 19 balls remaining in the Test.

That was when Graham Onions showed his stomach for a fight to save the day, even overcoming the fact Paul Collingwood messed up twice, leaving our number 11 exposed at the start of both the penultimate and final overs. Graeme Smith also gave us a helping hand, mind, with his sentimental decision to throw the ball to Makhaya Ntini, in his 100th Test, for the final over. Bunny kept him out and we saved the game by a hair's breadth.

It was pleasing to receive the man-of-the-match award but it also raised a smile because statistically my second half of the game was fairly atrocious. I managed nought for 91 and two, hardly figures to get excited about. The adjudicators must have thought it was a bloody good first half.

South Africa were vying to become the number-one-ranked Test team that winter, but we seriously jeopardised their hopes when we went to Durban and absolutely obliterated them in the Boxing Day Test. It was an amazing game because of the way it changed almost instantaneously on the opening day. They batted, and were progressing serenely on what was one of the hottest days I've ever played cricket – it was like being in Sri Lanka, the humidity was incredibly stifling. Such was the temperature, in fact, that I broke one of my regimented habits: I always like to bowl in long sleeves, but on this occasion I cut them to three-quarter length in one of the intervals.

The tipping point of that Test match proved to be just after tea on day one when I went around the wicket to Kallis and had him caught at slip for 75. South Africa were 160 for three and his departure changed things very quickly for us. We were soon on top and before we knew it had bowled them out. Had it not been for Dale Steyn's late rally of 47 from number 10 they wouldn't have made 300. As it was, we knew 343 was not a big score on that surface. All the talk when we got back into the changing room was about how incredibly true it was.

The rest of the chat revolved around how we should go about building a healthy advantage on it, and it was team policy to target both Makhaya Ntini and their spinner Paul Harris in that innings. Ntini by this stage of his career was a shadow of his former self, and had noticeably lost a yard or two of pace. Meanwhile, we were annoyed that we had let Harris dictate to us in the previous Test and Ian Bell, in particular, made a point of attacking him in Durban. The batters had spoken about the fact that he was reliant on creating pressure by bowling dot ball after dot ball, and they reckoned that as he was not a big spinner of the ball there would not be excessive danger in being really aggressive against him. After all, he was never going to beat the outside edge of the bat.

The plan was put into action effectively enough and that pair proved to be the most expensive of a six-man South African attack. Harris was not allowed to settle into his customary role as container, and that was integral to us getting a massive total. J.P. Duminy was even drafted in to bowl 24 overs after Harris was essentially hit out of the attack. Ntini's ineffectiveness heaped more work on their threat bowlers Morne Morkel and Dale Steyn.

Bell and Alastair Cook both churned out hundreds and, armed with a 231-run lead, we then had a storming session with the ball shortly before tea on the fourth day. Once again, I prised out Ashwell Prince with my second delivery of a spell, caught at silly point, and followed up by bowling Hashim Amla, who'd proved a real thorn in our side in Pretoria, through the gate.

With them two down at tea, we ran through the remainder of their top order in the final session. Broad produced another great spell to send back both Jacques Kallis and A.B. de Villiers shouldering arms, and when I trapped Smith leg before from around the wicket, South Africa were reduced to 50 for six. So, heading into the fifth day, we only needed four more wickets to go 1–0 up in the series. We cruised it.

The dismissals of Morne Morkel and Dale Steyn before lunch saw me take another five-wicket haul and claim a second consecutive man-of-the-match award. Most observers would have expected my role in the series to be to chip away at one end and get a few wickets here or there, but after two games I had 14. I guess when it's your time it's your time, and there was enough happening for me to suggest that this was mine. As if to emphasise it, a couple of bat-pads went straight off the face of the bat. Following my initial scepticism at changing to a four-man attack, by mid-series I had been won over. My mindset had always been that the role of a spinner was to influence the second innings of matches but I was learning to pick up first-innings successes too. As a Test spinner, if you are going at two and a half runs an over, even getting one or two wickets first dig you are doing your job for the team. In county cricket it's different because you usually have a couple of batsmen who can bowl seam-up, so they tend to send down the fill-in overs while your main men have a breather.

There was another accolade for me in the aftermath of that innings-and-98-run win, as it was revealed I had become the first English spin bowler to take 50 wickets in a calendar year. When I was informed of that achievement my thoughts turned, naturally enough, to the great pair of Fred Titmus and Derek Underwood – surely they must have done it? It led to me researching the claim myself. Of course, the statistic was correct and I was proud to take it, even overlooking the fact that the spinners of yesteryear would happily pick up 45 wickets before September, then spend the next three months on a paddle steamer. I also finished the year as second only to Mitchell Johnson in terms of Test victims.

Confidence was generally high among the England team as we went into the New Year – we always knew things would be tough out in South Africa but the unexpected one-day series win was a nice fillip at the start of a long tour and we had carried good form into the longer format. It was just a shame we were unable to hang on to our lead in the latter stages of the Test series.

The New Year's Test in Cape Town was remarkably similar to the match at Centurion, or at least its ending was. After relative parity on first innings, South Africa muscled us out of the game second time around and left us with four and a half sessions to survive. The pressure increased when we entered the fifth morning with seven wickets intact and 90 overs to negotiate.

So I needed the exchange I had with Graham Onions, sitting in the viewing gallery with my pads on, like a hole in the head. It came not long after we lost our sixth wicket, following 57 overs of defiance between Ian Bell and Paul Collingwood. I was due in at number 10 because we had used Jimmy Anderson as nightwatchman. Now, although I am generally relaxed before I go out, there is a reason for it. It is directly linked to me being superstitious – some would call it anal. As I sit waiting, my gloves rest in a certain place on my legs, my bat leans against my box and no one is allowed to touch my bat. I just need to know everything is in the right place, and if so all is calm in my little world.

The tense atmosphere was neither here nor there for me until Bunny turned to me and asked: 'Do you get nervous before you bat?'

'No, not really, mate.'

'You must be, man, look at the situation, we could lose this Test match,' he said, manically. 'There will be a lot of pressure when you get out there! I feel the pressure, man, I'm properly nervous sat back here.'

In the end I got up and moved.

After a flurry of late wickets, our conversation reconvened in the middle when he came out to bat for the final 17 balls. I thought it only right to make a point of checking whether he was still feeling that pressure. Dale Steyn was bowling at one end and Morne Morkel was at the other.

I faced the first three balls and then asked him what he wanted me to do – did he want me to get a single, how did he feel about things? To be fair, he had thought things through, and told me categorically that he didn't want to face Steyn.

'You block him out, and I'll take Morkel,' he announced.

As it happened, I was more than happy because Morkel had got me out a few times, including in the first innings of the match with an absolute snorter.

'Of course, if that's what you want, mate, no problem.'

'Aye, I'd just rather not face Steyn, if it's all the same to you.'

Our pact made, we both stuck to our sides of the bargain, and we managed to hold on once again.

It was the first series we had featured in with the amended Umpire Decision Review System and nowhere did that cause as much controversy as in the final Test in Johannesburg, where we got absolutely annihilated. When Strauss was out to the first ball of the Test, to a ridiculously good catch by Hashim Amla at short leg, diving away to his right to cling on one-handed off the face of the bat from the bowling of Dale Steyn, we should have known it wasn't to be for us. That kind of dismissal is freakish, and set the tone for what followed.

While it was probably justified that South Africa levelled things at the Wanderers – because they had played the better cricket over the course of the series, and we had to give them credit for that – they also had by far the better of the glitches thrown up by the UDRS. Or by Australian umpire Daryl Harper's employment of it, to be more accurate.

When Graeme Smith was caught behind on 15 cutting at Ryan

Sidebottom everyone could tell it was blatantly out. But somehow Tony Hill did not raise the finger and TV official Harper inexplicably upheld the not-out decision. It had been made clear at the start of the series that stump microphones would be used as one of the technology gadgets for edges behind, and that the default volume setting would be level four. But there was nothing to prevent Harper turning it up to the maximum 10 when adjudicating on a review, yet he simply refused to do so. Andy Flower went to see him in a rage at lunch on the second day – I have never seen him so angry – because we felt short-changed and it later led to us appealing, albeit in vain, for our used review to be given back. I was fully behind that move, because we needed to make a stand.

I felt A.B. de Villiers twice nicked off to me – and indeed twice in one ball for the first of them – to no avail. It was the third day and de Villiers was on 11, in a score of 242 for five, which represented a South African advantage of 62. We had just put in a leg slip and the ball clipped de Villiers's gloves, then his pads, then the back of his bat and went to Jimmy Anderson. Yet, although he was given out on the field, de Villiers referred it, probably because he thought he could walk on water at this stage, and Harper looked at it once and said not out.

These seemed to be signs that we were going to get hammered in this game, and we duly were. It would be ridiculous to blame those incidents for losing, of course, but they certainly didn't help. Getting bombarded out for less than 200 twice was the real reason we lost. But the teething trouble for reviews angered us a great deal. Nevertheless, my personal performances were recognised when I shared the man-of-the-series award with South Africa's Mark Boucher.

It had been a great start to the 2009–10 winter for me, but I was not looking forward to its conclusion because Bangladesh, Neil Foster once told me, was quite simply 'the ----hole of the earth'. When he had toured years earlier, the hotels weren't finished, rats ran amok in them and it was an uncomfortable few weeks away. In contrast, however, I loved the place. Admittedly, it was a good job it was a short tour because you weren't allowed to venture outside – doing so generally leads to you being mobbed, such is the Bangladeshis' enthusiasm for the game.

Without my best mate Jimmy, and our leader Andrew Strauss, both on rest periods, I courted Alastair Cook, the stand-in captain, as my new tour buddy. No flies on me, eh. As well as making him my alarm clock, we watched *Entourage* every night on the laptop, and had room service followed by a slab of Dairy Milk chocolate. How romantic.

Just as it had in South Africa, the cricket went really well for me out there. Of course, I would always expect to do well as a spinner in Asia, but with this tour came another kind of expectation – that I would be the major wicket-taker. I managed to cope with that pressure, however, despite the pitches being generally flat. There were certainly no gimmes on surfaces better for batting on than bowling and, after I claimed 16 wickets in the two-Test series in March, it angered me when I later heard on the grapevine that my success had actually gone against me when the International Cricket Council announced their nominations for the 2010 World Test Player of the Year. The view held by that panel, prior to a frantic backtracking, was that too many of my wickets were cheap Bangladeshi ones.

But Bangladesh proved nuggety opponents and so our victories, both completed on the final day, were much better than people gave us credit for. You are actually on a hiding to nothing when you tour there because you are expected to steamroller them. But they have some outstanding talent coming through and the oppressive heat is equally demanding.

I felt fairly senior on that trip, with only Stuart Broad among the bowlers having more international experience than me. I had only played 16 Tests prior to arrival but I enjoyed the extra responsibility as we blooded people like James Tredwell and Steve Finn. It was also a good laugh with Cook as captain, and I warned him every night over our squares of chocolate: 'Don't change my field tomorrow.' So, whenever he walked towards me when I was bowling – he did so with a grin on his face – I ordered him to go away. Keep walking, keep walking, I used to instruct him. Not sure I would ever dare do that with Strauss, as he looks like he could wrestle a bear.

Contrary to the thoughts of the ICC selection panel, I worked hard to become the first English spinner to take 10 wickets in a Test match since Jim Laker's famous 19-wicket haul at Old Trafford in the 1956 Ashes. Bangladeshi conditions make it a real war of attrition, and it took me 78.3 overs to reach double figures.

I am not a statistics man but the 50 wickets in a calendar year and emulating the great Laker were nice notches to achieve during that winter. They, along with my two man-of-the-series awards, will be on my CV when I hand it to my grandchildren in 30 years' time, in my bid to convince them that the washed-up bloke they see before them, who sings at Butlin's in skin-tight leather trousers, doing Shakin' Stevens covers, also played for England for a while.

16

PLANNED TO PERFECTION

STAPLEFORD PARK, a big old country house in leafy Leicestershire, was a picture of splendour on 29 January 2010 as my winter of content peaked with marriage to Sarah. When you are involved in international cricket you have to plan ahead to do anything socially, and so we got hitched between series in South Africa and Bangladesh. It was a case of lining up the Future Tours Programme and our own calendar and coming up with a date that was doable. No mean feat, I can tell you.

It was a brilliant occasion. Weddings generally are, I guess, but having 150 people there with us, comprising our best mates and family, was so special, and also unforgiving because some of them can party pretty hard. The champagne reception began at midday and most of my England team-mates made it. All but Steve Harmison and his missus Hayley, that is. Ironically, they had been the first of the cricket lot to confirm their attendance with a reply when we had dispatched the invites, and Harmy even went as far as telling me he couldn't wait. Well, I'm still waiting.

When we sat down, the story goes that Alastair Cook looked at the empty places to his left and wondered about the identity of the missing guests. His curiosity sated by a check of the seating plan, he put in a quick call to give his mate the hurry-up. Unfortunately, Harmy had completely forgotten and was away on holiday with the family. I didn't see him for months afterwards, but I popped into Trent Bridge when Durham played their County Championship fixture in the 2010 summer and left a note on his peg. It simply read: 'Do you still want these bangers and mash? I can keep them for a while longer but I think they're going a bit cold.' When I eventually bumped into him later in the year he was properly apologetic, and we had a good laugh about it.

My creative side was allowed expression on the big day. While Sarah was in charge of the decoration of the hall, I was allowed to choose the food. Which meant proper food – a bowl of soup to start, bangers and mash for the main course, and apple and blackcurrant crumble for afters. A magical menu. And I took it upon myself to be in charge of the drinks too, which led to a particularly embarrassing incident immediately after I returned home from Bangladesh. The hotel were as good as gold throughout our big day, and because we booked out virtually the whole place they said they would keep the bar open the entire night. As I say, my mates can set a ferocious pace, but when, weeks later, the hotel manager queried an unpaid £12,500 bill that I had allegedly signed for, I protested my innocence and agreed to drive down to examine it in person.

'Nonsense, someone's forged it, it's a joke,' I told the good lady on the phone. Unfortunately, it was not. Or if it was indeed a joke, it was now at my expense, as it turned out to be the invoice for the excess wine bill at the wedding breakfast. And to make matters worse, I had been so drunk when asked to settle up that evening that I thought I was being asked for my autograph. So here I was back near Melton Mowbray face to face with a genuine bill and, to make matters worse, not only had I signed it, I had written *Best Wishes Graeme Swann*, and finished it off with a kiss underneath. My bullish mood when I walked in, determined that no cash would be handed over, was followed by one of those try-to-act-casual moments. 'Yeah, of course it was me, I remember doing it now,' I said, through gritted teeth. Let's just say the look Sarah had given me in the reception a couple of months earlier contained a great deal more fondness.

The wedding was a proper day-nighter and we managed to see it through to 6 a.m., narrowly failing to take the honours as the last couple standing. We then squeezed in a 10-day honeymoon in the Maldives before England's next assignment in the United Arab

Emirates. As a coach, Andy Flower is very understanding when it comes to things like that, and he simply asked me to keep on top of my fitness ahead of departure. Given our ludicrously packed itinerary, it was a relief to be able to get away at all. Looking back, thank God I didn't get an Indian Premier League deal in the January auction because if I had, Sarah might have made me famous as the international cricketer with the shortest-ever marriage.

Officially no longer a singleton, my status was changing rapidly in other ways too. When I returned from Bangladesh, I was ranked third in the world Test bowling ratings and named as England Player of the Year and also a Wisden Cricketer of the Year. Being recognised by Wisden topped it all off for me from a playing perspective. My old man bought the Wisden Almanacks every year, they were all lined up on the shelves in our front room, and now here I was as one of the five players being presented with a commemorative leather-bound edition. My brother Alec was commissioned to write the piece on my career, which was both nice and weird in equal measure.

Prior to him composing it, he interviewed me for the first time. We went down the pub in Nottingham, which was nothing out of the ordinary, but when he sat there with a Dictaphone, and began asking questions, that threw me. Trying to talk sensibly with someone you have mucked about with all your life is a challenge, and treating the interview seriously was nigh on impossible. Neither of us could make eye contact, so we both kept staring at the floor as we chatted. But I was grateful for the glowing write-up.

A new-look England team was soon earning its own rave reviews as we began our campaign for the 2010 World Twenty20 crown in the Caribbean in late April. Its composition was conceived two months earlier in Dubai, where we stopped off on the way to Bangladesh to play a couple of 20-over matches against Pakistan. Crucially, as a warm-up we played England Lions, who were already out there playing Pakistan A in limited-overs matches. It was a match that defined our future selection.

After we managed a reasonable 157 for six, Michael Lumb and Craig Kieswetter charged the Lions towards their target. It seemed quite funny when Stuart Broad made an absolute hash of a simple skied catch at mid-off early on off Ryan Sidebottom – he positioned himself and the ball bounced about five yards behind him! – but there were also serious repercussions. Kieswetter only had four at the time but went on to smash 81 and Lumb also scored a half-century at a rate well in excess of a run a ball. On the back of those innings they got into the full squad. In fact, I would go as far as to say that their inclusion was one of the main reasons that we were successful, because suddenly we had players at the top of the order who threw caution to the wind and smacked it everywhere. It was what our team had been crying out for. I have always said everything happens for a reason. Good old Broady!

We clicked from the start in the World Twenty20, and played some great cricket in the warm-up games, to beat both Bangladesh and South Africa comfortably at the Kensington Oval, Barbados. We were drilled and there was a repetitive pattern to our play. We took wickets at the top of the order, primarily through Sidebottom and Broad, and that kept the brakes on. Michael Yardy and I were able to take wickets and keep it tight in the middle and we were the only team who really nailed bowling at the death over there. We didn't just bowl yorkers; there were a lot of slower balls and slower-ball bouncers thrown in, and they stifled the big hitters.

Not that our progress through the tournament was without its hiccups. In fact, had the rain relented against Ireland we may well have lost, and such a result would have been enough to oust us at the first group stage. The pitch in Guyana was not an easy one for batting and we managed a modest 120 for eight. Ireland were 14 for one in the fourth over of their reply when the showers became more persistent, and, after a brief dry spell, their target was readjusted to 61 runs from nine overs. We would probably have been all right, but when the wet weather readjusts scores in 20-over cricket, they are notoriously hard to defend. To be truthful, we were pleased to get away from the Guyanese climate because the rain plagued us there. Our opening defeat to West Indies was shaped by it. Having posted an excellent 191 for six, we were forced to try to defend a 60-run target from six overs, and went down by eight wickets.

However, from that point onwards, in virtually every game we played we seemed to take wickets at exactly the right time. When things are going well for you that tends to happen. We were almost destined to win it, it seemed, and after comfortable victories over Pakistan and South Africa in Barbados, we continued our winning streak when, in the last Group E game in St Lucia, we defeated New Zealand, a team that always play above their means in world events.

We hammered teams with our bowling more than anything, and even though I finished with 10 wickets out there, in my opinion the seamers were phenomenal. Tim Bresnan did a solid job but the other two, Siddy and Broady, were ridiculously unsung. Kevin Pietersen got a lot of the plaudits for his runs, rightly so, but the fact we always took wickets at the top meant we were able to rein in opposition totals – they claimed 18 wickets between them.

Their potency with the new ball certainly set up the comfortable semi-final win over Sri Lanka, also in St Lucia. The Sri Lankans really struggled up front – Sanath Jayasuriya nicked off to second slip from Siddy's first ball, and Mahela Jayawardene and Tillakaratne Dilshan also succumbed inside the powerplay period. It was a recurring theme in our performances. And we backed it with aggressive batting. That was all honed in training, which was really good fun. Practice was geared around us smashing the ball as far and as hard as we possibly could, and we spent long periods range-hitting: basically receiving underarm throws and trying to launch massive sixes. We had competitions to see who could hit it the furthest, and that kind of thing always appeals to me, even though I never make the top three. I'm rarely in the top 13, if I'm honest.

The day after we had qualified for the final via a seven-wicket victory, we watched the other semi-final on TV at our hotel. It was Pakistan v Australia and Pakistan absolutely walked all over the

Aussies for 95 per cent of the game. Then, from nowhere, Mike Hussey blasted an unbeaten 60 off only 24 balls. Chasing 192, Australia had been 105 for five when he walked in. They then needed 70 off the final five overs, 34 off the last two and 18 off one. He did it with a ball to spare. It was an incredible effort to get his team into the final, but if it had occurred a year later eyebrows would surely have been raised. At the time, it was real 'you're kidding me' stuff, watching every ball disappear out of the ground towards the death, and all of a sudden we were facing the Aussies, having been certain of facing the Pakistanis just minutes earlier.

Being thrown up against Australia might have daunted us if we'd dwelt on our record against them in limited-overs matches over the previous couple of years. Their dominance over us had been fairly exceptional, resulting in eight victories in our previous nine ODIs. However, the way we were playing combined with our assessment of how they were playing gave us real confidence. We knew, for example, that they would run in and bowl as fast as they possibly could up front, and we knew that Lumb, Kieswetter and Pietersen, our top three in the tournament, thrive against genuine pace.

I went into that game on 16 May with real belief we would win, and everything went right for us at the Kensington Oval from the moment we won the toss. We got a wicket in the first over when I caught Shane Watson at slip after the ball bobbled out of Kieswetter's gloves, David Warner was run out in the second, and Siddy got his second wicket when Brad Haddin edged behind to leave Australia eight for three in the third. The game had barely begun and we were all over them. Our formula had worked a treat once more. With the pressure applied, I sent down a four-over spell for 17 runs, including the dismissal of Michael Clarke, who was brilliantly caught at short midwicket by a diving Paul Collingwood.

Although David Hussey and Cameron White rescued them a bit towards the end of the innings, hauling them up to 147 for six, we knew it was still short of competitive if we batted well. Our attitude in the changing room at the halfway stage was that we would go for it 100 per cent. In other words, rather than try to pace the chase over 20 overs, simply attack. It worked to perfection. The top order went nuts, and the 111-run stand between Kiesy and KP was the best batting of the tournament.

I didn't leave the physio room throughout that innings. Not only did it provide a great view, it was also perfectly air-conditioned. I'd happened to be on the bench having some treatment when the innings started and, as you will appreciate by now, my superstitious nature did not allow me to move for the next hour or so. Before we knew it we had won a world event, England's inaugural world event.

Twenty20 happens in a flash and by three o'clock that afternoon we were on the way back to the hotel, three sheets to the wind from consumption of beers, with the World Twenty20 trophy in our grasp. Before the sun went down we had some photos taken on the beach where we were staying and our drunken smiles said it all. It wasn't as good a feeling as winning the Ashes, but it was up there with anything I have won in cricket since that Under-13 triumph at Irchester.

In Twenty20 you are certainly reliant on a modicum of good luck – you rarely win anything without decisions going your way, the opposition dropping the odd catch, or one of their key players losing form or making an error of judgement at a crucial time, all the little bits add up – but when we had got on the plane to go out there in late April, I looked around at the rest of the team and genuinely thought: 'You know, we can win this.' I certainly hadn't experienced that sort of feeling when we departed for the Champions Trophy eight months earlier. Back then I considered we could do all right, but never imagined we had a team good enough to actually win. And there is a massive difference between hoping to win – if everything falls in place for you – and feeling you should win, because of the team you have on paper. When I sized us up on that flight, I genuinely believed we were as good as or better than every other team in the world. More importantly, everyone else seemed to share that same belief.

*

Our surprise success landed us a date in Downing Street, and we were hosted by the recently appointed prime minister, David Cameron. Being inherently nosy, I had a quick look for Nick Clegg in the downstairs toilet while I was there. Mr Cameron, who officially congratulated us in the garden at Number 10, revealed himself to be a big cricket fan. But he did drop a clanger when we made our way onto the steps out front for a photo opportunity.

One of the press shouted out: 'Are you happy to be hosting the England cricket team, Mr Cameron?'

'Yes, of course, it makes me proud to stand out here with Colin Collingwood and all his boys,' he replied.

The rest of us began creasing up with laughter while Collingwood, who is renowned for his terrible banter, retorted with: 'Colin? Oh, that's okay, *David*!'

As he chuckled to himself, the rest of us were forced to remind him that the PM's first name was indeed David. Cue tumbleweed.

'Aww, Christ, man!' he chuntered.

Between them our two revered leaders made a complete balls-up that afternoon.

Recognition for services to my country provided the perfect ending to a hectic but rewarding spell of overseas assignments for me. For those of us centrally contracted and playing all forms of the game, the 2009–10 winter was unforgiving, and the manic schedule meant that I had precious little time to be of any service at home. In fact, Sarah and I had hardly had time to put our bits and pieces together in our marital home before I was off on international duty once more. Nine months later I was to become a proud father.

17

AN UNSAVOURY SUMMER

ONLY A matter of hours after our party at the PM's pad, we began what turned out to be a successful but ultimately sordid summer. The two-match Test series against Bangladesh was supposed to be a walkover, of course; mere fine-tuning for the four matches against Pakistan that followed. But as they had shown us in their own conditions, they have some emerging players of genuine world-class ability in Tamim Iqbal, Shakib Al Hasan and Mushfiqur Rahim. And despite being nullified by English conditions, they pushed us hard in the first Test at Lord's at the end of May, despite following on.

I can honestly say that my performance was one of the worst, if not the worst, of my Test career. Although we had only been playing white-ball cricket for a few weeks in the Caribbean, it was my first first-class match of the season and switching back to the red ball in different conditions was far from agreeable to me. My previous match had been the second Test in Mirpur two months earlier. I was completely out of sorts, and I wasn't alone. We bowled dreadfully as a team at Lord's that week and Tim Bresnan, especially, suffered the worst rhythm of his career. He just didn't know what he was doing.

When we took to the field it had the feel of one of those pre-season county games, when you are trying to brush the cobwebs away. Because of the incessant international itinerary, however, we were brushing ours off in a Lord's Test match. It was not an enjoyable experience, nor did it feel right that we were doing so. Nothing should be allowed to degrade international matches at Lord's. However, although we were undoubtedly suffering from a World Cup hangover, at least we won the game. Thankfully, our batsmen weren't undermined by the same switch-over problem – only two of the top seven had been to the World Twenty20 – and Jonathan Trott's double hundred set up the victory.

Despite our rustiness with the ball, defending a first-innings score of 505 allowed us to enforce the follow-on. But Tamim showed his talent with his hundred in the second, and at one stage Bangladesh were 321 for three, a position from which they could have made things decidedly difficult for us. In the end we were glad to restrict them to 382, and our subsequent chase to 160. We won comfortably, but I got what I deserved from the match – nothing. I had played an integral role in the Ashes win 10 months earlier but this time I left without a wicket to my name.

Normal service was resumed at Old Trafford, however, for both myself and the attack as a whole. We were soon back in the groove and the improvement within a week was discernible – we dismissed the Bangladeshis twice in the equivalent of a day's cricket to win by an innings with seven and a half sessions of the match unused.

I claimed five wickets in the first innings, and after my previous blank that was pleasing. But it was far from a pleasurable experience playing in Manchester that week. Anyone who has had the misfortune of coming face to face with Old Trafford's newest monstrosity will know exactly what I mean. Although the building is officially called The Point, it would be more aptly referred to as The Pointless. It's the single worst building in world cricket (although I made that judgement before I'd clapped eyes on Headingley's new pavilion) and it disappointed me so because it has been plonked next to the beautiful pavilion at one of my favourite grounds in the world. It dwarfs it, and I will happily volunteer my name as part of the demolition team in 25 years when the locals come to their senses and it is officially deemed a blot on the landscape.

Swing and bounce did for the Bangladeshis twice for fewer than our 419 all out. Steve Finn claimed another six wickets to add to his nine from the first Test, and depth in English cricket's bowling stocks was emphasised by a competent debut from Ajmal Shahzad. I hope there is a good England career ahead of Aj, as I believe he can develop into a top-class bowler. What he showed us inside his first six months around the full England team was an ability to reverse-swing the ball with great control, and a faultless attitude. He is the most intense trainer I've ever seen. In one way he is like a model because he is so paranoid about weight issues and what he eats. He actually counts calories by the mouthful and if he has so much as a slice of bread he wants to get down the gym to bash the carbs out of himself. He actually trains too much, I reckon, and that is why his body packs up every now and again and begs for a rest. If he gets the balance right, though, he will be awesome for England.

Physical management of players became an issue for the England coaching team during the 2010 summer. Concern over potential player fatigue meant they were desperate to look after us all as the Ashes drew nearer, and to be honest I held the same view. In my head, I was already prioritising that series five months before departure, and I began hoping that my body would hold out and that I wouldn't incur serious injury at the wrong time. At the end of the summer I was relieved when I walked away unscathed. I would play Ashes matches over anything else. With this in mind, I was okay for once when Andy Flower instructed me to rest instead of taking part in the three-match NatWest Series against the Bangladeshis. At least in theory, because when it came down to it I found it difficult to know what to do with myself. While going to Alton Towers with the missus, and stuff like that, made me happy, when you are an England cricketer and you are not around for England matches it can make you feel uncomfortable. But Andy reiterated what a big series we had ahead of us in the winter, and that they wanted to make sure I was in fine fettle for it. Others were also targeted for feet-up weeks throughout the season.

Everyone wants to play in England v Australia matches, although the one-day series we played against Ricky Ponting's team in midsummer 2010 was naturally unloved. The five-match campaign was no more than a money-making exercise, and nobody was hoodwinked by it. As players, we couldn't escape the feeling that instead of a NatWest Series we could all have been enjoying a fortnight of rest and recuperation at the halfway point of another hectic year.

We won the series, which was great for confidence, building on our World Twenty20 final victory. Charging into a 3–0 lead reaffirmed to us that we could beat them on a regular basis, but it was not a particularly enjoyable experience. If I was a fast bowler, that kind of series would make me give serious consideration to the wife's proposal for a midsummer holiday in Skegness. At the start of a fortnight like that you know you've got to bowl 50 overs competitively over a fortnight plus net every other day for a couple of hours, and all for a series that nobody wants to come and watch. I exaggerate slightly, but the fact was that I couldn't even give away my complimentary tickets. Even at Lord's, I had two unused. Normally, friends and family would be fighting over them.

On a personal note, I did okay. Four wickets in the pivotal match at Old Trafford, a one-wicket win, represented half my total of victims for the series. Regular tussles with Australia also provided the chance to assess the batsmen we would be facing in the future, how their games had developed since the last time I had bowled to them and whether there was any weaknesses in their technique. The one thing that did become apparent to me during that series was that Michael Clarke was in nowhere near the form he had been the year before, during the 2009 Ashes. That previous summer, every time he batted he looked unbelievable. But in this one-day series, he cut quite a different figure. Although he got a couple of scores, he struggled a bit against the short ball and Stuart Broad even bounced him out in the second match at Cardiff – I reckon I'm the only England player to have taken a catch at short leg in a one-day international in England. In addition to Clarke, I sensed that Ricky Ponting was not in the same frame of mind as he had been in the past.

The door then opened on what truly was a pretty horrible summer for English cricket. At the time, it seemed to be a good one for me, with 22 wickets in four Tests against Pakistan, one of them from the best ball I have ever bowled – only for those achievements to be tarnished when the apparent actions of our opponents, or at least a select few, were made public. The spot-fixing allegations that hit the headlines sullied the 3–1 win and the sport of cricket in general.

We were aware that Pakistan would offer a much sterner test of our credentials than Bangladesh and so the result of the first Test at the end of July, and how it came about, were ideal for both me and the team. To summarise, I stood at slip and therefore had one of the best seats in the house as Jimmy Anderson produced a swing master-class at Trent Bridge. I took four catches in the match and Jimmy bamboozled them with 11 for 71 in a 354-run win. My contribution with the ball was limited to a couple of overs.

Having been dismissed for 80 to lose the opening match, Pakistan struggled once more at Edgbaston, where they could muster only 72 batting first. But my first wicket of the series was definitely worth the wait. Twelve months earlier I had claimed, tongue padlocked in cheek, that the delivery that did for Ricky Ponting was the ball of the century, so there was some irony in the fact that it was back at the same ground that some eminent critics of the game branded my delivery to Imran Farhat exactly that, and compared it to 'that' ball to Mike Gatting from Shane Warne at Old Trafford in the 1993 Ashes.

Pakistan were 53 for one when I came on for my first over of the match, the 30th over of the second innings. My first ball turned a fraction, the second went pretty much straight on, but the third came out of the hand absolutely perfectly, fizzed, dipped, pitched outside leg stump and hit the top of off. I will never bowl a better ball than that. It left Imran Farhat groping with his hand on the floor, almost in disbelief. In one way he was unlucky, because I'll never be able to replicate it. Just once in a while everything falls in to place, like the perfect storm, I guess. The wind blows in the right direction, the sea swells properly, the air pressure and temperature is just right. This was one of those moments when a combination of factors made it the worst-case scenario for the batsman. The ball had enough revolutions on it to create that fizz and dip and hit the part of the wicket that was going to make it turn the absolute ideal amount to hit the top of off stump. A lot of deliveries turned that day but that was just perfect. Given that it was the third ball of a spell, I reckon it would have done for any batsman in the world. The only way I could envisage anyone surviving would have been if they had opted to sweep.

Pakistan are traditionally good players of spin bowling, but when you get a ball like the Farhat one it can send shockwaves through a dressing room. Everyone sits up and takes note. In one-day cricket, for example, if you get a ball to turn sharply early on, it's guaranteed to take 15 runs off your spell, no matter how you bowl, because batsmen become naturally more cautious against you. All it takes is the inevitable comment from the next bloke in to bat. One interjection of 'Cor, did you see how much that spun?' and doubt is implanted in all his team-mates' heads.

The pitches really turned in 2010 and when it rags square my eyes obviously light up – not that you want *every* delivery you send down to be as exaggerated in its sideways movement. When the surface proves as helpful as that, the fact that some turn and others do not is a much more useful weapon. Particularly dangerous balls, in fact, are the ones when the batsman plays for the turn that isn't there. The hardest thing to bat on is an inconsistent pitch, whether the variation is in the spin or the bounce. The trick is to get onlookers to believe you are varying the degrees of turn, but the truth is that a lot of your successes come when one goes square and the next goes straight on from virtually the same spot.

Certainly in my first two years in Test cricket such variations accounted for a number of my wickets, particularly to left-handers. Two-thirds of my first 50 wickets were against lefties, in fact, and there are reasons for that. Rather like a genuine fast bowler trying to generate maximum pace, as a spinner I try to spin everything as hard as I can. But if the ball doesn't grip, and therefore goes straight on, lbws come into the equation for me. If it does turn, then slip is in play. And since the Decision Review System has been applied, technology has shown that appeals umpires would routinely have turned down in the past are actually hitting the stumps. That has increased my wickets by a third, I reckon, and around half of my successes against left-handers are from balls which haven't turned as much as they were meant to.

Moments like the Farhat one at Edgbaston are genuinely thrilling, but what happened later in the series provided me with an inescapable feeling that my efforts had been downgraded in some way. I finished with six wickets in the victory in Birmingham, and then followed up with seven at The Oval, in a match that we lost. That sequence of three matches was probably a high point for me in Tests in terms of stringing consistent performances together. I was bowling very well, so the events of 29 August 2010, which turned out to be the final day of the four-match series, left me with a hollow feeling in the pit of my stomach.

Lord's is not a ground that offers massive turn, but I had brilliant fun in the fourth Test when I was switched from my usual Nursery End to the Pavilion End and for once it did. It was pleasing throughout the four matches to dismiss Pakistan captain Salman Butt, because he was not popular with our team even before the *News of the World* sting that implicated him in spot-fixing. The way he carried himself rubbed me up the wrong way. Aloof and arrogant are the best descriptions of him, and what made my dismissal of him with my first ball after tea on the third day all the more satisfying was the fact he pompously refused to leave the field despite being bowled. Of course, we all knew television replays would confirm his fate and I really enjoyed standing there in our little huddle taking the mickey out of him while he awaited it. He was adamant that the ball had rebounded off wicketkeeper Matt Prior's gloves and knocked the bails off. He probably had a bit too much on his mind to realise the ball had hit the stumps.

Toying with him as he stood his ground was hilarious. A lot of the Pakistani lads can't speak English but he most definitely can, and it was nice to know that he could understand every word of what I said – although, to be fair, I also taught him a few new ones.

Such was the speed with which we shot out Pakistan, for just 74 in 33 overs, that we had another go at them that evening. It meant that I actually dismissed Butt twice in the same session, the final one before the allegations emerged that he, in collusion with bowlers Mohammad Asif and Mohammad Amir, conspired for no-balls to be bowled at specific points in the match dictated by Butt's agent Mazhar Majeed. It was vile information to digest, and I would be lying if I said that it didn't take the edge off my performance in the match. The fourth and final morning was the most bizarre atmosphere I have ever played international cricket in. When we took wickets – and I took four of the final six – we genuinely didn't know how to celebrate. By the end we weren't celebrating at all, and nor were the crowd, the stony silence a confirmation that everyone in the ground was aware of that morning's headlines.

There was even some doubt whether the match would continue given what had happened on the first two days of the contest, but as a team we remained clinical. For example, when I bowled Amir with the first ball he faced from me, with an absolute snorter that pitched outside leg and hit the top of off, normally I would have gone absolutely bonkers. But because it was him, and came in those circumstances, I took no pleasure in it. None of us spoke to the opposition; we just couldn't wait to get off the field – we felt as if we wanted to get away and wash our hands of the series. We had been dragged into something that we simply did not want to be part of. Something that should have been sacrosanct – a Lord's Test match – had been ruined.

The after-match presentation was held away from the public glare, in the Long Room, and we just grabbed our winners' medals, and cheques, and got out of there. There was a worrying whisper that the records of the game would be expunged, and it would have been gutting not to have my name up on the honours board for my five second-innings wickets. It would have been even harder on Stuart there is a good England career ahead of Aj, as I believe he can develop into a top-class bowler. What he showed us inside his first six months around the full England team was an ability to reverse-swing the ball with great control, and a faultless attitude. He is the most intense trainer I've ever seen. In one way he is like a model because he is so paranoid about weight issues and what he eats. He actually counts calories by the mouthful and if he has so much as a slice of bread he wants to get down the gym to bash the carbs out of himself. He actually trains too much, I reckon, and that is why his body packs up every now and again and begs for a rest. If he gets the balance right, though, he will be awesome for England.

Physical management of players became an issue for the England coaching team during the 2010 summer. Concern over potential player fatigue meant they were desperate to look after us all as the Ashes drew nearer, and to be honest I held the same view. In my head, I was already prioritising that series five months before departure, and I began hoping that my body would hold out and that I wouldn't incur serious injury at the wrong time. At the end of the summer I was relieved when I walked away unscathed. I would play Ashes matches over anything else. With this in mind, I was okay for once when Andy Flower instructed me to rest instead of taking part in the three-match NatWest Series against the Bangladeshis. At least in theory, because when it came down to it I found it difficult to know what to do with myself. While going to Alton Towers with the missus, and stuff like that, made me happy, when you are an England cricketer and you are not around for England matches it can make you feel uncomfortable. But Andy reiterated what a big series we had ahead of us in the winter, and that they wanted to make sure I was in fine fettle for it. Others were also targeted for feet-up weeks throughout the season.

Everyone wants to play in England v Australia matches, although the one-day series we played against Ricky Ponting's team in midsummer 2010 was naturally unloved. The five-match campaign was no more than a money-making exercise, and nobody was hoodwinked by it. As players, we couldn't escape the feeling that instead of a NatWest Series we could all have been enjoying a fortnight of rest and recuperation at the halfway point of another hectic year.

We won the series, which was great for confidence, building on our World Twenty20 final victory. Charging into a 3–0 lead reaffirmed to us that we could beat them on a regular basis, but it was not a particularly enjoyable experience. If I was a fast bowler, that kind of series would make me give serious consideration to the wife's proposal for a midsummer holiday in Skegness. At the start of a fortnight like that you know you've got to bowl 50 overs competitively over a fortnight plus net every other day for a couple of hours, and all for a series that nobody wants to come and watch. I exaggerate slightly, but the fact was that I couldn't even give away my complimentary tickets. Even at Lord's, I had two unused. Normally, friends and family would be fighting over them.

On a personal note, I did okay. Four wickets in the pivotal match at Old Trafford, a one-wicket win, represented half my total of victims for the series. Regular tussles with Australia also provided the chance to assess the batsmen we would be facing in the future, how their games had developed since the last time I had bowled to them and whether there was any weaknesses in their technique. The one thing that did become apparent to me during that series was that Michael Clarke was in nowhere near the form he had been the year before, during the 2009 Ashes. That previous summer, every time he batted he looked unbelievable. But in this one-day series, he cut quite a different figure. Although he got a couple of scores, he struggled a bit against the short ball and Stuart Broad even bounced him out in the second match at Cardiff – I reckon I'm the only England player to have taken a catch at short leg in a one-day international in England. In addition to Clarke, I sensed that Ricky Ponting was not in the same frame of mind as he had been in the past.

The door then opened on what truly was a pretty horrible summer for English cricket. At the time, it seemed to be a good one for me,

Right: The celebrations begin.

Below: Flintoff runs out Ponting at The Oval, and the Ashes are as good as ours!

Left and above: Pinching Brett Lee's celebration after bowling him in a one-day game at the Riverside in 2009. Thankfully, he took the joke well!

Below: Watching the greatest team on earth with big Steve Harmison, one of my favourite men to go on tour with.

Victory in the second Test at Durban on the 2009-10 tour. My nine wickets earned me the man-of-the-match award.

Acknowledging a Test-best 85 at Centurion, December 2009. Jimmy Anderson and I shared a century partnership, during which I encouraged him to hit his first six in any form of cricket.

'Bunny' Onions does it again, by blocking out the last over from Morne Morkel to save the third Test at Cape Town's beautiful Newlands, January 2010.

Left: Sarah and I tied the knot in January 2010. What an amazing day!

Below: Victory in the World Twenty20, May 2010.

The trio responsible for our 517 for one declared in the first Test at the Gabba: Jonathan Trott (135*), Alastair Cook (235*), Andrew Strauss (110). I didn't move from my makeshift bed in the changing room for two days.

I reverted to a holding role in the final Test of the 2010–11 Ashes as the pace bowlers ran through the Australians twice.

Four nil against the Indians, and a new world ranking of number one. Jimmy and I seem delighted with our ability to pour champagne out of the bottle.

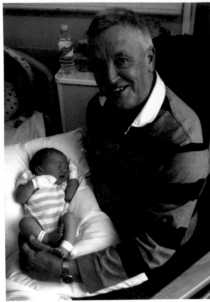

Mum and Dad both got to meet their new grandson in hospital. Wilf is one day old here.

Leaving Wilf and Sarah behind to play in the World Cup was incredibly hard. Skype provided some relief but the cats didn't seem too excited to see me!

Wilfred already has impeccable dress sense! Here we are in the famous black and white stripes of Newcastle United.

At David Cameron's house after our World Twenty20 win in 2010. Sarah is lurking in the background as I hand out political advice.

A proud moment for me as I toss the coin, in my role as England captain, at the Oval. It had taken more than a dozen years from my debut to be recognised as a natural leader...

Here I am walking off after taking 10 wickets in the second Test match against Sri Lanka in Colombo. It was 48 degrees. Yes, 48! Lunacy.

Broad, after his 169 rescued our innings, alongside Jonathan Trott, who weighed in with 184. I was glad they remained up on display because the guys in our dressing room knew that their team had not been trying to get out, or to bowl badly.

Some of the Pakistanis were probably as hacked off as we were at the end of that series, but not as hacked off as we were about to become. Ill feeling spilled over during the NatWest Series that followed when Pakistan Cricket Board chairman Ijaz Butt accused the England team of losing the third match of the series for cash. Being accused of match-fixing enraged us. I'm glad Butt didn't make his accusation in the same room as me. Being accused in that tit-for-tat manner – after an International Cricket Council inquiry was launched into the behaviour of the suspended Butt, Asif and Amir – was like being in a school playground, and it would have drawn a playground reaction from me. It was just so pathetic. His ludicrous and unfounded claims reminded me of the squabbles of six-year-olds.

'Why did you break that glass?'

'I didn't break it, you broke it.'

'No, I didn't, you did.'

Those comments, made on 19 September, the day before the fourth one-day international at Lord's, suggesting that we deliberately lost the third one-dayer in return for 'enormous amounts of money', were as offensive as they could possibly be. They went against everything I stand for as a professional sportsman. They left us feeling powerless because as soon as somebody says something like that and it is read by cricket followers, your name is smeared. You can't go around accusing people and pointing fingers with completely unsubstantiated claims. In the civilised world, it is not something that should happen, and I for one did not want to play on as a result. I lobbied that we should refuse as a team to carry on with the final two matches because I felt doing so was kowtowing to this clown. I thought we should distance ourselves from Butt and not play Pakistan while he was associated with them. Nor was I alone in my view. Andrew Strauss was of the same opinion prior to his meeting with the ECB and the

Professional Cricketers' Association, and Eoin Morgan was particulary vehement in speaking out against continuing. He was of the belief that you don't accuse people of things like that without any evidence.

As an England team, we released a statement expressing our disgust at Butt's comments, while our employers demanded an unreserved apology and retraction, or face a legal action. We retained our misgivings about competing in the final two matches – none of us wanted to play cricket against Pakistan in those circumstances – but Strauss persuaded us it was the right thing to do for the good of the world game and to avoid setting a precedent. 'We would like to express our surprise, dismay and outrage at the comments made by Mr Butt yesterday,' Strauss wrote. 'We are deeply concerned and disappointed that our integrity as cricketers has been brought into question. We refute these allegations completely and will be working closely with the ECB to explore all legal options open to us. We do, however, recognise our responsibilities to the game of cricket, and in particular to the cricket-loving public in this country, and will therefore endeavour to fulfil these fixtures to the best of our ability.'

Once again, however, you couldn't shake the feeling that the underlying motivation of the board to plough on was monetary – the scourge of the game. Whatever happens, we play on. We did so here and lost at Lord's, which meant that the series came down to a decider at the Rose Bowl. Eoin Morgan scored another hundred there to follow one earlier in the summer against Australia, and I took three for 26 as we won by a landslide 121 runs. After all that had gone before, victory felt as sweet as it could possibly get, and the team song that night was sung with a certain fervour, I can tell you. I would almost call it venom. It had been a dirty affair and a filthy end to the summer. I was glad it was all over.

It irritated me later when the ICC's anti-corruption tribunal meted out only five-year bans to the trio, with extra terms suspended for Butt and Asif. If that is the level of punishment, where is the deterrent? The problem is never going to go away unless life bans are handed out. That is what happened to the England and Sheffield

Wednesday footballer Peter Swan in the 1960s. He bet on his own team to lose in a match at Ipswich, at the peak of his career, and his suspension meant he never played for his country again. His best years were taken away from him.

Whatever the outcome of their impending court case – they protest their innocence in the face of corruption charges – and appeal against the ICC's decision to ban them, the likelihood is that all three of these Pakistani cricketers will play again, and in the case of Amir, he will get the chance of a lengthy career. Some even made excuses for him as he was only 18 when he transgressed. But just because someone is young, and talented, it doesn't make them exempt. Age can never be an excuse. He is playing for his country at full international level and when you do that you have to be a grown man. It is not a valid excuse that he was being led by his elders and that he didn't know better. The ICC have promoted a zero-tolerance policy on match-fixing, yet the length of the bans appears to have been tailored so that they can play again. If they are guilty, and have cashed in, then they have ruined the integrity of the game, so get rid of them. Let them find another game to play. Tell them to go and play chess, just keep them away from cricket. There should never be leniency for age. Rules are rules whether you are 18 or 58. Life means life to me. One thing's for sure, if I ever came up against Amir again I would be having plenty to say. Although, I guess I'd better be careful because he bowls at 90 miles an hour and is prone to running through the crease.

The funny thing was – excuse this figure of speech because none of it was in the slightest amusing – that at the time when Amir bowled the massive no-ball to Jonathan Trott, Paul Collingwood looked at the replay and said: 'Flippin' hell, that looks like match-fixing, that. It looks like he might be taking cash to bowl a no-ball.' He was laughing and joking about it, but it sparked a debate as to whether it was possible to bowl a no-ball like that by accident. There was a lot of scepticism but Stuart Broad argued that it was possible if you knackered up your run-up and tried to rectify it by changing your stride pattern. So, of course, later that week, Colly claimed to be the all-seeing-eye. 'Aah know I was only jokin' but I got it right,' he insisted.

It was during the Pakistan Test series that a lot was made of my exclusion from the ICC's long list for their 2010 Cricketer of the Year award. Like Jimmy Anderson, I had made the Test list, and went on to be named in the composite team of the year, but being snubbed by a selection committee chaired by Clive Lloyd, and including former England coach Duncan Fletcher and ex-England bowler Angus Fraser, drew plenty of attention. Not from me especially but from the British press. Within hours of their 19 August announcement, I had been added, with an apology for the oversight. I had enjoyed a good 12 months, with 49 Test wickets and 28 in one-day internationals, and was pleased with my performance at the World Twenty20. But this wasn't just about me. There was a feeling that the England team had received next to no credit for their achievements. Nasser Hussain was particularly riled, writing in the *Daily Mail*: 'It is astonishing to me that there were no Englishmen in the list of 16 names who will contest the ICC Cricketer of the Year award. In fact, it's an absolute joke. It's unbelievable,' he claimed. 'There must be something wrong with the system if no player from a side who have won the Ashes, the World Twenty20, one-day series against South Africa and Australia, and drawn a Test series in South Africa can make the long list.'

Only three days earlier my name had drawn attention for a different reason, as I appeared in court for the first time following a drink-driving charge. The incident occurred in the early hours of 2 April, following the Black Tie Opening Dinner for Ryan Sidebottom's benefit year at the Nottingham Belfry Hotel, the previous evening. Renovation work was being done on my house that week and the floorboards had been taken up by the builders in the process. Mindful of the fact that our cats Max and Paddy can get everywhere, Sarah and I shone a torch into the gaps and shouted for them both before the floorboards were put back down, just in case either of them had wandered down there. Of course, there was no response, and so when Paddy failed to show up for a full day we were concerned enough for me to be making 'Lost Cat' posters and posting them up and down our street. It was 36 hours later, in fact, after Sarah and I returned from Siddy's do, that we heard this ridiculously faint squeaking. We had no idea where, but it was evident that Paddy was stuck somewhere beneath our feet.

In a panic we looked for some screwdrivers but we couldn't find any, so Sarah asked me whether I thought I was over the limit. I had drunk a few glasses of wine over a number of hours but we had been back a while, and so, having told her I was okay, I jumped into her Porsche heading on a mission to the 24-hour Asda. However, on the way back I got pulled over by the police because, in their words, I was driving a high-performance car in an area that had recently experienced a high number of thefts and burglaries. Off I was carted to the police station by this copper who was giving it the big 'un routine. 'What do you pull in then, you cricket boys? What are you making a year? Yeah, I could have been a professional sportsman. I could have been a professional footballer. But I chose the force instead,' he told me. 'Did you hell,' I thought. When he got out of the car, he showed himself to be all of 5 ft 1 in. Only Sammy Lee played at that height, pal.

Within a couple of hours of my leaving the cells later that morning, a *Daily Mirror* reporter knocked on my front door. The following day I was to read a story riddled with inaccuracies: apparently I had been out belatedly celebrating my birthday, and I had been out with my girlfriend, which my wife was understandably concerned about, chiefly because I had been with her. Then for the whole of the 2010 summer I had to put up with inane shouts from the stands. People meowed or yelled things at me like: 'Swanny, where's your cat?' I didn't hear one amusing thing either, which was naturally a source of disappointment.

Over the next few months I had to go back to Nottingham Magistrates' Court on numerous occasions, after it was admitted that the police had used the wrong blood sample to take a reading of the alcohol level in my blood. They were supposed to use the first sample they took but neglected to do so, throwing it away and using the second sample instead. The case was adjourned a number of times on this issue, with the Crown persistently arguing that they had not messed up when they had, and because of my England commitments, it was not resolved until the eve of the 2011 World Cup. When I visited the court building all the press would be lined up waiting outside and I loved playing mind games with them. In my head everything has to be a competition, so I started coming up with different ways I could walk past them. There is an expanse of 200 yards of open ground to get to the courtroom door, so it is almost impossible to evade being spotted, yet once I did actually manage to sneak in. Swann 1 Paparazzi 0.

There were happier times ahead at home and further afield, however, as the 2010 domestic season finished. Sarah and I discovered that we would be having a baby boy in the new year, which meant I had a month to get the nursery decorated and buy some little outfits, including the obligatory Newcastle kit with 'Wilf 66' on the back. There was also a responsibility to ensure I was in good physical shape for the most demanding of England tours that winter.

My thoughts were nothing but positive in the build-up to departure for Australia, and I was extremely confident that our bowling attack would dismiss them regularly. That confidence had grown considerably over the course of the summer because Jimmy Anderson had bowled like a dream against the Pakistanis. He had swung the ball at good pace over the course of the Test series, although in one way his success served to put extra pressure on him, because every so-called expert was harping on about the fact it had come with the Duke's ball and the Kookaburra version would be used in the Ashes.

But I recognised a quiet confidence in Jimmy that he could do well out in Australia. He knew he was a better bowler than he had been on the previous Ashes tour in 2006–07, and though mindful that it would not swing as much as it had done in England over the summer, he had by this point learned a lot more tricks of the trade. And the fact that Australians everywhere had written him off as a no-hoper made it all the sweeter when he turned out to have such a great Ashes. I was made up for him. He is a grumpy bastard if he is not doing well – you should see him when he gets dropped for a game if we are on tour – whereas when he's doing well he still looks grumpy on the pitch but is a good laugh off it. If he wasn't he would be permanently unbearable.

Jimmy produced some of the best conventional swing bowling I have ever seen to run through Pakistan at Trent Bridge. And seeing my other close mate in the team, Alastair Cook, come out of his form slump was equally timely. Cooky endured a stinking summer, a difficult one for batting because of the aerial and lateral movement on offer for bowlers. But his hundred in the third Test at The Oval came at just the right time. The press were starting to get on his back following a run of low scores and that innings halted the hounding and eased the pressure on his place in the starting line-up for Australia. However, even in his wildest dreams he wouldn't have envisaged the series he was about to have – then again, probably none of us could.

18

THE ASHES RETAINED

WHEN WORD of a pre-Ashes bonding mission filtered its way into the England dressing room during the first Test against Pakistan in late summer 2010 it kiboshed a rare chance for me to get away with my mates. Having already been given a list of all the crucial dates for the rest of the year in mid-season, I had arranged to head off to Las Vegas for a few days with the lads shortly after our one-day matches against the Pakistanis concluded on 22 September. There was no chance any other commitments would be tagged on after that date, I thought, so imagine my surprise when Stuart Broad approached me in a panic after getting wind of the management's plans.

'Can't believe it, mate, can't believe it,' he chuntered, ashen-faced.

'What on earth are you babbling on about, Broad?'

'Haven't you heard? We are going on a team bonding trip straight after the one-day series.'

Concerned that my four-day jolly was in jeopardy – if you have seen the film *The Hangover*, I anticipated creating carnage on a similar level – I told Broad to come with me and marched to Andy Flower's office. Coincidentally, Broady was also due to be in Vegas that week, on Luke Wright's stag do.

'A word please, Andy,' I said, as I poked my head around the door. 'There is a nasty rumour flying around that immediately after the season you are sending us away on a bonding trip. Tell us it isn't true.'

With a wry smile on his face, he simply said: 'I wouldn't book anything if I were you.'

Broady explained his Luke Wright commitments. 'And I'm kinda going on a beer-drinking and gambling trip with my mates to Vegas too,' I said.

'I'd kinda get your money back,' he told us.

I couldn't, so that meant three grand out of the window, and I was at the mercy of ECB holidays instead. The international summer had only been put to bed 36 hours earlier, and to a man we felt we needed this trip like a hole in the head. As it happened, I felt as if I did have a hole in my head as we set off for Gatwick Airport, having only just got back from a very late one at the Professional Cricketers' Association awards dinner at the Hurlingham Club in London. After a tumultuous end to the summer, that night was a rare occasion for us to let our hair down, and we got mullered. A few of us literally just made it back to the hotel in time to change into our tracksuits before our red-eye departure. Eoin Morgan hadn't made it back at all, in true Irish style.

We were ferried down to Gatwick, passports at the ready, as instructed, in the early hours of Friday, 24 September, having been given a list of essential items to pack – army fatigues, sleeping bags and stuff like that. Briefly, however, when we were handed our boarding passes, we dared to dream that it had all been a double bluff. Apparently, we were on our way to Munich, and in that dazed 6 a.m. state, the mind slowly cranked into gear: 'Munich . . . late September . . . Oktoberfest!'

Having been to Stuttgart's beer festival for my stag do, I was temporarily the most excited man on the planet at the thought that we were heading to the most renowned drinking festival in western Europe. I couldn't wait to get there. Unfortunately, however, when we landed in Germany, we were met by two Australian blokes, who were blatantly special forces dudes. Menacingly, they did not speak a word to us, aside from demanding we clamber into their minibuses, and proceeded to drive us two hours to a field in the middle of nowhere.

That was the start of our four-day boot camp. For boot camp is what it was, no two ways about it. We put up tents, hiked, carried logs and went through exercise drills, all at the behest of these mean-spirited Aussies. If anyone swore, the whole group had to stop their activity and do 50 press-ups. If you called someone by their first name, the group had to stop and do 50 press ups. It was 'Mr Anderson' that week; any muttering of 'Jimmy' resulted in us down on our fronts, arms pumping.

For me, it was easily the worst four days of my life. I hated every minute of it. The idea was to teach us all about teamwork, and what we could achieve as a group, but it even tested the resolve of Andy Flower as early as halfway through the first day. As we carried bricks up a hill, I glanced over at him, open-mouthed.

'What the hell am I doing here?' he said. 'Why did I agree to this?'

The trip was the brainchild of our security expert, Reg Dickason, and was designed to test our limits, both as individuals and as a team. I am sure some people enjoyed the challenge of that discovery, and as a team it didn't do us any harm, but I couldn't have cared less about the whole experience. For someone like me who absolutely detests authority, being frogmarched around and told what to do was purgatory. Mobile phones were confiscated, our meals came from ration packs and we slept in tents. I am a genial and affable bloke, but I resented being there.

We were just a few weeks away from leaving for the Ashes tour and I wanted to spend some time at home with my pregnant wife, as I was going to see very little of her over the next four months. Put it this way, I wouldn't have suffered the guilt trip Jonathan Trott experienced when Andy Flower told him he was excused from coming. His wife Abi was due to give birth while we were there, but it was explained to him that once we'd departed, no one would be able to get hold of him. Because he was so keen to be part of the team, and did not want to miss out, it was with a certain degree of reluctance that Trotty agreed to stay put in England. I would have given a million pounds to do the same. Once I got there and found out exactly how degrading the experience felt, I would have upped it to two million.

In the evenings we sat around in the pitch black, a big bonfire and a torch the only light sources, and held group discussions. On one occasion we were split into separate groups and briefed to give presentations in whatever way we wished on certain subjects. My group's subject was mental fortitude, so I grasped the opportunity and completely took over. I turned our presentation into a mock game show, with me as the over-the-top American host. 'Hi, I'm the completely non-pompous Giles Clarke III,' I said, by way of introduction. Lots of my team-mates got a panning, although I am not sure those serious Aussie chaps were overly impressed. However, humour was my escape route.

That brief levity definitely helped my mood but reality hit home when it was time for bed, which meant sharing a tent with four other people. Mark Bawden, the team psychologist, was pressed right up next to me and snored like a deranged gibbon in my ear all night. By 3 a.m. I was punching him as hard as I could to stop the din. He would briefly stir, say 'Sorry, cocker' in his West Country drawl and then immediately fall back into his snoring slumber. When I finally got to sleep, it was broken by these two Aussie maniacs who awoke the whole camp by barking a two-minute warning for duty. So, here we were, suffering from sleep deprivation, tramping down the road with our arms held in front of us for 20 minutes, at four o'clock in the morning. And in the flipping rain too. Next time I get the slightest inkling that we might be doing that kind of thing, expect to read in the newspapers that I passed out at the airport and was sent home on medical grounds. Or that I have flat feet. That excuse got people out of the war, didn't it? I would gladly be England cricket's first conscientious objector.

How kind it was of Reg to organise that trip for us. Joking aside, he is a really popular bloke among our squad, but it safe to say there was a lot of resentment towards him that week, most of it emanating from the fact that while we roughed it, he stayed in a hotel down the road. Alastair Cook only arrived for the last couple of days because he had been to his brother's wedding, and Reg stayed out on his own so that he could pick him up from the airport and transport him to us. So when Cook reported sightings of empty McDonald's bags in the car, we were left fuming. He had been troughing on fast food while we were eating out of packets for a week. My ire was fuelled by the fact that I'd never been hungrier. If he'd stood next to the edge of a cliff that week, there would have been a queue of 15 people waiting to push him off. It is safe to say that the three-hour wait at Munich airport for our return flight involved some serious pigging. I have never seen so many Big Macs smashed in my life. Obviously, that damage was inflicted by the rest of the lads, while my choice was couscous and feta in a sun-dried tomato wrap.

Cooky was quite shocked when he first saw the state we were in, and I confessed to him that I was seriously depressed by the week's events. In contrast, he's the kind of bloke who always lands on his feet and it was typical that his only full day with us was one of outdoor pursuits. He couldn't fathom what all the moaning was about as we were thrown headlong into abseiling and rock climbing.

It was during the camp finale, of course, that Jimmy Anderson incurred his famous pre-Ashes injury, one that was feared might rule him out of the series. We were all put into pairs for boxing, the idea being that your partner was of a similar size. But in that scenario, who on earth was going to go with Chris Tremlett? Jimmy drew the short straw, took one big punch to his torso and walked away with a broken rib. I sparred with Ajmal Shahzad, and he also landed a killer blow – on my conk. There was supposed to be no hitting in the head, but he threw an uppercut at my body and missed. How on earth his glove got past that chin of mine, I'll never know. My nose rang for about two weeks after that and it still clicks now. Thanks, Aj.

Of course, with the benefit of hindsight, and a glance through rose-tinted spectacles, some might say that the break in Germany was essential for forging togetherness ahead of our big winter. But I reckon that had long been established, and that our sense of team was already our biggest strength. For example, while critics, Shane Warne most eminent amongst them, claimed that we had no chance of dismissing Australia regularly unless I took the majority of the wickets, I was convinced they were wrong. Warne reckoned I would need 40 victims for us to win, subscribing to the notion that I would be the difference between two evenly matched teams. Some people would have had you believe that I was single-handedly going to win the Ashes for England, based on the two years of success behind me.

I did not feel that these opinions were very informed, however, because when you looked at the places in which we were going to play, the pitches we would find there and the guys we were going to play against, it seemed likely that what lay ahead for me was a lot of hard work. Spinners just don't go to Australia and take 40 wickets in five Test matches. Sure, Warne himself had managed that feat against England in England, in 2005, but we're talking about one of the most special players the game has ever seen. So while I was confident of having a decent Ashes, I knew, even before a ball was bowled, that my role was going to be similar to what it had been in South Africa rather than a series-defining one. My main aim in South Africa had been to hold down one end, and I expected more of the same. If in fulfilling the requirements of the team my own successes swelled to five-wicket hauls then great, but that would be a bonus.

Of course, I would be lying if I said that it was not nice to have my ego massaged by comments such as Warne's, but any suggestion that I was England's greatest hope in Australia since Ian Botham in the 1980s was complete tosh. Deep down I knew that I could be successful against the Australians because I had the experience of bowling to them, and I had been successful in my Test career to that point. There wasn't going to be anyone who would surprise me – it was only Phil Hughes I hadn't really bowled at and that was because he kept getting out early in the previous Ashes. I had game plans for all their top-order batsmen, and although I knew we wouldn't be playing on raging bunsens, Australian grounds are big and that is always a positive thing for a spinner. So, just as I'd been against South Africa, I was confident that I would do well.

Contrary to sceptical Aussie opinion, I was convinced that, as a collective, we would bowl Australia out regularly. Jimmy Anderson had been bowling brilliantly throughout the whole of 2010, not just for a fleeting spell at the end of the summer, and even when the ball didn't swing for periods against Bangladesh and Pakistan, our pace bowlers still looked dangerous with their lengths, lines and variations. So whereas others expressed reservations about our potency, I had none, and I was of a firm belief that we would win matches with big runs in the first innings. When you are playing on good wickets there are no two ways about it, if you don't get 400 in the first innings you are going to struggle. The reason that we went on to win so convincingly over there was that although we bowled really well, and dismissed Australia twice in four of the Test matches, we absolutely piled on the runs. When you consistently get into positions where you cannot lose, you hold all the aces.

Alastair Cook was absolutely phenomenal with his 766 runs, it was the series of his life, and Jonathan Trott was not far behind him in consistently churning out scores. Andrew Strauss, meanwhile, was in the crazy position of having a sound campaign himself but not even managing half as many runs as his opening partner. Ian Bell and Kevin Pietersen weighed in with big scores too, and the best way to summarise our displays was that we batted in the way Australia have traditionally batted against us. All a bowling unit wants is scores to bowl at and if your batsmen give you a chance to win three or four out of five Test matches then you are doing really well. Without claiming to be a soothsayer, the formula I suspected we needed to win out there is the one that helped us to our 3–1 success.

Thankfully, Jimmy recovered from his cracked rib in the nick of time, and we went into the first tour game against Western Australia with a fully fit squad. For a few minutes during our first net session, however, I feared that we would not, after Tim Bresnan struck me on the end of the thumb while I was batting. I feared the worst, but you always do whenever you get hit, I guess. Initially, I thought I had cracked it and panic set in that I would be out of the Ashes, but my fears proved unfounded and I had only suffered bruising. However, throughout the rest of the series I was forced to wear a protective sheath over my thumb, almost like a condom – a metal strip with neoprene around it – whenever I was in the field. Even then, in catching practice, whenever I took one too close to the joint I knew about it. It felt like a red-hot poker in the eyeball.

The three-day game against Western Australia in Perth started on 5 November 2010, and Stuart Broad's first over, the second of the tour, set the tone for what was to follow. From his fourth ball, Western Australia's opening batsman Liam Davis edged to me at second slip. It wasn't an easy catch – in fact, being slightly to my left and fairly low down, it was the kind you could easily drop in the first few overs of a tour – but rather than rattle around in my fingers, it went straight into the palm, as clean as you like. Michael Swart was bounced out next ball and we were up and running.

My first-innings contribution was dire, however, as I just couldn't shake the rustiness out of my bowling. Physically, I felt dreadful: stiffness from the first few days of training restricted my movement and discomfort in my back was a concern. The garbage I sent down was not spinning, drifted the wrong way and lacked any real threat. I swapped ends for the second innings, and it was a completely different story, so I decided to put my struggle on the opening day down to a lengthy lay-off, and the psychological trauma of my brief stint as GI Joe in Deutschland.

Four wickets in Western Australia's second innings contributed to the hosts being dismissed for 223, and set up a run chase of 243 in four hours. We displayed our intent by completing it at a rate of five runs per over. What was eye-opening afterwards, though, was the reaction of the Australian media to our victory. This, they were quick to tell us, was the worst Western Australian team for 30 years. But the plain fact was that we hammered them on an unbelievably good wicket.

There was a significant change at the start of the 2010–11 Ashes in the England team's approach to the state games. On previous tours we had treated these warm-ups as glorified practice, but one of Andy Flower's big objectives was to develop a winning culture quickly and attempt to maintain it through the whole tour. So we approached the first three matches as if they were a mini-series, and set out to try to win it 3–0. There was a real desire to achieve that, although we kept our own counsel about it rather than blurt it out as a statement of intent.

We manufactured another push for victory at the Adelaide Oval the following week when, despite only losing nine wickets in the match, declarations in each innings left South Australia a 308-run target on the final day. I was satisfied with my four for 68 in South Australia's first-innings 221, and that was the one ground I was able to get a feel for ahead of the five-Test series. Our attitude in that match – which was terminated by torrential rain with the state side 48 for two shortly after lunch on the final day – shocked a couple of our opponents. Chatting afterwards, they couldn't believe how hard we had gone at them to try to win – they had expected us to use the latter stages as batting practice. Instead, Stuart Broad bowled seriously fast and bombed them: it was pretty hostile stuff and indicative of our tour ethos. Australian state sides of days gone by had done their utmost to undermine England, but the tables had been turned.

Much was made of our attention to detail and the fact that the Test attack was dispatched to Queensland early rather than heading to Tasmania for the final first-class fixture before the real stuff began on 25 November at the Gabba. It was a fine piece of outside-the-box thinking, and not the sort of thing that had been done before on overseas tours. Our Australian bowling coach, Dave Saker, flagged the idea up as soon as he saw the itinerary. He recognised the cunning of the schedule Cricket Australia had devised for us. Playing in Hobart is just like playing in England climate-wise, whereas Brisbane could not be more of a contrast. It's tropical, hot and sticky. Saker's logic was that it would be better to send the bowlers up there early to get used to the demands of the temperature and humidity.

It was a move that provided a double whammy as far as we were concerned. While Tim Bresnan, Ajmal Shahzad, Chris Tremlett and Monty Panesar made mincemeat of Australia A thousands of miles away, we acclimatised at the Allan Border Oval, where Queensland play most of their state cricket. Wet weather meant that we were unable to get onto the Gabba itself so close to the first Test, but bowling down the road was the next best thing. The getaway was also good from a bonding point of view, as Jimmy Anderson, Steve Finn, Stuart Broad and I socialised every night. One evening in Brisbane was one of my favourites of the whole tour. Dave had come out to dinner with the four of us and we introduced him to Jäger Bombs as his one for the lift shaft. 'Bloody great! We'll have another one of those,' he announced, after necking his maiden shot. One hour later we were all in a nightclub, and I am ashamed to say that after falling over several times I left the youngsters to it.

We were in good spirits when the touring party was reunited, and the fact that our second-string attack was up and running, having bowled us to a 10-wicket win, upped our confidence. It had been a perfect build-up, and we sensed the changing mood of the Australians as the weeks passed and our number of wins increased. We had been prepared for the usual media-led Pommie-bashing – as soon as you land the whole country seems against you, even people walking their dogs in the street are prone to stopping to abuse you for being an English cricketer – yet by now there was a distinct lack of it. It was a sign that the cricket-loving folk of Australia were impressed with how we had gone about our business. In contrast, their own team were copping heaps. Defeat in India meant Ricky Ponting's captaincy was under massive pressure, while big question marks hung over the heads of three or four of their top batsmen. So, as has often been the case, the two teams competing in the opening Ashes match seemed to have come from different worlds – only this time we were not the ones under pressure. It was heavenly to hear positive things said about us in the local press: we were a credit to England, had banished the memories of poor English tourists before us – you get my drift. The Australian team, on the other hand, were portrayed as an embarrassment to their country.

The 2010–11 Australians had the weight of history on their shoulders. This was not the all-conquering team of four years previously, and they were reminded of that at every turn. Their predecessors contained half a dozen superstars, and only one of them, Ponting, was left. There was no Matthew Hayden, no Justin Langer, no Adam Gilchrist, no Shane Warne, no Glenn McGrath. Let's face it, take those five out of any team and you would be struggling. Or, looking at it another way, put them into any team in the last 30 years and you've probably got the best team in the world at that time. There is no doubt Australia were learning what mortality feels like on a cricket field. A trained chimp could have thrown the ball to Warne and demanded a six-for to win a Test match, but that was no longer an option.

The Gabba had been such a treacherous venue for overseas opponents over the past two decades that it had been nicknamed the Gabbattoir, but aside from losing captain Andrew Strauss in the first over, the first Test actually started all right for us. Things weren't going too badly at all until Stuart Broad allowed his youthful exuberance – nay, naivety – to jinx us. I was hanging out with Jimmy and Broady in the changing room – we lay on various physio beds and benches with rolled-up towels for pillows – when the youngest among us declared what a good day it had been, and how great it would be if we were only four down at the close. Ten minutes later, Broad was involved in the most frantic scene imaginable, his pads and thigh pad on the floor as he prepared himself to bat in record time. A 100-yard stroll later, he became Peter Siddle's hat-trick victim.

Being dismissed for 260 inside a day was a bit of a shock, given how well we were progressing, but in response we produced a good bowling performance at the start of Australia's innings that evening, even if the scoreboard didn't reflect it. Jimmy bowled ridiculously well both then and the following morning, probably as well as he bowled in the entire series, but without luck. For the first one and a half hours, Australia did not lose a wicket, yet we were completely on top. You couldn't keep up with the number of times Australia's batsmen were playing and missing, or getting away with borderline lbw shouts. Jimmy showed off the full repertoire – inswinger, away-swinger, bouncer – in a display that told everyone he could cut it Down Under. He didn't get his just rewards in that game, but he cashed in later in the series.

Jimmy did get our first two wickets of the Test winter, Shane Watson and Ricky Ponting either side of lunch on the second day, and we made significant inroads to reduce Australia to 143 for five. He then had Mike Hussey, who only secured his place in the Australian team with a Sheffield Shield hundred the previous week, stone-dead lbw but we had already used up our two permitted reviews. Hussey went on to score a big hundred, and shared a 307-run stand with fellow centurion Brad Haddin. I eventually dismissed Haddin, having had Marcus North caught at slip on day two, but I was not happy with my bowling in Brisbane.

All the talk in the build-up had been about how Australia were going to hit me out of the attack in a bid to expose our four-bowler policy. To be honest, that goes with the territory for a spinner anyway. As it happened, there was no need to target or unsettle me, because I bowled so many bad balls that they could just wait for them. I could not get my approach to the crease right, and I was genuinely disappointed that we had not had the chance to practise on the Gabba itself beforehand. Because it has a sand-based outfield, the approach to the crease is quite heavy, and I never got any rhythm into my run-up. It felt uncomfortable, and Hussey used his feet well early on to hit the ball over the top and then pulled anything I dropped short. I just couldn't get the pace of the wicket right. The only saving grace for me was that I'd bowled better than I had done on my first day in the 2009 Ashes.

Faced with a 221-run deficit, there was a lot of pressure on us when we batted for a second time, but it was tempered by the fact that the pitch was still phenomenally good. If its quality was in any doubt, Andrew Strauss and Alastair Cook demonstrated it with tremendous application. Usually, as a Test match goes on, the pitch deteriorates and there is a bit more in it for the bowlers, but there was nothing on offer here and so us bowlers enjoyed a brilliant two days lying in the changing room laughing and joking amongst ourselves. Broad kept his match-summarising to a minimum this time, thank goodness, and we entered into competitions as to who could make the best playlists on the iPod. Obviously, I won, Jimmy was second and Broad was declared an absolute shambles. Who the hell is Chipmunk, by the way?

When we closed the fourth day on 309 for one we simply needed more of the same, and that included the preparation. So Alastair Cook was told in no uncertain terms that it was roast lamb again for him for his evening meal. It was what he had eaten the previous evening when he was unbeaten on six, so why have anything different now he was still going on 132? Cook batted for 10 and a half hours for his double hundred, and our second innings of 517 for one proved very significant for the rest of the series. To see the opposition bowling attack labouring for 152 overs and being blunted to that extent obviously filled all our batsmen – not just centurions Cook, Strauss and Jonathan Trott – with no end of confidence. Before a ball was bowled they were in good spirits, but you never know how things will go until you begin. When a few got in and inexplicably got out on the first day, it would have been easy for everyone to question how we were going to score runs in the series. But during the second innings our top three created a positive mood because they showed we could cash in on good wickets.

In psychological terms, Strauss landed another significant blow when Australia suffered the ignominy of having to bat again. I considered Strauss's declaration, when he could easily have allowed the game to drift to an inevitable conclusion, to be clever because it emphasised the point that Australia had not beaten us. He was sending a message to Ricky Ponting that his team had not been able to bowl us out, so we would have to pull out on our own terms. We got Simon Katich's wicket early, Shane Watson was dropped at slip and overall we showed good intent with the ball. Although Ponting scored his only fifty of the series, it was the England team that made the significant statement.

The only negative English thoughts coming out of that first Test belonged to Steve Finn. He hadn't bowled as well as he had done during the previous summer but he'd picked up six wickets, not that you would have known it from his reaction. Here he was with a six-for on his Ashes debut and he'd walked away from the Gabba genuinely disappointed.

'Nah, fact is I didn't bowl well, Grae,' he told me that evening.

'Fair enough, I've seen you bowl better, but you've got six wickets, for goodness sake,' I told him. 'If I ever see you like this again when you've got six wickets in an Ashes Test, I'm going to smack you on the nose. Just be happy that you've got the wickets. Sure, have high standards and be disappointed that you haven't bowled as well as you could, but don't ever be gutted about wickets, because there are days when you will bowl like a dream, just as Jimmy Anderson has done, and get none. That's the game.'

I have never met a young bloke as hard on himself, to be honest. Some people might see that as a good thing, but I don't because there is enough pressure already without manufacturing more of your own. He obviously sets really high standards, and while it is great to set those standards, you can't always reach them. If you want to improve your performance then go away and work to make it better, but no one can ever take your successes away from you, so give me the chance to bowl like a drain and get six and I'm over the moon.

There is a long-standing theory about the Adelaide Oval, the venue of the second Test, that batting first is essential to control a match, and having just batted so well at Brisbane, it would have been ideal for us to bat again, maintain our momentum and make the running. But within our team meetings in the build-up, we tried to play down this theory. Of course we would have preferred to have won the toss, but we tried to prepare ourselves to see the positives if we lost it and were asked to bowl first. For example, we thought it might swing a bit and there might be a little moisture for the first hour or so. It is always important to be ready for either side of the coin dropping. Nevertheless, after losing the toss, our captain walked into the dressing room and was met by a chorus of 'Bloody hell, Strauss, you've only got one job to do and you've messed it up!'

Yet we couldn't have got off to a better start in that match. Now, Jonathan Trott himself will admit he was not one of our better fielders on the park, so for him to run out Simon Katich, who had not even faced a ball, in the manner he did was unheard of: a direct hit with one stump to aim at was ridiculous. That gave us an early shot at Ponting, of course, and he edged his first ball from Jimmy straight to me at second slip. Broad then ran up and bowled a very fast over that had Michael Clarke jumping around the crease. When Jimmy nicked Clarke off with the first ball of his second over, only the third of the innings, Australia were two for three and we had grabbed control of the game, but not in the way one would usually associate with Adelaide. We dismissed our hosts for 245 before the close.

One of my strengths is the ability to put poor performances to one side and survey the next challenge. I have never seen the point of dwelling on negatives, and even though I was far from distraught with my Brisbane display, it was below the standard I set myself. At Adelaide, however, I was pleased to get on and tie things down at one end. Having already bowled there in a tour game, I felt a lot more comfortable. The outfield is absolutely impeccable, it's like a billiard table when you are running up to the crease, so I didn't have any of the rhythm problems I had experienced the previous week. The pitch also turned a bit, not a great deal, but enough to pick up a couple of first-innings wickets.

One of them was rather fortuitous, however. After snaring Mike

Hussey at slip agonisingly close to a hundred, I had Ryan Harris lbw first ball. Only later did I discover that he smashed the cover off it! Yet when he immediately signalled for a review it caused consternation among our team. 'Why are you doing that?' someone asked him, incredulously.

'Because I hit it,' was the no-nonsense response.

To be fair, when it was shown on the big screen you could tell he had hit it, yet there was no evidence to prove that he had from the TV technology available. Hot Spot showed nothing and the same could be said for the Snickometer. Harris must have been seething, as it contributed to him bagging a king pair.

So, despite all the pre-match drooling over this batting paradise, we managed to bowl them out before the end of the first day. The formula of racking up 600 and grinding your opponents down had gone out of the window – we began our first innings late that evening. Nobody would have believed that would be a possibility, and despite Andrew Strauss getting out in the first over of the following morning to Doug 'The Bald Git' Bollinger – I refuse to call him 'The Rug' as a matter of principle – we ended up posting another monster total. Every other member of the top seven got in – Alastair Cook churned out another hundred, Kevin Pietersen hit 227 – and we declared on 620 for five.

There were other benefits from batting for more than 11 hours, and they had repercussions for me. The foot-holes that Bollinger made were perfectly placed for an off-spinner. Not all left-arm pace bowlers create decent rough outside the off stump – Mitchell Johnson must bowl in ballet shoes and on tiptoes because he leaves nothing for you to play with. In contrast, Ryan Sidebottom was always the perfect foil for me because he made these great omelettes on the pitch. Full credit to Doug, though, because I can reveal he did have an impact on the Ashes after all. For future reference, Australia, he should always be selected against us for Test matches. His scarring of the surface gave me plenty to work with as we pressed for victory, and the pitch became increasingly more difficult to bat on, because one ball would hit the lip of the crater and turn massively and the next one would go straight on. That is how we got Ricky Ponting caught at slip: a couple really ripped and then the one that went straight on nicked the edge.

Our lead of 375 runs meant the pressure was always on Australia, but we also seemed to have that priceless knack of picking up wickets at crucial times in that Test. Never was that exemplified better than when Hussey and Michael Clarke batted together for a couple of hours on the fourth evening. It was the one occasion in the series that Clarke looked in command and that was probably because it was when the conditions made him feel most at home. While the ball didn't really swing, it did turn and that meant plenty of work for me. As everybody will acknowledge, Clarke is a fine player of spin bowling, and just as he had throughout 2009 he played me really well. The crucial point of the match, in fact, was when Strauss sidled up to me to inform me that he wanted to end my marathon 34-over spell. It was getting near the close of play and he told me he wanted to give Kevin Pietersen a couple of overs. Would you believe it – he got Clarke out with just his eighth delivery. The Australian vice-captain went to turn one nonchalantly on the leg side – sometimes you take your foot off the gas when a part-time bowler comes on – and got himself in a tangle as the ball kissed the edge of his bat and ballooned off his thigh pad to short leg. We all knew he had hit it, as the subsequent review showed, but for some reason he didn't walk and was initially given not out. How he thought he was going to get away with it, I will never know. He was clearly in denial, and perhaps like us celebrating Englishmen, he knew the Test was ours now.

That fourth wicket signalled the end of the fourth day, and despite our positivity, we were also acutely aware of the weather forecast, and the threat that it would hose it down the following afternoon. When the rain comes down in Australia it really comes down, but we had also learned that forecast rain does not always materialise. Sometimes the prediction of wet weather simply means that the temperature is 40 degrees instead of 42.

In the circumstances, we made a cracking start next morning when Hussey misjudged a pull off Steve Finn in the sixth over. In fact, what we didn't realise at the time was that we really were bowling against the clock. But it was the rush of wickets that kept us focused as Jimmy Anderson sent back Brad Haddin and Ryan Harris in consecutive balls.

It was then my turn to take centre stage – oh, how I hate that! – as I once again exposed Marcus North's uncertainty against me from around the wicket and followed up with two more to finish with a five-for and complete the Test match win. I bowled Xavier Doherty with one that found its way through bat and pad, and Peter Siddle was bowled through the gate. We had wrapped things up, and taken a 1–0 series lead, by claiming six wickets in 20 overs that final morning. It was a nice personal feeling too because, having taken four a few times, this was my first five-wicket haul against Australia in Tests. Statistics don't do much for me but that is the kind of stat I like – every bowler recognises five-fors. Yet I got abused afterwards by Jimmy and Alastair Cook for saluting our fans with my fists in the air. They reckoned I had wandered into Freddie Flintoff territory.

Later in the dressing room, our celebrations were still relatively young, following the post-match presentations, when Paul Collingwood urged us to put down our beers and look outside. It was around 2.30 p.m., the match had finished a little over two hours earlier, and so we trooped down towards the pitch – it is a long walk from the dressing room at the Adelaide Oval, because you are housed in the belly of the stand, so you have to walk about 30 metres down a ramp to get to the opening. The noise in the distance initially sounded something like an old washing machine rumbling, then a panel-beating convention, and as we got closer it might as easily have been a jumbo jet flying too low. Of course, we were soon to discover that it was none of these but the rain absolutely hoying down; the sort of rain that completely washes out an entire day's play. Australia had probably only needed to cling on for another hour and a half and that would have been that. As it was, it kept raining and we kept drinking. We had something to celebrate, and Colly provided some late-afternoon entertainment when he joined some of the Barmy Army and produced a Gazza-style dive onto the covers. Our fans' support throughout was absolutely phenomenal and they showed their staying power by remaining at the ground in world's-end weather, sliding down the mud banks and generally revelling in the fact that England were ahead with three matches remaining.

At that point in the tour I reckon our supporters, and cricket followers in general, recognised that we could win the Ashes. We were doing our best to convince people with our performances, and the evidence we presented was compelling. We had saved the first Test from the kind of position that in years gone by would have been a lost cause. Yet we saved it with ease. In Adelaide we had simply hammered them, and that is perhaps what made the Barmy Army feel things were going to go our way.

We had had to finish off the second Test match with a three-man attack after Stuart Broad injured his side, and within hours he was ruled out for the rest of the tour. He had pulled a muscle and when he took his shirt off it looked as if someone had cooked a fried egg on him. It was all yellow and horrible. But his misfortune – and I was gutted for him because he is a close mate – really opened the door for Chris Tremlett, or Twiggy as he is known in the dressing room.

Tremlett made an immediate impact in the third Test at Perth as we dismissed Australia inside the first day once more, this time for 268, but we were then brought back down to earth with a huge bump. Things deteriorated rapidly following a solid start to our reply. The ball suddenly began swinging for Mitchell Johnson and we batted like 11-year-olds with blindfolds on. In general, Johnson had another poor Ashes, but he bowled really well that day. When he gets it right, as he did at the Waca, there is no doubt he is superb – because he pushes the ball across, pushes the ball across and then swings one back in from nowhere. Perhaps sometimes he doesn't know it is going to happen himself, which actually makes him the hardest type of bowler to play against. It is not dissimilar to me when I am bowling to left-handers: when it is turning, turning, turning, if one goes straight on it can be dangerous. Without any discernible change you have become twice the bowler. From 78 without loss, we were bundled out for 187 thanks to Johnson's six-wicket burst, and we went on to get hammered.

There was not much good that came out of that Test from an English perspective, but Tremlett's performance was a huge positive. He had taken Broad's place and showed enough with his eight wickets to oust Steve Finn for the Boxing Day Test, after the management decided to select Tim Bresnan for the conditions in Melbourne. Tremlett's performance in Perth had hinted at what both he and the rest of our attack could achieve during the remainder of the trip. We were already without our original first-choice unit and now Finn had been dropped, but in had come a guy who was bowling quickly and extracting plenty of bounce. From his very first spell he'd looked really threatening.

There was not a great deal of despondency after that defeat, if I am honest, because we knew we had suffered one of those below-par displays, and there was nothing that couldn't be put right. My biggest disappointment in the aftermath, in fact, was that my online video diaries, which had been universally applauded earlier in the tour, were now a target for displeasure. A month earlier, my behind-the-scenes fun was viewed positively; people reckoned the diaries emphasised what a great team spirit existed within the England dressing room. That togetherness had been a key factor in our escaping in Brisbane and winning in Adelaide, was the theory. But now, at the first hint of a blip, a couple of people questioned its role in print. Former England bowler Angus Fraser wrote a piece in the *Independent* suggesting that our antics were a sign of cockiness. Apparently, having fun and doing the sprinkler dance meant we weren't treating the tour with the gravity it deserved.

Never one to take things lying down, I immediately produced

another diary so that I could make my retort. I have always been one that lives by the sword, dies by the sword and if I have made a mistake I will always hold my hand up. I would like to think I am quite an honest character like that. But to be blamed – and what's more for the sprinkler to be blamed – for that defeat was ridiculous. From that moment I resolved to make the diary less and less refined and to be more out there with every episode. For the seventh instalment of *Swanny's Diary* I even called in one of my celebrity pals to appear, David Hasselhoff. If we were going to win the Ashes it would be because we played the better cricket, and you play your best cricket when you are in your best frame of mind. Having a laugh has always been conducive to creating that for me.

The sprinkler became a real tour symbol for us, and the craze had begun in the tour game against South Australia in the early weeks of the trip. Its first outing came on the final day there when rain came in after lunch and consigned us to the dressing room. Every so often a messenger would head down the tunnel to assess the weather and return with a report. Once it gets to the point when a game has lost its meaning no one really wants to play, and although we had knocked over a couple of early wickets in our victory bid, lost time had virtually scuppered our hopes already. So whenever anyone came back with a declaration of 'It's still raining, lads!' it would be met with general giddiness. All the old dance-floor classics came out in a disco-style celebration as it became more and more obvious we wouldn't have to spend futile time in the field. There were some moonwalks, some robot dances and then Paul Collingwood walked in from his check and said: 'Hey, what about the sprinkler?'

Now, if you've seen Colly doing the sprinkler, it looks like someone having an epileptic fit. Everyone was in stitches and it led others to get up and do their own version. From that moment the sprinkler was born for us, and that night a couple of the lads re-enacted it on the dance floor in an Adelaide bar. People have suggested that we invented it, but we can make no such claim. The dance is years old. I had a mate from Australia who used to do it when I was about 15 or 16. But what I can say is that the England cricket team made it fashionable. Not that all our lads wanted to join in with the fun, particularly when they knew it would be filmed. The fact every one of our squad made it onto one of my early videos providing their own versions was seen as a show of unity. However, the truth is that the only reason we had everyone up was down to the persuasive nature of the cameraman. The majority didn't mind making fools of themselves but there are always one or two party-poopers. Neither Jimmy Anderson nor Stuart Broad would do it at first, because they are the vainest people in the team. 'Why would I do that? Are you trying to make a t--- of me?' moaned Jimmy. Broady said with disdain: 'Sorry, er, do what?' Of course, careful editing provided the feel of spontaneity, but there was a large degree of reticence because deep down that pair think they're Brad Pitt and Johnny Depp. They find it very hard to laugh at themselves, particularly Jimmy.

On a serious note, we had to put the Perth game into perspective and move on quickly. The facts were simple: we were bowled out because the ball swung, and that cost us the match. Mitchell Johnson was outstanding in the first innings and Ryan Harris bowled impressively in the second. But we knew it was a one-off, so we had to turn our attention forwards and not backwards. It was frustrating that we had once again been undone by the swinging ball because ultimately our failings against Pakistan the previous summer stemmed from our inability to deal with the aerial movement of Mohammad Asif and Mohammad Amir. That weakness had resurfaced at Perth, where it was neither as quick nor as bouncy as you would expect. It bounced a bit, and probably more than any of their other pitches, but there was nothing untoward. So it was criminal to finish with scores of 187 and 123.

We have a debrief after every Test match, win, lose or draw, and the one post-Perth was quite constructive. My uncomplicated contribution to our discussion was that we shouldn't get downhearted. If the ball swung again we needed to find a way of combating it, I said. That was about the level of my input. Because, from my perspective, we hadn't played bad cricket overall on the tour. We had actually played very good cricket, so why worry about one bad game? That was now out of our systems, and although the scores were now level at one apiece we technically still had our noses in front with two matches to play. Two draws would see us retain the urn.

All the talk heading to Melbourne was that there would be a similar pitch awaiting us at the MCG – the groundsman had apparently tried to replicate Perth – but we knew it wouldn't really be like that. Our research told us that it would be low and slow and that the ball would reverse-swing. There was a bullishness about the Australian public too that the series had just changed, but I for one certainly didn't buy into the theory that Australia were now showing exactly who was boss and were therefore going to walk the series.

By this point I had become one of the singletons on tour because Sarah had to fly home. Her enforced departure – she could not fly home any later than 32 weeks pregnant under medical orders – almost took a dramatic twist because of the heavy snow back in Britain that restricted the number of aeroplanes landing during the run-up to Christmas. Desperate not to have my first child born in Australia, I had already begun contingency plans to boat her over to New Zealand (I have some friends in Christchurch) for the birth. A Kiwi has to be better than an Aussie offspring, surely, and Wilf would then naturally have been good at rugby. As you can tell, I'd thought it through. Thankfully for Sarah, her flight managed to get off before her deadline and so I was by myself as I awaited one of those matches that sound so magical when you are a kid. I had heard so much about the feted Boxing Day Ashes Tests, and so I spent Christmas Day clock-watching.

It went painfully slowly. I sat down to Christmas dinner on the top floor of a Melbourne hotel with my adopted family – Monty Panesar, Twiggy, Steve Davies and Ajmal – wondering why we weren't having a proper Christmas meal. There were no parsnips, no sprouts, they didn't have roast potatoes, I am not sure they even had turkey.

Christmas is always rubbish when you're away from home; anyone who says they cannot believe how good it must be to have sun on Christmas Day doesn't know what they're talking about. Give me a freezing cold, snowy Christmas any day. Back home there was a white carpet over the whole of the country. How special is that? I longed to be wrapped up, off down the pub, having a couple of pints, before getting home to realise we'd burnt the potatoes; who cares, get through a mound of turkey, bubble and squeak for tea, chicken sandwich, Bond film. That's Christmas. Throwing a shrimp on the barbie and reaching for the board shorts definitely isn't.

Carlsberg don't do first days of Test cricket, but if they did it would probably be the one at Melbourne. It was almost perfect. Give me a morose Christmas Day any year if that is what comes next. Paul Collingwood put down a difficult catch at slip in the first over, off Jimmy Anderson, Shane Watson smashed an even harder chance to Kevin Pietersen at gully, with the same result, and when their opening batsmen responded with a couple of early boundaries the noise from the 85,000 crowd was deafening, the whole experience was incredible. I have never sampled an atmosphere like it. Three hours later, however, there was complete silence, as we completed the task of bowling them out.

You could hear a pin drop. It was amazing. Because of the size of the ground and crowd, the Barmy Army were spread out, and so their usual catalogue of songs was conspicuous by its absence. To be honest, this silence was of the golden variety. There was no time to rue the two dropped chances because Tremlett did for Watson with one that bounced and struck the glove, and when I caught Ponting at slip, diving in front of Andrew Strauss, Australia were 37 for three. Good job I held that one as it would have hit Strauss in the face if I hadn't got my hands on it.

We had begun to pick up wickets, and once started we never stopped. When Jimmy got Mike Hussey out for nought, there was a feeling on the field that we were through Australia. When Huss walked out to bat I couldn't resist having a word with him. He doesn't normally get distracted if you engage him in conversation but I reckoned there was a way of unsettling one of the most focused players you will ever come across. In mid-series, Mr Cricket had altered the stickers on his bat – the bat with which he had scored more than 500 runs in three matches against us.

'What you doing, mate, you got both those hundreds and a ninety with your normal kit, what you playing at?' I asked him, referring to the frightful orange stickers and orange trim on his pads, gloves and bat grip. Now, Mr Cricket never talks back – he always tries to ignore me – but I always try to engage him nevertheless. Even on this occasion he still walked past me, but I knew he could hear me and I hoped it would unsettle him. 'It's a very dangerous game you're playing, messing with the cricketing gods,' I continued. So when he nicked off to Jimmy, I excitedly screeched at him: 'I flaming told you!' After the match he told me that Kookaburra, his sponsors, had enforced the change because their new range was out on 1 January, and he was their prime advertisement.

By the end of that refreshing first day the scoreboard told you that England would win the game. Australia 98; England 157–0. There is no way there was going to be any other result, even though the local theory seemed to be that all Australia had to do was turn up, take all 10 wickets for a further 100 runs and then bat big to win the game. The pitch was a lot better than that, though, and everything fell into place for our batsmen to post the kind of total we had made in our early Ashes exchanges.

The surface put our bowling display into perspective but unfortunately our seamers did not get the credit they deserved. They kept the ball in disciplined channels and it was one of those days when the batsmen nicked it rather than missed it. The ball was in the right area often enough, and perhaps it just skidded off the pitch a bit more than they expected, because all 10 dismissals were nibbles behind the wicket. So it was disappointing, while watching the Channel 9 highlights that night, to hear former wearers of the baggy green cap rip their successors' techniques to shreds. Had they played and missed, nothing would have been made of it. It was just one of those days that occur in cricket sometimes. We bowled, they nicked it.

A lot of cricketers don't watch the highlights, and don't read the newspapers, or at least don't admit to it, but I always have done. It is cathartic if you've done badly and can be an ego massage if you've done well. So I found myself tuning in to the replay of the day's action regularly during the Ashes – unless there was an episode of *Family Guy* on another channel. That night, the criticism of the Australians by their own former players seemed very old-school English, and very negative. None made allowance for the skill of Anderson, Bresnan and Tremlett. The only point they made was that the England team had caught well, but that was strange to me because it was not the catchers who prised them out for less than 100. For me, that demonstrated their reluctance to accept that they were being outplayed by an English team.

Jonathan Trott's big unbeaten hundred that followed was incredible. The television station showed a graphic of his first 100 runs during that innings and something like two of them had come through the off side. The Australians bowled wider and wider to him but he just kept nipping across and flicking them off his legs. Matt Prior got 85, and if you needed any further proof that this was a game in which everything went wrong for the Aussies, it came when Mitchell Johnson got Matt out only for him to be reprieved by the umpires as he was walking off. They wanted to check whether it was a no-ball; it was and that summed it up for them. We ended up with 513, and had two and a half days to bowl them out.

As it was, we completed our task in three sessions, and I have never bowled a more disciplined spell for England than in that second innings. It wasn't spinning a jot but I was able to get some drift, and my job was to keep things tight at one end while the pace trio rotated in a bid to exploit the reverse swing on offer at the other. In terms of fulfilling the role asked of me, I have never done a better job. Of course, it helped that we had the 415-run advantage on first innings in the bank, but in terms of reading and executing my role it was the best I have managed.

Early on, I had Michael Clarke missed from a stumping chance – Matt Prior's one blemish for the whole tour, I think – but I recall sending down only one bad ball, a short one that Clarke put away for four. Everything felt so natural and I bowled for ages at Clarke over the wicket without him being able to score off me, which is no mean feat against a player of his calibre. I had bowled five maidens to him when I changed my angle of attack to round the wicket and told Andrew Strauss to move himself from short midwicket to second slip. Fourth ball he nicked it straight to him! When things like that happen you feel amazing, and I walked off that day with a glow about my performance. Yes, I have bowled better balls and better individual overs, but for consistency over a two-hour period that is right up there.

I finished with figures of 27–11–59–2 on a pitch that was as flat as a pancake. The surface was rock hard – every time one of the big lads hit it huge chunks came off the leather – yet didn't offer a great deal of bounce. We had to work really hard on the ball to keep one side shiny, and because the other one was so wrecked, the ball reverse-swung a lot. We had Bres and Jimmy, who are both fine exponents of that art, but it was not until this Ashes series that we realised that so too is Chris Tremlett. Although Australia managed 258 in their second innings, we probably bowled better as a collective than in their first-innings capitulation because all 11 of their guys had been given the chance to go away and think about how they were going to combat us on that surface. The seamers were nothing short of exceptional.

Australia opted to field an all-pace attack at the MCG, and they had a really uneasy relationship with their spinners throughout the series. Whatever his identity, he was always the outsider. Before a ball was bowled they completely lost faith in Nathan Hauritz, and seemed reluctant to recall him. It made you think he must have had a fall-out with one of their selectors or something. So they originally went with left-armer Xavier Doherty because of his decent one-day record and the fact that he had bowled well in a Sheffield Shield game that Ricky Ponting had played in. He is a nice bowler who puts it on the spot but he doesn't turn it that much, or at least doesn't seem to try to. So he was unceremoniously axed after two games, despite bowling on two batsman-friendly pitches. They didn't play a spinner in the third Test, so when they won at the Waca, they maintained their one-dimensional attack for Melbourne, much as they had done when they moved from Headingley to The Oval in 2009. On both occasions it seemed as though they had made their selections regardless of what the pitch was like.

Then in the last Test, they offered this Michael Beer chap a game when 95 per cent of Australia had never heard of him. He had only played seven first-class games for Western Australia, and one of those had been against us, so he was more recognisable to us than half their team when he turned up for practice in Sydney. Word got round that some of the Australians didn't even know what he looked like. It all seemed like a throwback to England in 1993 when they used 24 players in one six-match Ashes series. I felt sorry for him. Nor did it help that his first wicket in Tests was scrubbed because he'd bowled a no-ball to Alastair Cook. Talk about a baptism of fire – he was the one bloke you didn't want to give a second chance to. I actually thought Beer bowled okay, if I am honest, but you simply don't get selections like his in winning teams. His call-up told its own story and indicated that they didn't have a clear idea of who their best bowlers were.

Australia also drafted in Steve Smith halfway through the series. Someone told me they had brought him into the team to be like me. 'What? Dashingly handsome with a 1940s Hollywood jaw?' I checked. Unfortunately, that was not their assessment. His role, according to the man himself, was to be funny and provide energy to their game. If those were the credentials I had been picked for, I certainly wouldn't have revealed them at a press conference, as he did. Fancy confessing that you had been selected on the strength of telling a few jokes. Could he not see what was coming when he stepped onto the field?

Surely it was fairly obvious that as soon as he started playing and missing at Perth his funny-man persona was going to be the basis for our sledges. 'Is this what they meant when they said you were in for your jokes?' he was asked, as another one whistled passed his outside edge. 'You were supposed to provide them with your mouth not your bat, you clown.' I think that was Jimmy, to be fair. I was less subtle. Every time I walked past him I begged him: 'Tell me a joke, Smiffy.'

How Australia managed only 280 at the SCG in the final Test I will never know. It was an absolutely belting pitch and the match should have been 500 plays 500 on first innings. They had the best of the batting conditions, but we showed the true nature of the wicket with our 644, the highest England total ever registered in Australia in an Ashes Test. The way the entire team applied themselves with the bat demonstrated our determination not simply to retain the Ashes but to win the series emphatically.

Obviously, we'd enjoyed a massive party in Melbourne, and no one could begrudge us the opportunity to toast our achievement there. A few beers in the MCG changing rooms were followed by hitting the town, but as soon as we arrived in Sydney we felt it was a case of unfinished business. Andrew Strauss was very keen to reiterate the point to us.

'You can be the team that goes home having retained the Ashes with a draw, and people will refer to you in that way, or we can go back and forever be remembered as winners. It has been a fantastic effort by everyone, but going home with a draw will take some of the gloss off. It is not how I want us to be remembered,' he told us.

So we headed into the final match on 3 January 2011 as if it was a win-at-all-costs affair. That is a style that suits us, as it happens. Try to play for a draw, and we don't do very well. Every single one of us was desperate to round things off at 3–1, and when we began batting on the second afternoon, none of us wanted to field for another couple of days. The resolve with which everyone strode to the crease was tangible. Strauss is a big one for placing your foot on the opposition's throat when they are down, and it was felt that we could get into that position if we applied ourselves. Apart from Kevin Pietersen, who never really bats in this way, everyone seemed intent on occupying the crease for as long as possible. Cook took his incredible tally to 766 runs for the series, with his 189, and Matt Prior hit another hundred. Even I got my first decent runs out there, and although I only made 36 not out, I was robbed of my maiden Ashes hundred when Twiggy nicked behind. I was only 30-odd balls away.

The intensity in the batting was matched by our efforts in the field on the penultimate day of the series. To be honest, intensity is easy to keep up when you are doing well. Initially, there was a half-hour period in the second innings when we didn't take the wicket that we wanted, and normally in those circumstances it takes a few looks around the field and a few gee-ups to get people going. On this occasion, we didn't need a thing. When you looked around at your colleagues, you saw 10 blokes intent on finishing the job.

It was fitting that Jimmy Anderson bowled so supremely again in the 10th and final Australian innings to finish with a 24-wicket haul. Afterwards, when the series was over and we went for a drink in what the Australians call their rooms, Mike Hussey confessed that he just could not pick Jimmy during that final Test. He would run in hiding the ball, and with exactly the same action, the ball would duck either in or out. Huss reckoned it was an unbelievably high-quality spell of bowling, and I would agree from my vantage point at second slip.

Once again we just kept chipping away with regular wickets, rewarded for our patience and discipline. The crowd were fully behind our quest and became particularly animated when Mitchell Johnson came out to bat for the final time. Johnson is undoubtedly the Australian version of KP, and the pantomime villain suffered a cacophony of unsettling abuse as he strolled to the crease at 171 for six. He did so to the loudest possible rendition of the Barmy Army song about him.

'He bowls to the left, he bowls to the right, that Mitchell Johnson, his bowling is sh---,' they roared.

There were 25,000 Englishmen singing that at the top of their voices and it sounded like St James' Park on a packed derby weekend. The noise was ridiculous. And it got even louder when Chris Tremlett ran in and cleaned him up first ball. I still get goose bumps thinking about that moment. I felt genuinely sorry for him on this occasion as he shuffled back. He must have felt two inches tall. He must have wanted to scurry off and hide in his cricket bag.

That was a fair cop in my book, but I could not condone the treatment meted out to Johnson the following morning, at the after-match award presentation and the handing-over of the urn. The Barmy Army had been brilliant all the way through the series but when halfway through the presentations they started singing that song at the mere mention of his name, it was rubbish. I have a massive thing about being humble in victory and I hate people who aren't. You celebrate properly. You don't rub it in the faces of the team you've beaten.

Australia didn't need mocking, although even their own were seemingly out for Ricky Ponting, who missed the last Test with a broken bone in his hand, upon the conclusion of our 3-1 win. Cricket Australia announced a post-Ashes inquest into their failings, but I could sum up where they went wrong very quickly. The major difference between the teams throughout the series was that we had people in form and they didn't. Simple as that. Especially in the batting department. We had Cook and Trott in the form of their lives, and Strauss in seriously good nick. Aesthetically you will not find a top three less pleasing on the eye than ours, in fact they would all have a decent claim to being the ugliest batsman in the world, but I wouldn't swap any of them. Without the referral system Cook might only have made 300 runs, but he was due a change of fortune and used it to his great advantage.

In contrast, Australia had Clarke and Ponting in the worst form of their lives, Simon Katich got injured, Phil Hughes was dropped once more because of poor form, and Shane Watson resumed his routine of getting 50 and out. To a lesser extent, the same applied in the bowling. Jimmy Anderson was in great shape with the ball, whereas their strike bowler Peter Siddle started off really well on the first day of the series but did nothing after that.

One of the best things about the SCG is that it is a proper old-school cricket ground, and you can smell the atmosphere of the changing room from 100 years ago. Everything is wooden, including the lockers, and there is a tradition of players signing them. So I took the opportunity to scribble *Swanny Ashes 2010–11, Winners 3–1* on mine before the families came in to visit.

Later, when everyone had cleared the ground, at around 5 p.m., we went and sat on the outfield, right by the square, while the sprinklers were on. We got sprayed a bit but nobody cared less. There we all were, beers in hand, smoking big fat cigars, when David Saker started reminiscing about the events of the past few months. It came about in the most organic way possible but for the next hour, the group of us, one by one, started revealing our favourite moments of the Test series. One spoke, the rest listened intently. Virtually everyone had spoken when it got round to my turn.

'Look,' I told the others. 'My favourite part of this entire Ashes is right now, sat here on the SCG, with a cold beer and a big fat cigar, having won 3–1. We are celebrating the fact we've won three Tests by an innings. Do we understand the magnitude of our achievements here? This is amazing.' There was a lot of nodding of heads and smiling at that point. I think we all loved relishing that moment.

Twenty-four years earlier, Elton John had been involved in the after-show party thanks to his friendship with Ian Botham. This time young punks like Broad and Pietersen went to hang out with Tinie Tempah in the city. That's not my scene, so I headed off to a pub the Barmy Army had requisitioned for the week, with Bresnan and Cook. We were made to feel like movie stars as we sat on the balcony of the fourth floor and had drinks thrown at us all night. Everyone wanted a picture, and I loved the attention.

It was an amazing night. Some of the hardcore among the Barmies later dragged me back to Star City, the casino complex where the England team were staying. For some reason I saw fit to take $500 out of the cashpoint and head to the tables at around 6 a.m. with my new mates in tow. I might as well have just handed the wedge straight to the croupier because I didn't even know what game we were playing as I went for broke and put the whole lot on one hand. When he turned the final card over, I meekly asked: 'Have I won anything?' That was me, goodnight. But nothing could have taken the gloss of those 24 hours. They were just brilliant.

19

WORLD CUP WILF

How on earth are you supposed to maintain your level of performance when you have just reached the zenith of your career? After winning an Ashes series in Australia, everything that follows is understandably inferior, and it was impossible for me to pretend that the subsequent Twenty20 and one-day internationals meant anywhere near as much to me as those five Test matches. No matter how much you persuade yourself that you are trying your butt off, and that they are as every bit important as the Sydney finale, you can't fool yourself deep down.

Initially, once we got back onto the field, it felt as if we were on such a roll that we would win every game we played against the Australians. The confidence was certainly at a high as we went into the first of two Twenty20 matches at Adelaide, and even when it turned out to be the closest of games, we still had that touch of something going for us. Chris Woakes came in and had an astonishing debut; his batting under pressure was unbelievable, and I am sure that was something to do with the positive environment he walked into. Some late wickets threatened to deny us a new world record of eight straight 20-over international wins – but he kept his head and swung the pendulum back our way.

It was during my brief innings in that one-wicket victory that I incurred the knee injury that was to sideline me during the one-day series. I was hit on the knee by a Brett Lee full toss, and the ball just chipped my kneecap slightly. During the second Twenty20 in Melbourne, which we narrowly lost, and the opening ODI on the same ground, I developed real problems with it, and although I tried to play through the discomfort, it forced me to leave the field during the latter match.

It was no more than badly bruised but, with the 2011 World Cup in mind, the medics advised a fortnight's rest. It was a precautionary measure more than anything, the idea being that I would recuperate while staying with the squad, then return to play for the last couple of games in the seven-match series. That way I would be both relatively fresh for the tournament in Asia and match-sharp.

So I stayed for a week and worked on strengthening my upper body. But in the changing room in Tasmania, I innocently bent down to pick my shorts up and my tour came to an abrupt halt. I suffered a back spasm. Now, if you have ever had one you will know they are the most ridiculous things in the world. They make you look like an 80-year-old with rickets. I spent my last few hours in Australia doubled over in pain, and my final evening meal in Australia was obtained by crawling on all fours to my hotel room door to receive room service.

In the end I was sent home to Sarah, who at eight months pregnant was suffering with her back too. So there we were, both of us laid up on the couch for a week. Any expectant father will recognise the frustration of those final days when your wife is nesting. All you want her to do is sit down while you make her a cup of tea or head off to the chip shop. But I couldn't even put the kettle on without a grimace.

I also felt uncomfortable being away from the action. As soon I left the England tour, I felt like an outsider, so I refrained from watching the rest of our 6–1 series defeat and instead concentrated on getting my fitness right for both Wilf's arrival on 17 February and my departure for the World Cup two days later.

Physically I was fine by the morning of the 17th but emotionally I was all over the place, as we went down to the hospital for our Caesarean section appointment. Because there had been a couple of emergencies during the night, we had been pushed back from 9 a.m. to one o'clock that afternoon, and the next four hours seemed like the longest of my life: I read the same article in *The Times* about 50 times, and not once did I finish it. These were nerves like I'd never known. I was panicking in case Wilf came out looking like me, or his fingers and toes didn't each add up to 10, or he had inherited my massive chin.

Leaving Sarah and Wilf behind was the worst thing I have ever had to do. It was absolutely gut-wrenching. Walking out of the house was truly horrible, and because I hadn't organised my kit, I just picked up my bag from the end of the Ashes tour – I knew there was coloured clothing inside but didn't know whether it was clean or not – and hoped for the best. We had only had about three hours together back at the house, after the short stint in hospital, and I spent the majority of it standing, holding Wilf, thinking how much I wanted to stay put. To have to hand him over to Sarah and say 'See ya later, I'm off to Nagpur' was tough. I certainly didn't want to be 6,000 miles away from my family so soon after such a life-changing event, and although that is the lot of an international cricketer, for the first game against the Netherlands on 22 February, I have to admit my heart was not in it.

I might not even have made it to Nagpur, had it not been for bumping into Nick Hoult of the *Daily Telegraph*. Without him I would still be walking round Mumbai's domestic airport, looking for details of my connecting flight. I had no idea where I was going, no one spoke English and it made me appreciate Phil Neale, the England team's operations manager, that little bit more. He sorts out all the minutiae of our travel arrangements and ensures we are properly pampered. We depart without our bags, because they've been shipped on the night before, and arrive with everything waiting for us in the hotel. It all runs perfectly. Now, when I had been left on my own, and to my own devices, it was a shambles. I was walking around like a lost puppy until Nick pointed me in the right direction.

My journey to and arrival in India had all been a bit of a whirl-wind, and as any new parent will testify, jet lag is not something exclusively contracted from long-haul flights. Once you've got a baby in your life you tend to keep strange hours. And the baby in my life occupied my thoughts constantly during our first Group B game against the Netherlands. It was still only a matter of hours after my arrival and although I bowled well to finish with figures of two for 35, I dropped the most straightforward catch of my life in the final over of their innings. The Dutch number eight batsman, Mudassar Bukhari, spooned one to short third man and I clanged it. Not through any lack of focus, I can assure you, it was just a cock-up, although Jimmy Anderson, the bowler, was not best pleased.

Coincidentally, I was switched on for the business end of their innings. Although the same could not be said of the period that had preceded it. Fifty overs is quite intense in that you are always thinking – about field placings, how you're going to stop the batsman scoring, the most likely way to get someone out, stuff like that. But I was thinking about Wilf every few balls. A couple of times I had to snap myself out of it and realised I was in the wrong fielding position. The only time it was easy was when I was bowling because then I was fully engaged with what I was doing. The heat didn't help either, and after 10 days at home, I found it difficult to acclimatise. The change of temperature really does hit you hard, and after 20 overs I looked up at the board, desperate for it to be 45 overs gone. The three and a half hours in the field felt like three and a half months. To tell the truth, I was nodding off halfway through the Dutch innings of 292 for six, but I was no worse than the rest of the England team. We performed like imbeciles with our fielding and we didn't bowl well as a unit. My dropped catch was by no means in isolation, and Ryan ten Doeschate's hundred, although a fine effort, should have been denied. For some unknown reason, when he hit one straight up in the air off me in the 40s, Jimmy and Kevin Pietersen left it to each other. They jogged towards each other from long on and long off and then glared when the ball landed in the middle. When your best two fielders do that, you can imagine what everyone else is doing.

We knocked off the runs comfortably enough, and although the six-wicket win caused us more grief than we would have wished for, we were up and running in the tournament, and the next fixture made us all feel part of a World Cup. It was against India, the co-hosts, and turned out to be a hell of a game. The wicket at the M. Chinnaswamy Stadium, the best we played on while we were out there, was almost perfect for one-day cricket. Limited-overs games are about runs and there were plenty of them in this match. In fact, we came back really well towards the end of India's innings to restrict them, because from 180 for one in the 30th over they should have gone on to get a bigger score than 338 all out. Sachin Tendulkar's hundred was masterful but, when it was our turn to bat, we put the favourable conditions into perspective.

During the mid-innings break in that match, I experienced something that I never like to see in a game of cricket: gloating from the opposition. They seemed to be crowing about their score, and they gave off the impression that they thought they were going to walk all over us. Perhaps it was because that is exactly what they had done to us in the one-day series in India 15 months earlier. Nevertheless, it was not behaviour that endeared them to us.

It was not our motivation, but there is nothing quite like silencing an Indian crowd. You certainly don't want them screaming all day because it really can be ear-shattering. Andrew Strauss got us moving swiftly out of the blocks, and his outstanding 158 was deserving of the man-of-the-match award. It also proved that, contrary to some so-called experts' opinions, he had the ability to adapt to the pace of one-day cricket.

At 281 for two in the 43rd over we were cruising that chase and undoubtedly should have won the game. But it turned out to be such a dramatic see-saw of a conclusion that in the end we were grateful for a tie. Ian Bell and Strauss fell in consecutive Zaheer Khan deliveries and when Michael Yardy was dismissed to leave us on 307 for seven, we needed 32 off only 15 balls. Tim Bresnan contributed massively to keeping us in with a chance as both he and I hit sixes off Piyush Chawla, but when he fell with 14 required from seven balls, it left me and Ajmal Shahzad at the crease for the final over of the match.

When Ajmal extraordinarily launched his first ball, and third of the over from Munaf Patel, into the stands at long on, it was our game once more, but with me back on strike and needing four off two, and then two off one, we came up agonisingly short. I hit the final delivery all right, as it happened, but extra cover dived across and stopped it. Yet, for all its twists and turns, that game probably had the correct result.

It was also a result that shocked a few people because that Indian team had been built up to be unbeatable in their own conditions. However, we showed that, while their batting was phenomenal, their bowling was comparatively weak. Zaheer Khan was an exceptional bowler and Harbhajan Singh worthily deemed world-class, but as a unit their bowling did not have the authority that their top six batsmen possessed.

In contrast, there was not such a large disparity between the quality of our batting and bowling – our World Cup problem was that the quality of our performances yo-yoed so violently. People made excuses for us, such as fatigue from the heavily congested fixture list on the tour of Australia, but that was rather convenient. It was far too easy to say that we were knackered. Delve deeper and you would have found evidence that we had just not been consistent enough. It's hard to explain how our fortunes could swing so violently from game to game and also within games. We cruised that match against India for four-fifths of the chase and yet had as good as thrown it away before Bres, Aj and I got together and dashed for the finish line. I guess that short passage of play summed us up. Not once in the same 100 overs did we bat well and bowl well – it was either one or the other.

But reaction to our surprise defeat to Ireland on the same Bangalore ground on 2 March really angered me. If we believed ourselves to be the disgrace that half the people on Twitter thought we were, following that three-wicket defeat, there would have been no point in playing on. A few days earlier, after going toe to toe with invincible India, the whole world was saying: 'Oh my God, England can win this.' But we certainly became aware of the fickle nature of supporters that week. Every now and again someone wakes up and simply has the best day of their life. Kevin O'Brien was that guy against us and, yes, it was annoying in the extreme and painful to be on the wrong side of, but when someone hits a hundred off 50 balls, you have to hold your hands up and say well done. Sure, we should not have lost with a score of 327 for eight, and we had the game won when they were 111 for five in the 25th over. But we failed to finish things off.

Ireland never stopped believing they could win that game, despite being underdogs. The same could be said of our attitude in the tense win over South Africa that followed in Chennai. Despite defending only 171, we knew there was life in the pitch for us, and we knew how difficult it had been to score when we batted, particularly at the end of the innings. It was an added bonus that we walked off a field for once without one of the opposition taking a hundred off us.

It was typical of our tournament, though, that we salvaged our group standing with an enthralling six-run win like that, only to lose to Bangladesh. Not that I believed that match was contested on a level playing field. I am very passionate in the way that I play and I completely lost it when I was asked to bowl with a ball that was saturated in dew. Some will argue that you should just get on with it, but I'd like to invite them to bowl spin with a ball that's sodden. It made a farce of the contest between bat and ball. That wicket in Chittagong was a spinner's paradise and I couldn't land the ball. I had no idea where it was going. I had a chance to win the game for England but was being hamstrung by the conditions.

When I asked for the ball to be changed I was told it wasn't wet enough. That is what caused me to blow, but I know I should not have sworn at umpire Daryl Harper when he instructed me to get on with things. It cost me 10 per cent of my match fee, and let's face it my punishment for being caught swearing on a stump microphone wasn't just for an act of petulance – kids would have been watching and listening at home. Nor do I condone bad language being directed towards officials. I apologised to Harper afterwards, and got my just deserts with the reprimand. But I maintain that it was ridiculous to play a day-night match in the World Cup that was so heavily influenced by the dew. The ball was so wet it was like trying to bowl with a bar of soap. It felt like playing football with both hands tied behind my back. Surely, when you have a ground with a history of dew you do not schedule night matches there.

The two-wicket defeat left our requirements for progression simple: we now needed to beat West Indies and rely on other results going our way. We managed our half of the bargain in what turned out to be a great game, not necessarily for the way we played – because that wasn't very different from any of the others – rather for the feeling it gave us after we managed to defend a relatively small score at Chennai once more. For raw emotion it was up there with the Ashes as we claimed four wickets in a rush to halt the West Indians in their tracks.

When Jonathan Trott's head brushed the rope taking a tumbling catch at long on, off my bowling, to give Andre Russell six rather than dismiss him, our opponents needed only 34 more runs in 12.4 overs to knock us out. But the late drama was simply captivating. James Tredwell and I rotated towards the end of the innings and as a team we claimed four wickets for three runs in a little over three overs. Fittingly, Trott's throw ran out Sulieman Benn to complete an 18-run win.

Even though we had held our nerve, however, I don't think even the most fervent England supporter could have claimed we were genuine contenders for that trophy. We had beaten two good teams in low-scoring matches on spinner-friendly surfaces and pushed India all the way, but we showed no signs of being capable of producing three good performances in a row, and unless we could do that from the quarter-final stage onwards we stood no chance.

Our failings were cruelly exposed by Sri Lanka in the last-eight meeting in Colombo. It was another belting surface we were faced with and a score of 229 was well under par. In contrast to other games, both our suits matched up this time as our bowlers failed to contain our aggressive opposition. Had we put a complete perform-ance together, we would have stood a good chance of progress to the semi-finals, but we didn't play a good enough standard of cricket to stay in, this time from start to finish.

It's true that our build-up was not ideal – for example, heading into the tournament without Eoin Morgan, who I reckoned to be the best one-day batsman in the world in the preceding 12 months, and losing Kevin Pietersen midway through to another injury, after we had plumped for him as an opening batsman. But one player does not make a team and the absence of those two at various points shouldn't have changed the way the collective played. It wasn't as if they scored hundreds when they played, either. Your world-class players are only truly world-class if they're in top form. But they weren't and as a team we posted horrendously substandard scores on three occasions, and then two or three times our bowling got hit for way too many.

We certainly didn't need a seven-match one-day series in Australia after the Ashes. It just took us too close to the World Cup. Of course, it filled the coffers of the Australian board, but if in doing so it contributed in any way to eliminating both England and Australia from a global tournament then it was surely false economy. In the future, I reckon there should be a limit on the number of matches allowed in a one-day series. Three should be standard – because you would only ever have one dead rubber per series – five the absolute maximum.

Ever since watching the 1992 final I have wanted England to win a World Cup. But although the 2011 version held some personal fondness for me – I love bowling, and what better pitches to bowl on than turning ones; I love Chennai because it's where I made my Test debut – it proved a generally uninspiring four weeks. Our batsmen were not scoring good runs. We didn't have anyone who looked as if they could take an attack apart. We'd hit a few fours, the occasional six and a few singles, but unfortunately the way we played felt very English. Nor did our bowling have that *je ne sais quoi*, that X-factor, so we were far removed from the Twenty20 England team of 10 months previously. Back then there was a feeling that we could win games from anywhere.

It would have been great to have recreated the camaraderie and team spirit that we had in the Caribbean but there just wasn't the same feel. We had become a bit conservative again in our outlook compared to how we had played in the 2010 World Twenty20 event. Our brand of cricket was nowhere near as attacking as it had been there. I am not talking about directives from the coach or captain here, either. Being able to play a certain way is confidence-driven and comes directly from players. In the World Twenty20 we had enough players confident enough to throw caution to the wind, but in this World Cup we lacked exactly that.

And if I am honest, while the World Cup is the biggest deal going for other nations, for me there is no use pretending that it feels anywhere near as important as an Ashes series. Perhaps it's because I was raised on its rich tradition – but there is certainly no comparison. Even the biggest World Cup matches are not a patch on beating Australia, and so there remained a certain contentment at the winter's work when it was all over and we stepped onto the plane to fly home from Sri Lanka.

It will be a winter that I will remember for ever, and one that has left an indelible mark on the Swann family. For it was while we sat toasting our 3–1 success on the grass at the SCG that a thought struck me. Sarah and I had been seeking a suitable second middle name for Wilf for quite a while – he would be Wilf after my grandad and Richard is a name which recurs in Sarah's family – so what about Sydney? It came to me on the spur of the moment, and I couldn't help proudly telling the other lads I would be naming my first son after our achievement. Obviously, I couldn't back down after that, there were too many witnesses, so after some checking that Sydney with a 'y' could be used as a male name – temporarily forgetting that the great Sydney Barnes spelt his name that way – Sarah and I vowed to go with it.

And so we have our very own walking piece of Ashes memorabilia, and more importantly a boy who has enough initials to qualify for the captaincy of England. Everyone knows that to be a proper England captain one needs three forenames. Hopefully Wilfred Richard Sydney Swann will be inspired to follow in the family business.

20

MISSION ACCOMPLISHED

I T WAS incredible when we looked back at the end of the 2011 Test summer to reflect on how far we had come during the Andrew Strauss–Andy Flower era. Our whitewashing of India was the crowning moment of two and a quarter years of unprecedented success and led to official confirmation that we were the best Test team on the planet. But it didn't just happen by chance.

As with most things involving our coach Andy Flower, it was meticulously planned. Almost spookily so, in fact, because amazingly at the start of the 2009 summer we had sat down as a team at the National Performance Centre in Loughborough and discussed our targets. It was during that initial address by Strauss and Flower, who had just been appointed permanently following his interim period in the Caribbean, that we spoke about wanting to be number one in the world.

So we mapped out what we had to do to achieve our goal: the series results that would help us climb from fifth place to the summit of Test cricket. We would have to win the Ashes that summer, retain it by a 3–0 or 3–1 margin, draw at the very least against South Africa and beat everyone else, including India, handsomely. Having just lost away to West Indies, we must have looked at what was being asked of us and thought 'Yeah, right.' Not that we lacked belief in our ability as a team, but everything would have to go to plan perfectly. Our stats people had worked out that this was the quickest we could get to number one, but it meant we couldn't afford to lose a single series. It might have seemed pretty ludicrous at the time, yet if anything, we ended up surpassing the targets.

At the beginning of the 2011 summer, one thing we knew, or at least thought we knew, was that our first opponents, Sri Lanka, would not be interested if it was cold. We expected that to be a big distraction for them and, sure enough, I don't remember the sun coming out too often in Cardiff in the first Test at the end of May. However, despite all the rain, and the far from ideal batting conditions, Sri Lanka showed a real willingness to adapt and dug in to get exactly 400 in the first innings.

All in all, it was a rather slow start to the summer. The backdrop to the match was a bit like a county game – there wasn't much of a crowd in – and the weather restricted the flow of the contest. So much so that when the rain finally relented on the afternoon of the fifth day we were still in the first innings of the game. The match was going nowhere, so Andrew Strauss allowed Ian Bell, unbeaten on 98 overnight, to get to three figures, something he wasn't originally going to do. The initial decision was to be rather hard-nosed and emphasise that the team always comes first with an immediate declaration. But Strauss had a change of heart and reckoned it wasn't going to make much difference to allow Belly to get a hundred. In the grand scheme of things, it wouldn't really matter whether we began bowling a dozen or 15 overs before tea – we knew that if we were going to make any impression we would have to do it quickly.

But I don't think that either Andy Flower or Strauss really expected us to win from that position 96 runs ahead; they just wanted us to go out there with the right attitude, give it everything and get some wickets. Of course, you never know what might happen if you do that, but none of us could have envisaged the crazy couple of hours that followed.

We were without Jimmy Anderson, who was nursing a side strain for this innings, and so I knew I would be on a little earlier than usual. Indeed, I was introduced into the attack for the over before tea, and bowled in tandem with Chris Tremlett for quite some time. When Tremmers took his third wicket in the first over after the interval – the prize one of Mahela Jayawardene, caught at slip – there were still 38 overs remaining in the day, but we couldn't have foreseen what was to come.

It was when Thilan Samaraweera chopped into his stumps off me, to leave them 36 for four, that the chatter in our huddle turned positive. 'God, they're four down now, imagine that; this will be a surprise to all their lads who didn't expect to bat.' And the mood improved further in my next over when two edges left Sri Lanka six down: Kumar Sangakkara was taken low at slip by Andrew Strauss and Farveez Maharoof bizarrely used up a review despite being clearly caught at the wicket. It was then that everybody started to get excited.

Another review went our way two balls later after Billy Doctrove had initially turned down an appeal for a gloved pull by Prasanna Jayawardene off Chris Tremlett, and the manner in which the little left-hander Rangana Herath then played highlighted how the panic had set in. He was playing massive shots from the off and it was almost inevitable when he was lbw, to give me a fourth success. Things were happening so quickly now that it was hard to take in quite what was going on.

The brief respite in the fall of wickets lasted five overs and probably coincided with us realising that we were going to pull off a victory. Then Stuart Broad came on to finish the job with the last two wickets and complete one of the craziest 25-over periods I have ever been involved in. My spell of four for two in 10 balls came out of nowhere, but it's contributing to wins that pleases me more than anything.

It was nevertheless a rather surreal environment in which to win a Test match. There was barely a soul in the SWALEC Stadium by that stage, so it was not so much like a county game as a club training night. The few hundred that were there were probably the guys who had downed a few too many at lunchtime when it was pouring with rain, and had nothing better to do. When we got back to the dressing room, everyone burst out laughing. How the hell did we win a Test match there? From that situation we had absolutely no right to win.

As it turned out, it was a good job that we did, because rain plagued

the series and denied us the chance to force results in either of the
two remaining games. They were completely ruined as contests and
ended up as boring draws. To be fair, Sri Lanka showed a lot of fight
at both Lord's and Southampton. They have some world-class players
and losing that first game was a proper kick up the backside for them.
I am not sure their coach, Stuart Law, would have been too happy
if the Cardiff capitulation had happened again, and with their talent
and application, they proved quite difficult to bowl out. Given the
time restrictions, our only chance of winning either of the games
was for them to collapse in a heap again. But they showed some
resolve and we were thankful that the madness of Cardiff averted a
drawn series.

One of the pleasing things about the series was that our top seven
appeared to have picked up where they had left off in Australia over
the winter. You never know what is going to happen after a break,
and the World Cup had been played in between, so it was important
for us to win that first series of the summer, one that, no matter
which way you looked at it, was a precursor to the series against
India. Even though we would never treat it as anything but a series
in its own right, there was an overwhelming feeling from everybody
– the press, media, the crowds – that the Indian series was the big
one.

The Sri Lanka series was also great for us in terms of getting us
ready in cold and wet conditions, the same conditions we would
potentially face when we came up against India. Whereas the Indians
were in the West Indies playing in 100-degree heat, our team was
acclimatising with some big scores in English conditions. Jonathan
Trott began 2011 with another double hundred, and Alastair Cook
and Ian Bell both hit two hundreds during the 1–0 series victory.
Matt Prior also showed how crucial he is for us with a brilliant
counter-attacking 126 after we had wobbled in the first innings of
the draw at Lord's.

Everyone recognises how important Adam Gilchrist was to
Australia. Matt holds the same value to England, because whenever

he goes in, his natural game is an attacking one. He looks to score at every opportunity and he is an absolute pain to bowl to. I gained first-hand knowledge of that back in 2008, when he was dropped from the Test team. During that season people spoke about him as being the best player in county cricket by an absolute country mile, whether you were talking about batsmen or wicketkeeper-batsmen. He scored 131 and 64 for Sussex against us at Trent Bridge, the two highest scores in a bowler-dominated County Championship match, and so it has been no surprise to me that he has gone on to do so well. He is a class player, a game changer, someone you would always want on your team.

It is very rare he is involved in anything that isn't positive, but such was the dull nature of the second and third Tests against Sri Lanka that the most memorable event followed a rare failure for Matt. We were pushing for a quick declaration in the second innings at Lord's and Matt went in with the intention of helping the scoring rate along. Unfortunately, he was run out for just four and, being a proper batsman – someone who cherishes his average, and wants to keep it in decent nick – he was pretty annoyed. Into the dressing room he stormed, and you could see he was angry.

Now, a lot of rubbish was talked about him throwing his bat – particularly after an erroneous press statement was put out saying that he had thrown a glove – but I witnessed what happened next and no throwing took place whatsoever. Matt changes by the window and rests his bats up against the window frame. As he put down the bat he'd been using, with about 10 per cent more force than normal – he did not throw it by any means – one rubber grip bounced off another and the bat he had been using fell into the window. It was not much more powerful than if you had made a flick with your finger, so he was so unlucky, and the 150-year-old window must have been desperate to break because the bat just went straight through it. A massive hole appeared and most of a pane of glass rained down on a couple sitting on a bench below.

It's a decent drop, probably about 30 feet, and it can't be very

pleasant to be showered with Victorian-age glass, so they were understandably shaken by the incident. Of course, apologies were hastily
offered to them by Matt, but at around the same time a few other
members closer to the front looked round at the balcony, where
Jonathan Trott and Kevin Pietersen were sitting, and had a go at
them. Let's just say that Trott gets fairly defensive when criticised, so
when this chap turned round and, in an archetypal MCC member's
voice, said: 'Your behaviour's disgusting,' Trott looked at him incredulously and said: 'What?' None of the players on the balcony could
have had a clue what was going on, so Trott didn't take it kindly
when this bloke started saying things like: 'I'll tell your father!' 'What
the hell did you say about my father?' barked Trott. The situation
eventually calmed down, but it says something about the Lord's game
that this was the one memorable issue from it.

In fact, the best part of the whole episode was when, with team-
mates biting arms trying not to laugh as an infuriated Matt took
shape as Public Enemy Number One, the new pavilion attendant
walked into the dressing room. Our usual guys, Pete and Cameron,
were not on duty for some reason, so this new bloke wandered in to
assess what had happened. To set the scene, there are four big windows
in the dressing room, and obviously three of them were fine and the
other had a huge cartoon-style hole in it. 'Excuse me,' he said, 'which
is the window that's broken?' Of course, everybody just fell about
– it was like that Mike Gatting TV interview moment in the 1980s
when, sporting a badly broken nose after being struck by a bouncer
in the Caribbean, he was asked: 'Where did it hit you?' However, we
didn't laugh too loudly near Matt in case he threw a punch at us.

Despite our progress in Test cricket, we still have some way to go to
replicate it in one-day internationals. We've won the World Twenty20,
numerous Test series over the past few years and reached the pinnacle
over five days, but as a 50-over side we remain perennial under-
achievers. We are better than we have been in the past, but it is fairly
obvious that one-day cricket will now get a lot of attention from our

management because it is the area that needs most improvement. I don't think we are a bad one-day team; there are just other teams around the world who are a lot more consistent than we are.

As usual, our first post-World Cup one-day assignment, a five-match NatWest Series against Sri Lanka, was viewed as something of a new era – a time for rebuilding and introducing fresh faces at the start of a four-year cycle. One of the new faces was Alastair Cook as captain, following Andrew Strauss's retirement from one-day international cricket, and I was thrilled for him when he had an incredible series and proved those who doubted his ability to adapt to the shorter form of the game wrong.

Cook is a close mate of mine and he phoned me during the interview process to ask for my thoughts: should he go for it, was it a problem that he was being asked to captain even though he wasn't in the team at the time, and was it the right thing to accept if he was offered it? Of course you should, I told him. For one, he was, in my opinion, more than good enough to do exactly what Strauss had done before him and reinvent himself as a one-day batsman. I also told him it would be good for his future as an England player because it would make him a shoo-in for the Test captaincy when Strauss takes a seat in the House of Lords.

He was understandably nervous going into his maiden series as official captain, but his leadership was outstanding in those five games – aside from his team talks. He can get quite nervous, he stumbles and stammers a lot when he speaks and he is renowned for starting one sentence and jumping into another before he has finished. He's best summed up as a bit of a rambler, so I always have to stare at the floor during his team talks in a bid not to laugh. Scoring runs as he did always helps a captain start off well, though, and he made his series total of 298 at a tad under a run a ball to boot.

I have never pretended to be the biggest fan of 50-over cricket, but this series turned into a proper competition, because we went 2–1 down before drawing level at 2–2 – turning the fifth match into a bit of a final. Particularly after the drubbing Sri Lanka had given us during the World Cup, this was a chance for us to get our own back. Completing the job was pleasing on many levels. It was the first time we'd won a one-day series by coming from behind for quite a while, and the Old Trafford pitch was very similar to the style that you get in Colombo – and the one on which we lost that quarter-final in April.

Even though we failed to make the 350 we should have, when we fouled up an electric start by managing to throw wickets away at regular intervals, and then allowed them back into it after claiming three of their wickets in the mandatory powerplay, we were able to derail them from a dominant position when Jade Dernbach came on and demonstrated how exciting he is going to be for England. They needed 36 with five wickets in hand heading into the final four overs, but Jeevan Mendis hauled a Samit Patel delivery to Kevin Pietersen in the deep to start the trickle of wickets, and two overs later Jade finished things off with wickets in consecutive balls. As one of the new faces, he surprised me because I didn't realise how skilled he was when he was first called in. I had only played against him once in a county game, when we just abused each other the whole time. He rubbed me up the wrong way and I rubbed him up the wrong way, so I didn't think I would get on with him at all. But he came into our dressing room and was an absolute hoot. I loved him to bits. He also performed very creditably.

The series was a good one for me personally. I took eight wickets and generally bowled well – sufficiently well, in fact, to displace Daniel Vettori as number one in the world ODI bowling rankings. The first I knew of this was on the night after the series when I received a text from my mum asking me whether I realised I was number one. 'Yes, Mum, of course I do,' was my reply, and then I saw the story for myself on Sky Sports News. People weren't shy in asking how the heck I'd done it, mind you. (Actually, that was just my brother Alec.) The great thing for me, though, was that with no one-day cricket around the world for the following couple of months there was no chance of anybody knocking me off the top!

*

During that one-day hiatus, I was asked to record an advert at Lord's to promote Sky's coverage of the forthcoming Tests against India. All summer, whenever people stopped me in the street, their conversations had focused on the India series. This was the one they had been waiting for. That had been true from a playing perspective too, and the glitz of this ad emphasised its importance. It was full of bhangra dancers, very Bollywood-influenced, and all I had to do was walk up to the camera (official direction was walk up, take glasses off, look quizzically, smile warmly and walk away). It only took four hours to nail. And all the time I was filming, people were driving past, honking their horns and shouting 'Come on England' as if the game was starting that morning.

The series had obviously grabbed the public's attention because India were coming over with top billing and we had a chance to take over as number one if we could win. That head-to-head competition really captured people's imaginations, but some people took it too far. Jimmy, KP and I started getting abused regularly on Twitter: arrogant and racist, we were going to be destroyed. This was serious.

There were a lot of subplots too. There was Sachin Tendulkar's pursuit of a 100th international hundred; Andrew Strauss's lack of runs against Sri Lanka and alleged struggles against left-arm pace bowlers were being discussed almost as much, with his personal challenge against Zaheer Khan a by-product of that; and England were up against former coach Duncan Fletcher for the first time. So there was plenty of hype before a ball was bowled, but the funniest pre-series event for me was Strauss heading off to play for Somerset against the tourists at Taunton. It made me wonder who would experience the bigger culture shock – the prematurely balding, Radley College and Durham University-educated England captain, or the 4,500 cider drinkers welcoming him for one match. I must say, though, that he looked wonderful in the maroon helmet, so much so that I have told him he must play for Northamptonshire for a couple of years and help them win something once he's finished with England.

The pleasing thing was that he made 78 and an unbeaten 109 in his guest appearance, and as a result went into the four-match campaign in good form. It meant that the entire batting unit were in good nick, which played a part in how we confronted difficult situations – situations in which, 12 months previously, we might have fallen over like a pack of cards. Against Pakistan in 2010, even though we were winning games and generally playing well, as soon as the ball did something it almost felt like just a matter of time until we got rolled. But this summer there seemed to be a real resilience in our team.

To be fair, when someone like Kevin Pietersen gets 200, as he did in the first Test against India at Lord's at the end of July, it does bring a real sense of calm to everyone else who goes in to bat behind him. Even though the ball is moving about, it tends to move onto the middle of the bat rather than the edge when KP is in form, and I must have been relaxed, because I remember having a lovely sleep in the changing room during our first innings of 474 for eight declared. It is the nicest changing room in the country for knocking out some Zs, thanks to the very long leather benches, and as it's a big changing room you get a decent amount of square footage per person around you. That is crucial for me in particular because I change next to Alastair Cook and he is the messiest colleague you could ever have. Such was my blissful time – when I rolled up a few towels and put my head down – that Andy Flower had to order me to be woken at one point because he wanted to do a team talk. I'd dropped off with us three down on the second day and when I was roused three hours later we were only five down.

It had been a tricky start to the match for us, having lost the toss in overcast conditions, but we came through it. One of the things Andy told us prior to playing at Lord's was that although we should not be in awe of the opposition, we had to give them credit and remember that they were number one for a reason. However, at the same time he stressed that we should go out and make sure it was *them* not wanting to play against *us*. So our approach was no different from any other series. Rather than worrying about the challenges thrown down, we were excited by them. We fully expected to perform and win.

The only thing that niggled me in the build-up to Lord's was the scrutiny Stuart Broad was being put under for his place. When someone starts having a go at a member of our team – because it is genuinely a close-knit one – it does tend to get on your nerves. You feel that the criticism is unwarranted, particularly when the team is winning, and I thought that people just had it in for Broady. He seemed to have inherited the bad-boy-of-the-month tag and Bob Willis, pontificating on Sky Sports, was desperate for him to get dropped. Numerous journalists wrote about his petulance and suggested that he didn't deserve his place. As far as I was concerned, one of my best mates was getting a raw deal and I wished the bunch of opinionated so-and-sos would leave off.

Ironically, it was at this time that a television documentary about the Ashes summer of 1981 was shown, and a few of us watched it in the changing room. It featured a 30-year-old video clip of Bob Willis as a player and he was claiming, following some similar criticism he had received, that: 'The media has gone completely down the pan these days; they look for small quotes from players under pressure to write stories.' Broad turned round to everyone and simply said: 'What's changed there then, Bob?'

So the rest of us were delighted when Broady bowled so well at Lord's – it began what was an exceptional second half of the summer for him. To be honest, he should have started that series with a five-for but both Strauss and I dropped catches off him. Then again, he already has a hundred on the Lord's honours board, so he probably doesn't deserve one! But joking aside, his bowling on that third day was impressive. He profited from bowling a fuller length, that much was there for everyone to see, but the barrage of criticism he received while people deconstructed his bowling in mid-summer had still been disappointing. There were so many I-told-you-sos, and everyone seemed to have an opinion on the subject, yet Broad had not bowled badly at all against Sri Lanka, in my opinion. He had been used specifically to bomb the living daylights out of them, and it irked me that these old-school bowlers had forgotten what it was like to bowl fast. I am sure they used to bowl bouncers in their day as well, but they chose to neglect that fact and acted as if it was best practice to run up and bowl half-volleys all day.

It wasn't just that Stuart bowled fuller; he also got his wrist in a better position and therefore moved the ball more. It is no good pitching it up all the time if you are not doing anything with the ball, but luckily the bloke who knows most about bowling in the country is our bowling coach, David Saker. He never gets too worried about what others say; he just works on plans to get batsmen out, and that's what he did to help turn Stuart around.

At times, that first Test was closely fought, and when we were six down in the second innings, 295 runs ahead, India may even have fancied their chances of forcing a result themselves. But Matt Prior and Broadsword recovered the situation in typical style, and to such a degree that I didn't get to bat, despite being next in. When something like that happens it completely changes the atmosphere around the team. It lifts everyone to go from a potentially precarious situation to one where there is only going to be one winner, and it's you.

At the end of the series, Andy Flower told us during his debrief that in this country people are quick to diminish your achievements or rubbish what you've done. Our win was downgraded by some because of a judgement that it was the worst Indian team we'd seen for ages – they just hadn't shown up – yet Andy told us never to believe that kind of thing. His opinion was that we had faced a world-class opposition, but we had not allowed them to play or given them a sniff of winning the series. Whenever we got into tricky positions, as we had in the first Test, we dug deep and played some really good cricket to regain the initiative.

There will always be people out there ready to shoot you down and tell you they were better in their day, but we were rightly proud of our achievements, and as a team I felt we played some top-class cricket. Our batsmen churned out three double hundreds, a couple of our other hundreds in the series were daddies, and we scored big totals as a team in each match. To back it up, our seamers bowled unbelievably throughout, and even when Chris Tremlett was forced out because of injury, Tim Bresnan made the transition effortlessly. The fact that we had someone of Bresnan's quality highlighted our current strength in depth. Such was the start to his Test career that he was walking around in late August calling himself Eldine Baptiste II. Just as his fellow all-rounder Baptiste had managed during West Indies' glory years, Bresnan had played 10, won 10 by the time the summer was out. In a ridiculous attempt at a Caribbean accent, he would tell Andy Flower: 'Ten from ten for me, coach. You can't drop me now, man!'

Asked to bat first for the second consecutive match, we faced the prospect of India taking the game away from us on two occasions in the first half of the second Test at Trent Bridge. But we showed our customary fight.

Before I went out to bat with Stuart Broad at a position of 124 for eight, Andrew Strauss said to me in the changing room: 'It would be good to get up to 160 here.' I told him he had clearly forgotten that Broad and I had a hundred partnership in Test cricket. Obviously, I was being flippant in a bid to relax both him and myself, but there was truth in what I said and our attitude has always been to take the game to the opposition and see what happens. That is exactly what we did when we walked out after tea, having survived four balls before it. I hit a few fours to get India on the back foot, and Broady needs the least persuasion out of anyone I have ever known to join in with some fun. Once again, if the ball was anywhere near us we were going to try to swing through it.

I thoroughly enjoyed watching Broady teeing off from the other end and he dominated the scoring as we shared 73 in the opening 11 overs of the evening session. However, no sooner had I considered that we could get up to 300 if we batted sensibly than I got a ball that went through the top, cracked a bone in my left hand and looped into the air. It immediately put me in a stinking mood, as not only was I out and in pain but I couldn't catch any more, which meant I was ruled out of the slips and consigned to the boundary for the rest of the game. The lads said afterwards that we could never allow that situation to arise again because I am so useless in the deep that I don't even concentrate on the game. And yes, I can confirm it is true that I would rather be in the stand drinking beer than having it thrown on me.

The break in question, revealed later in a scan, was to a metatarsal, and there is nothing you can really do for an injury like that. You can't fix it, so it was a matter of padding it up, reinforcing my batting glove and getting on with it for the rest of the series. It was a pain in the backside that it hurt so much, but by the final innings at The Oval, it had healed sufficiently for me to remove the protection, and I took a catch and didn't feel a thing.

I suppose I could easily use the excuse that the injury affected my bowling, but to say that the pain in my left hand restricted me would be nonsense. Afterwards others tried to make that excuse for me, but the truth is I just bowled like a clown at Trent Bridge. It always riles me when people look for excuses rather than admit they were a bit rubbish. I had a stinking game – sometimes it just doesn't come out of your hand very well – and that was a shame on my home ground. Unfortunately, my international record at Trent Bridge is pretty woeful, about on a par with my batting record at Worcester.

A score of 221 at least gave us something to bowl at, but when India batted they cruised past us with only four down, and they had gained a 46-run lead by the time Broady produced an unbelievable spell of bowling with the second new ball. Having separated Rahul Dravid and Yuvraj Singh when the latter nicked behind, he produced a first England Test hat-trick since Ryan Sidebottom three years earlier in New Zealand. After Mahendra Singh Dhoni was well held by Jimmy Anderson, substituting for me in the slips, there was a bitter-sweet moment in the middle of his three-in-three when Harbhajan

Singh was adjudged lbw by umpire Marais Erasmus despite the chunkiest of inside edges. Because of the noise of the crowd none of us heard it at the time and when we saw it replayed on the big screen, a couple of lads in the huddle were uncertain why he hadn't called for a review. As Harbhajan trudged off it was a source of great amusement to us to recall that it was India who had not wanted the DRS used in the series. Praveen Kumar was castled by a full delivery next ball and the incredible spell of wickets shifted the momentum back our way. We never looked back.

There were a lot of good contributions in our second innings, led by Ian Bell's 159. His innings meant we posted a truly massive score. However, in some ways it is unfortunate that it will be remembered for the bizarre incident on the stroke of tea when the ball was struck to the boundary and semi-stopped by Praveen Kumar. Most people will have seen the ball retrieved from next to the rope and relayed back to the middle in a most lackadaisical manner, which gave the impression that it had gone for four. So when the Indians took the bails off, it was blatantly obvious to me that it should not have been out. I don't care what anybody says – 'India did nothing wrong, the decision should have stood' – there is no way, when you watch replays of the incident, that Ian Bell is going for a run. He was walking up to Eoin Morgan to wander off together and have some tea.

As we sat in our changing room at teatime, the general feeling was that if India were going to uphold the appeal, and wanted to play in that manner, the whole series would descend into farce, just like the one against Pakistan the previous year. To put it into perspective, if I was of a mind to tally up, I'd lose count of the number of times in an innings that I could run out the non-striker, out of his ground gardening, when I field balls patted back to me off my own bowling. As the rules state, I could whip off the bails and he'd be out. But nobody ever does that because it would just ruin the game.

So it was a pretty tense 20-minute tea break on that third afternoon and Bell, on 137 at the time, did not learn of his reprieve until right at the very end of it, literally as the players were due to go back out.

Third umpire Billy Bowden came into our dressing room and told him that India had rescinded the appeal. The interval had begun with Andrew Strauss heading down to the Indian changing room to have a talk with Dhoni and India coach Duncan Fletcher. He simply asked them whether they really wanted the game to be played in that manner. Fletcher was fine with it, though, and didn't see anything wrong with standing by the dismissal, because he was adamant that Belly had been attempting a fourth. So when Strauss returned to our dressing room, he informed us that the Indian captain and coach thought the decision should stand. But they had agreed to put it to the floor and take the opinion of the rest of their team into account. Word later got back to us that Sachin Tendulkar and Rahul Dravid were of the opinion that they ought to call him back because it was not how they should be playing the game.

India walked out after tea to intensive boos, which were replaced as they stood in a team huddle on the outfield by huge cheers as Bell emerged a minute later. I think those few seconds showed that India had done the right thing in the end because there was every chance that they would have been booed mercilessly for the rest of the summer had they gone along with it. In my opinion, you just can't do that kind of thing. There are so many passages of play where you could try to bend the rules or go against the spirit of the game to get an edge, but if you want to do that then play rugby or football, just don't play cricket.

As it happened, Bell had already established the platform and only added a further 22 runs himself, but the middle and lower order kicked viciously once more to set India a mammoth 478-run victory target. What happened next, to my mind, was one of the most crucial contributions to us winning the series 4–0. It was the spell of bowling from Tim Bresnan when he just ran up and bombed the hell out of Suresh Raina and Yuvraj Singh. We had men out on the hook and a Bodyline-esque field – and it worked, because he got them both out. He had bullied them into submission on a cricket field.

When things like that happen and the opposition come out fighting in response it can really fire up a series, but they can also retreat into their shells instead. That is more or less what happened, and when opponents react like that it gives you a feeling of invincibility. If nothing else, we knew that we always had that plan to fall back on if things were not going well. In a fight, if you are 6 ft 5 in and you are taking on a guy who is 5 ft 1 in, and built like a rake, you are always going to feel confident. It was a bit like that from then on; we just felt as if we had an edge over them.

No bullying was required at Edgbaston for the third Test as the ball swung around in overcast conditions. Although India were theoretically strengthened by the return of Virender Sehwag, he was out first ball to Stuart Broad. Our three pace bowlers kept putting it in the right place and catches were taken behind all day. But for 77 from Dhoni, they would have been bowled out for an absolute pittance.

In fact, it looked like a really good wicket to bowl on until we went out to bat. Then suddenly it looked like a formidable batting wicket. But I guess that this was because of the confidence of our team. Our batsmen believed they could score hundreds every time they went in to bat and our belief in them was demonstrated by the fact that on the second morning all the bowlers decided to go for a kip in the new dressing rooms at Edgbaston, which are more like luxury apartments. So I can't profess to have witnessed too much of Alastair Cook's 294. Now, that might sound lazy, but it is permitted in our team rules – the deal is that if the batters give us time off, a good period to rest and recover, we have to win the game the following day. You should see some of the weird and wonderful positions Jimmy Anderson gets into when he falls asleep. He is like a three-year-old kid: he can nod off picking his nose, one leg over the edge of the sofa, head dangling towards the floor. It's brilliant.

Jimmy was incredible for us all summer, carrying on where he left off last year. He has developed into such a potent weapon. He has the knack of getting wickets early, swings it and has enough pace.

After completing Sehwag's king pair on the third evening, he really deserved a five-for next morning and was only denied it by me performing a diving-Swann act at slip when one of their tail-enders was in. I went to catch it and fell over my own feet.

Although Jimmy bowled magnificently, the real turning point for us was obviously when I ran out Sachin Tendulkar backing up. Everyone has since said that deflecting that return drive from Dhoni into the stumps was a fluke, but I stand by my quick-thinking genius. You can see quite clearly on the replay: it is not a horrible misfield at all, it is a clever bit of angling the hand a few degrees at the right time to get the ball to flick it. No one in the team believes me, but I can sleep safe in the knowledge that I single-handedly won that Test match with one piece of magic! Jimmy Anderson knows I try it all the time in the nets and in one-day games, yet when he asked me if I had done it on purpose, and I told him yeah, he said: 'Course you did . . . !' Then again, people didn't recognise Van Gogh's genius until after he was dead. So I expect my reaction fielding will be acknowledged approximately 100 years after my untimely death.

That innings win, achieved inside four days, guaranteed that we would displace India at the head of the world rankings. On a personal note, I bookended the summer with a pleasing performance at The Oval as we completed our 4–0 series victory. I'd played a decent hand in the first Test win of 2011 against Sri Lanka in Cardiff and this was the final Test, with our goal achieved, so not having had the most productive summer myself – there were times when I hardly bowled at all during that India series – it was nice to contribute.

The portents were good. As had happened before that final Ashes Test two years earlier, two or three turned square past the edge in net practice. After several seamer-friendly surfaces, it was a refreshing change and a quick chat to the groundsman, Scott Patterson, confirmed that my optimism was not misplaced. I quizzed him on whether it would turn, and he told me it would both turn and bounce, and that I would absolutely love it. So it proved.

This time, Andrew Strauss won the toss and batted, and despite rain ruling out two-thirds of the opening day and a third of the third, we were always going to go all out for a whitewash once we reached a position of 591 for six, on the back of Ian Bell's 235 and 175 from Kevin Pietersen. Even with that many runs on the board we knew it would be tough, however, and after rain gave way to sunshine late on the afternoon of Saturday, 20 August, as we finished our warm-up session, Andy Flower called us over for a team talk on the outfield. He wanted to get it into our heads that we had a couple of really hard days' graft ahead of us if we were to fulfil what he expected of us. The only chance of winning would be to bowl them out for less than the follow-on target of 392, so he wanted us to go out there, try our socks off and give it everything. He told us that although the wicket was flat – and we all knew it was – we had one over on the Indian team psychologically and so we had to make that count. To complete our task, he said, we would have to field for 200 overs consecutively. Later, there were those within the team who thought we should have a quick bat after we bowled them out for 300, but the only real way to win the game was to stick them back in and make one last big push for the series.

I loved the battle I had with Sachin Tendulkar in that final Test. I got him out sweeping in the first innings, and so quite naturally I wanted him to play the same stroke again in the second innings. Only he didn't play it at all. You see, with Tendulkar, if something doesn't work for him, he just puts it to bed, and that makes him very hard to bowl at. But even then, during that second innings, when he held us at bay for so long alongside nightwatchman Amit Mishra, I had him dropped at short leg and at the wicket, and he survived a couple of lbws we were confident were out.

They repelled us for 30 overs that final morning and were only 29 runs in arrears when my dismissal of Mishra left them four down. But it has become customary for this England team to pull things out of the bag. We have learned that when you are on a wearing wicket, no matter how long a partnership goes on, if you dig in and remain patient, it will pay dividends when a breakthrough is made. It is just a matter of patience and being able to utilise the conditions when you get the chance. It was similar to the Ashes finale against Australia in 2009, when they had that marathon partnership between Mike Hussey and Ricky Ponting, and their separation had marked the opening of the floodgates.

One end was now open, although it was Tim Bresnan who struck an even heavier blow four balls later when he dismissed Tendulkar agonisingly shy of his hundred. What I found weird that week was that there were so many people in the crowd who wanted him to get there. When I did the press conference in the build-up to the game they were all talking about how nice it would be for Sachin to get his 100th hundred in this match. 'This is his chance and surely you would like him to get a hundred, but England to go on and win? Wouldn't that be the perfect scenario?' someone asked me. But I just didn't get that. If you have played sport at any level, you simply do not want someone on the opposition to do well. Afterwards you might acknowledge someone's outstanding performance, or be pleased that a mate has done well, but you never go into a contest with that attitude. As a team, we certainly didn't want Sachin Tendulkar to reach his milestone in that Test match.

I soon followed up by trapping Suresh Raina leg before, and when Gautam Gambhir later sliced to backward point to leave India nine down, I was urged to mimic the Australian habit of holding the ball up to the crowd to acknowledge a five-wicket haul. The seamers had been doing it throughout 2011, but whereas people automatically clap when a batsman reaches 50 and then you raise your bat, as a bowler you have to stand there and get the crowd to notice you. It is the ultimate milking of applause. The other guys had been amazingly sheepish doing it, particularly Broad at Trent Bridge, although Jimmy Anderson looked as if he really meant it. He just stood with an arrogant stare on his face similar to the one that El Hadji Diouf has when he scores a goal.

After I'd been pressured into it, primarily by Bressie, who handed me the ball, it took ages until anyone noticed, and when they did it reminded me of the time Freddie Flintoff ran out Ricky Ponting in 2009 and just stood there, chewing his gum, arms outstretched. Naturally, I decided to pay homage to him with a similar pose.

Of my nine wickets in the match, the one I savoured most was that of Rahul Dravid, in the second innings, after he had carried his bat in the first. To have him caught at short leg was doubly satisfying for me because I hadn't got him out previously in the series and he'd batted unbelievably well throughout. Although there is something incredibly special about the way Sachin picks up the length of the ball the instant you let go of it, the one who played the best all series for India was Dravid. He was undoubtedly the player in the most impressive form and he had probably never batted better throughout an entire series than that – he was phenomenal.

Getting Sehwag too on that fourth evening gave me a good feeling because it was a classic off-spinner's dismissal: pitching outside off and turning in through the gate to hit middle. You don't get many of those, probably three or four a year if you are lucky, and it is a delivery that Matt Prior calls the cheese ball. Matt is known as The Cheese within our dressing room and back in the mid-noughties I cleaned him up in exactly that way, so every now and again, if it is turning, you will hear him shout: 'C'mon, Swanny, give us the cheese!' That one and Dravid's were the most pleasing dismissals for me, not just in the series but in the first eight months of 2011.

After wrapping things up by bowling Shanthakumaran Sreesanth, I was able to drive home to Nottingham that night with the extra special feeling that comes from providing a major contribution to an important win, and it was the first time I'd been able to say that since Cardiff in May. I was pretty chuffed with my personal return of taking five wickets or more in a Test innings at The Oval for the first time.

On the outfield after the game Andy Flower spoke emotionally about his pride in our achievement. He is 100 per cent committed to his job, and that comes across whenever you hear him speak. He is a hard man – you just don't mess about with Andy; you get the feeling he used to be an assassin or something like that, and we have all been called horrific things by him when we've played against him – but it is great that he can be so passionate that he chokes up the way he did over a couple of beers that glorious Monday night.

It was there, after we had been presented with the ICC's Test mace – a trophy that confirmed us as world number ones, and looks as if it should have the magical powers to keep us there – and completed several laps of honour, with 'Jerusalem' playing on loop, that he told the team to ignore anyone wanting to bemoan the Indian standard of play. Just look at the names on their list, look at the players you did not allow to have good series, and be proud of what you have done. Enjoy it, look each other in the eye and say well done, he told us.

21

CHANGING TIMES

M Y MUM Mavis always said I would be England captain one day. I dismissed this prophecy as one of those things that mums say, but in mid-September 2011 she was proved right. Of course she was – mums tend to be right about everything, don't they? – and having sworn to my dad for years that it would come true, she really enjoyed her told-you-so moment.

The news was delivered to me during the ICC Awards dinner at the Grosvenor House Hotel in London. Although it was a bit of a swanky do, and I was one of five England players named in the World Test XI, I was not overly keen on being there, as it was held only 24 hours after the one-day international against India at Lord's, and all I really wanted to do was get home and see Sarah and Wilf. As it was, I did a deal with the management that I would turn up for the dinner, show my face on the red carpet and make an idiot of myself with Jimmy Anderson in media interviews, but then disappear after the formalities rather than hang around and hobnob.

As I sat through the awards announcements, my eyes were more or less fixed on my watch. My thoughts were on the journey home, and I was actually gazing down at my wrist when Andy Flower asked me for a word in private. He led me out of the room and behind a curtain.

'What the hell have I done now?' I thought. When I was a kid at school, being summoned out of a room like that meant a minor rebuke at best and a meeting of slipper and buttocks at worst.

Then it suddenly dawned on me: Stuart Broad had been sidelined with an injured shoulder and Eoin Morgan, the vice-captain of the

Twenty20 team, was out too. Could it be good news for a change?

As Andy looked at me and started smiling, I failed to suppress one of my own.

'I know what you're about to ask me,' I said. 'You're going to ask me to be captain, aren't you?'

He rolled his eyes and said, 'Well, yes, we are!' After a pause, he added, 'In all seriousness, we think you are the ideal man to do it.'

Even though I knew it was only an interim job for back-to-back 20-over matches against West Indies while Broad was injured, I still felt giddy – I was that excited. Temporary or not, I was still captain – England captain.

As I drove home up the M1, I couldn't help chuckling to myself and reflecting on how my career had gone full circle. The bloke at the steering wheel was quite different from the idiot who had been fined for missing the bus and had been considered the least mature cricketer of his generation. Graeme Swann the captain would never pick Graeme Swann the kid. But at 32, even though the young lunatic was still in there, I managed to hide him most of the time, and had done so successfully enough to allow the England management to select me as their on-field leader. Don't get me wrong: there is a time for messing around, and I still indulge in it, but this was a time to be serious.

A measure of exactly how seriously I took it was the fact that aside from my wife – who threatened Chinese water torture – I did not tell anyone about my appointment. She always knows when I'm hiding something from her, so I made her the one exception to the instruction from Andy to keep it top secret until the official announcement was made 36 hours later. Perhaps they had factored in that time to organise a more suitable replacement; who knows?

There were a couple of journalists who, by process of elimination, had worked out that I had got the job, and that meant avoiding their calls and messages. I was asked directly in one text message, but I opted to ignore it and let time take its course. When I was questioned by John Etheridge of the *Sun*, things got a little uncomfortable because of my working relationship with him and the newspaper, but it seemed to me that a reply of 'No, mate, they'd never let me do it' was a fairly believable defence.

Of course, under normal circumstances, a Twenty20 series against West Indies in Siberian conditions would be about as appealing as a mud-wrestle with Pat Butcher, but it is amazing how a bit of power and responsibility can sharpen the focus. I was genuinely excited about doing the job. This was proper poacher-turned-gamekeeper stuff, and I began to see things in a totally different light.

In terms of pre-match preparation, in one way it is easier being captain than in the ranks because you have 101 things to occupy your thoughts. Normally, the night before a match I would be thinking about who I would be bowling at the following day, where I wanted to bowl at them and the fields I would set. Now I was thinking about which bowlers to use when, while trying to come up with a Plan B in addition to my Plan A and working out who would field at mid-off – as well as more important stuff like who to put as far away from me as possible. I began to see how people get power-crazy after just a couple of days in office, and why certain individuals are drawn to positions of authority.

I obviously relished the team talks, because there is nothing more soothing to me than the sound of my own voice, and I loved every minute of leading the team on the field. In fact, once I was at the ground I enjoyed it all: getting to put a spin on selection, deciding who bowled when, the field settings. Being able to shape a game other than with the ball was appealing

However, there were other parts of the job that proved more of a pain. Primarily these were off-field responsibilities, the man-management duties that leadership entails. Having to tell people that they weren't playing was not nice, but nor for that matter was having to go to others' rooms to tell them that they were in the XI. I recall going to see Scott Borthwick with good news but feeling a complete idiot in delivering it. It should have been straightforward telling a young lad that he was playing for England the next day, but it proved an uncomfortable experience, probably because I was not used to being the one delivering a yes or a no like that Simon Cowell chap.

One of those omitted was Jimmy Anderson, and I admit to cowardice when it came to his fate. I actually chickened out of telling him, and instead of sidling up for a quiet word, I saved the disappointment for when I read out the team at final practice. I can't imagine he was expecting to play, as he hadn't been involved in Twenty20 internationals for a couple of years, yet his face told me that he was not best pleased at the prospect of sporting an orange bib for a few days.

Situations like that I found particularly awkward, in Jimmy's case doubly so because I drove to and from The Oval with him each day. Even though we are great mates, we can both still be petulant and childish at times, and our journey back to the hotel was frosty for a good five minutes – until one of us cracked a joke or farted. I can't recall which, but everything was rosy again after that (which probably suggests it was the former rather than the latter).

I also didn't really appreciate the criticism that came my way after the second game, when we lost a ridiculously low-scoring match. Dean Wilson, the *Mirror*'s cricket correspondent, and someone I consider a friend, had been full of praise for my innovative captaincy following the 10-wicket win in the opening contest, but he back-pedalled after the second, suggesting that what I had done was formulaic and predictable, and that I was perhaps not a good captain after all.

As a rule, I tend not to get hacked off when people write negative stuff about my batting or bowling, but this really got under my skin. I considered it absolute pigswill, and told him as much in a message. As a captain, if your team has restricted the opposition to 113 in 20 overs, you've generally done a good job. So I challenged him to produce a Twenty20 scorecard between two teams of decent standard in which a first-innings score of 113 had proved successful.

'I will happily concede I didn't do a good job if you can find one,' I told him.

To his credit, he went away and looked, and came back to tell me that he couldn't track down an example. But his comments in print had hurt me, and this episode opened my eyes to what Andrew Strauss and Alastair Cook have to go through. Every decision they make is analysed, and as we have seen with Strauss recently, their form is questioned with little regard for the great jobs they do as on-field leaders.

As captain, you become an easy target for criticism, and with people looking for someone to blame for this defeat – they couldn't justify criticising young lads so early in their careers – they chose me as a scapegoat. But I couldn't see that it was justified.

To be fair, there were very few defeats to pick over in 2011, and denying India a single success on their tour was particularly pleasing. Moreover, the 3–0 NatWest Series win represented the first one-day series I had played in where, every time we got into a position to take the game on, we did so.

During limited-overs matches you often get points at which the contest can swing either way – with, say, a quick 40-run partnership or a key wicket – and this was the first time in my experience that we always took the right turn. Previously, when we faced these 50–50 game-breaking situations, they turned out to be exactly that. Half the time we would make the positive move and prosper; the other half we would flunk it, which made it almost pot luck whether we won games or not. In this series, every time it reached a crucial stage, we came out on top. All of a sudden, we were winning games from all kinds of positions.

Although the weather played its part in the tied Duckworth-Lewis match at Lord's – when we contrived to lose two wickets in as many balls to bring India back into the equation at the end of a stop-start finale – we were actually helped by the elements in the series. Rain, or the threat of it, certainly forced our hand in a couple of batting situations and made us go about our innings more aggressively than we might have otherwise. Both at the Rose Bowl and Sophia Gardens we batted with the intention of staying well ahead of the rate, so that if Messrs Duckworth and Lewis had their say, we would be the ones celebrating.

It was refreshing, because a number of young lads came into the middle order and, with Eoin Morgan injured, showed similarly adventurous natures. I had never seen Jonny Bairstow bat before he walked in at number six in Cardiff, so it was a pleasant surprise to see him hitting it everywhere from the word go. He struck his fifth ball in international cricket for six, then reverse-swept his seventh ball for four and never looked back in an unbeaten 41. It was really positive to see this kind of approach and it made it a fun series.

From a personal perspective, it had been a fairly lean summer wicket-wise, so it was doubly enjoyable to pick up a few in that one-day series. Things had begun to go my way during the last Test at The Oval, when a nine-wicket haul seemed to alter my luck. Wickets came regularly again, which was a very nice touch, because I was not bowling at the top of my game or anything like it. For example, my three at the Rose Bowl came in a reduced-overs game, when the Indian batsmen were going for their shots. First, a brilliant catch at short midwicket by Jimmy Anderson to get rid of Rahul Dravid; then Virat Kholi came down the wicket, got to the pitch, went to hit a straight six and fluffed it to long on; and finally I somehow clung to a return drive by Ajinkya Rahane above my head.

Sometimes in limited-overs cricket you become the beneficiary of batsmen trying to score against the clock, and here was another example. Cricket is not always about form; occasionally, something just goes your way and you have to take advantage of it when it does. It sounds cheesy to say that if you keep persevering things will eventually go your way, but then again the quantity of your successes is not always commensurate with your efforts as a spin bowler.

If luck was with me, the dice were definitely rolling in England's favour too during this five-match series, and we unearthed a team of young guys brought up on a diet of Twenty20 cricket. A handful have the potential to become megastars. We had merely the slightest glimpse of Bairstow's ability in Cardiff; we know all about Ben Stokes's potential; and then there are people like Alex Hales and Jos Buttler. All in all, England have the potential for the most exciting top six in world cricket within a few years.

Had the summer ended there, things would have been damn near perfect. As it was, I set off for India in early October with a bit of a heavy heart. We had walked away from Cardiff with a 3–0 series win and an unbeaten record against India – not forgetting the number one ranking in Test cricket. But there was no time for reflection. After everything we had achieved, it would have been a lovely point at which to stop and have a break. Instead, we were flying out to play another five one-day internationals against the same opponents. It is a dreadful thing to say – because you should always cherish every minute of playing for your country – but I simply couldn't find the enthusiasm.

It didn't help that they hammered us. In contrast to the home series, we just couldn't get into any positions of control at all. We went from churning out wins to not being able to buy one for love nor money. All the progress we seemed to have made since the World Cup was unpicked in just over a fortnight. It wasn't an enjoyable tour by any means. I didn't do particularly well and found myself longing to return home. The only thing that kept me going was the two-month break on the horizon.

Not that we travelled to India with anything other than a resolution to win over there. Victory would have put us one step closer to our target, because we genuinely believe that this England team has an opportunity to get to number one in one-day as well as Test cricket. But we found our opponents were well equipped to counter us in their own conditions. Guys that we had smashed around the park just a few weeks earlier were being treated like world-beaters now. We were either letting them get us out or going into our shells against them, and overnight we became an easy team to beat. It was bizarre how our form dropped so dramatically, but I believe it was partly the result of an extremely long season, one that had followed the gruelling programme of the Ashes and a World Cup campaign back to back. Perhaps some of the younger guys suffered from nerves – whatever the reason, we hardly put up a fight and we were thrashed 5–0.

Before the solitary Twenty20 fixture, even though I was preparing to be England captain for a third time, whenever I saw a plane fly over Eden Gardens in Kolkata during pre-match practice sessions, I wished myself on it. Once we were on the field, however, things could hardly have gone better. Where we had struggled to take advantage of our opportunities in the longer form of the game, now we seized them, removing the same batsmen we had struggled against in the 50-over format and restricting the target to 120-odd, before Kevin Pietersen walked in and smashed it everywhere. Job done.

The months of November and December 2011 provided us with some rare rest, but when the post-mortem was carried out into our failure against Pakistan in the United Arab Emirates the following January and February, I was reluctant to buy into the theory that it had anything to do with that break. There may have been a grain of truth in the suggestions that it had caused rustiness, but after such a heavy schedule over the previous year, it was a necessity. Not having that opportunity to put the feet up for a few weeks might have shaved 18 months off a few of our careers – certainly mine. Fatigue catches up with you eventually on the international circuit, but I believe there were more relevant contributing factors in our 3–0 loss.

For three years we had scored really well as a batting team all around the world, but suddenly we were unable to put decent totals together. I am not sure that we didn't underestimate Pakistan in those conditions, too. The facts suggest we did, because in the first Test in Dubai Sports City they dismissed us cheaply twice on what, as my innings of 34 and 39 will testify, was a very good batting wicket.

Even after that poor start, we should have come roaring back in the remaining two matches, but although we got ourselves into positions to win, we blew it. It was very frustrating, because recent history had demonstrated our ability to come back strongly. We only had to think of how well we had performed after setbacks in Jamaica and Leeds in 2009, and then again in Perth in late 2010, to remind ourselves how we normally reacted to adversity. Everyone expected us to come back, and as a team we expected it too.

In one way we did just that, because in the second Test at Abu Dhabi we controlled the game – until the fourth innings. How we managed to mess up a chase of 145 on what remained a true surface, I am still not sure. It was inexplicable. It was arguably a mixture of poor form and loss of confidence, with a dollop of panic thrown in as well. And to lose the third Test after bowling them out for 99 in the afternoon session of the opening day was mind-boggling. It was a defeat of phenomenal magnitude. We were always going to lose that first Test, because of how well Pakistan played. They totally blew us out of the water. But I will forever look back at the other two and think, 'Christ, we should have won that series.'

In no other series has so much attention been placed on the Decision Review System. It has changed the game, and certainly its use got into batsmen's heads during those three matches, when spin was so prevalent. The system has vindicated those of us who have argued with umpires over the years that certain balls were going on to hit the stumps. Too often in the past, batsmen got the benefit of the doubt when struck on the pad and now us twirlers have been proved right.

Batsmen have become increasingly susceptible to lbw decisions, and the game has undoubtedly changed. Yet as Younis Khan showed with his brilliant hundred during that final Test, you can still counter the questions asked of you by using your bat. He simply refused to let anything hit his pad, swept really well and watched the ball like a hawk. It wasn't a bad set of principles for the modern player.

Not that I consider that my fellow spinners and I will dominate from now on. I suspect that within a couple of years batsmen will have adjusted and will discover a new way of playing spin. The balance is bound to shift back in their favour at least a little, because cricket has a habit of being cyclical. A particular set of specialists tend not to dominate for long.

The combination of the ball doing just enough off the pitch to catch the edge and skidding on as well proved lethal. On some pitches, the ball can do too much, but the amount it spun in this series was just enough. That meant both edges were vulnerable, and batsmen were also susceptible to deliveries that didn't spin as anticipated. If the ball was coming into you, it proved very difficult to deal with early in an innings.

We got ourselves into positions to win two Tests, and you can only do that by bowling out the opposition. Our issues were not with the ball, however, but with the bat. Not that I want to point fingers. Ultimately, you cannot blame the batsmen, because there have been plenty of times when they have got us out of trouble. It was just strange that so many were struggling with poor form at the same time.

Throughout the previous couple of years, whenever anyone was out of nick, they were covered by the rest of the batting group. For example, during the entire Ashes of 2010–11, we were able to carry Paul Collingwood because Alastair Cook and Jonathan Trott were scoring so heavily. That's what good teams do, and when a couple of batsmen are churning out the runs, it makes it much easier for everyone else, whatever form they're in. Yet on this particular assignment, half a dozen guys were struggling at the same time.

From a bowling perspective, a lot was made as to whether it was me or Monty Panesar who was fulfilling the role of number-one spinner, but I was surprised by this media talk because from a cricketing perspective it was fairly straightforward. As Pakistan's top order were predominantly right-handers, Monty was the more dangerous option, because he takes the ball away from a right-hander's bat, and therefore he got to bowl the majority of overs – simple as that. Similarly, whenever a left-hander walked in, I tended to be brought on to bowl, because as a spin bowler you are always trying to locate the outside edge.

I claimed 13 wickets at 25 runs apiece, a return comfortably better than my career average of 28. So without setting the world on fire – it was obviously nothing compared to the 22 I had taken against them during four Tests in England in 2010 – I had made a contribution. Furthermore, my performances were compared to those of Pakistan's spinner Saeed Ajmal, who all credit to him, was brilliant throughout the three matches. Fair play to him. However, even the most myopic of observers would have to concede that Saeed Ajmal and I are very different types of bowlers. Well, we certainly have very different actions, and he doesn't bowl the sort of traditional spin that I bowl, relying instead on his deceptive doosra and pace off the pitch as his major weapons.

When batting against him, I found the extent of the challenge depended largely on the state of the light. In bright sunshine during mid-afternoon, you could see the ball coming down at you and that made it considerably easier. But because of the big stands behind the bowler's arm at the grounds in Dubai and Abu Dhabi, and the fact that the sun went down while play was still in progress, shadows covered the middle at times. With a mystery spinner, it is normal practice to watch the wrist at the point of delivery, but because of Ajmal's unique action, you see more of his elbow than his wrist when he lets the ball go. When visibility was good, I would try to watch the rotations on the ball, but when there were patches of dark and light, it was almost impossible. We struggled against him all the way through the series. He was difficult enough to read at the best of times and a complete menace at others.

So we headed into the limited-overs section of the tour amid murmurings that our rise to the top had been a fluke. There were those who couldn't wait to say 'I thought it was too good to be true; we're effing useless.' And that was just in the commentary box.

The one-day matches gave us a chance to banish a few demons, not least the drubbing in India before Christmas. I also had an extra incentive to show my worth to the team. After that 5–0 defeat in India, I'd had some disparaging things to say about one-day cricket, and as a result was rebuked face-to-face at Lord's by my bosses. A mixture of tiredness and petulance, worsened by our displays on the subcontinent, had led to me spouting off in a press interview, and questioning the wisdom of playing a five-match series against Australia in the summer of 2012 when we were playing only three Tests against South Africa. I was rightly hauled over the coals to explain my comments. It was perfectly understandable that NatWest, as sponsors, would not have been happy to hear one of the England team's established players talking in those terms.

During my disciplinary meeting, one thing that Andy Flower stressed was that as I was a senior player my thoughts would be picked up on by the younger lads. What impression was I giving to them? It was a fair enough question to ask, and I felt like a spoilt brat afterwards. No individual should ever pick and choose what series they play in, what's important and what's not. There will always be personal preference for where you want to play and what you want to play in, and I can hardly pretend that I love one-day cricket as much as Test cricket, because I just don't. But some things are best left unsaid. I'd worked that out before I got down to London, and as Sarah had already given me a huge telling-off for getting into trouble, I was quite contrite with my apology. So whatever my thoughts on the 50-over game, I will keep them to myself from now on, for fear that Andy metes out six firm strokes of the cane.

Before the trip, most cricket-following folk would have assumed that we would win the Test series and struggle in the one-dayers, but expectation was turned on its head as we produced the kind of solid performances that had eluded us in the five-day games. As an opening partnership, Alastair Cook and Kevin Pietersen were both outstanding, and we played good basic cricket to ensure any advantage we opened up was exploited.

By the time that one-day series finished – as a rare 4–0 win – and we were preparing for the Twenty20 series, we were back to the point where we thought we could win any game of cricket, which is obviously a very good place to be. Added to the fact that we are good at Twenty20, it suggested our winning streak would continue. We had played Pakistan in two 20-over games in the Middle East immediately prior to our World Twenty20 success in 2010 and departed with a sense we had let ourselves down by drawing 1–1; a series victory would have been a fairer reflection of where we were as a team. Similarly, in this three-match campaign, the fact that we lost the first game came as a big surprise to us all. But in the other two low-scoring matches on slow pitches, we managed to come out on top.

The winter's up-and-down character continued in Sri Lanka in March and April, and I would have to say that the first Test defeat there was our worst result of the whole winter.

Though Abdur Rehman had bowled well against us in the UAE, our problems against Pakistan had stemmed from the difficulty in picking Ajmal. We spent so much time and energy trying to determine whether he was bowling his doosra or off-spinner that it distracted us from the job in hand. As often happens in cricket, Rehman picked up the rewards of us being demoralised by his partner. Perhaps not facing Ajmal meant our batsmen relaxed for a few moments. But what was certain was that Rehman was good enough to cash in.

Sri Lanka, however, possessed no such quality amongst their spin bowlers, so I was genuinely surprised that Rangana Herath managed to get 12 wickets in the first match in Galle. With all due respect to him, he is a good bowler, with lovely control, but he is not a mystery bowler. You can judge exactly what each ball is going to do, and yet we failed to combat the straightforward armoury he possesses. Yes, it was a good pitch to bowl spin on, but it was not a bad pitch to bat on. There was some turn and bounce on offer, but it was far from impossible to score runs.

Having bowled out the Sri Lankans for 318 in the first innings, we should have scored 400–500 in response to take control of the game, but we messed up big style, making only 193. Even then, dismissing them for 214 gave us half a chance going into the final dig – and it would have been even better if Stuart Broad's wicket-taking delivery to Prasanna Jayawardene had not been a no-ball. They were nine down at the time and ended up getting another 47 runs. As it was, we lost by 75, but it would have been a psychological boost to be chasing sub-300 in those conditions rather than 340. Things like that going against you certainly test your mental strength.

Each night we faced an hour's drive from the ground back to our hotel, and normally on a journey like that people have their head-phones on or watch Tim Bresnan attempt to play Pictionary on an iPad (which is just genius, by the way, and to be thoroughly recom-mended should you ever get a chance), but the journey that followed our defeat was dominated by an air of grave disappointment. You could feel just how fed up everyone on that bus was. It was distinctly different from the feeling in Pakistan, and a lot more difficult to deal with. This was the kind of defeat that left you wringing your hands and screaming in frustration, almost demanding to be allowed to turn back the clock and put things right. You knew you couldn't possibly make the same mistakes twice.

When it came to the second Test in Colombo, there seemed to be a collective determination not to allow a repeat showing. Come hell or high water, we were going to win that Test. Not even the most physically demanding conditions in world cricket would get in our way. You see, if you are a fully signed up member of the ginger club, as I am – thanks, Mum – you want to stay out of any heat above about 23 degrees. This was 48. Anything over 40 per cent humidity can feel harsh, almost unbearable, and yet here we were close to 100 per cent.

The one bloke who was able to deal with this was Superman Bresnan, he of the 100 per cent Test record. You see, it was only Bres who seemed to have no problem with the extremity of the heat. We had been discouraged from talking about it, although it was inevitable the subject would come up, and at our first net session of the tour, I said to him, 'This place is ridiculous, isn't it? It's just so humid. I'm sweating like a cornered virgin.'

'It's no different from Yorkshire 'ere,' Bres bizarrely insisted. 'It feels exactly the same as Harrogate or Bradford.'

This observation became the in-joke of the tour. In that Test match, it was stinking hot one afternoon and when Bres threw the ball back in, Matt Prior greeted it with 'It's just like Keighley this, eh Bres? Just like Doncaster, big lad?'

There were days when I walked out of the hotel and I would have given my tour fee to walk straight back in, lounge around in my air-conditioned room and stay there all day playing on the Xbox or reading a book. Playing in those conditions is such hard work, and alien for English cricketers, but we had vowed not to allow it to become an excuse for poor performances. So the warpaint went on – I looked as if I had half a tin of Dulux across my nose each morning – and so did the sweatbands. Now, I was brought up to believe that anyone who wore sweatbands was some horrific show pony, yet here I was with one on each wrist! Needs must, though.

Six wickets in the second innings at Galle suggested I was bowling okay and the biggest challenge I encountered was keeping the ball dry. Every other delivery, I would be removing my Oakley glasses and wiping them on my shirt just to get the sweat off. Otherwise it was streaming down your nose. After a few overs out in the sun there would be barely a dry part of your body left. If you fell over, you looked as if you'd hang-glided into a sewage farm.

The pitch provided some assistance as the match drew on and we were able to capitalise on another burst of three wickets from Jimmy Anderson with the new ball. Having dismissed Sri Lanka for 275, we realised that winning was on the cards if we pulled our fingers out. It represented a bloody good achievement to do so. You couldn't take anything away from the batsmen in this last game of the winter; they were brilliant. KP in particular smashed it everywhere, with six sixes in his 151, and when he is in the mood there is simply no one to compare, but in general the top six played with the kind of arrogance and abandon they had displayed against Australia the previous winter. The old swagger was back, and with a 185-run advantage this time, we were able to pressurise the Sri Lankan batsmen.

Selection meant I had only Samit Patel for company rather than specialist spinner Monty Panesar, but I enjoyed having the onus on me. When the ball turned a little on the first day, everyone was looking to me to perform, and thankfully I managed four wickets in that first innings and was able to add another half-dozen to my tally in the second. To take a ten-for is a big thing for a bowler – I've only managed it five times in my first-class career – and when personal success contributes to an important victory it feels all the sweeter.

That win, by eight wickets, retained our top-of-the-tree status in Test cricket. We could enjoy the view for a little while longer.

CAREER STATISTICS

Compiled by Victor Isaacs

TEST CAREER

Record

M	Inns	NO	Runs	HS	Avge	SR	100	50	Ct	Overs	M	Runs	Wkt	Avge	5	10	Best	Econ	SR
41	49	6	947	85	22.02	74.85	–	4	34	1719.5	324	5091	182	27.97	13	2	6/65	2.96	56.6

Series by series

	M	Inns	NO	Runs	HS	Avge	SR	100	50	Ct	Overs	M	Runs	Wkt	Avge	5	10	Best	Econ	SR
England in India 2008/09	2	3	0	11	7	3.66	30.55	–	–	2	100.3	16	316	8	39.50	–	–	3/122	3.14	75.3
England in West Indies 2008/09	3	2	2	31	20*	–	110.71	–	–	1	180.2	52	457	19	24.05	2	–	5/57	2.53	56.9
West Indies in England 2009	2	1	1	63	63*	–	70.78	–	1	3	39	10	119	7	17.00	–	–	3/16	3.05	33.4
Australia in England 2009	5	8	1	249	63	35.57	83.27	–	2	1	170.2	30	567	14	40.50	–	–	4/38	3.32	73.0
England in South Africa 2009/10	4	7	1	171	85	28.50	95.53	–	1	3	210.2	25	659	21	31.38	2	–	5/54	3.13	60.0
England in Bangladesh 2009/10	2	2	0	38	32	19.00	122.58	–	–	–	144.4	31	404	16	25.25	2	1	5/90	2.79	54.2
Bangladesh in England 2010	2	2	0	42	22	21.00	140.00	–	–	–	67.2	15	210	6	35.00	1	–	5/76	3.11	67.3
Pakistan in England 2010	4	6	0	48	28	8.00	44.44	–	–	9	106.5	38	269	22	12.22	2	–	6/65	2.51	29.1
England in Australia 2010/11	5	5	1	88	36*	22.00	88.88	–	–	6	219.1	43	597	15	39.80	1	–	5/91	2.72	87.6
Sri Lanka in England 2011	3	1	0	4	4	4.00	80.00	–	–	3	103.2	16	283	12	23.58	–	–	4/16	2.73	51.6
India in England 2011	4	3	0	55	28	18.33	73.33	–	–	4	142	18	529	13	40.69	1	–	6/106	3.72	65.5
Pakistan v England 2011/12 (in United Arab Emirates)	3	6	0	105	39	17.50	65.62	–	–	1	114.5	17	326	13	25.07	–	–	4/107	2.83	53.0
England in Sri Lanka 2011/12	2	3	0	42	24	14.00	61.76	–	–	1	121.1	13	355	16	22.18	2	1	6/82	2.92	45.4

Test record at each ground

	M	Inns	NO	Runs	HS	Avge	SR	100	50	Ct	Overs	M	Runs	Wkt	Avge	5	10	Best	Econ	SR
Lord's, London	6	6	1	117	63*	23.40	81.81	–	1	7	196.3	37	554	24	23.08	1	–	5/62	2.81	49.1
Kennington Oval, London	3	4	0	95	63	23.75	81.89	–	1	3	169.2	35	484	24	20.16	1	–	6/106	2.85	42.3
Edgbaston, Birmingham	3	2	0	28	24	14.00	62.22	–	–	3	87	25	298	10	29.80	1	–	6/65	3.42	52.2
Dubai International Cricket Stadium	2	4	0	90	39	22.50	63.82	–	–	–	69.5	10	208	8	26.00	–	–	4/107	2.97	52.3
Trent Bridge, Nottingham	2	4	0	61	28	15.25	64.21	–	–	4	17	10	109	0	–	–	–	–	6.41	–
W.A.C.A., Perth	1	2	0	20	11	10.00	55.55	–	–	2	25	0	103	2	51.50	–	–	2/52	4.12	75.0
Rose Bowl, Southampton	1	–	–	–	–	–	–	–	–	1	27	6	69	2	34.50	–	–	1/12	2.55	81.0

Ground	M	Inns	NO	Runs	HS	Avge	SR	100	50	Ct	Overs	M	Runs	Wkt	Avge	5	10	Best	Econ	SR
Old Trafford, Manchester	1	1	0	20	20	20.00	117.64	–	–	–	29.2	4	110	6	18.33	1	–	5/76	3.75	29.3
Trent Bridge, Nottingham	1	2	0	30	28	15.00	62.50	–	–	4	2	1	12	0	–	–	–	–	6.00	–
Headingley, Leeds	1	2	0	62	62	31.00	71.26	–	1	–	16	4	64	0	–	–	–	–	4.00	–
Old Trafford, Manchester	1	1	0	20	20	20.00	117.64	–	–	1	29.2	4	110	6	18.33	1	–	5/76	3.75	29.3
Sydney Cricket Ground	1	1	1	36	36*	–	138.46	–	–	–	44	12	112	2	56.00	–	–	1/37	2.54	132.0
Woolloongabba, Brisbane	1	1	0	10	10	10.00	111.11	–	–	1	51	5	161	2	80.50	–	–	2/128	3.15	153.0
Riverside, Chester-le-Street	1	–	–	–	–	–	–	–	–	1	17	4	64	1	64.00	–	–	1/13	3.76	102.0
Melbourne Cricket Ground	1	1	0	22	22	22.00	78.57	–	–	1	29	12	60	2	30.00	–	–	2/59	2.06	87.0
Shere Bangla National Stadium, Mirpur	1	1	0	6	6	6.00	100.00	–	–	–	66.1	12	187	6	31.16	–	–	4/114	2.82	66.1
Kensington Oval, Bridgetown	1	–	–	–	–	–	–	–	–	–	50.4	8	165	5	33.00	1	–	5/165	3.25	60.8
Queen's Park Oval, Port-of-Spain	1	1	1	11	11*	–	100.00	–	–	1	66.4	25	143	6	23.83	–	–	3/13	2.14	66.6
Antigua Recreation Ground	1	1	1	20	20*	–	117.64	–	–	1	63	19	149	8	18.62	1	–	5/57	2.36	47.2
MA Chidambaram Stadium, Chennai	1	2	0	8	7	4.00	29.62	–	–	2	38.3	14	145	4	36.25	–	–	2/42	3.76	57.7
Punjab CA Stadium, Mohali	1	1	0	3	3	3.00	33.33	–	–	–	62	14	171	4	42.75	–	–	3/122	2.75	93.0
Kingsmead, Durban	1	1	0	22	22	22.00	157.14	–	–	–	56	6	164	9	18.22	1	–	5/54	2.92	37.3
SuperSport Park, Centurion	1	2	0	87	85	43.50	90.62	–	1	2	72.2	13	201	5	40.20	1	–	5/110	2.77	86.8
New Wanderers, Johannesburg	1	2	0	47	27	23.50	106.81	–	–	1	23	0	93	2	46.50	–	–	2/93	4.04	69.0
Newlands, Cape Town	1	2	1	15	10*	15.00	60.00	–	–	1	59	6	201	5	40.20	–	–	3/127	3.40	70.8
Zahur Ahmed Chowdhury Stadium, Chittagong	1	1	0	32	32	32.00	128.00	–	–	–	78.3	19	217	10	21.70	2	1	5/90	2.76	47.1
Adelaide Oval	1	–	–	–	–	–	–	–	–	2	70.1	14	161	7	23.00	1	–	5/91	2.29	60.1
Galle International Stadium	1	2	0	25	24	12.50	71.42	–	–	1	53	8	174	6	29.00	1	–	6/82	3.28	53.0
P Sara Oval, Colombo	1	1	0	17	17	17.00	51.51	–	–	–	68.1	5	181	10	18.10	1	1	6/106	2.65	40.9
Sheikh Zayed Stadium, Abu Dhabi	1	2	0	15	15	7.50	78.94	–	–	1	45	7	118	5	23.60	–	–	3/52	2.62	54.0

Test record against each opponent

	M	Inns	NO	Runs	HS	Avge	SR	100	50	Ct	Overs	M	Runs	Wkt	Avge	5	10	Best	Econ	SR
Australia	10	13	2	337	63	30.63	84.67	–	2	7	389.3	73	1164	29	40.13	1	–	5/91	2.98	80.6
Bangladesh	4	4	0	80	32	20.00	131.14	–	–	–	212	46	614	22	27.90	3	1	5/76	2.89	57.8
India	6	6	0	66	28	11.00	59.45	–	–	6	242.3	34	845	21	40.23	1	–	6/106	3.48	69.2
Pakistan	7	12	0	153	39	12.75	57.08	–	–	10	221.4	55	595	35	17.00	2	–	6/65	2.68	38.0
South Africa	4	7	1	171	85	28.50	95.53	–	1	3	210.2	25	659	21	31.38	2	–	5/54	3.13	60.0
Sri Lanka	5	4	0	46	24	11.50	63.01	–	–	4	224.3	29	638	28	22.78	2	1	6/82	2.84	48.1
West Indies	5	3	3	94	63*	–	80.34	–	1	4	219.2	62	576	26	22.15	2	–	5/57	2.62	50.6

Wicket breakdown

	Batting	Bowling
Bowled	6	37
Caught keeper	6	9
Caught fielder	21	77
LBW	9	52
Run out	1	0
Stumped	–	7
Not out	6	–
Total	49	153

Five wickets in an innings (13)

5/57	v West Indies at Antigua 2008–09
5/165	v West Indies at Barbados 2008–09
5/110	v South Africa at Centurion 2009–10
5/54	v South Africa at Durban 2009–10
5/90	v Bangladesh at Chittagong 2009–10
5/127	v Bangladesh at Chittagong 2009–10
5/76	v Bangladesh at Old Trafford 2010
6/65	v Pakistan at Edgbaston 2010
5/62	v Pakistan at Lord's 2010
5/91	v Australia at Adelaide 2010/10
6/106	v India at The Oval 2011
6/82	v Sri Lanka at Galle 2011/12
6/106	v Sri Lanka at Colombo (PSS) 2011/12

ONE–DAY INTERNATIONAL CAREER

Record

M	Inns	NO	Runs	HS	Avge	SR	100	50	Ct	Overs	M	Runs	Wkt	Avge	4	Best	Econ	SR
67	44	12	468	34	14.62	89.82	–	–	25	534	24	2385	92	25.92	4	5/28	4.46	34.8

Series by series

	M	Inns	NO	Runs	HS	Avge	SR	100	50	Ct	Overs	M	Runs	Wkt	Avge	4	Best	Econ	SR
England in South Africa 1999/00	1	–	–	–	–	–	–	–	–	–	5	0	24	0	–	–	–	4.80	–
England in Sri Lanka 2007/08	4	3	0	83	34	27.66	87.36	–	–	4	40	5	156	7	22.28	1	4/34	3.90	34.2
England in New Zealand 2007/08	2	2	0	8	7	4.00	36.36	–	–	–	5	0	44	0	–	–	–	8.80	–
NatWest Series v NZ 2008	5	4	1	45	29	11.25	63.38	–	–	3	39	2	163	7	23.28	–	2/33	4.17	33.4
England in India 2008/09	3	2	1	10	5*	10.00	111.11	–	–	–	19	0	124	4	31.00	–	2/21	6.52	28.5
West Indies in England 2009	2	–	–	–	–	–	–	–	–	1	16	1	64	2	32.00	–	1/26	4.00	48.0
Ireland v England 2009	1	1	0	5	5	5.00	71.42	–	–	–	4	0	21	1	21.00	–	1/21	5.25	24.0
NatWest Series v Aus 2009	5	4	0	33	14	8.25	73.33	–	–	2	40	1	171	9	19.00	1	5/28	4.27	26.6
ICC Champions Trophy 2009/10	4	3	1	37	18	18.50	84.09	–	–	2	17	0	97	1	97.00	–	1/43	5.70	102.0
England in South Africa 2009/10	2	1	1	6	6*	–	100.00	–	–	1	9	0	49	0	–	–	–	5.44	–
England in Bangladesh 2009/10	3	1	0	2	2	2.00	66.66	–	–	2	30	0	122	7	17.42	–	3/32	4.06	25.7
Scotland v England 2010	1	–	–	–	–	–	–	–	–	2	10	0	29	2	14.50	–	2/29	2.90	30.0
NatWest Series v Aus 2010	5	4	1	54	33	18.00	114.89	–	–	1	36	1	163	8	20.37	1	4/37	4.52	27.0
NatWest Series v Pak 2010	5	2	0	12	12	6.00	70.58	–	–	2	47	4	209	11	19.00	1	4/37	4.44	25.6
England in Australia 2010/11	1	1	0	4	4	4.00	40.00	–	–	–	10	0	42	1	42.00	–	1/42	4.20	60.0
ICC World Cup 2010/11	7	6	4	60	16	15.00	117.64	–	–	1	68	5	309	12	25.75	–	3/36	4.54	34.0
NatWest Series v SL 2011	5	4	3	31	13*	31.00	114.81	–	–	1	45	4	164	8	20.50	–	3/18	3.64	33.7
NatWest Series v Ind 2011	4	2	1	40	31	40.00	142.85	–	–	2	33	1	147	8	18.37	–	3/33	4.45	24.7
England in India 2011/12	4	3	1	25	10*	12.50	92.59	–	–	–	36	1	191	2	95.50	–	1/35	5.30	108.0
Eng v Pakistan (in UAE) 2011/12	3	1	1	13	13*	–	108.33	–	–	2	25	3	96	2	48.00	–	2/19	3.84	75.0

One Day International record against each opponent

	M	Inns	NO	Runs	HS	Avge	SR	100	50	Ct	Overs	M	Runs	Wkt	Avge	4	Best	Econ	SR
Australia	12	10	1	109	33	12.11	93.16	–	–	3	91	2	407	18	22.61	2	5/28	4.47	30.3
Bangladesh	4	2	0	14	12	7.00	127.27	–	–	1	40	1	164	9	18.22	–	3/32	4.10	26.6
India	12	8	4	90	31	22.50	123.28	–	–	3	97	3	521	15	34.73	–	3/33	5.37	38.8
Ireland	2	2	1	14	9*	14.00	116.66	–	–	–	14	0	68	4	17.00	–	3/47	4.85	21.0
Netherlands	1	–	–	–	–	–	–	–	–	–	10	0	35	2	17.50	–	2/35	3.50	30.0
New Zealand	8	7	0	64	29	9.14	56.63	–	–	5	44	3	207	7	29.57	–	2/33	4.70	37.7
Pakistan	8	3	1	25	13*	12.50	86.20	–	–	4	72	3	305	13	23.46	1	4/37	4.23	33.2
Scotland	1	–	–	–	–	–	–	–	–	2	10	0	29	2	14.50	–	2/29	2.90	30.0
South Africa	5	3	2	30	16	30.00	85.71	–	–	1	32	2	145	2	72.50	–	1/29	4.53	96.0
Sri Lanka	11	8	3	114	34	22.80	92.68	–	–	5	98	9	404	15	26.93	1	4/34	4.12	39.2
West Indies	3	1	0	8	8	8.00	100.00	–	–	1	26	2	100	5	20.00	–	3/36	3.84	31.2

Four wickets in an innings (4)

4/34	v Sri Lanka at Dambulla 2007–08
5/28	v Australia at Chester-le-Street 2009
4/37	v Australia at Old Trafford 2010
4/37	v Pakistan at Lord's 2010

Wicket breakdown

	Batting		Bowling
Bowled	10		20
Caught keeper	6		7
Caught fielder	8		43
LBW	2		10
Run out	6		–
Stumped	–		11
Hit wicket	–		1
Not out	12		–
Total	44		92

FIRST–CLASS CAREER

Record

M	Inns	NO	Runs	HS	Avge	SR	100	50	Ct	Overs	M	Runs	Wkt	Avge	5	10	Best	Econ	SR
227	309	27	7233	183	25.64	72.88	4	35	171	6892.5	1390	20614	650	31.71	28	5	7/33	2.99	63.6

Season by season

Season	Venue	Team	M	Inns	NO	Runs	HS	Avge	SR	100	50	Ct	Overs	M	Runs	Wkt	Avge	5	10	Best
1998	England	Northants	14	18	2	548	111	34.25		1	2	7	199.4	41	666	22	30.27	1	–	5/29
1998/99	Zimbabwe	England 'A'	3	5	0	115	48	23.00		–	–	5	103.1	23	292	9	32.44	–	–	4/52
1998/99	South Africa	England 'A'	2	4	1	61	21	20.33		–	–	3	98.4	20	246	12	20.50	1	–	5/77
1999	England	Northants	18	27	4	727	130*	31.60		1	4	13	560.1	131	1641	57	28.78	2	1	6/41
1999/00	South Africa	England XI	2	1	0	13	13	13.00		–	–	–	52.4	9	210	1	210.00	–	–	1/79
2000	England	Northants	16	24	0	597	72	24.87		–	3	8	467.3	92	1366	41	33.31	2	–	6/118
2000/01	West Indies	England 'A'	4	6	0	95	49	15.83		–	–	3	144.3	48	362	18	20.11	1	–	5/27
2001	England	Northants	15	25	0	543	61	21.72		–	3	9	422.3	87	1365	30	45.50	1	–	5/34
2002	England	Northants	11	16	0	539	183	33.68		2	1	5	270.5	60	884	31	28.51	2	1	6/126
2003	England	Northants	9	13	1	256	69	21.33		–	2	9	238.2	37	759	33	23.00	3	–	7/33
2004	England	Northants	14	22	0	485	54	22.04		–	2	13	403.2	71	1168	30	38.93	–	–	4/94
2004/05	Sri Lanka	England 'A'	2	3	0	85	71	28.33		–	1	3	78.5	19	238	10	23.80	1	–	5/79
2005	England	MCC/Notts	16	17	2	322	63	21.46		–	2	7	413.2	89	1307	33	39.60	1	–	6/57
2006	England	Notts	15	21	1	546	85	27.30		–	3	9	439.5	95	1247	28	44.53	–	–	4/54
2007	England	Notts	16	20	4	516	97	32.25		–	3	15	487.2	93	1503	45	33.40	2	1	7/100
2008	England	Notts/Eng Lions	14	18	2	586	82	36.62		–	5	16	360.5	73	959	32	29.96	–	–	4/25
2008/09	India	England	2	3	0	11	7	3.66		–	–	2	100.3	16	316	8	39.50	–	–	3/122
2008/09	West Indies	England	4	3	2	43	20*	43.00		–	–	1	222.2	54	625	19	32.89	1	–	5/57
2009	England	Notts/England	10	12	2	352	63*	35.20		–	3	6	269.2	55	824	27	30.51	–	–	4/38
2009/10	South Africa	England	4	7	1	171	85	28.50		–	1	3	210.2	25	659	21	31.38	1	–	5/54
2009/10	Bangladesh	England	2	3	1	38	32	19.00		–	–	–	144.4	31	404	16	25.25	2	1	5/90
2010	England	Notts/England	7	9	0	91	28	10.11		–	–	9	200.1	58	567	30	18.90	3	–	6/65
2010/11	Australia	England	7	7	2	150	37*	30.00		–	–	9	290.4	55	826	24	34.41	1	–	5/91
2011	England	Notts/England	9	8	0	101	28	12.62		–	–	8	287.2	39	956	28	34.14	1	–	6/106
2011/12	U.A.E.	England	5	9	2	144	39	20.57		–	–	4	180.1	26	567	20	28.35	2	1	6/82

			M	Inns	NO	Runs	HS	Avge	100	50	Ct	Overs	M	Runs	Wkt	Avge	5	10	Best
2011/12	Sri Lanka	England	4	5	1	80	31*	20.00	–	–	3	184.5	27	531	18	29.50	13	2	4/107
2012	England	Notts	2	4	0	18	12	4.50	–	–	1	61	16	126	7	18.00	3	–	3/26

First-class record for each team

	M	Inns	NO	Runs	HS	Avge	100	50	Ct	Overs	M	Runs	Wkt	Avge	5	10	Best
England	41	49	6	947	85	22.02	–	4	34	1719.5	324	5091	182	27.97	13	2	6/65
England 'A'	11	18	1	356	71	20.94	–	1	14	425.1	110	1138	49	23.22	3	–	5/27
England Lions	1	2	–	61	52	30.50	–	1	1	35	7	94	0	–	–	–	–
England XI	10	10	4	178	37*	29.66	–	–	9	300.1	47	1035	19	54.47	–	–	4/68
Marylebone Cricket Club	1	–	–	–	–	–	–	–	2	46	10	166	3	55.33	–	–	2/124
Northamptonshire	97	145	7	3695	183	26.77	4	17	64	2562.2	519	7849	244	32.16	10	2	7/33
Nottinghamshire	66	85	9	1996	97	26.26	–	12	47	1804.2	373	5241	153	34.25	2	1	7/100

First-class record against each team

	M	Inns	NO	Runs	HS	Avge	100	50	Ct	Overs	M	Runs	Wkt	Avge	5	10	Best
Australia	10	13	2	337	63	30.63	–	2	7	389.3	73	1164	29	40.13	1	–	5/91
Bangladesh	4	4	0	80	32	20.00	–	–	–	212	46	614	22	27.90	3	1	5/76
Border and Eastern Province Combined XI	1	–	–	–	–	–	–	–	–	17	3	79	1	79.00	–	–	1/79
Cambridge University	2	1	0	12	12	12.00	–	–	–	37	9	126	4	31.50	–	–	2/39
Derbyshire	7	10	0	327	91	32.70	–	3	7	172.5	31	653	29	22.51	2	1	7/33
Durham	8	9	1	315	109	39.37	1	2	3	205.3	46	573	12	47.75	–	–	4/81
Durham U.C.C.E.	3	4	1	127	50	42.33	–	1	6	40	14	79	5	15.80	–	–	3/48
Essex	8	10	1	216	97	24.00	–	1	6	267.3	52	828	25	33.12	1	–	4/47
Gauteng XI	1	2	1	34	18	34.00	–	–	–	42.5	9	110	7	15.71	1	–	5/77
Glamorgan	12	18	0	305	48	16.94	–	–	6	404.3	77	1204	34	35.41	2	1	7/100
Gloucestershire	8	9	0	313	183	34.77	1	–	3	191	36	595	20	29.75	1	–	6/118
Guyana	1	2	0	12	8	6.00	–	–	1	36	14	105	4	26.25	–	–	4/84
Hampshire	8	11	2	151	54	15.10	–	1	3	242.2	42	710	16	44.37	–	–	4/46
ICC Combined Associate & Affiliate XI	1	2	2	15	14*	–	–	–	1	33	1	132	3	44.00	–	–	2/99
India	6	6	0	66	28	11.00	–	–	6	242.3	34	845	21	40.23	1	–	6/106
Jamaica	1	1	0	0	0	0.00	–	–	–	39	12	106	5	21.20	–	–	4/79
Kent	9	13	0	310	85	23.84	–	1	7	218.5	35	741	12	61.75	–	–	3/66
Lancashire	12	16	1	309	54	20.60	–	1	8	340	71	1008	33	30.54	–	–	4/81
Leeward Islands	1	2	0	34	21	17.00	–	–	2	33	8	89	0	–	–	–	–

Opponents	M	I	NO	Runs	HS	Avge	100	50	Ct	O	M	R	W	Avge	5i	10m	Best
Leicestershire	6	9	0	311	111	34.55	1	1	–	178.2	47	509	24	21.20	3	1	6/41
Loughborough U.C.C.E.	1	1	0	63	63	63.00	–	1	–	3	2	1	0	–	–	–	–
Marylebone Cricket Club	1	1	0	8	8	8.00	–	–	–	22	7	92	1	92.00	–	–	1/88
Middlesex	13	18	1	416	78	24.47	–	3	–	261.1	46	829	14	59.21	–	–	2/49
New Zealand	1	2	0	61	52	30.50	–	1	–	35	7	94	0	–	–	–	–
Northamptonshire	2	3	0	71	51	35.50	–	1	–	82.3	17	186	7	26.57	–	–	4/90
Nottinghamshire	5	5	0	62	25	12.40	–	–	–	112.1	22	315	10	31.50	–	–	3/55
Oxford Universities	2	2	0	73	57	36.50	–	1	–	22	3	73	0	–	–	–	–
Oxford U.C.C.E.	2	3	1	54	38	27.00	–	–	–	37.4	15	102	7	14.57	–	–	3/13
Pakistan	7	12	0	153	39	12.75	–	–	–	221.4	55	595	35	17.00	2	–	6/65
Pakistan Cricket Board XI	1	1	0	24	24	24.00	–	–	–	37	9	73	2	36.50	–	–	1/24
Somerset	7	9	0	202	61	22.44	–	1	–	188.3	41	607	17	35.70	–	–	4/85
South Africa	4	7	1	171	85	28.50	–	2	–	210.2	25	659	21	31.38	2	–	5/54
South African Board President's XI	1	2	0	27	21	13.50	–	–	–	55.5	11	136	5	27.20	–	–	3/58
South African Invitation XI	1	1	0	13	13	13.00	–	–	–	35.4	6	131	0	–	–	–	–
South Australia	1	1	0	25	25	25.00	–	–	–	22.4	4	68	4	17.00	–	–	4/68
Sri Lanka	5	4	0	46	24	11.50	–	–	–	224.3	29	638	28	22.78	2	1	6/82
Sri Lanka 'A'	3	5	2	290	130*	96.66	1	1	–	82.5	19	258	10	25.80	1	–	5/79
Sri Lanka Board XI	1	1	0	7	7	7.00	–	–	–	32	9	80	3	26.66	–	–	3/33
Sri Lanka Cricket Development XI	1	1	1	31	31*	–	–	–	–	27	4	132	1	132.00	–	–	1/30
Surrey	9	12	2	306	82	30.60	–	2	–	205	38	689	17	40.52	–	–	4/94
Sussex	10	16	1	391	54	26.06	–	1	–	330.5	68	904	35	25.82	1	–	5/29
Warwickshire	13	20	2	463	72	25.72	–	2	–	358.5	85	1030	31	33.22	2	–	6/57
West Indies	5	3	3	94	63*	–	–	1	–	219.2	62	576	26	22.15	1	–	5/57
West Indies 'A'	1	1	0	12	12	12.00	–	–	–	42	8	168	0	–	–	–	–
Western Australia	1	1	3	37	37*	–	–	–	–	48.5	14	161	5	32.20	–	–	4/101
Windward Islands	1	1	0	49	49	49.00	–	–	–	36.3	5	62	9	6.88	1	–	5/27
Worcestershire	9	15	1	265	69	18.92	–	2	–	235.3	50	701	25	28.04	2	–	6/66
Yorkshire	8	14	0	430	68	30.71	–	3	–	256.4	49	692	22	31.45	–	–	4/25
Zimbabwe 'A'	2	3	0	36	24	12.00	–	–	–	66.1	20	176	8	22.00	–	–	4/52
Zimbabwe Cricket Union President's XI	1	2	0	79	48	39.50	–	–	–	37	3	116	1	116.00	–	–	1/116

Wicket breakdown

	Batting	Bowling
Bowled	46	127
Caught keeper	36	51
Caught fielder	147	314
LBW	46	125
Run out	4	–
Stumped	3	32
Hit wicket	0	1
Not out	27	–
Total	309	650

Five-wickets in an innings (28)

5/29	Northamptonshire v Sussex at Northampton 1998
5/77	England 'A' v Gauteng XI at Johannesburg 1998–99
5/85	Northamptonshire v Leicestershire at Northampton 1999
6/41	Northamptonshire v Leicestershire at Northampton 1999
6/118	Northamptonshire v Gloucestershire at Cheltenham 2000
5/55	Northamptonshire v Worcestershire at Northampton 2000
5/27	England 'A' v Windward Islands at Castries 2000–01
5/34	Northamptonshire v Leicestershire at Northampton 2001
6/126	Northamptonshire v Derbyshire at Derby 2002
7/33	Northamptonshire v Derbyshire at Northampton 2003
5/37	Northamptonshire v Glamorgan at Cardiff 2003
6/66	Northamptonshire v Worcestershire at Northampton 2003
5/79	England 'A' v Sri Lanka 'A' at Colombo (CCC) 2004–05
6/57	Nottinghamshire v Warwickshire at Edgbaston 2005
7/100	Nottinghamshire v Glamorgan at Swansea 2007
5/57	England v West Indies at Antigua 2008–09
5/165	England v West Indies at Barbados 2008–09
5/110	England v South Africa at Centurion 2009–10
5/54	England v South Africa at Durban 2009–10
5/90	England v Bangladesh at Chittagong 2009–10
5/127	England v Bangladesh at Chittagong 2009–10
5/76	England v Bangladesh at Old Trafford 2010
6/65	England v Pakistan at Edgbaston 2010
5/62	England v Pakistan at Lord's 2010
5/91	England v Australia at Adelaide 2010–11
6/106	England v India at The Oval 2011
6/82	England v Sri Lanka at Galle 2011/12
6/106	England v Sri Lanka at Colombo (PSS) 2011/12

Centuries (4)

111	Northamptonshire v Leicestershire at Leicester 1998
130*	Northamptonshire v Sri Lanka 'A' at Northampton 1999
109	Northamptonshire v Durham at Northampton 2002
183	Northamptonshire v Gloucestershire at Bristol 2002

GRAEME SWANN IN TEST CRICKET

TEST CAREER RECORD

M	I	NO	Runs	HS	Avge	Overs	Maids	Runs	Wkts	Avge	Best	5wI	10wM
41	49	6	947	85	22.02	1719.5	324	5091	182	27.97	6/65	13	2

1. **v India at Chennai 11-15 December 2008 – India won by 6 wickets**
Toss: England
Man of the match: V.Sehwag
England 316 (A.J.Strauss 123) & 311-9dec (A.J.Strauss 108, P.D.Collingwood 108)
India 241 & 387-4 (S.R.Tendulkar 103*)

| 1st innings | c R.Dravid b Harbhajan Singh | 1 | 10 0-42-2 |
| 2nd innings | b Z.Khan | 7 | 28.3-2-103-2 |

2. **v India at Mohali 19-23 December 2008 – Match drawn**
Toss: India
Man of the match: G.Gambhir
India 453 (G.Gambhir 179, R.Dravid 136) & 251-7dec
England 302 (K.P.Pietersen 144) & 64-1

| 1st innings | b Z.Khan | 3 | 45-11-122-3 |
| 2nd innings | did not bat | | 17-3-49-1 |

3. **v West Indies at St. John's 15-19 February 2009 – Match drawn**
Toss: West Indies
Man of the match: R.R.Sarwan
England 566-9dec (A.J.Strauss 169, P.D.Collingwood 113) & 221-8dec
West Indies 285 (G.P.Swann 5-57) & 370-9 (R.R.Sarwan 106)

| 1st innings | not out | 20 | 24-7-57-5 |
| 2nd innings | did not bat | | 39-12-92-3 |

4. **v West Indies at Bridgetown 26 February-2 March 2009 – Match drawn**
Toss: England
Man of the match: R.R.Sarwan
England 600-6dec (A.J.Strauss 142, R.S.Bopara 104) & 279-2dec (A.N.Cook 139*)
West Indies 749-9dec (R.R.Sarwan 291, D.Ramdin 166, G.P.Swann 5-165)

| 1st innings | did not bat | | 50.4-8-165-5 |
| 2nd innings | did not bat | | |

5.   v West Indies at Port of Spain 6-10 March 2009 – Match drawn
Toss: England
Man of the match: M.J.Prior
England 546-6dec (A.J.Strauss 142, P.D.Collingwood 161, M.J.Prior 131*) & 237-6dec (K.P.Pietersen 102)
West Indies 544 (C.H.Gayle 102, S.Chanderpaul 147*, B.P.Nash 109) & 114-8

1st innings	not out	11	45.4-12-130-3
2nd innings	did not bat		21-13-13-3

6.   v West Indies at Lord's 6-8 May 2009 – England won by 10 wickets
Toss: West Indies
Man of the match: G.P.Swann
England 377 (R.S.Bopara 143, F.H.Edwards 6-92) & 32-0
West Indies 152 (G.Onions 5-38) & 256 (following on)

1st innings	not out	63	5-2-16-3
2nd innings	did not bat		17-4-39-3

7.   v West Indies at Chester-le-Street 14-18 May 2009 – England won by an innings and 83 runs
Toss: England
Man of the match: J.M.Anderson
England 569-6dec (A.N.Cook 160, R.S.Bopara 108)
West Indies 310 (R.R.Sarwan 100, J.M.Anderson 5-87) & 176 (following on)

1st innings	did not bat		14-4-51-0
2nd innings			3-0-13-1

8.   v Australia at Cardiff 8-12 July 2009 – Match drawn
Toss: England
Man of the match: R.T.Ponting
England 435 & 252-9
Australia 674-6dec (S.M.Katich 122, R.T.Ponting 150, M.J.North 125*, B.J.Haddin 121)

1st innings	not out	47	38-8-131-0
2nd innings	lbw b B.W.Hilfenhaus	31	

9.   v Australia at Lord's 16-20 July 2009 – England won by 115 runs
Toss: England
Man of the match: A.Flintoff
England 425 (A.J.Strauss 161) & 311-6dec
Australia 215 & 406 (M.J.Clarke 136, A.Flintoff 5-92)

1st innings	c R.T.Ponting b P.M.Siddle	4	1-0-4-0
2nd innings	did not bat		28-3-87-4

10.   v Australia at Edgbaston 30 July-3 August 2009 – Match drawn
Toss: Australia
Man of the match: M.J.Clarke
Australia 263 (J.M.Anderson 5-80) & 375-5 (M.J.Clarke 103*)
England 376

1st innings	c M.J.North b M.G.Johnson	24	2-0-4-1
2nd innings			31-4-119-1

11. **v Australia at Headingley 7-9 August 2009 – Australia won by an innings and 80 runs**
Toss: England
Man of the match: M.J.North
England 102 (P.M.Siddle 5-21) & 263 (M.G.Johnson 5-69)
Australia 445 (M.J.North 110, S.C.J.Broad 6-91)

1st innings	c M.J.Clarke b P.M.Siddle	0	16-4-64-0
2nd innings	c B.J.Haddin b M.G.Johnson	62	

12. **v Australia at The Oval 20-23 August 2009 – England won by 197 runs**
Toss: England
Man of the match: S.C.J.Broad
England 332 & 373-9dec (I.J.L.Trott 119)
Australia 160 (S.C.J.Broad 5-37) & 348 (M.E.K.Hussey 121)

1st innings	c B.J.Haddin b P.M.Siddle	18	14-3-38-4
2nd innings	c B.J.Haddin b B.W.Hilfenhaus	63	40.2-8-120-4

13. **v South Africa at Centurion 16-20 December 2009 – Match drawn**
Toss: England
Man of the match: G.P.Swann
South Africa 418 (J.H.Kallis 120, G.P.Swann 5-110) & 301-7dec (H.M.Amla 100)
England 356 (P.L.Harris 5-123) & 228-9

1st innings	c G.C.Smith b P.L.Harris	85	45.2-10-110-5
2nd innings	lbw b M.Morkel	2	27-3-91-0

14. **v South Africa at Durban 26-30 December 2009 – England won by an innings and 98 runs**
Toss: South Africa
Man of the match: G.P.Swann
South Africa 343 & 133 (G.P.Swann 5-54)
England 574-9dec (A.N.Cook 118, I.R.Bell 140)

1st innings	c A.G.Prince b D.W.Steyn	22	35-3-110-4
2nd innings			21-3-54-5

15. **v South Africa at Cape Town 3-7 January 2010 – Match drawn**
Toss: England
Man of the match: G.C.Smith
South Africa 291 (J.H.Kallis 108, J.M.Anderson 5-63) & 447-7dec (G.C.Smith 183)
England 273 (M.Morkel 5-75) & 296-9

1st innings	c G.C.Smith b M.Morkel	5	22-1-74-2
2nd innings	not out	10	37-5-127-3

16. **v South Africa at Johannesburg 14-17 January 2010 – South Africa won by an innings and 74 runs**
Toss: England
Man of the match: D.W.Steyn and M.Morkel
England 180 (D.W.Steyn 5-51) & 169
South Africa 423-7dec (G.C.Smith 105)

1st innings	c M.V.Boucher b J.J.Morkel	27	23-0-93-2
2nd innings	A.B.de Villiers b D.W.Steyn	20	

17. v Bangladesh at Chittagong 12-16 March 2010 – England won by 181 runs
Toss: Bangladesh
Man of the match: G.P.Swann
England 599-6dec (A.N.Cook 173, P.D.Collingwood 145) & 209-7dec
Bangladesh 296 (G.P.Swann 5-90) & 331 (Junaid Siddique 106, G.P.Swann 5-127)

1st innings	did not bat		29.3-8-90-5
2nd innings	c Junaid Siddique b Shakib Al Hasan	32	49-11-127-5

18. v Bangladesh at Mirpur 20-24 March 2010 – England won by 9 wickets
Toss: Bangladesh
Man of the match: Shakib Al Hasan
Bangladesh 419 & 285
England 496 (I.R.Bell 138) & 209-1 (A.N.Cook 109*)

1st innings	run out (Shakib Al Hasan)	6	36.1-5-114-4
2nd innings	did not bat		30-7-73-2

19. v Bangladesh at Lord's, 27-31 May 2010 – England won by 8 wickets
Toss: Bangladesh
Man of the match: S.T.Finn
England 505 (I.J.L.Trott 226; Shahadat Hossain 5-98) and 163-2
Bangladesh 282 and 382 (Tamim Iqbal 103; S.T.Finn 5-87) (following on)

1st innings	c Rubel Hossain b Shakib Al Hasan	22	11-6-19-0
2nd innings	did not bat		27-5-81-0

20. v Bangladesh at Old Trafford, 4-6 June 2010 – England won by an innings and 80 runs
Toss: England
Man of the match: I.R.Bell
England 419 (I.R.Bell 128; Shakib Al Hasan 5-121)
Bangladesh 216 (Tamim Iqbal 108; G.P.Swann 5-76) and 123 (S.T.Finn 5-42) (following on)

1st innings	lbw b Abdur Razzak	20	22.1-4-76-5
2nd innings			7.1-0-34-1

21. v Pakistan at Trent Bridge, 29 July-1 August 2010 – England won by 354 runs
Toss: England
Man of the match: J.M.Anderson
England 354 (E.J.G.Morgan 130; Mohammad Asif 5-77) and 262-9dec (M.J.Prior 102*)
Pakistan 182 (J.M.Anderson 5-54) and 80 (J.M.Anderson 6-17)

1st innings	lbw b Mohammad Asif	2	2-1-12-0
2nd innings	lbw b Danish Kaneria	28	

22. v Pakistan at Edgbaston, 6-9 August 2010 – England won by 9 wickets
Toss: Pakistan
Man of the match: G.P.Swann
Pakistan 72 and 296 (G.P.Swann 6-65)
England 251 (Saeed Ajmal 5-82) and 118-1

1st innings	c and b Saeed Ajmal	4	
2nd innings			37-20-65-6

23. **v Pakistan at The Oval, 18-21 August 2010 – Pakistan won by 4 wickets**
Toss: England
Man of the match: Mohammed Aamer
England 233 (Wahab Riaz 5-63) and 222 (A.N.Cook 110; Mohammad Aamer 5-52)
Pakistan 308 and 148-6

1st innings	c Umar Akmal b Mohammad Asif	8	27.2-9-68-4
2nd innings	b Saeed Ajmal	6	18.4-4-50-3

24. **v Pakistan at Lord's, 26-29 August 2010 – England won by an innings and 225 runs**
Toss: Pakistan
Man of the match: S.C.J.Broad
England 446 (I.J.L.Trott 184, S.C.J.Broad 169; Mohammad Aamer 6-84)
Pak 74 and 147 (G.P.Swann 5-62) (following on)

1st innings	c Azhar Ali b Mohammad Aamer	0	8-3-12 4
2nd innings			13.5-1-62-5

25. **v Australia at Brisbane, 25-29 November 2010 – Match drawn**
Toss: England
Man of the match: A.N.Cook
England 260 (P.M.Siddle 6-54) and 517-1dec (A.J.Strauss 110, A.N.Cook 235*, I.J.L.Trott 135*)
Australia 481 (M.E.K.Hussey 195, B.J.Haddin 136; S.T.Finn 6-125) and 107-1

1st innings	lbw b P.M.Siddle	10	43-5-128-2
2nd innings	did not bat		8-0-33-0

26. **v Australia at Adelaide, 3-7 December 2010 – England won by an innings and 71 runs**
Toss: Australia
Man of the match: K.P.Pietersen
Australia 245 and 304 (G.P.Swann 5-91)
England 620-5dec (A.N.Cook 148, K.P.Pietersen 227)

1st innings	did not bat		29-2-70-2
2nd innings			41.1-12-91-5

27. **v Australia at Perth, 16-19 December 2010 – Australia won by 267 runs**
Toss: England
Man of the match: M.G.Johnson
Australia 268 and 309 (M.E.K.Hussey 116; C.T.Tremlett 5-87)
England 187 (M.G.Johnson 6-38) and 123 (R.J.Harris 6-47)

1st innings	c B.J.Haddin b R.J.Harris	11	16-0 52-2
2nd innings	b M.G.Johnson	9	9-0-51-0

28. **v Australia at Melbourne, 26-29 December 2010 – England won by an innings and 157 runs**
Toss: England
Man of the match: I.J.L.Trott
Australia 98 and 258
England 513 (I.J.L.Trott 168*; P.M.Siddle 6-75)

1st innings	c B.J.Haddin b B.W.Hilfenhaus	22	2-1-1-0
2nd innings			27-11-59-2

29. v Australia at Sydney, 3-7 January 2011 – England won by an innings and 83 runs
Toss: Australia
Man of the match: A.N.Cook
Australia 280 and 281
England 644 (A.N.Cook 189, I.R.Bell 115, M.J.Prior 118).

1st innings	not out		36	16-4-37-1
2nd innings				28-8-75-1

30. v Sri Lanka at Cardiff, 26-30 May 2011 – England won by an innings and 14 runs
Toss: Sri Lanka
Man of the match: I.J.L.Trott
Sri Lanka 400 (H.A.P.W.Jayawardene 112) and 82
England 496-5dec (A.N.Cook 133, I.J.L.Trott 203, .I.R.Bell 103*)

1st innings	did not bat			24.4-2-78-3
2nd innings				7-1-16-4

31. v Sri Lanka at Lord's, 3-7 June 2011 – Match drawn
Toss: Sri Lanka
Man of the match: T.M.Dilshan
England 486 (M.J.Prior 126) and 335-7dec (A.N.Cook 106)
Sri Lanka 479 (T.M.Dilshan 193) and 127-3

1st innings	c N.T.Paranavitana b U.W.M.B.C.A.Welagedara	4	32.4-5-101-3
2nd innings	did not bat		12-2-19-0

32. v Sri Lanka at Southampton, 16-20 June 2011 – Match drawn
Toss: England
Man of the match: C.T.Tremlett
Sri Lanka 184 (C.T.Tremlett 6-48) and 334-5 (K.C.Sangakkara 119)
England 377-8dec (I.R.Bell 119*)

1st innings	did not bat		2-0-12-1
2nd innings			25-6-57-1

33. v India at Lord's, 21-25 July 2011 – England won by 196 runs
Toss: India
Man of the match: K.P.Pietersen
England 474-8dec (K.P.Pietersen 202, P.Kumar 5-106) and 269-6dec (M.J.Prior 103*)
India 286 (R.Dravid 103*) and 261 (J.M.Anderson 5-65)

1st innings	b S.K.Raina	24	19-3-50-1
2nd innings	did not bat		22-3-64-1

34. v India at Trent Bridge, 29 July-1 August 2011 – England won by 319 runs
Toss: India
Man of the match: S.C.J.Broad
England 221 and 544 (I.R.Bell 159)
India 288 (R.Dravid 117, S.C.J.Broad 6-46) and 158 (T.T.Bresnan 5-48)

1st innings	c A.Mukund b P.Kumar	28	12-0-76-0
2nd innings	c sub (W.P.Saha) b I.Sharma	3	3-0-21-0

35. v India at Edgbaston, 10-13 August 2011 – England won by an innings and 242 runs
Toss: England
Man of the match: A.N.Cook
India 224 and 244
England 710-7dec (A.N.Cook 294, E.J.G.Morgan 104)

1st innings	did not bat		4-0-22-0
2nd innings			13-1-88-2

36. v India at The Oval, 18-22 August 2011 – England won by an innings and 8 runs
Toss: England
Man of the match: I.R.Bell
England 591-6dec (I.R.Bell 235, K.P.Pietersen 175)
India 300 (R.Dravid 146) and 283 (G.P.Swann 6-106) (following on)

1st innings	did not bat		31-5-102-3
2nd innings			38-6-106-6

37. v Pakistan at Dubai (DSC), 17-19 January 2012 – Pakistan won by 10 wickets
Toss: England
Man of the match: Saeed Ajmal
England 192 (Saeed Ajmal 7-55) and 160
Pakistan 338 and 15-0

1st innings	lbw b Saeed Ajmal	34	29.5-3-107-4
2nd innings	c Asad Shafiq b Saeed Ajmal	39	

38. v Pakistan at Abu Dhabi, 25-28 January 2012 – Pakistan won by 72 runs
Toss: Pakistan
Man of the match: Abdur Rehman
Pakistan 257 and 214 (M.S.Panesar 6-62)
England 327 and 72 (Abdur Rehman 6-25)

1st innings	lbw b Abdur Rehman	15	18-2-52-3
2nd innings	lbw b Saeed Ajmal	0	27-5-66-2

39. v Pakistan at Dubai (DSC), 3-6 February 2012 – Pakistan won by 71 runs
Toss: Pakistan
Man of the match: Azhar Ali
Pakistan 99 and 365 (Azhar Ali 157, Younis Khan 127, M.S.Panesar 5-124)
England 141 (Abdur Rehman 5-40) and 252

1st innings	c Abdur Rehman b Saeed Ajmal	16	1-1-0-1
2nd innings	c Asad Shafiq b Umar Gul	1	39-6-101-3

40. v Sri Lanka at Galle, 26-29 March 2012 – Sri Lanka won by 75 runs
Toss: Sri Lanka
Man of the match: H.M.R.K.B.Herath
Sri Lanka 318 (D.P.M.D.Jayawardene 180, J.M.Anderson 5-72) and 214 (G.P.Swann 6-82)
England 193 (H.M.R.K.B.Herath 6-74) and 264 (I.J.L.Trott 112, H.M.R.K.B.Herath 6-97)

1st innings	c T.M.Dilshan b S.Randiv	24	23-3-92-0
2nd innings	lbw b H.M.R.K.B.Herath	1	30-5-82-6

41. v Sri Lanka at Colombo (PSS), 3-7 April 2012 – England won by 8 wickets
Toss: Sri Lanka
Man of the match: K.P.Pietersen
Sri Lanka 275 (D.P.M.D.Jayawardene 105) and 278 (G.P.Swann 6-106)
England 460 (K.P.Pietersen 151, H.M.R.K.B.Herath 6-133) and 97-2

1st innings	c T.M.Dilshan b H.M.R.K.B.Herath	17	28.1-4-75-4
2nd innings	did not bat		40-1-106-6

GRAEME SWANN IN ONE-DAY INTERNATIONALS

ONE-DAY INTERNATIONAL CAREER RECORD

Up to and including Sri Lanka at Southampton 2011

M	I	NO	Runs	HS	Avge	Overs	Maids	Runs	Wkts	Avge	Best	4wI	Econ
67	44	12	468	34	14.62	534	24	2385	92	25.92	5-28	4	4.46

1. **v South Africa at Bloemfontein 23 January 2000 – England won by 9 wickets**
   Toss: South Africa
   Man of the match: D.Gough
   South Africa 184 (49.5 overs) (J.H.Kallis 57, D.Gough 4-29)
   England 185-1 (39.3 overs) (N.Hussain 85, N.V.Knight 71*)

   did not bat   5-0-24-0

2. **v Sri Lanka at Dambulla 1 October 2007 – Sri Lanka won by 119 runs**
   Toss: Sri Lanka
   Man of the match: M.F.Maharoof
   Sri Lanka 269-7 (50 overs) (D.P.M.D.Jayawardene 66)
   England 150 (34.5 overs) (M.F.Maharoof 4-31)

   c S.L.Malinga b T.M.Dilshan   24 (71)   10-0-47-1

3. **v Sri Lanka at Dambulla 4 October 2007 – England won by 65 runs**
   Toss: England
   Man of the match: O.A.Shah
   England 234-8 (50 overs) (O.A.Shah 82)
   Sri Lanka 169 (44.3 overs)

   run out (W.U.Tharanga/C.R.D.Fernando)   34 (37)   10-3-27-2

4. **v Sri Lanka at Dambulla 7 October 2007 – England won by 2 wickets (D/L)**
   Toss: Sri Lanka
   Man of the match: G.P.Swann
   Sri Lanka 164 (41.1 overs) (T.M.Dilshan 70, G.P.Swann 4-34)
   England 164-8 (46.5 overs)

   b C.R.D.Fernando   25 (37)   10-2-34-4

5.   v Sri Lanka at Colombo (RPS) 10 October 2007 – England won by 5 wickets
Toss: Sri Lanka
Man of the match: A.N.Cook
Sri Lanka 211-9 (50 overs) (K.C.Sangakkara 69, L.P.C.Silva 67)
England 212-5 (46.5 overs) (A.N.Cook 80, K.P.Pietersen 63*)

did not bat   10-0-48-0

6.   v New Zealand at Wellington 9 February 2008 – New Zealand won by 6 wickets
Toss: England
Man of the match: S.B.Styris
England 130 (49.4 overs)
New Zealand 131-4 (30 overs)

run out (J.M.How/B.B.McCullum)   7 (16)   3-0-17-0

7.   v New Zealand at Hamilton 12 February 2008 – New Zealand won by 10 wickets (D/L)
Toss: New Zealand
Man of the match: J.D.Ryder
England 158 (35.1 overs) (A.N.Cook 53)
New Zealand 165-0 (18.1 overs) (J.D.Ryder 79*, B.B.McCullum 80*)

c B.B.McCullum b D.L.Vettori   1 (6)   2-0-27-0

8.   v New Zealand at Chester-le-Street 15 June 2008 – England won by 114 runs
Toss: England
Man of the match: K.P.Pietersen
England 307-5 (50 overs) (K.P.Pietersen 110*, P.D.Collingwood 64)
New Zealand 193 (42.5 overs) (P.D.Collingwood 4-15)

did not bat   10-1-45-2

9.   v New Zealand at Edgbaston 18 June 2008 – No result
Toss: New Zealand
Man of the match: None
England 162 (24 overs) (L.J.Wright 52)
New Zealand 127-2 (19 overs) (B.B.McCullum 60*)

c G.J.Hopkins b T.G.Southee   1 (2)   5-0-26-0

10.   v New Zealand at Bristol 21 June 2008 – New Zealand won by 22 runs
Toss: England
Man of the match: K.D.Mills
New Zealand 182 (50 overs) (G.D.Elliott 56)
England 160 (46.2 overs) (T.G.Southee 4-38)

c L.R.P.L.Taylor b S.B.Styris   29 (46)   4-0-10-1

11.   v New Zealand at The Oval 25 June 2008 – New Zealand won by 1 wicket
Toss: New Zealand
Man of the match: S.B.Styris
England 245 (49.4 overs) (R.S.Bopara 58, O.A.Shah 63)
New Zealand 246-9 (50 overs) (S.B.Styris 69)

c J.M.How b K.D.Mills.   3 (7)   10-1-49-2

12. v New Zealand at Lord's 28 June 2008 – New Zealand won by 51 runs
Toss: England
Man of the match: S.B.Styris
New Zealand 266-5 (50 overs) (S.B.Styris 87*, J.D.P.Oram 52)
England 215 (47.5 overs) (O.A.Shah 69)

c B.B.McCullum b K.D.Mills   12 (16)   10-0-33-2

13. v India at Kanpur 20 November 2008 – India won by 16 runs (D/L)
Toss: England
Man of the match: Harbajan Singh
England 240 (48.4 overs) (R.S.Bopara 60)
India 198-5 (40 overs) (V.Sehwag 68)

not out   5 (5)   10-0-47-1

14. v India at Bangalore 23 November 2008 – India won by 19 runs (D/L)
Toss: England
Man of the match: V.Sehwag
India 166-4 (22 overs) (V.Sehwag 69)
England 178-8 (22 overs) (O.A.Shah 72)

run out (M.M.Patel)   5 (4)   2-0-21-2

15. v India at Cuttack 26 November 2008 – India won by 6 wickets
Toss: India
Man of the match: V.Sehwag
England 270-4 (50 overs) (K.P.Pietersen 111*, O.A.Shah 66*)
India 273-4 (43.4 overs) (V.Sehwag 91, S.R.Tendulkar 50, M.S.Dhoni 50, S.K.Raina 53*)

did not bat   7-0-56-1

16. v West Indies at Bristol 24 May 2009 – England won by 6 wickets
Toss: England
Man of the match: P.D.Collingwood
West Indies 160 (38.3 overs) (D.J.Bravo 50; S.C.J.Broad 4-46)
England 161-4 (36 overs)

did not bat   8-1-26-1

17. v West Indies at Edgbaston 26 May 2009 – England won by 58 runs
Toss: West Indies
Man of the match: M.J.Prior
England 328-7 (50 overs) (A.J.Strauss 52, M.J.Prior 87, O.A.Shah 75)
West Indies 270 (49.4 overs) (S.Chanderpaul 68)

did not bat   8-0-38-1

18. v Ireland at Belfast 27 August 2009 – England won by 3 runs (D/L)
Toss: England
Man of the match: D.T.Johnston
England 203-9 (50 overs) (J.L.Denly 67; D.T.Johnston 4-26)
Ireland 112-9 (20 overs)

b A.C.Botha   5 (7)   4-0-21-1

19. v Australia at The Oval 4 September 2009 – Australia won by 4 runs
Toss: England
Man of the match: C.J.Ferguson
Australia 260-5 (50 overs) (C.L.White 53, C.J.Ferguson 71*)
England 256-8 (50 overs)

c T.D.Paine b S.R.Watson   4 (5)   7-0-29-0

20. v Australia at Lord's 6 September 2009 – Australia won by 39 runs
Toss: England
Man of the match: M.G.Johnson
Australia 249-8 (50 overs) (C.J.Ferguson 55)
England 210 (46.1 overs) (P.D.Collingwood 56)

b N.W.Bracken   14 (22)   8-0-31-2

21. v Australia at Southampton 9 September 2009 – Australia won by 6 wickets
Toss: England
Man of the match: C.L.White
England 228-9 (50 overs) (A.J.Strauss 63)
Australia 230-4 (48.3 overs) (C.L.White 105, M.J.Clarke 52)

lbw b S.R.Watson   3 (3)   5-0-35-1

22. v Australia at Trent Bridge 17 September 2009 – Australia won by 111 runs
Toss: Australia
Man of the match: T.D.Paine
Australia 296-8 (50 overs) (T.D.Paine 111, M.E.K.Hussey 65; J.M.Anderson 4-55)
England 185 (41 overs)

b N.W.Bracken   12 (15)   10-0-48-1

23. v Australia at Chester-le-Street 20 September 2009 – England won by 4 wickets
Toss: England
Man of the match: G.P.Swann
Australia 176 (45.5 overs) (R.T.Ponting 53; G.P.Swann 5-28)
England 177-6 (40 overs) (J.L.Denly 53)

did not bat   10-1-28-5

24. v Sri Lanka at Johannesburg 25 September 2009 – England won by 6 wickets
Toss: England
Man of the match: P.D.Collingwood
Sri Lanka 212 (47.3 overs) (S.H.T.Kandamby 53, A.D.Mathews 52)
England 213-4 (45 overs) (E.J.G.Morgan 62*)

did not bat   4-0-23-0

25. v South Africa at Centurion 27 September 2009 – England won by 22 runs
Toss: England
Man of the match: O.A.Shah
England 323-8 (50 overs) (O.A.Shah 98, P.D.Collingwood 82, E.J.G.Morgan 67)
South Africa 301-9 (50 overs) (G.C.Smith 141)

not out   8 (9)   8-0-43-1

26. v New Zealand at Johannesburg 29 September 2009 – New Zealand won by 4 wickets
Toss: New Zealand
Man of the match: G.D.Elliott
England 146 (43.1 overs) (G.D.Elliott 4-31)
New Zealand 147-6 (27.1 overs) (M.J.Guptill 53; S.C.J.Broad 4-39)

c B.B.McCullum b G.D.Elliott   11 (20)   did not bowl

27. v Australia at Centurion 2 October 2009 – Australia won by 9 wickets
Toss: England
Man of the match: S.R.Watson
England 257 (47.4 overs) (T.T.Bresnan 80)
Australia 258-1 (41.5 overs) (S.R.Watson 136*, R.T.Ponting 111*)

run out (N.M.Hauritz)   18 (15)   5-0-31-0

28. v South Africa at Cape Town 27 November 2009 – South Africa won by 112 runs
Toss: South Africa
Man of the match: A.B.de Villiers
South Africa 354-6 (50 overs) (H.M.Amla 86, G.C.Smith 54, A.B.de Villiers 121,
A.N.Petersen 51*; S.C.J.Broad 4-71)
England 242 (41.3 overs) (P.D.Collingwood 86; W.D.Parnell 5-48)

not out   6 (6)   9-0-49-0

29. v South Africa at Port Elizabeth 29 Nov 2009 – England won by 7 wickets
Toss: South Africa
Man of the match: J.M.Anderson
South Africa 119 (36.5 overs) (A.N.Petersen 51; J.M.Anderson 5-23)
England 121-3 (31.2 overs) (I.J.L.Trott 52*)

did not bat   did not bowl

30. v Bangladesh at Mirpur 28 February 2010 – England won by 6 wickets
Toss: England
Man of the match: Tamim Iqbal
Bangladesh 228 (45.4 overs) (Tamim Iqbal 125)
England 229-4 (46 overs) (A.N.Cook 64, P.D.Collingwood 75*)

did not bat   10-0-32-3

31. v Bangladesh at Mirpur 2 March 2010 – England won by 2 wickets
Toss: England
Man of the match: E.J.G.Morgan
Bangladesh 260-6 (50 overs) (Imrul Kayes 63, Mushfiqur Rahim 76)
England 261-8 (48.5 overs) (A.N.Cook 60, E.J.G.Morgan 110*)

b Shakib Al Hasan   2 (3)   10-0-52-2

32. v Bangladesh at Chittagong 5 March 2010 – England won by 45 runs
Toss: Bangladesh
Man of the match: C.Kieswetter
England 284-5 (50 overs) (C.Kieswetter 107)
Bangladesh 239-9 (50 overs) (T.T.Bresnan 4-28)

did not bat   10-0-38-2

33. v Scotland at Edinburgh (Grange) 19 June 2010 – England won by 7 wickets
Toss: Scotland
Man of the match: none
Scotland 211 (49.5 overs) (K.J.Coetzer 51)
England 213-3 (33.4 overs) (A.J.Strauss 61, C.Kieswetter 69)

did not bat   10-0-29-2

34. v Australia at Southampton 22 June 2010 – England won by 4 wickets
Toss: Australia
Man of the match: E.J.G.Morgan
Australia 267-7 (50 overs) (M.J.Clarke 87*)
England 268-6 (46 overs) (E.J.G.Morgan 103*)

did not bat   8-0-44-0

35. v Australia at Cardiff 24 June 2010 – England won by 4 wickets
Toss: Australia
Man of the match: S.C.J.Broad
Australia 239-7 (50 overs) (S.R.Watson 57, C.L.White 86*; S.C.J.Broad 4-44)
England 243-6 (45.2 overs) (A.J.Strauss 51, E.J.G.Morgan 52)

not out   19 (14)   4-0-19-0

36. v Australia at Old Trafford 27 June 2010 – England won by 1 wicket
Toss: England
Man of the match: G.P.Swann
Australia 212 (46 overs) (S.R.Watson 61; G.P.Swann 4-37)
England 214-9 (49.1 overs) (A.J.Strauss 87)

b D.E.Bollinger   1 (10)   10-1-37-4

37. v Australia at The Oval 30 June 2010 – Australia won by 78 runs
Toss: England
Man of the match: R.J.Harris
Australia 290-5 (50 overs) (R.T.Ponting 92, M.J.Clarke 99*)
England 212 (42.4 overs) (M.H.Yardy 57; R.J.Harris 5-32)

c T.D.Paine b D.E.Bollinger   1 (2)   6-0-31-1

38. v Australia at Lord's 3 July 2010 – Australia won by 42 runs
Toss: Australia
Man of the match: S.W.Tait
Australia 277-7 (50 overs) (T.D.Paine 54, S.E.Marsh 59, M.E.K.Hussey 79; S.C.J.Broad
4-64)
England 235 (46.3 overs) (P.D.Collingwood 95; S.W.Tait 4-48)

c R.J.Harris b S.W.Tait   33 (21)   8-0-32-3

39. v Pakistan at Chester-le-Street 10 September 2010 – England won by 24 runs
Toss: Pakistan
Man of the match: S.M.Davies
England 274-6 (41 overs) (S.M.Davies 87, I.J.L.Trott 69; Saeed Ajmal 4-58)
Pakistan 250-9 (41 overs) (Kamran Akmal 53)

did not bat   8-0-50-2

40. v Pakistan at Headingley 12 September 2010 – England won by 4 wickets
Toss: Pakistan
Man of the match: A.J.Strauss
Pakistan 294-8 (50 overs) (Kamran Akmal 74, Asad Shafiq 50; S.C.J. Broad 4-81)
England 295-6 (49.3 overs) (A.J. Strauss 126, I.J.L.Trott 53)

did not bat   10-0-43-1

41. v Pakistan at The Oval 17 September 2010 – Pakistan won by 23 runs
Toss: Pakistan
Man of the match: Umar Gul
Pakistan 241 (49.4 overs) (Fawad Alam 64)
England 218 (45.4 overs) (A.J.Strauss 57, E.J.G.Morgan 61; Umar Gul 6-42)

c Shahid Afridi b Umar Gul   0 (8)   10-0-53-1

42. v Pakistan at Lord's 20 September 2010 – Pakistan won by 38 runs
Toss: Pakistan
Man of the match: Abdul Razzaq
Pakistan 265-7 (50 overs) (Mohammad Hafeez 64; G.P.Swann 4-37)
England 227 (46.1 overs) (A.J.Strauss 68; Umar Gul 4-32)

b Umar Gul   12 (9)   10-0-37-4

43. v Pakistan at Southampton 22 September 2010 – England won by 121 runs
Toss: England
Man of the match: E.J.G.Morgan
England 256-6 (50 overs) (E.J.G.Morgan 107*)
Pakistan 135 (37 overs)

did not bat   9-0-26-3

44. v Australia at Melbourne 16 January 2011 – Australia won by 6 wickets
Toss: England
Man of the match: S.R.Watson
England 294 (49.4 overs) (A.J.Strauss 63, K.P.Pietersen 78)
Australia 297-4 (49.1 overs) (S.R.Watson 161*)

c X.J.Doherty b M.G.Johnson   4 (10)   10-0-42-1

45. ICC World Cup 2011 v Netherlands at Nagpur 22 February 2011 – England won by 6 wickets
Toss: Netherlands
Man of the match: R.N.ten Doeschate
Netherlands 292-6 (50 overs) (R.N.ten Doeschate 119)
England 296-4 (48.4 overs) (A.J.Strauss 88, I.J.L.Trott 62)

did not bat   10-0-35-2

46. ICC World Cup 2011 v India at Bangalore 27 February 2011 – Match tied
Toss: India
Man of the match: A.J.Strauss
India 338 (49.5 overs) (S.R.Tendulkar 120, G.Gambhir 51, Yuvraj Singh 58; T.T.Bresnan 5-48)
England 338-8 (50 overs) (A.J.Strauss 158, I.R.Bell 69)

not out   15 (9)   9-1-59-1

47.   ICC World Cup 2011 v Ireland at Bangalore 2 March 2011 – Ireland won by 3 wickets
Toss: England
Man of the match: K.J.O'Brien
England 327-8 (50 overs) (K.P.Pietersen 59, I.J.L.Trott 92, I.R.Bell 81; J.F.Mooney 4-63)
Ireland 329-7 (49.1 overs) (K.J.O'Brien 113)

not out	9 (5)	10-0-47-3

48.   ICC World Cup 2011 v South Africa at Chennai 6 March 2011 – England won by 6 runs
Toss: England
Man of the match: R.S.Bopara
England 171 (45.4 overs) (I.J.L.Trott 52, R.S.Bopara 60; Imran Tahir 4-38)
South Africa 165 (47.4 overs) (S.C.J.Broad 4-15)

c J-P.Duminy b Imran Tahir	16 (20)	10-2-29-1

49.   ICC World Cup 2011 v Bangladesh at Chittagong 11 March 2011 – Bangladesh won by 2 wickets
Toss: Bangladesh
Man of the match: Imrul Kayes
England 225 (49.4 overs) (I.J.L.Trott 67, E.J.G.Morgan 63)
Bangladesh 227-8 (49 overs) (Imrul Kayes 60)

c and b Shakib Al Hasan	12 (8)	10-1-42-2

50.   ICC World Cup 2011 v West Indies at Chennai 17 March 2011 – England won by 18 runs
Toss: England
Man of the match: J.C.Tredwell
England 243 (48.4 overs) (A.D.Russell 4-49)
West Indies 225 (44.4 overs) (J.C.Tredwell 4-48)

b A.D.Russell	8 (8)	10-1-36-3

51.   ICC World Cup 2011 v Sri Lanka at Colombo (RPS) 26 March 2011 – Sri Lanka won by 10 wickets
Toss: England
Man of the match: T.M.Dilshan
England 229-6 (50 overs) (I.J.L.Trott 86, E.J.G.Morgan 50)
Sri Lanka 231-0 (39.3 overs) (W.U.Tharanga 102*, T.M.Dilshan 108*)

lbw b B.A.W.Mendis	0 (1)	9-0-61-0

52.   v Sri Lanka at The Oval 28 June 2011 - England won by 110 runs (D/L)
Toss: Sri Lanka
Man of the match: J.M.Anderson
England 229-8 (32 overs) (C.Kieswetter 61)
Sri Lanka 121 (27 overs) (J.M.Anderson 4-18)

not out	2 (2)	5-0-18-3

53.   v Sri Lanka at Headingley 1 July 2011 – Sri Lanka won by 69 runs
Toss: England
Man of the match: D.P.M.D.Jayawardene
Sri Lanka 309-5 (50 overs) (D.P.M.D.Jayawardene 144, K.C.Sangakkara 69)
England 240 (45.5 overs) (E.J.G.Morgan 52)

not out	13 (12)	10-0-42-2

54. v Sri Lanka at Lord's 3 July 2011 – Sri Lanka won by 6 wickets
Toss: England
Man of the match: L.D.Chandimal
England 246-7 (50 overs) (A.N.Cook 119)
Sri Lanka 249-4 (48.2 overs) (D.P.M.D.Jayawardene 79, L.D.Chandimal 105*)

not out   11 (4)   10-0-32-2

55. v Sri Lanka at Trent Bridge 6 July 2011 – England won by 10 wickets (D/L)
Toss: England
Man of the match: A.N.Cook
Sri Lanka 174 (43.4 overs) (K.C.Sangakkara 75)
England 171-0 (23.5 overs) (A.N.Cook 95*, C.Kieswetter 72*)

did not bat   10-2-31-0

56. v Sri Lanka at Old Trafford 9 July 2011 – England won by 16 runs
Toss: England
Man of the match: I.J.L.Trott
England 268-9 (50 overs) (I.J.L. Trott 72, E.J.G.Morgan 57; H.K.S.R.Kaluhalamulla 5-42)
Sri Lanka 252 (48.2 overs) (L.D.Chandimal 54, A.D.Mathews 62)

run out (T.M.Dilshan K.M.D.N.Kulasekara)   5 (9)   10-2-41-1

57. v India at Southampton 6 September 2011 – England won by 7 wickets
Toss: England
Man of the match: A.N.Cook
India 187-8 (23 overs) (A.M.Rahane 54)
England 188-3 (22.1 overs) (A.N.Cook 80*)

did not bat   5-0-33-3

58. v India at The Oval 9 September 2011 – England won by 3 wickets (D/L)
Toss: England
Man of the match: R.A.Jadeja
India 234-7 (50 overs) (M.S.Dhoni 69, R.A.Jadeja 78)
England 218-7 (41.5 overs) (C.Kieswetter 51)

not out   9 (5)   10-0-31-0

59. v India at Lord's 11 September 2011 – Match tied (D/L)
Toss: England
Man of the match: R.S.Bopara and S.K.Raina
India 280-5 (50 overs) (S.K.Raina 84, M.S.Dhoni 78*)
England 270-8 (48.5 overs) (I.R.Bell 54, R.S.Bopara 96)

run out (M.M.Patel)   31 (23)   9-1-49-2

60. v India at Cardiff 16 September 2011 – England won by 6 wickets (D/L)
Toss: England
Man of the match: J.M.Bairstow
India 304-6 (50 overs) (R.Dravid 69, V.Kohli 107, M.S.Dhoni 50*)
England 241-4 (32.2 overs) (A.N.Cook 50, I.J.L.Trott 63)

did not bat   9-0-34-3

61. v India at Hyderabad (Deccan) 14 October 2011 – India won by 126 runs
Toss: India
Man of the match: M.S.Dhoni
India 300-7 (50 overs) (S.K.Raina 61, M.S.Dhoni 87*)
England 174 (36.1 overs) (A.N.Cook 60)

b U.T.Yadav   8 (9)   10-1-35-1

62. v India at Delhi 17 October 2011 – India won by 8 wickets
Toss: England
Man of the match: V.Kohli
England 237 (48.2 overs) (R.Vinay Kumar 4-30)
India 238-2 (36.4 overs) (G.Gambhir 84*, V.Kohli 112*)

b R.Vinay Kumar   7 (7)   8-0-52-0

63. v India at Mohali 20 October 2011 – India won by 5 wickets
Toss: England
Man of the match: A.M.Rahane
England 298-4 (50 overs) (I.J.L.Trott 98*, K.P.Pietersen 64, S.R.Patel 70*)
India 300-5 (49.2 overs) (A.M.Rahane 91, G.Gambhir 58)

did not bat   10-0-59-1

64. v India at Kolkata 25 October 2011 – India won by 95 runs
Toss: England
Man of the match: R.A.Jadeja
India 271-8 (50 overs) (M.S.Dhoni 75)
England 176 (37 overs) (C.Kieswetter 63, A.N.Cook 60, R.A.Jadeja 4-33)

not out   10 (11)   8-0-45-0

65. v Pakistan at Abu Dhabi 13 February 2012 – England won by 130 runs
Toss: England
Man of the match: A.N.Cook
England 260-7 (50 overs) (A.N.Cook 137, R.S.Bopara 50, Saeed Ajmal 5-43)
Pakistan 130 (35 overs) (S.T.Finn 4-34)

not out   13 (12)   7-3-19-2

66. v Pakistan at Abu Dhabi 15 February 2012 – England won by 20 runs
Toss: England
Man of the match: A.N.Cook
England 250-4 (50 overs) (A.N.Cook 102, R.S.Bopara 58)
Pakistan 230 (49 overs) (S.T.Finn 4-34)

did not bat   8-0-33-0

67. v Pakistan at Dubai (DSC) 18 February 2012 – England won by 9 wickets
Toss: Pakistan
Man of the match: K.P.Pietersen
Pakistan 222 (50 overs) (Umar Akmal 50, Shahid Afridi 51)
England 226-1 (37.2 overs) (A.N.Cook 80, K.P.Pietersen 111*)

did not bat   10-0-44-0

INDEX